THE ESSENTIAL
BOOK OF MORMON
COMPANION

Cover images:
Cover Top Left—*The Title of Liberty* © Jeremy Winborg. For more information, visit www.jeremywinborg.blogspot.com.
Cover Top Right— Etching by Fredrick Catherwood.
Cover Bottom Right—*Nephi Hunting* © Gary E. Smith.
Cover Bottom Center—Photograph © Sheryl Lee Wilson.
Cover Bottom Left—*His Father Rejoiced* by Walter Rane. © By the Hand of Mormon Foundation.
Spine Top—*Ye Shall Have My Words* © Judith Mehr. For more information, visit www.judithmehr.com.
Spine Bottom—*Samuel the Lamanite* by Jerry Thompson © Intellectual Reserve, Inc.
Back Cover—*Nephi and Lehi Encircled by Fire* © Gary Kapp. For more information, visit www.garykapp.com.

Cover and interior design copyrighted 2011 by Covenant Communications, Inc.
Published by Covenant Communications, Inc.
American Fork, Utah

Authored by Kathryn B. Jenkins
Copyright © 2011 by Covenant Communications, Inc.

Printed in China
First Printing: October 2011
20 19 18 17 16 15 14 13 12 11   10 9 8 7 6 5 4 3 2 1

ISBN 978-1-60861473-8

THE ESSENTIAL
BOOK OF MORMON
COMPANION

KEY INSIGHTS TO YOUR GOSPEL STUDY
Main Themes, Prominent People, Key Concepts about the Savior, and more

KATHRYN B. JENKINS

Covenant Communications, Inc.

Introduction

The Essential Book of Mormon Companion is the first in a new series of scripture commentaries offered by Covenant Communications. Unlike traditional commentaries that provide a verse-by-verse explanation or an in-depth interpretation of the scripture, this *Companion* is meant to be exactly that—a user-friendly fellow traveler on your journey through the Book of Mormon.

Between its covers you'll find a two-page spread for each chapter in the Book of Mormon (with the exception of a handful of chapters in the latter part of Alma, which are combined two to a spread). Each two-page spread contains a key scripture from that chapter, a one- or two-sentence explanation of the major concept, a quick list of the prominent people in the chapter, and an overview of what happens in that chapter.

You'll also find a paragraph giving some interesting facts about something in the chapter, a "Who Was?" paragraph about a prominent individual in the chapter, or both.

Of greatest significance are two bulleted lists you'll find on each two-page spread. The first, "Main Themes," provides a summary of how that chapter applies to us today—what we can incorporate into our lives from those pages in the

Book of Mormon. Read and applied, they will help you "liken all scripture" to yourself (1 Ne. 19:23). Most important is "Key Insights about the Savior," a bulleted list of what that chapter tells us about Jesus Christ—His character, His way of dealing with us, His desires, His mission for all of us.

You'll quickly determine the best way for you to use this *Companion*. You might find it helpful to get a quick overview of the chapter before you read the actual scripture, or you might find it helpful as a guide while you are reading the Book of Mormon itself. You might also find that it's a beneficial tool to help you put the scriptures into perspective after you finish reading each chapter. Maybe you'll find it helpful in all three ways.

I am deeply indebted to Covenant authors and personal friends Ed J. Pinegar and Richard J. Allen for their magnificent insights into the Book of Mormon; in many cases, those insights have inspired the "Interesting Facts About" sections in this book. In all cases, their thorough offerings in *Book of Mormon Who's Who* and *Old Testament Who's Who* were condensed or adapted for the "Who Was?" sections of this book. Their scholarship, gifts of expression, and personal example have been powerfully influential in my life, and I express my sincerest gratitude.

I also owe sincere thanks to Todd Parker, who read these pages not only for doctrinal accuracy, but who made helpful suggestions that improved the text and who suggested additional sources that verify what is written here.

The greatest message of this *Companion* is that the Book of Mormon is indeed another testament of Jesus Christ. He is called by 101 different names throughout the book, and one of those names is mentioned an average of once every 1.7 verses (see Black, 60–61). An average of one in every eight verses—12.6 percent of the Book of Mormon—contains speech texts from and about the Savior. And its pages confirm the fact that all prophets since the beginning of time—some who have given their lives as a result—have testified of Jesus Christ and His atoning mission. All we are, and all we ever hope to be, we owe to our Savior, Jesus Christ.

Since its first publication in 1830, more than 140 million copies of the Book of Mormon have been published and distributed in 107 languages. It continues to go throughout the world as a testimony of He who has us graven on His palms (see 1 Ne. 21:16)—He who rose from the tomb with our names on His lips, providing for us the opportunity to repent and return to live in His presence. No matter our failures and weaknesses in mortality, we can become pure again because of His infinite sacrifice on our behalf if we will experience a mighty change of heart. The Book of Mormon shows us how.

It is my hope that as you read the pages of the Book of Mormon and ponder the insights offered in this *Companion,* your own testimony of both the Savior and the Book of Mormon will become deeper and richer. I know that examining it again to prepare this *Companion* has given me even greater knowledge that it is a book translated from ancient records by the Prophet of the Restoration, Joseph Smith. Those who wrote and abridged it truly are speaking to us as voices from the dust, bearing their own solemn witness of the Savior and pleading with us to live by its words (see Morm. 8:35). It was written not for their contemporaries, but for us in our day—and may we never take for granted the unparalleled blessing of having the Book of Mormon: Another Testament of Jesus Christ.

—Kathryn Jenkins

1Nephi 1

OVERVIEW The Lord, who can see all things, may give instructions that seem to make little sense to us. In this case, He instructs Nephi to keep two separate records: he is to record historical events on one set of plates and a religious or spiritual record on a separate set of plates. Since it was very difficult to engrave on the metal plates, Nephi may have wondered at the purpose for these separate records. Nevertheless, he obeys. The reason for the Lord's instruction became very clear when Joseph Smith began translating the Book of Mormon. Once he had translated the book of Lehi from the large plates—the historical account—he was persuaded to give the 116-page manuscript to Martin Harris. As we know, those records were stolen. Now the Lord's purpose becomes very clear: because Nephi kept a separate account of the spiritual experiences of his people, we know of the things that happened to Lehi and his family—despite the loss of the 116 pages.

PROMINENT PEOPLE

- Lehi
- Nephi

MAIN THEMES

- Affliction, while difficult when it is upon us, is a powerful teacher that can strengthen and enable us to meet future challenges.

- The influence of good and righteous parents is significant.

- The keeping of records is key in preserving the faith of those who come after us; our own personal records should be patterned after what we find in the scriptures.

- Lehi was not the first to prophesy of the destruction of Jerusalem, a prophecy that was considered blasphemous; Jeremiah, Nahum, Habakkuk, and Zephaniah had also warned the people of the need to repent to escape the destruction of their city.

- The only way to be delivered from bondage is through Jesus Christ.

- Lehi's experience in this chapter symbolizes God's pattern of revelation to His prophets.

over all those whom he hath
them mighty even unto the

INTERESTING FACTS ABOUT EGYPTIAN INFLUENCE The Jews at the time of Lehi used Egyptian in their written communication. While Nephi was also fluent in Hebrew and the Aramaic language, he followed tradition and used Egyptian in making his record. (The language used to abridge the records much later was reformed Egyptian—a type of shorthand combining Egyptian and Hebrew—that was more compact than Hebrew so more to be recorded on the plates.) This coincides with Nephi's statement that the record he made consists of both the learning of the Jews and the language of the Egyptians. There was significant Egyptian influence in Jerusalem at this time that impacted not only written communication but also cultural, social, and diplomatic affairs.

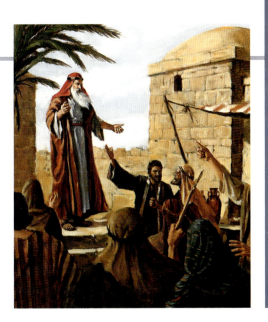

WHO WAS LEHI? A descendant of Joseph through the lineage of Manasseh (see Alma 10:3), Lehi was a native of Jerusalem and a contemporary of Jeremiah, Daniel, and Ezekiel. Threatened with his own life because he called the people of Jerusalem to repentance, Lehi followed the Lord's counsel to depart into the wilderness in 600 BC. (He knew of Urijah, who prophesied against Jerusalem in 605 BC and was driven out and executed [see Jer. 26:20–24]). A man of means, he left his riches behind and took only his family and the provisions they needed to survive in the wilderness. He eventually led his family to the promised land, where he endured faithfully to the end. Lehi was the right man for the right time: he was an experienced caravaneer, trader, and desert traveler who had significant survival experience. As far as spiritual preparation, Lehi's worthiness allowed him to commune with the Lord; he received through revelation a prophetic view of the plan of salvation and the coming of the Messiah, which enabled him to act as a witness of the divinity to the Savior.

KEY INSIGHTS ABOUT THE SAVIOR

- Just as the Lord cares for and delivers those chosen to do His work, He does not forsake those who trust and obey Him.

- The Lord has a clear view of the past, present, and future, and gives specific direction that will help the faithful accomplish His purposes, though the results of that direction may not be obvious for hundreds or even thousands of years.

- The tender mercies of the Lord are provided to those who are faithful, and He will make His chosen ones mighty.

- The Lord answers fervent prayer.

- The Lord speaks through prophets in behalf of his people.

1Nephi 2

"Blessed art thou, Nephi, because of thy
as ye shall keep my commandments, ye
led to a land of promise. . . ." (1 Ne.

MAJOR CONCEPT

The Lord guides and directs us in paths of righteousness for our own good; our obedience to His commandments assures our eternal safety and protection.

OVERVIEW In response to a commandment of the Lord, Lehi departs Jerusalem and travels into a foreboding wasteland, leaving behind his considerable lands, gold, silver, and other possessions. He takes with him only his family and those provisions needed for survival. Laman and Lemuel, his two oldest sons, murmur and rebel against their father, doubting his visions and feeling resentful about leaving behind their wealth. Nephi seeks spiritual confirmation of his father's vision and is given strength and understanding. Because of his faith he is to be made a ruler and a teacher over his brothers.

PROMINENT PEOPLE

- Lehi
- Sariah
- Laman
- Lemuel
- Nephi
- Sam

INTERESTING FACTS ABOUT RIVERS A "river of water" (see verse 6) is a Semitic phrase that indicates ancient origin, further evidence that the Book of Mormon was translated and not just written by Joseph Smith. Joseph would have referred to a simple "river." In addition to the Semitic construction of the phrase,

MAIN THEMES

- Our family is our greatest and most valuable possession, worth much more than any worldly wealth.

- We have the opportunity to gain our own testimony of the truths taught to us by our parents and Church leaders through seeking confirmation of those truths from the Lord.

- The Lord visits us according to our desires and His will.

- Obedience allows us to prosper in the Lord and in the land; disobedience and rebellion cause us to be cut off from the presence of the Lord.

- Keeping the commandments is the key by which we will prosper; just as Lehi and his family were promised that they would be led to a land of promise because of their righteousness, we will be led to our own land of promise as a result of our individual righteousness.

600 BC   90 BC

faith. . . . And inasmuch
shall prosper, and shall be
2:19–20)

there is another consideration: there are two types of "rivers" in the Middle East: rivers of water, which have water in them continually, and *wadis,* which are dry streambeds that are occasionally swollen by heavy rains. Year-round rivers of water are scarce.

WHO WAS LAMAN? Laman, the eldest son of Lehi, is a model of murmuring and deception. When Lehi heeded the warnings of the Lord and took his family into the wilderness to escape destruction, Laman led his brother Lemuel in accusing Lehi of being a "visionary man" who had foolishly led them out of Jerusalem and caused them to lose their riches and their inheritance. As Nephi assumed leadership, Laman reacted with jealousy, torturing Nephi and even attempting to kill him on several occasions. Even after being rebuked by an angel (see 1 Ne. 3:29), he immediately began to murmur again. Not even the voice of the Lord was effective in turning Laman to righteousness (see 1 Ne. 16:39). After reaching the promised land, Laman again rejected the gospel of Jesus Christ and was cast off from the presence of the Lord; he and his followers became the nation of the Lamanites.

KEY INSIGHTS ABOUT THE SAVIOR

- The Savior seeks trustworthy and faithful people who are obedient and humble to be His servants and leaders.
- The Lord often visits us or provides answers to our prayers according to our desires; how intent are we in seeking the Lord?
- The Lord will preserve us against our enemies if we keep His commandments; when we fail to keep His commandments, we have no promise.

Image: One of the many wadis along the path Lehi's family traveled.

1Nephi 3

"I will go and do the things which the giveth no commandments unto the that they may accomplish the thing

MAJOR CONCEPT

While the Lord's commandments may sometimes seem daunting, He will always prepare a way for us to obey and will never ask anything of us that we cannot do if we remain faithful and diligent.

OVERVIEW After Lehi and his family travel for a time in the wilderness, the Lord commands Lehi to send his sons back to Jerusalem to obtain from Laban plates of brass that contain the records of Adam through Jeremiah and a genealogy of Lehi's forefathers. Such a request is difficult to consider: the family has already traveled for fourteen days—probably between 160 and 180 miles—through hot, barren country infested by venomous insects and dangerous marauders. Laman and Lemuel murmur (complain), but Nephi responds with the now well-known promise that he will go and do the things the Lord has commanded. Considering what they faced, the real wonder is not that Laman and Lemuel murmured but that Nephi did not.

MAIN THEMES

- The scriptures and our family records are of great importance, not only for us but for the generations that will follow.
- In obeying the commandments, we often sacrifice immediate reward for permanent joy.
- Obedience requires great faith.
- One of the greatest tests of mortality is the test of obedience.
- The brass plates helped preserve the language of Lehi and his family and the words of the prophets.

PROMINENT PEOPLE

- Lehi
- Nephi
- Sam
- Laman
- Lemuel
- Laban

Their initial attempts at obtaining the records are unsuccessful.

INTERESTING FACTS ABOUT BIRTH ORDER During Lehi's time, the firstborn son in a family was given the leadership role in the family and was expected to "rule" over his brothers and sisters. As the firstborn in Lehi's family, Laman would normally have had that leadership position—but because of his exactness in keeping the commandments, Nephi instead was given that position by the Lord (see 1 Ne. 2:22). The same thing happened in the Old Testament when Joseph replaced Reuben (see Gen. 35:22) and Jacob replaced Esau (see Gen. 27). Nephi assumed leadership during their mission to obtain the plates from Laban, which caused Laman to accuse him of trying to usurp power. Laman made this same accusation on several other occasions (see 1 Ne. 16:37, 38; 1 Ne. 18:10).

Lord hath commanded, for I know that the Lord children of men, save he shall prepare a way for them which he commandeth them." (1 Ne. 3:7)

WHO WAS LABAN? A descendant of Joseph of Egypt and a distant relative of Lehi, Laban was living in Jerusalem when Lehi and his family departed into the wilderness. Laban and his forefathers had kept records on plates of brass that began with the creation of the world and continued to the time of Jeremiah, a contemporary of Lehi; those records were stored in Laban's house. He was a powerful and influential man; according to Hugh Nibley, Laban commanded a garrison of fifty, met in full ceremonial armor with Jewish elders for secret consultations by night, and had control of the treasury. He was also a man to be feared: Nibley described him as a large man who was short-tempered, crafty, dangerous, cruel, greedy, unscrupulous, and given to drink. He was slain by Nephi, who was directed by the Spirit to kill Laban in order to obtain the plates of brass (see *Lehi in the Desert and the World of the Jaredites*, 111).

KEY INSIGHTS ABOUT THE SAVIOR

- The Lord always rewards faith and faithfulness.
- There are various ways the Lord communicates with us; one way is through dreams.
- The Lord will never command us to do anything without providing a way for our obedience.

1 Nephi 4

"It is better that one man should perish should dwindle and perish in unbelief."

MAJOR CONCEPT

We always have safety in obeying the Lord's commandments and following the direction provided by the Spirit.

OVERVIEW After several failed attempts to obtain the plates of brass from Laban, Nephi asks his brothers to remain outside the city walls while he goes back into the city under cloak of darkness. Led by the Spirit, and not knowing ahead of time what he will do, he encounters Laban drunk and passed out in the street. Nephi slays Laban under direction of the Spirit, puts on Laban's clothing and armor, and gains entry to the treasury when the guard, Zoram, assumes he is Laban. Nephi takes the plates of brass and instructs Zoram to follow him. When they reach Nephi's brothers and Zoram discovers the truth, Zoram takes an oath to depart into the wilderness and remain with Lehi's family.

PROMINENT PEOPLE

- Nephi
- Sam
- Laman
- Lemuel
- Laban
- Zoram

INTERESTING FACTS ABOUT OATHS When Zoram discovered he had actually helped Nephi obtain the plates of brass, his immediate response was to try to flee back to Jerusalem. Nephi restrained him and quickly administered an oath: Zoram would be protected and given his freedom

MAIN THEMES

- We must be willing to obey and follow the Lord even if we don't understand the process or know the outcome.

- The Lord destroys the wicked to bring forth His righteous purposes.

- Obedience brings strength.

- Relying on valiant examples from the scriptures—as Nephi did when he remembered Moses—can provide us with the inspiration to go forward under even the most difficult circumstances.

- We must obey the voice of the Spirit.

600 BC   90 BC

if he would accompany Nephi into the wilderness. Zoram's instant acceptance of that oath makes sense when we realize that the oath is most sacred and unbreakable among the desert people. Hugh Nibley points out that the only way Nephi could possibly have pacified the panic-stricken and struggling Zoram in an instant was to utter an oath on the life of the Lord ("as the Lord liveth"), the most solemn of all oaths (see *An Approach to the Book of Mormon,* 109–110).

WHO WAS ZORAM? Zoram was a servant employed by Laban to guard his vast treasury of wealth. At first Zoram was terrified to realize he had given the plates not to Laban, but to Nephi. However,

Nephi promised by an oath to spare Zoram's life and to grant him freedom if he joined their group in the wilderness. Zoram complied and returned with Nephi and his brothers to the tent of Lehi. Zoram married the oldest daughter of Ishmael, whose family was journeying with Lehi, and traveled with them to the promised land (see 1 Ne. 16:17). When the aging Lehi gave blessings to his sons after reaching the promised land, he included Zoram (see 2 Ne. 1:30–32). Zoram maintained his allegiance to Nephi's group and stayed with them when Nephi separated himself from Laman and Lemuel (see 2 Ne. 5:6–7).

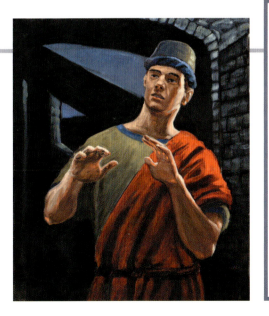

KEY INSIGHTS ABOUT THE SAVIOR

- The Savior knows the beginning from the end and will direct us in paths that will be for our good even though He does not always reveal the outcome.
- The Lord protects us when we obey His commandments and follow the promptings of the Spirit.
- The Lord will do whatever is necessary to fulfill His righteous purposes.
- The Lord provides deliverance to the faithful, even as Israel was delivered from Egypt.

1Nephi 5

"And we had obtained the records which us . . . insomuch that we could preserve Lord unto our children." (1 Ne. 5:21)

MAJOR CONCEPT

The scriptures are of tremendous value to us, providing not only an account of the Lord's dealings with His people throughout the history of the world, but revealing the prophecies of holy prophets from the beginning of time.

OVERVIEW The return of Nephi and his brothers results in great rejoicing. Sariah, who had been waiting for her sons to return for more than a month, feared that they had perished in the wilderness and had dealt harshly with Lehi for sending them back to Jerusalem. While Lehi trusts in God even when his sons are gone, Sariah gains a deep testimony of Him only after she knows her sons are safe. After giving thanks for his sons' safe return, Lehi examines the plates of brass and prophesies that they will go forth to all nations, kindreds, tongues, and people who are of his seed and that the records will never perish or be dimmed by time.

INTERESTING FACTS ABOUT THE PLATES OF BRASS At first

PROMINENT PEOPLE

- Lehi
- Sariah
- Nephi

MAIN THEMES

- The natural man is prone to murmur and doubt God.
- True faith and trust in the Lord is manifest during times of adversity, not just in retrospect after the adversity has passed.
- The plates of brass Nephi obtained contained more than what we find in the current Old Testament.
- The scriptures give us much more than a simple history; they are of great worth because they preserve the commandments of the Lord.

glimpse, it seems that the plates of brass simply contained the records we know as the Old Testament. But as Lehi examined them, it becomes clear that they contained not only the five books of Moses (Genesis, Exodus, Leviticus, Numbers, and Deuteronomy) but also a record of the Jews and the prophecies of the holy prophets from the beginning. Handed down from generation to generation among the Nephites, the plates of brass were valuable to Lehi and his descendants for other reasons as well: they enabled the Nephites to preserve their language, their civilization, and their religion. The very wording—*plates of brass*—is further evidence that the book was translated from an ancient record. When one noun follows another in the English language, the first serves as an adjective, such as *brass plates*. In Hebrew, however, the same phrase would be *plates brass*; in order to make sense in English, the word *of* is added, making the phrase *plates of brass* instead of the simpler brass plates (see Sorenson and Thorne, 79).

WHO WAS SARIAH? Sariah was the wife of the prophet Lehi and the mother of Nephi and his siblings. Nephi described both his mother and his father as "goodly" (see 1 Ne. 1:1), and Sariah remained loyal and faithful to the Lord despite severe tribulation. Though her worries about her children did cause her to murmur in agony (see 1 Ne. 5:2–3), she remained loyal to her husband in his prophetic calling. While there are only scant details about Sariah's life in the Book of Mormon, we know that she was the mother of at least six sons and at least two daughters and that she was a conscientious and devoted mother. She also exhibited great faith in abandoning her significant wealth—which included a house, gold, and silver, among other "precious things"—to follow her husband into the wilderness.

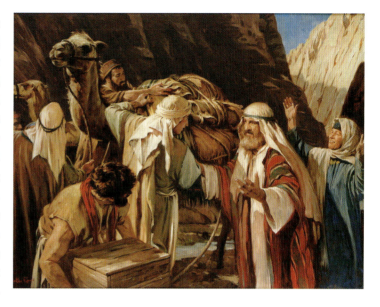

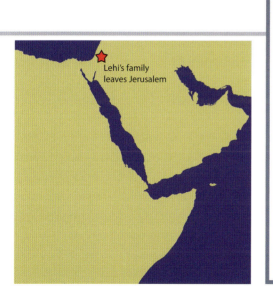

Lehi's family
leaves Jerusalem

Key Insights about the Savior

- The Lord directs us in paths for our good and rewards our determined efforts to obey.

- The role of women, although not often recorded, is very important to the Lord, as shown by the fact that Lehi and Sariah together offered sacrifice to the Lord.

1 Nephi 6

"Wherefore, the things which are pleasing write, but the things which are pleasing who are not of the world." (1 Ne. 6:5)

MAJOR CONCEPT

The things that Nephi wrote in the Book of Mormon were carefully chosen and were designed to persuade men to come unto God.

OVERVIEW In this chapter, which is a break in the historical narrative, Nephi explains that he is writing the things of God on the small plates. He also explains that his intent is not to give a full account of the history of Lehi and his people but to save room for writing things that will persuade readers to come unto Christ. Finally, he indicates that he will instruct his descendants to record only those things that are of worth.

INTERESTING FACTS ABOUT WRITING HISTORIES In this brief chapter, consisting of a mere six verses, Nephi provides an elegant list of criteria for us as we write our personal and family histories. A genealogy is important, but it can be brief and certainly should not take up the

PROMINENT PEOPLE

- Nephi

entire history. Nephi indicates, instead, that we should keep three things in mind: Our histories should contain those things that will persuade our descendants to come unto the Lord, that are pleasing to the Lord, and that are of worth. We are then tasked with determining what is of worth as it pertains to the descendants who will read and use our histories. Nephi's experience suggests that it may be wise to keep a record of sacred things in a separate place in addition to historical data.

WHO WAS NEPHI? A great prophet-servant, Nephi was born in Jerusalem to Lehi and Sariah; large in stature and mighty in spirit, he was a peer of Daniel and a contemporary of Jeremiah and Ezekiel. He left Jerusalem with his family around 600 BC, and went onward via ocean travel to the promised land. There he became a colonizer, nation-builder, historian, teacher and preserver of the word of God, spiritual leader, temple-builder, and

MAIN THEMES

- Nephi and the other writers and abridgers of the Book of Mormon used great selectivity in what they chose to include in the records.

- Nephi's criteria governing what he included in the record provides us with a list of what we should include in our personal and family histories.

- The value of the Book of Mormon is great because of what was included in it.

- In our lives, we should focus on the things that are pleasing to God, not those that are pleasing to man.

600 BC

90 BC

prophet. An untiring disciple of Christ, he was commanded to separate his people (the Nephites) from those of his brothers (the Lamanites). He went on to build a temple (see 2 Ne. 5:16) and lead his people in the manner of happiness. Before he died, he ordained his brother Jacob to succeed him as spiritual leader and keeper of the records.

KEY INSIGHTS ABOUT THE SAVIOR

- The Lord desires that we record the events of our lives in a way that will inspire our descendants to come unto Him.
- The fulness of Nephi's intent is to bring people to Christ, which is the whole purpose of the Book of Mormon.

1Nephi 7

" . . . the Lord is able to do all things the children of men, if it so be that they (1 Ne. 7:12)

Major Concept

As we are led by and respond to the Spirit, we become important instruments in the hands of the Lord in fulfilling prophecy and in setting the stage for future events.

OVERVIEW Lehi is inspired to invite Ishmael and his family to leave Jerusalem and to travel into the wilderness with him and his family. He sends his sons, under the leadership of Nephi, back to Jerusalem to persuade Ishmael and his family to join them on their trek. Ishmael's heart is softened, and the journey back to Lehi's family begins. During the journey—probably 360 miles, which takes about a month round-trip—Laman and Lemuel rebel and want to return to live in Jerusalem; they bind Nephi with cords and plan to leave him in the wilderness to be devoured by wild beasts. Strengthened by the Lord, Nephi bursts the cords that bind him. Still angry, his brothers again attempt to lay their hands on him but are persuaded by members

Prominent People

- Lehi
- Nephi
- Sam
- Laman
- Lemuel
- Ishmael and his family

Main Themes

- The natural man tends to forget the Lord and rebel against Him even after significant spiritual experiences.

- We are delivered from our enemies in this life or the next when we obey the commandments and follow the Lord.

- The influence of one righteous member of a family can significantly alter the outcome for all family members.

- We should follow promptings of the Spirit, which are given to direct us in paths that can save us and our descendants.

of Ishmael's family to spare Nephi. They repent, and Nephi forgives them.

INTERESTING FACTS ABOUT THE JOINING OF TWO FAMILIES Before traveling any farther into the wilderness, Lehi was inspired to invite Ishmael and his family to accompany him and his family on their travels. He sent his sons back to Jerusalem—even though they had just completed the round-trip journey to obtain the plates of brass—to convince Ishmael and his family to join them on their trek into the wilderness. Ishmael's heart was softened, and he accepted the invitation. Later, his daughters' marriages to Lehi's sons was the fulfillment of an important prophecy that the descendants of Abraham and Isaac would grow together on the American continent (see Gen. 48). Ishmael and his family were of the lineage of Ephraim, while Lehi and his family were

according to his will, for
exercise faith in him. . . ."

of the lineage of Manasseh, thereby joining the descendants of Abraham and Isaac. An important reason for the journey was so members of both families could marry in the covenant, which was a commandment under the law of Moses (see Deut. 7:3–4).

WHO WAS ISHMAEL? Ishmael, a descendant of Ephraim, was living in Jerusalem at the time of Lehi's departure in about 600 BC. At the time he was invited to join Lehi and his family in the wilderness, Ishmael's family included his wife, five daughters, and two sons who were presumably married with children. While Ishmael was supportive of the exodus with Lehi's group, there was a division of opinion among his children; both of his sons and two of his daughters rebelled but eventually the group did complete the journey. Ishmael's five daughters of marriageable age married Laman, Lemuel, Sam, Nephi, and Zoram. Ishmael did not live to complete the journey to the promised land; he died in the wilderness and was buried in a place called Nahom (see 1 Ne. 16:34), which means "to sigh or moan." The combined families went on to establish mighty nations. Nephi, Sam, Jacob, Joseph, and Zoram stood at the head of the Nephite nation; Laman, Lemuel, and the two sons of Ishmael established the Lamanite nation.

KEY INSIGHTS ABOUT THE SAVIOR

- The Lord protects and comes to the rescue of those who obey and follow Him in faith and righteousness.
- The Lord knows the beginning from the end and directs His servants to accomplish those things that advance His cause.
- The Savior will forgive whom He will forgive, but we are to forgive all men.

1 Nephi 8

"And as I partook of the fruit thereof it joy; wherefore, I began to be desirous that for I knew that it was desirable above all

MAJOR CONCEPT

By clinging to the word of God and avoiding the pride and temptations of the world, we and our families can partake of the Atonement and experience the love of God, which is the sweetest of all experiences.

OVERVIEW In the vision of the tree of life, one of the most significant visions ever recorded, Lehi is privileged to see in a dream the process by which we gain exaltation. By holding steadfastly to the iron rod (the word of God, or the gospel), we travel safely through the large and spacious field (the world), avoiding the river of water (the depths of hell) and the mist of darkness (the temptations of the devil). We are also able to avoid entering the great and spacious building (the pride and vanity of the world) and at last come to the tree of life, where we partake of its fruit (the love of God), which is most desirable above all else. Lehi sees in vision that Nephi, Sam, and their families are saved and partake of the fruit but feels great fear for Laman and Lemuel, who have refused to embark on the path.

PROMINENT PEOPLE

- Lehi
- Nephi
- Sam
- Laman
- Lemuel

INTERESTING FACTS ABOUT SYMBOLISM Lehi's vision of the tree of life is a significant exercise in symbolism. The Lord often teaches using symbolism; Elder John A. Widtsoe wrote, "The holy endowment is deeply symbolic. Going through the temple is not a very good phrase, for temple

MAIN THEMES

- Any significant undertaking in life should be done with adequate and careful preparation, just as Lehi prepared to travel in the wilderness.

- The word of God that keeps us safe from the snares of evil includes the scriptures, the gospel plan, and the words of living prophets.

- Mocking, ridiculing, and finger-pointing are ways the wicked try to make the righteous feel ashamed.

- Our first concern should be to share truth with our family.

- A child's rejection of the truth as taught by righteous parents is a product of the child's unwise use of agency rather than a reflection of the parents' efforts.

- Different categories of people have different approaches for coming unto Christ.

filled my soul with exceedingly great my family should partake of it also; other fruit." (1 Ne. 8:12)

worship implies a great effort of mind and concentration if we are to understand the mighty symbols that pass in review before us. . . . No man or woman can come out of the temple endowed as he should be, unless he has seen, beyond the symbol, the mighty realities for which the symbols stand. The endowment which was given by revelation can best be understood by revelation; and to those who seek most vigorously, with pure hearts, will the revelation be greatest" (Widtsoe, 62).

WHO WAS SAM? Sam was Nephi's next older brother. Nephi offered insight into Sam's character when he testified of Lehi's message from God, saying, "And I spake unto Sam, making known unto him the things which the Lord had manifested unto me by his Holy Spirit. And it came to pass that he believed in my words" (1 Ne. 2:17). From that time on, Sam was loyal to Nephi and endured in the faith. Just before he died, Lehi gave Sam a special blessing, promising that he would be blessed in all his days (see 2 Ne. 4:11). When Nephi separated from his brothers, sometime between 588 and 570 BC, Sam and his family went with Nephi and became part of the Nephite nation. Sam and his posterity remained united with the posterity of Nephi, where they grew in strength and faith because they "lived after the manner of happiness" (2 Ne. 5:6).

KEY INSIGHTS ABOUT THE SAVIOR

- The Lord uses symbolism to reveal truth to those who are spiritually ready and to conceal spiritual truths from those who are not prepared to receive them.
- The Lord cares deeply about each of His children and will provide answers to our questions.
- The tree represents Christ; the tree—Christ—is the focus of the dream, just as Christ is the central focus of life and the universe.

1Nephi 9

"But the Lord knoweth all things from the
way to accomplish all his works among
hath all power unto the fulfilling of all

MAJOR CONCEPT

The Lord knows ahead of time what will take place and will guide and counsel us to be
instruments in His hands in helping accomplish His will.

OVERVIEW In another break from the historical narrative, Nephi gives some insight into his efforts in engraving the plates. At this point, Nephi has finished abridging Lehi's records. He tells of his intention to make two sets of records, both called the plates of Nephi. The larger plates contain a secular, historical account; the smaller plates mostly contain a spiritual account of Nephi's ministry among his people.

INTERESTING FACTS ABOUT THE TWO SETS OF PLATES Nephi is careful in this chapter to explain that he is preparing two separate sets of plates. The first, also known as the large plates, were made in 590 BC and contain a

PROMINENT PEOPLE

• Nephi

MAIN THEMES

- It is crucial that we obey the promptings of the Spirit, even if we don't know beforehand what the outcome will be or why the direction is given.

- Generations will be blessed by our efforts to record our personal and family histories.

secular history—a "full account" that contains the reign of the kings, the wars and contentions of the people, and other historical details. The second set of plates— our current 1 Nephi through Omni—was made in 570 BC and contains a spiritual or ecclesiastical history. Nephi explains that the Lord commanded him to make two separate sets of plates "for a wise purpose in him, which purpose I know not" (1 Ne. 9:5). But, as he also states, "the Lord knoweth all things from the beginning" (1 Ne. 9:6)—and He knew the first 116 pages of the manuscript, which were the translation of the large plates (the book of Lehi), would be stolen by Satan-inspired men. Despite that loss, we still have the history (this one spiritual) of Nephi and his family because of the account on the small plates (see D&C 10:8–11, 40–45).

WHO WAS NEPHI? Among the most recognized and admired of the Lord's

beginning; wherefore, he prepareth a
the children of men; for behold, he
his words." (1 Ne. 9:6)

prophet-servants, Nephi was an example of
faith, obedience, steadfastness, leadership,
and valor in upholding a testimony of Jesus
Christ as Redeemer and Savior. As a peer of
Jeremiah, Daniel, and Ezekiel, Nephi was
a first-hand witness of the cultural unrest
and spiritual decline in the Holy Land
immediately prior to the destruction of
Jerusalem by the Babylonians around 587
BC. His journey with his family through
the wilderness of what is now Saudi Arabia
and then via ocean transit to the promised
land is a stunning chronicle of suffering and
sacrifice. After arriving in the promised land, he grew in stature
and wisdom to become a powerful leader who established the
great Nephite nation.

Image: The Lord prepared for Martin Harris losing the 116 pages with
His commandment that Nephi make a second record.

KEY INSIGHTS ABOUT THE SAVIOR

- The Lord knows what lies ahead and will guide and direct
  us to fulfill His purposes.
- The Lord has all power when it comes to the fulfilling of
  His words.

1 Nephi 10

"For he is the same yesterday, to-day, all men from the foundation of the unto him." (1 Ne. 10:18)

MAJOR CONCEPT

Salvation is possible only through Jesus Christ, who came to redeem all mankind from their sins.

OVERVIEW In this chapter, Lehi delivers powerful prophecies regarding the Babylonian captivity and the eventual scattering and gathering of Israel. He also prophesies of John the Baptist, "a prophet who should come before the Messiah, to prepare the way of the Lord" (1 Ne. 10:7) and who would baptize the Messiah. Finally, he prophesies of Jesus Christ, who will redeem all mankind. Nephi testifies that the Holy Ghost bears witness of all truth and that those who diligently seek will find through the power of the Holy Ghost.

INTERESTING FACTS ABOUT THE ALLEGORY OF THE OLIVE TREE This chapter is not the only place in which

PROMINENT PEOPLE

- Nephi
- Lehi
- Jesus Christ
- John the Baptist
- The Holy Ghost

MAIN THEMES

- The house of Israel will be scattered upon the face of the earth but will be physically gathered again after coming to a knowledge of the Messiah (which represents a spiritual gathering).
- We will be judged for all our acts in mortality. If we seek wickedness, we will be found unclean and will not be able to dwell in the presence of God.
- If we repent and come unto Christ, the way is prepared for us to gain exaltation.
- We can know all things by the power of the Holy Ghost, which is the gift of God to all those who seek Him.

the house of Israel is compared to an olive tree. Readers of the Book of Mormon are familiar with the allegory of the olive tree detailed in Jacob 5, which is based on the prophecies of Zenos, a Hebrew prophet who was slain because he testified with great boldness about the things the Lord revealed to him. We now find this same comparison given by Lehi. It is likely that Lehi was familiar with the allegory of the olive tree, since it would have been found on the plates of brass retrieved from Laban's treasury and since Lehi was known to have read and studied the plates early in his exodus into the wilderness. The Apostle Paul probably had access to the same records of Zenos (see Rom. 11:16–25).

WHO IS THE HOLY GHOST? The Holy Ghost, the third member of the Godhead, is a personage of spirit who does not possess a body of flesh and bones. He is

and forever; and the way is prepared for
world, if it so be that they repent and come

often referred to as the Spirit, the Spirit
of the Lord, the Holy Spirit, and the
Comforter. The power of the Holy Ghost
was manifest among all the dispensations
prior to the Savior, during which time the
Holy Ghost guided, bore witness, and
revealed truth. Once the Savior came, He
established the gift of the Holy Ghost;
that gift is conferred following baptism,
by proper authority and the laying on of
hands, and entitles a worthy recipient to
the companionship of the Holy Ghost.
While the Holy Ghost has a number of
roles, the primary one is as a convincing
witness of the truth.

Key Insights about the Savior

- The Lord is the same yesterday, today, and forever, and will
  never change in the way He deals with us on earth.
- The course of the Lord is one eternal round.
- All mankind would remain in a lost and fallen state if it
  were not for the Atonement of Jesus Christ.

1Nephi 11

" . . . thou shalt also behold a man witness; and after ye have witnessed God." (1 Ne. 11:7)

MAJOR CONCEPT

Jesus Christ, the Son of God, was born in the flesh, baptized, ministered unto the people, and was slain for the sins of the world.

OVERVIEW Nephi has been taught by his father, Lehi, and believed all the things he has been taught—providing a powerful example of honoring his parents. However, he has a real desire to know for himself all the things he has been taught, including Lehi's remarkable vision of the tree of life. As he ponders, he is caught up in the Spirit and shown for himself the vision of the tree of life. He is also shown the circumstances of the Savior's birth, ministry, and crucifixion. Verses 12 through 26 of this chapter constitute the central message of the Book of Mormon.

INTERESTING FACTS ABOUT CONDESCENSION The word *condescend* means to voluntarily descend from a superior rank, position, or dignity to one that is lesser—generally, to stoop or yield. In this chapter, two different verses refer to "the condescension of God," but each has a specific and unique meaning. As used in verse 16 the word refers to the condescension of God the Father, which occurred when He became the father of a man born to a mortal woman. Verse 26 refers to the condescension of Jesus

PROMINENT PEOPLE

- Nephi
- Jesus Christ

MAIN THEMES

- We can know for ourselves the truths taught by others.
- Quiet study and meditation are of tremendous value and can lead to great spiritual insights.
- The tree of life represents the love of God, which is personifed in the Savior; only through repentance and accessing the Atonement can we come unto Christ.
- The word of God always manifests the will of God.

- Nephi's vision of Christ's mortal ministry provides a second witness to the Bible.
- The Lord's covenant people, after falling into apostasy, led the fight against the Twelve.

600 BC

90 BC

descending out of heaven, and him shall ye
him ye shall bear record that it is the Son of

Christ, which occurred when He submitted
Himself to all mortal trials and suffering.

WHO WAS JESUS CHRIST IN THE BOOK OF MORMON? The central figure of the Book of Mormon is Jesus Christ; everything in the book testifies of the Lamb of God and His love and mercy for all of God's children. Prophecies about His divine nature and His redeeming mission abound. He was seen by many Book of Mormon prophets, including Nephi, Jacob, the brother of Jared, and Moroni; in His resurrected state, He was seen by thousands in Bountiful. The most compelling section of the Book of Mormon is the account of Jesus' visit to His "other sheep" on the American continent following His crucifixion and resurrection.

Images: Photo and sketch of Izapa Stela 5, thought to represent Lehi's dream.

KEY INSIGHTS ABOUT THE SAVIOR

- Jesus Christ—the Lamb of God—was born in the flesh to a virgin.
- The Savior was baptized by John the Baptist and went forth ministering to and healing the people of all their afflictions.
- The Redeemer was crucified on a cross and slain for the sins of the world.
- The Savior was sent among men as a manifestation of God's love for all mankind.

1 Nephi 12

"And it came to pass that I looked together in multitudes against the together to battle." (1 Ne. 12:15)

MAJOR CONCEPT

The forces of wickedness will always strive and battle against the forces of righteousness.

OVERVIEW This chapter is a continuation of Nephi's vision that began in 1 Nephi 11. In this chapter, Nephi sees the division between his seed—the Nephite nation—and the seed of his brethren, the Lamanites; he also sees that the main interaction between the two groups will be one of wars and great slaughters. Nephi is shown the result of dwindling in unbelief among both the Nephites and the Lamanites. He is also shown what will happen on the American continent when the Savior is crucified, a vision that is fulfilled in 3 Nephi 8–9, and sees the appearance of the Savior to the people at Bountiful.

PROMINENT PEOPLE

- Nephi
- The Twelve Apostles
- The Nephites
- The Lamanites

INTERESTING FACTS ABOUT PRIDE In his vision, Nephi sees great strivings and battles between his seed (the Nephites) and the seed of his brethren (the Lamanites). Much of the time, these battles represent a clear-cut distinction between good and evil. However, Nephi then sees in vision a disturbing

MAIN THEMES

- Because prophecies come from the Lord, the same prophecies are uttered by various prophets in different dispensations.

- The continued righteousness of the Twelve Apostles qualifies them to take part in the last judgment.

- Satan hardens the hearts of men and causes them to battle against righteousness.

- Those who become blinded by pride are subject to the temptations of the devil.

- Those who dwindle in unbelief become a filthy and loathsome people.

development: when the Nephites become prideful, they are overcome by temptation and are defeated by the Lamanites, who then go forth in multitudes upon the face of the land (see 1 Ne. 12:19–20). The Nephite church is actually destroyed from within, due to the wickedness of its own members, instead of from outside forces. It is our duty to guard against this same thing in our own time; Elder Daniel H. Wells prophesied, "There will come a time in the history of the Saints when they will be tried with peace, prosperity, popularity, and riches" (*Journal of Discourses,* 19:367), all of which can contribute to pride.

WHO WERE THE LAMANITES? Throughout the Book of Mormon, the descendants of Laman (the son of Lehi) are called Lamanites. The descendants of other family lines were also integrated into this group, including the descendants of Lemuel and Ishmael. Instead of trying to distinguish between Lamanites, Lemuelites, and Ishmaelites, Jacob wrote that all those who sought to destroy the people of Nephi were called "Lamanites" (see Jacob 1:14). Much of the Book of Mormon consists of wars between the Nephites and the Lamanites. Following the apostasy of the Nephites toward the end of the Book of Mormon record, the Lamanites become a faithful and righteous people in fulfillment of prophecy, though they do not remain so.

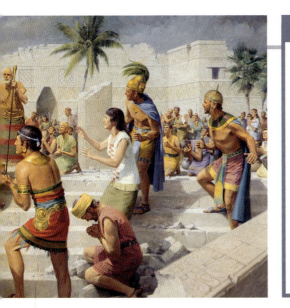

KEY INSIGHTS ABOUT THE SAVIOR

- Faith in the Savior and obedience to His commandments cause us to become clean and pure.
- The death of the Savior caused terrible earthquakes, tempests, tumults, and destruction in the promised land in fulfillment of prophecy.
- The Savior's Twelve Apostles will judge the twelve tribes of Israel.

1Nephi 13

"These last records, which thou hast
tongues, and people, that the Lamb
world; and that all men must come

MAJOR CONCEPT

The gospel has been restored and is evident in the coming forth of modern-day scripture
and the building up of Zion.

OVERVIEW Nephi's vision continues, and he sees the
establishment of the church of the devil, which is all of
Satan's dominions and followers; Christopher Columbus's
discovery of America and its subsequent colonization and
the loss of many plain and precious truths from the Bible,
which leads to the subsequent apostasy of the Gentiles. He
is also shown in vision the restoration of the gospel and
the coming forth of the latter-day scripture we know as the
Book of Mormon, the Doctrine and Covenants, and the
Joseph Smith Translation.

INTERESTING FACTS ABOUT CHRISTOPHER COLUMBUS
Christopher Columbus—who called himself an "emissary

PROMINENT PEOPLE

• Nephi
• The Gentiles
• Christopher Columbus

of the Holy Ghost"—said that the Lord
"unlocked" his mind as he studied histories
and maps in preparation for his voyages. Of
his initial journey to the American continent,
he wrote, "Who can doubt that the Holy
Ghost inspired me?" (see Petersen, 3, 26).
Nephi saw in vision not only Columbus (see

MAIN THEMES

• The church of the devil is the world and consists of all the evil and carnality to which fall-
en man is heir; it includes every false religion
and every church that does not exalt man.

• The Old Testament originally contained the
fulness of the gospel.

• Plain and precious things—scriptures that testified of Christ—were removed from the Old
Testament and the New Testament by people
who first took plain and precious things out of
the gospel and who took away many covenants.

• The Book of Mormon is another testament
of Jesus Christ.

• The brass plates (covering the period from
Adam through Jeremiah) contained more information than our present-day entire Bible.

seen among the Gentiles . . . shall make known to all kindreds, of God is the Son of the Eternal Father, and the Savior of the unto him, or they cannot be saved." (1 Ne. 13:40)

1 Ne. 13:12), but the European colonists who followed (see 1 Ne. 13:13) and who interacted with the descendants of Book of Mormon people. Nephi saw in vision that the seed of his brethren (the Lamanites) was scattered before the Gentiles and was smitten. The fulfillment of that prophecy is stark. When Columbus arrived, there were an estimated 10 million Indians living in North America; by the beginning of the twentieth century, there were only 235,000. When he arrived in Haiti, there were on the island an estimated 300,000 Indians; only fifty years later, there were fewer than 500 (see *Book of Mormon Student Manual,* 35).

WHO WAS CHRISTOPHER COLUMBUS?

Born in 1451 in the Republic of Genoa (present-day northwestern Italy), Christopher Columbus was a maritime navigator and explorer; a Roman Catholic, he had great interest in the Bible and biblical prophecies, which he often quoted. In 1492, he developed a scheme to sail from Europe to Asia—severely underestimating the circumference of the earth—and received funding from Isabella I of Castile, who hoped to gain an advantage in the spice trade. His first voyage across the Atlantic landed somewhere in the Bahamas; his later voyages molded the future of European colonization. He died on May 20, 1506, in present-day Spain.

KEY INSIGHTS ABOUT THE SAVIOR

- The Lord intervened in the founding of America, preparing a place where the gospel could be restored.
- The covenants of the Lord and the fulness of the gospel, once contained in the Old Testament, are now contained only in the Book of Mormon.
- The Lord's gospel is plain and precious.
- The Lord restored the truth to Joseph Smith.
- Other books (the Doctrine and Covenants, Pearl of Great Price, and Joseph Smith Translation) would come forth to make known that Jesus is God's Son and that all men must come unto Him.

1Nephi 14

"For the time cometh, saith the and a marvelous work among the everlasting. . . ." (1 Ne. 14:7)

MAJOR CONCEPT

There will be only two churches in the latter days: the Church of the Lamb of God and the church of the devil.

OVERVIEW Nephi's vision concludes in this chapter; he is told of the blessings and cursings that will come to the Gentiles. He also sees in vision the establishment of two churches—the Church of the Lamb of God and the church of the devil—and sees the great opposition that will exist between the two. Finally, he is given a vision of our day but is constrained from recording what he sees because an Apostle of Jesus Christ (John the Revelator) will be called to write the revelations. Nephi writes only a small part of what he sees in vision, and it is contained in the sealed portion of the Book of Mormon.

PROMINENT PEOPLE

- Nephi
- The Gentiles
- John the Beloved

INTERESTING FACTS ABOUT THE TWO CHURCHES The fourteenth chapter of Nephi distinguishes between the two churches that will exist in our day: the Church of the Lamb of God and the church of the devil (see 1 Ne. 14:11–15). The church of the devil, Nephi writes,

MAIN THEMES

- Whenever the church of God has been on the earth, the church of the devil has also been here.

- Great opposition will always exist between the Church of God and the church of the devil.

- The Church in the last days will be spared by the power of God and the righteousness of the Saints.

- No one can be neutral in regard to righteousness; we are either for or against the kingdom of God.

- When originally written, the Bible was plain and pure and easy to understand.

has dominion over all the earth, among all nations, kindred, tongues, and people; it is known as the whore of all the earth. It is every evil and worldly organization on earth (see McConkie, *The Millennial Messiah,* 54–55). It will gather multitudes and will be characterized by wickedness and abominations. The wrath of God will eventually be poured out upon it. In contrast, the Church of the Lamb of God will be upon all the face of the earth, though its members will be few in number. Despite its smaller numbers, it will be armed with righteousness and the power of God, and the power of the Lord will descend upon it and protect it from destruction.

WHO WAS JOHN? The son of Zebedee and the brother of James, John was one of the Lord's Twelve Apostles in the meridian of time. He was one of three Apostles—along with Peter and James—who had a special place of leadership among the Twelve. John exercised considerable energy and boldness in ministering on behalf of the Savior and was present at the Transfiguration, the Crucifixion, and the empty tomb. It is believed that he wrote the Gospel of John. Promised by the Lord that he would linger on the earth until the Savior comes again, John was eventually exiled to the isle of Patmos, where he wrote the book of Revelation.

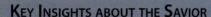

KEY INSIGHTS ABOUT THE SAVIOR

- The power of the Lord enables a few to triumph in battle against many.
- The Lord always prepares the way for the fulfilling of His covenants.
- The Lord assigned His Apostle John to write the revelations of the last days.
- The Lord will descend with great power to buoy up His Church in the last days.

1 Nephi 15

"Yea; they shall be remembered again grafted in, being a natural branch of (1 Ne. 15:16)

MAJOR CONCEPT

The descendants of Lehi—those broken off from the house of Israel—will receive the gospel in the latter days and will be saved.

OVERVIEW After his remarkable vision, summarized in the last four chapters, Nephi returns to Lehi's tent, where he finds his brothers disputing once again. Nephi explains the necessity of asking the Lord for clarification on matters hard to understand. He then repeats the symbolism of the olive tree, saying that the Gentiles will eventually be grafted in, or restored, and with all the kindreds of the earth will be blessed.

INTERESTING FACTS ABOUT GRAFTING AN OLIVE TREE If the green slip of an olive tree is merely planted and allowed to grow, it develops into a wild olive that produces only a small, worthless fruit. To become a productive tree, the main stem of the wild tree must be cut back completely, and a branch from a tame olive tree must be grafted into the stem of the wild one. With careful pruning and cultivating, the tree will begin to produce its first fruit in about seven years and will become fully productive in about fifteen

PROMINENT PEOPLE

- Nephi
- Lehi
- The Gentiles
- The Jews

MAIN THEMES

- Unless we inquire of the Lord, we will not fully understand the gospel.
- The tribes of Israel have a specific mission and will be scattered and go through difficult trials before being gathered again.
- The Abrahamic covenant promises that all the people of the earth will be blessed.
- The Jews will be restored in the latter days, indicating that they will be converted to the true Church and will assemble in Zion.
- Those who die in their wickedness will be cast off spiritually and will not be able to inherit the kingdom of God.
- In the last days, the fulness of the gospel will be brought forth from the Gentiles to the Lamanites.

years. Grafted and pruned, it will continue to produce fruit for centuries.

WHO WERE THE GENTILES? The word *Gentiles* used in scripture generally refers to those people who were not of the house of Israel. The term *gentile* can also refer to nations that do not yet have the gospel, even though there may be those of Israelite lineage among them. They are "cultural Gentiles." In the Book of Mormon, as in other scripture, the word *Gentiles* is largely used in context of the unfolding of the gospel message beyond those of Israelite heritage to encompass the entire world, as the Savior directed.

Image: Grafted olive tree.

KEY INSIGHTS ABOUT THE SAVIOR

• The Lord assures us that if we ask of Him in faith, with diligence in keeping the commandments, He will provide answers.

• Through the coming forth of the Book of Mormon, the Lamanites of the latter days will come to a knowledge of the Redeemer.

• No unclean thing can enter into the presence of the Savior.

• The Savior was sent to atone for our sins as a manifestation of God's great love for us.

1Nephi 16

"And it came to pass as my father arose tent door, to his great astonishment ball of curious workmanship. . . ."

MAJOR CONCEPT

If we exercise faith, affliction makes us strong.

OVERVIEW This chapter was written thirty years after Lehi left Jerusalem (ten years after arriving in the promised land), so it contains only highlights of the journey. As Lehi and his family prepare to journey farther into the wilderness, they discover the Liahona, a round ball of curious workmanship that serves as a type of compass to direct them in their travels. Lehi's sons, along with Zoram, marry the daughters of Ishmael. As he attempts to hunt for food, Nephi breaks his steel bow and subsequently has to fashion a bow out of wood. In one of the great lessons of the Book of Mormon, he asks his father, Lehi, where he should hunt, showing confidence in his struggling father. Ishmael dies on this part of the journey and is buried in Nahom; his family

PROMINENT PEOPLE

- Lehi
- Nephi
- Laman
- Lemuel
- Ishmael and his daughters

mourns, and Laman uses Ishmael's death as a chance to sow affliction among the family.

INTERESTING FACTS ABOUT NEPHI'S BOW In Nephi's time, bows were symbols of political power. Thus, when Nephi's steel bow broke and those of his brothers lost their spring, Nephi fashioned a new bow—and, as the only person in the group who now had a bow, he was accused by his brothers of having political ambitions. There is another curious detail in this account that further proves that the Book of Mormon was translated, not written by Joseph Smith. Nephi mentions that his bow broke but does not mention that any of his arrows were damaged. Yet he specifies that he fashioned new arrows from straight sticks. Why didn't he just use the old arrows with the new bow? His original bow was made of steel—and would have required heavier, thicker arrows than could be used with a wood bow, something that wouldn't have

MAIN THEMES

- Those who are unrighteous find it more difficult to hear the words of the Lord.

- The guilty take the truth to be hard, for it cuts them to the very center; the righteous are justified by the truth.

- How we react to adversity determines its outcome for us.

- We need to remember the Lord and give thanks to Him at all times, not just after our problems are resolved.

- True conversion requires an inner change—a contrite spirit and a broken heart.

600 BC

90 BC

in the morning, and went forth to the he beheld upon the ground a round (1 Ne. 16:10)

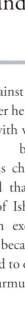

Lehi's family travels along the Red Sea

WHO WERE THE DAUGHTERS OF ISHMAEL?
When Nephi and his brothers returned to Jerusalem for a second time to persuade Ishmael and his family to join their exodus to the promised land, Ishmael and his entire family readily left their home in Jerusalem. Ishmael had two sons and five daughters; the five daughters eventually married Nephi, Sam, Laman, Lemuel, and Zoram. Ishmael's sons also married Lehi's daughters (information in the lost 116 pages; see *Journal of Discourses,* 23:184). One of the daughters was instrumental in defending Nephi against his brothers after he burst the bands with which they had bound him. In this chapter, we are told that the daughters of Ishmael did "mourn exceedingly" at his death; they are specifically mentioned because among the desert Arabs, only the women were allowed to officially mourn. The death of their father caused them to murmur against Lehi and to express regret over leaving Jerusalem.

been known by those (like Joseph Smith) unfamiliar with archery (see Welch, 41–42).

KEY INSIGHTS ABOUT THE SAVIOR

- The Lord chastens those whom He loves.
- The Lord will direct us in all things as we ask Him and exercise faith in Him.
- Just as the Liahona led Lehi's family to the promised land, so will the words of Christ lead us to a land of promise.
- By small things the Lord can bring about great things.
- As we repent and change, the Lord pours out blessings upon us.

1Nephi 17

"And if it so be that the children of doth nourish them, and strengthen can accomplish the thing which he

MAJOR CONCEPT

Even when the Lord requires hard things of us, He will prepare the way and make it possible for us to obey.

OVERVIEW After wandering for eight years in the wilderness, Lehi's family arrives at the land they call Bountiful, where they pitch their tents by the seashore. The Lord commands Nephi to build a ship that will carry the family across the many waters; though Laman and Lemuel first ridicule him and then try to prevent him from building the ship, Nephi is filled with the power of the Lord and shocks his brothers when they try to lay hands on him. His brothers repent and acknowledge the hand of the Lord. Throughout the chapter, Nephi compares the situation of his family to that of the children of Israel under the leadership of Moses.

PROMINENT PEOPLE

- Nephi
- Laman
- Lemuel
- Moses

INTERESTING FACTS ABOUT BOUNTIFUL There is only one place along the 1,400-mile Arabian peninsula that meets the description of Bountiful as given in the Book of Mormon—a place with a mountain, a shoreline, a cliff overlooking the sea, water, grass, flowers, honeybees, large trees from which to construct a ship, and metal ore. That place is Salalah, in present-day Dhofar in the Sultanate of Oman. This small sickle of land curves around a 28-mile bay and is backed by a little range of mountains—a condition that causes significant rainfall to this isolated area but to none other on the peninsula. Stretching away from it in all directions is solid barrenness. The same geography has existed there for at least two thousand years (see Brown, 46).

MAIN THEMES

- Adversity strengthens and toughens us to meet even greater challenges, just as eight years in the Arabian peninsula prepared Lehi's colony to establish the New World.
- The Book of Mormon substantiates accounts in the Bible and is a second witness.
- Nothing is accomplished without the Lord, but with the Lord all things are possible.
- We can become past feeling such that we are not perceptive to the still, small voice.

WHO WAS MOSES? Moses was the prophet of God who liberated the Israelites from Egyptian bondage, sustained them in their journeys in the wilderness, received the Ten

men keep the commandments of God he
them, and provide means whereby they
has commanded them. . . ." (1 Ne. 17:3)

Commandments and the law of Moses, established the Tabernacle among the people, authored the first five books of the Old Testament, and led the Israelites to the promised land. Under Moses's leadership, the Lord blessed the people with manna from heaven so they would not starve and parted the waters of the Red Sea, enabling them to escape the Egyptian soldiers and cross on dry land. In our day, it was Moses who appeared to Joseph Smith and Oliver Cowdery in the Kirtland Temple on April 3, 1836, to restore the keys of the gathering of Israel. Of major significance as a theme in the Book of Mormon is the fulfillment of the law of Moses through the ministry and Atonement of the Savior.

KEY INSIGHTS ABOUT THE SAVIOR

- The Lord nourishes and strengthens those who obey Him and provides the way for them to accomplish the things He commands.
- The Lord will serve as our light in the darkness and will prepare the way before us.
- The Lord regards all mankind as having equal value, but He favors the righteous.
- The Savior created the earth to be inhabited and for us.
- The Lord is the source of all power.
- By looking to the Savior, the Israelites bitten by serpents in the wilderness were saved. We too can be saved from fiery serpents of our day by looking to the Savior.

Image: Salalah in Dhofar.

1Nephi 18

"And it came to pass that after we did arrive at the promised land; and pitch our tents; and we did call it

MAJOR CONCEPT

The Lord blesses those who are obedient and willing to sacrifice.

OVERVIEW Nephi finishes the ship and Lehi and his family depart for the promised land after gathering abundant provisions. During the journey, the sons of Ishmael and their wives engage in revelry and then became rebellious, binding Nephi and threatening his life. While Nephi is bound the ship is driven back by a ferocious storm; only after he is freed and has offered prayer does the storm cease. The entire company arrives safely in the promised land, where they begin to till the earth, plant seeds, and mine ore.

INTERESTING FACTS ABOUT HORSES Verse 25 in this chapter provides solid evidence that Joseph Smith did not write the Book of Mormon: when mentioning the beasts

PROMINENT PEOPLE

- Lehi
- Nephi
- Laman
- Lemuel
- Jacob
- Joseph

MAIN THEMES

- Forgetting the Lord is the root of rebellion.
- The actions of one or two can dramatically affect an entire family.
- "Exceeding rudeness" can cause our personal Liahonas to stop working.
- Faith can control the elements.
- We should bear affliction with courage and faith and should not murmur against the Lord as we go through trials.

that were found in the promised land, he includes "the horse." In 1830, around the time that the Book of Mormon was translated, historians had stated that there were no horses on the American continent until recent times. Had he written—instead of translated—the Book of Mormon, Joseph Smith would have adhered to the knowledge of his day and would not have included horses in his list. Only later did archaeological evidence prove that horses were on the American continent as early as 2600 BC.

WHO WAS JACOB? Jacob, Nephi's younger brother and successor as leader of the Nephites, is considered among the greatest of the doctrinal analysts and preachers in the Book of Mormon. Born during Lehi's journey through the wilderness, Jacob lived the life of a wanderer; he wrote at the end of his life that they were "a lonesome and a solemn people, wanderers, cast out

had sailed for the space of many days we we went forth upon the land, and did the promised land." (1 Ne. 18:23)

from Jerusalem, born in tribulation, in a wilderness, and hated of our brethren" (Jacob 7:26). As one of the two youngest children, he keenly felt the effects of Laman and Lemuel's wickedness. Nevertheless, with trust in the Messiah, Jacob built a lifelong ministry, preserved the history of his people on the plates, witnessed angels, was nourished by the Spirit continually, and beheld the Redeemer.

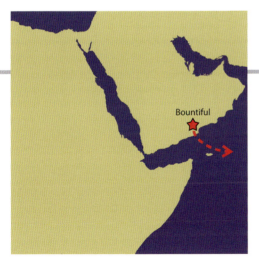

KEY INSIGHTS ABOUT THE SAVIOR

- The Lord often relies on people who have less formal education or experience but greater spiritual strength.

- The Lord protects those who are faithful and obedient.

- The Lord guides and instructs us; Nephi did not build the ship after the manner of men, but after the manner the Lord showed him.

1Nephi 19

"And I did read many things unto Moses; . . . for I did liken all scriptures and learning." (1 Ne. 19:23)

MAJOR CONCEPT

The prophecies about Jesus Christ are veiled in the Old Testament, but the plates of brass are bold and unmistakable in testifying of Him.

OVERVIEW Situated in the promised land, Nephi makes plates of ore (the large plates of Nephi) and begins to record the history of his people. In this chapter, Nephi again testifies of the coming of Jesus Christ—prophesying that He will be born into mortality six hundred years from the time Lehi's family left Jerusalem—and focuses on His crucifixion and resurrection. He also prophesies of the scattering and eventual gathering of the Jews.

INTERESTING FACTS ABOUT THE PLATES The plates of ore referred to in verse 1 are the large plates, but in 1 Nephi 19 we are reading from the small plates. A great deal of evidence shows that people in the Middle East often wrote on metal plates so that their writing would be preserved. We know that Nephi knew how to smelt metal (see 1 Ne. 17:9–11, 16). The "plates of ore" that Nephi made were actually gold—the ore found on the American continent at that time contained a high percentage of gold—and were the

PROMINENT PEOPLE

- Nephi
- Jesus Christ
- Zenos
- Zenock
- Neum
- The Jews

MAIN THEMES

- We are sometimes commanded to do things without knowing the reason.

- Nephi followed the pattern of those who went before in determining what to write on the plates.

- Peoples are scattered because they reject the gospel, defile the priesthood, forsake the Church, depart from the kingdom, turn from the Lord, and worship false gods.

- The Jews were scattered because they turned their hearts aside and despised the Savior.

- Revelations of our day have been shown to numerous prophets.

- We should liken all scriptures unto ourselves.

smaller plates that contained the spiritual record and prophecies. Until 722 BC the brass plates that were obtained from Laban were the scriptures of the house of Israel; they contained significant prophecies about the Savior, debunking the myth that Christianity started with Christ and His Apostles. Many of the characters on the Anthon transcript—a one-page document copied from the plates from which the Book of Mormon was translated—are similar to those of the Old North Arabian dialect, a dialect that would have been used in the area where Lehi's family set up their first camp in the wilderness (see *Echoes,* 86–88).

WHO WAS ZENOS? Zenos was a Hebrew prophet of the lineage of Joseph whose writings were included in the brass plates and were thus available to the Book of Mormon prophets. Gospel scholars Sidney B. Sperry and Robert L. Millet believe that Zenos was one of the prophets of the lost ten tribes. Zenos prophesied of the Savior's resurrection and of the three days of darkness and the widespread natural calamities that would occur on the American continent at His death. Zenos was the author of the all-encompassing allegory of the tame and wild olive trees that was retold by Jacob. Next to Isaiah, the prophet Zenos is quoted more extensively in the Book of Mormon than any other ancient Hebrew prophet.

KEY INSIGHTS ABOUT THE SAVIOR

- The Lord suffered the scourging and smiting of the Jews because of His loving kindness and long-suffering toward the children of men.

- The Lord yielded Himself into the hands of wicked people who crucified Him.

- At the last day the Lord will visit all His people, who will receive Him with joy and salvation because of their righteousness.

- When the day comes that the Jews no longer turn their hearts against the Savior, He will gather them—first in a spiritual, and then in a temporal gathering.

- The Lord showed prophets of old things concerning the Jews ("them") and concerning the Nephites ("us").

1Nephi 20

"For, behold, I have refined thee, furnace of affliction." (1 Ne. 20:10)

Major Concept

Those who have been chosen by the Lord will be tried in the furnace of affliction so they can go forward with strength and righteousness.

OVERVIEW Nephi pauses in his record on the small plates to quote from the plates of brass the prophecies of Isaiah, who reminds Israel that they must listen with intent to the Lord. In this chapter he quotes Isaiah 48, in which the Lord reveals His purposes and tells His people that they have been chosen in the furnace of affliction—a message that is relevant to Saints of every age and dispensation.

INTERESTING FACTS ABOUT ISAIAH Isaiah played a profound role in the Book of Mormon. His inspired words accompanied Lehi and his family on the plates of brass obtained from Laban. For Lehi and Nephi, looking back in time from the vantage point of 600 BC, the voice of Isaiah

Prominent People

- Isaiah
- Jesus Christ

was still vibrant, for he had prophesied of the Savior only a century and a half earlier. Put into perspective, that's like Saints of our day looking back at the mission of the Prophet Joseph Smith. The style of Isaiah is unique; not only did he use a great deal of symbolism, but he intermingled references of his own day with those of future times.

Main Themes

- In choosing our path through mortality, we must constantly listen to the Lord.
- The righteous need not fear.
- Obedience and righteousness bring us peace of heart and mind.
- There is no peace for the wicked.
- The Jews are invited to hearken to the Lord.

WHO WAS ISAIAH? Isaiah, the son of Amoz and chief advisor to King Hezekiah, was one of the greatest prophets of the Lord in any dispensation and is the most quoted of all the prophets in the scriptures (see "Quotations," LDS Bible Dictionary, 758). The book of Isaiah is one of the major prophetic books of the Old Testament; in it, Isaiah captures the sweeping contours of the Lord's plan for mankind. Isaiah often spans the entire range of man's existence in a verse or two, always returning to the central theme of the Messiah. At the core of Isaiah's writing is a vision of the mission

I have chosen thee in the

of the Redeemer and the atoning power of the Father's plan of salvation. His is the age-old prophetic message that wickedness never was happiness and that good will eventually triumph in the last days. The Savior Himself said of him, "Great are the words of Isaiah" (3 Ne. 23:1).

KEY INSIGHTS ABOUT THE SAVIOR

- The Lord will not allow His name to be polluted.
- The Lord will not allow His glory to be given to another.
- Israel is a peculiar treasure to the Lord, one He will never abandon.
- Christ is the first and the last, Alpha and Omega.
- The Lord foretold the destiny of Israel to the Jews through His prophets.
- The Lord will not cut off Judah.

1Nephi 21

"Behold, I have graven thee upon walls are continually before me."

MAJOR CONCEPT

No matter what else happens, the Lord will never forget or forsake us.

OVERVIEW Nephi continues quoting the prophet Isaiah in this chapter, which is taken from Isaiah 49. He teaches that the Gentiles will receive the gospel and will then take the word of the Lord to the house of Israel. Israel—the covenant people of the Lord—will accept the gospel and will be gathered in power in the last days. The information in this chapter lets us know that the house of Israel has an important mission to the world.

INTERESTING FACTS ABOUT RIGHTEOUSNESS As Nephi finishes up the section we know now as 1 Nephi, he cautions that the things he has written "testify that a man must be obedient to the commandments of God" (1 Ne. 22:30). He

PROMINENT PEOPLE

- The house of Israel
- The Gentiles
- Jesus Christ

further instructs us that only by obedience will we be able to endure to the end and be saved at the last day (see 1 Ne. 22:31). Righteousness is the key for saving not only us as individuals, but the world as a whole. President Spencer W. Kimball stated, "There is only one cure for the earth's sick condition. That infallible cure is simply righteousness, obedience, godliness, honor, integrity. Nothing else will suffice" (*The Miracle of Forgiveness*).

WHO IS "ISRAEL"? Generally, the term *Israel* is used to describe all those who are true believers in Christ. It is also used to denote all those belonging to the covenant people of God—either literally or through adoption according to their obedience to gospel principles. As an example, the "new song" for the redemption of Zion, revealed to the Prophet Joseph Smith, states in part, "The Lord has redeemed his people, Israel, According to the election of grace, Which was brought to pass by the faith And covenant of their fathers" (D&C 84:99).

MAIN THEMES

- It is not enough for us to strengthen each other; we must become an ensign of truth to all the nations.

- A massive number of people are still waiting to be gathered.

- Through conversion, the children of Israel will realize who they are and will recognize their place in the royal family.

- As the people of Israel embrace the word of God, they will know that the Lord is their Savior.

- The gospel will be a standard to the nations in the last days.

the palms of my hands; thy
(1 Ne. 21:16)

Image: Orson Hyde dedicates the Holy Land.

1Nephi 22

"And he gathereth his children from his sheep, and they know him; and he shall feed his sheep, and in him

MAJOR CONCEPT

In the last days the righteous will be gathered and saved, and the kingdom of the devil will be destroyed.

OVERVIEW Repeating a theme he addressed earlier, Nephi teaches that Israel will be scattered upon the face of the earth, but will be taught and nourished by the Gentiles in the last days. As Israel is gathered and saved in those days, the wicked will be destroyed, and Satan himself will be bound.

PROMINENT PEOPLE

- Nephi
- The Gentiles
- Jesus Christ
- The house of Israel
- Satan

INTERESTING FACTS ABOUT SCATTERING AND GATHERING Scattering can mean three different things: first, people lose their identity and are lost to history (as happened to the Ten Tribes); second, people leave the main group but maintain their identity (as happened to Lehi's colony); and third, people are dispersed and scattered among other people (as happened to the Jews). Gathering takes place when people gain knowledge or truth. There will be three main kinds of gathering in the last days: the Jews will return to Jerusalem, the Ten Tribes will be restored, and all the inhabitants of the earth will gain knowledge of the truth regarding

MAIN THEMES

- Through the missionary work that we do, all the people of the earth will be blessed.

- Those who are lost will be brought out of captivity, obscurity, and darkness.

- All of the house of Israel will know that Jesus Christ is the Savior and Redeemer.

- The church of the devil will destroy itself through its wickedness.

- The gospel and the priesthood keys have been restored and will be the key to gathering the house of Israel.

- Our righteousness is what will bind Satan.

the four corners of the earth; and he numbereth there shall be one fold and one shepherd; and they shall find pasture." (1 Ne. 22:25)

Jesus Christ. Joseph Smith taught that the main purpose of gathering at any time is to build a temple so people can receive the ordinances of exaltation.

WHO IS SATAN? Satan—also called Lucifer, "son of the morning," Perdition, fallen angel, "old serpent," and devil—is the primary enemy of God. As an angel in authority in the premortal realm who rebelled against the Almighty God, he lost forever the divinely appointed opportunity to receive an inheritance of glory and exaltation. In exacting vengeance, he hopes to gain as many of the Father's children as he can through sin. Satan enticed Adam and Eve to partake of the forbidden fruit, conspired with Cain to murder Abel, motivated the building of the Tower of Babel, and spread darkness across the globe in countless other cases. Ultimately, Michael (Adam) and his forces will dispel Satan and his followers forever (see D&C 88:111–116).

KEY INSIGHTS ABOUT THE SAVIOR

- The Lord will do a marvelous work in the last days (restoring the gospel) as He gathers all those who are lost.
- All who fight against the Lord will be destroyed.
- The Lord will not allow the wicked to destroy the righteous.
- The Lord will reign in dominion, might, power, and great glory forever.
- The Lord will raise up a mighty nation among the Gentiles (the United States of America).
- All things that will come to pass are made known to His prophets by the Lord.
- The prophet of whom Moses spoke is Christ.

2 Nephi 1

> "Inasmuch as ye shall keep my in the land; but inasmuch as ye will shall be cut off from my presence."

MAJOR CONCEPT

Only by righteousness and obedience will we continue to prosper in a land of liberty—a land choice above all other lands that was given by the Lord as a land of inheritance.

OVERVIEW This chapter—the first in the book of 2 Nephi—contains the words of Lehi's final blessing to his sons Laman and Lemuel. Lehi expresses his grave concern for his two sons, who had continually rebelled since the family left Jerusalem, and cautions them that if they continue to do so they will be scattered and smitten. Lehi pleads with his sons to put on the armor of righteousness and to arise from the dust. Prior to blessing his sons, it is as if Nephi gives a "patriarchal blessing" to the land of America.

INTERESTING FACTS ABOUT VERSE 14 Critics of the Book of Mormon try to use 2 Nephi 1:14 to show that Joseph Smith could not have possibly translated the plates from ancient records. Their reasoning is that Joseph Smith lifted "lay down in the cold and silent grave, from whence no traveler can return" from Shakespeare's *Hamlet*—obviously written far after 570 BC. In reality, however, these sentiments were common during Lehi's day and were used in Job

PROMINENT PEOPLE

- Lehi
- Laman
- Lemuel
- Sam
- Nephi
- Zoram

MAIN THEMES

- Prophets are able to see in vision the exact nature of events.

- If the citizens of America obey the commandments and serve the Lord, this nation will not be conquered.

- If the citizens of America dwindle in unbelief and reject the Lord after having a knowledge of Him, this nation will be conquered and smitten through bloodshed.

- Those with hardened hearts will be cut off and destroyed forever.

- We can inherit covenant blessings through righteousness regardless of lineage.

commandments ye shall prosper
not keep my commandments ye
(2 Ne. 1:20)

10:21, Job 16:22, and by the Roman poet Catulus.

WHO WERE LAMAN AND LEMUEL? The two eldest of Lehi's children, Laman and Lemuel have become prime examples of murmuring and rebellion. While Laman should have been the leader of his siblings, since that right fell to the firstborn, Nephi was given that position—not only because of his own faithfulness, but because of Laman's constant rebellion and iniquity. Numerous times after leaving Jerusalem, Laman and Lemuel tried to kill Nephi but were restrained by the Lord. On his deathbed, Lehi expressed the desire that his two eldest sons would repent

and become choice and favored people of the Lord. After Lehi died they became so wicked that Nephi and his followers were forced to separate themselves from them; the result was the establishment of the separate nations of the Nephites and the Lamanites, which civilizations continued to war against each other for centuries.

KEY INSIGHTS ABOUT THE SAVIOR

- The Lord brought Lehi and his family out of Jerusalem to save them.

- The Lord has consecrated America for those who obey Him.

- If the day comes that the inhabitants of the United States reject the true Messiah (Jesus), they will feel the judgments of God upon them.

2 Nephi 2

"Wherefore, the Lord God gave unto himself." (2 Ne. 2:16)

MAJOR CONCEPT

We have been given freedom of choice—the same freedom that resulted in the Fall—which we can use to choose liberty and eternal life or to choose captivity and death.

OVERVIEW In this chapter, Lehi explains why we were given agency, why law is necessary, why opposition is part of the plan, and why repentance is essential. He bears powerful testimony of the Savior and His role in redeeming us from the Fall. This important chapter is the basis of LDS doctrine on the Fall.

INTERESTING FACTS ABOUT THE BOOK OF MORMON IN EXPLAINING THE FALL President Ezra Taft Benson gave insight to the importance of this chapter in establishing our doctrine regarding the Fall when he said, "No one adequately and properly knows why he needs Christ until he understands and accepts the doctrine of the Fall and its effects on mankind. No other book in the world explains this vital doctrine nearly as well as the Book of Mormon" (*Conference Report,* April 1987, 106).

WHO WAS EVE? Eve was the first woman of humankind and the divine helpmeet given to Adam (see Gen. 2:18). President Joseph

PROMINENT PEOPLE

- Lehi
- Adam and Eve
- Jesus Christ
- Satan

MAIN THEMES

- If Adam had not fallen, all would have remained as it was in Eden (there would be no joy, no misery, no goodness, and no sin).

- If Adam had not fallen, we would not be here; Adam and Eve would still be in the garden, and we would still be in our premortal existence.

- Because afflictions strengthen us and are consecrated for our gain, we should not ask the Lord to remove them.

- No matter how righteous we are and how much we achieve, we cannot return to God without the Savior.

- There must be opposition in all things.

- The Fall was part of the eternal plan.

- Mortality is the time during which we should repent.

- We are free to choose, but we are not free to escape the consequences of our choices.

- Satan has power over us only as we allow it.

man that he should act for

F. Smith, in his latter-day vision concerning the work of salvation in the spirit world, described Eve as "glorious" (D&C 138:39). Like Adam, she was created in the image of God, and she used her God-given agency in wisdom and in the best interests of her children for generations. After learning of the plan of salvation from the Lord, Eve expressed that had she not partaken of the forbidden fruit, "we never should have known good and evil, and the joy of our redemption, and the eternal life which God giveth unto all the obedient" (Moses 5:11).

KEY INSIGHTS ABOUT THE SAVIOR

- The Savior redeems all mankind from the Fall.
- Jesus Christ paid the penalty for our sins if we will repent; His was an infinite and eternal sacrifice.
- Redemption comes only through the Savior, who is full of grace and truth.
- No one can dwell in the presence of God except through the merits, mercy, and grace of Jesus Christ.
- The Savior made intercession for all mankind.

Image: Eve.

2 Nephi 3

"For Joseph truly testified, saying: A God raise up, who shall be a choice my loins." (2 Ne. 3:6)

MAJOR CONCEPT

Joseph Smith was chosen before the foundation of this world to restore the gospel in these latter days, and prophets for dispensations foretold of him and his mission.

OVERVIEW In this chapter, Lehi tells his young son Joseph that their civilization—the Nephites—was seen in vision by Joseph of Egypt, from whom they descended. Lehi then prophesies of another Joseph, Joseph Smith, who will restore the gospel and bring forth the Book of Mormon. He bears powerful testimony that Joseph Smith will perform a saving work that will preserve Joseph's seed forever.

INTERESTING FACTS ABOUT JOSEPH SMITH Joseph Smith was seen in vision by prophets long before his birth. When Joseph Smith Sr. gave Joseph Smith his patriarchal blessing, he said that Joseph of Egypt sought diligently to know who would bring the word of the Lord, "and his eyes beheld

PROMINENT PEOPLE

- Joseph, the son of Lehi
- Moses
- Joseph of Egypt
- Joseph Smith Jr.
- Joseph Smith Sr.
- Mormon

MAIN THEMES

- Lehi was a descendant of Joseph of Egypt—a righteous branch of the house of Israel—and was promised his seed would never be destroyed.

- Joseph Smith was prophesied of millennia before his birth.

- Like Moses, Joseph Smith would deliver people out of bondage.

- Joseph Smith was an instrument in the hand of God.

- The LDS edition of the scriptures helps fulfill the prophecy that the Bible and the Book of Mormon will grow together.

thee, my son; his heart rejoiced, and he was satisfied" (see Joseph Smith Sr., "Patriarchal Blessing"). Referring to Joseph Smith, Brigham Young wrote that "the Lord had his eyes upon him, and upon his father, and upon his father's father. . . . He was fore-ordained in eternity to preside over this last dispensation" (see *Discourses of Brigham Young,* 108). Joseph Smith translated the Book of Mormon, laid the foundations of the Church, brought the truth out of darkness, preached the gospel, and received the sealing power of the priesthood; he did more than anyone other than the Savior for the salvation of mankind (see D&C 135:3).

WHO WAS JOSEPH? Joseph was the youngest son of Lehi and Sariah; like his brother Jacob, he was born in the wilderness after Lehi fled Jerusalem. His family experience was one of extreme contrasts—the example of rightous parents and brothers (Nephi, Sam, and Jacob) on the one hand, and the rebellious and wicked behavior of Laman and Lemuel on the other. Joseph followed his father and brothers in righteousness and accompanied Nephi when he separated himself from the wickedness of Laman and Lemuel. He, along with Jacob, was consecrated by Nephi as a priest and teacher, and he devoted himself to the building up of the kingdom of God.

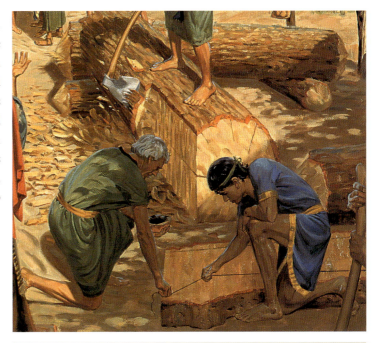

KEY INSIGHTS ABOUT THE SAVIOR

- The Lord raises up righteous servants to perform His work.
- The Lord covenants with His righteous people.

2 Nephi 4

"My God hath been my support; afflictions; and he hath preserved me deep." (2 Ne. 4:20)

Major Concept

We should glory in the Lord's goodness to us.

OVERVIEW Knowing he is about to die, Lehi blesses all of his children, praying that they will not perish; he then dies and is buried. Following Lehi's death, Laman, Lemuel, and the sons of Ishmael again become angry with Nephi; as he ponders the scriptures and his love of the Lord, Nephi delights in the Lord's goodness and places his trust in the Lord forever.

Prominent People

- Lehi
- Nephi
- Joseph of Egypt

INTERESTING FACTS ABOUT NEPHI'S PSALM Known as "Nephi's Psalm," verses 15 through 35 comprise a magnificent psalm of praise that expresses Nephi's personal religious experiences and feelings, including the delight he takes in the scriptures. It is actually poetry, and is intended to be read aloud. Typical of a psalm, it contains themes of sorrow in sin, communion with God, the search for perfection, and triumph over evil. Gospel scholar Sidney B. Sperry points out that its rhythm is comparable to David's psalms; he wrote, "it not only praises God, but lays bare to us the very depths of Nephi's soul" (Sperry, "Types of Literature in the

Main Themes

- We should continue to counsel and bless our children, even after they are married.

- We should write our personal and family histories for the learning and profit of our children.

- The more righteous and closer we are to perfection, the more clearly we perceive sin and the greater our despair over sin.

- Anger saps our strength and interferes with our spirituality.

- Our most appropriate fear is that of sin.

- We can pray for help even in the most difficult extremities.

Book of Mormon," 69–80). While Nephi used typical Hebrew parallelism in the psalm, clearly the spiritual insights he provided are more important than its literary style.

WHO WAS JOSEPH OF EGYPT? The son of Jacob and Rachel and holder of the birthright in Israel, Joseph was sold into slavery in Egypt by his jealous older brothers, who then convinced their father that Joseph had been killed. Once in Egypt, Joseph became overseer of the house of Potiphar, captain of Pharaoh's guard. When Joseph refused the advances of Potiphar's wife (see Gen. 39), he was wrongly accused and imprisoned. Released after interpreting dreams for Pharoah, he eventually became a ruler over all of Egypt; when his brothers came to Egypt looking for food during the famine, Joseph demonstrated an extraordinary capacity to forgive. Joseph married Asenath, and they had two sons, Ephraim and Manasseh. Joseph Smith received some of the writings of Joseph on papyri that were included with a mummy purchased from Michael Chandler (which also included the writings of Abraham); he translated the writings but did not publish them because they were "too great" for the people of our day (see Ludlow, *A Companion to Your Study,* 130, 131).

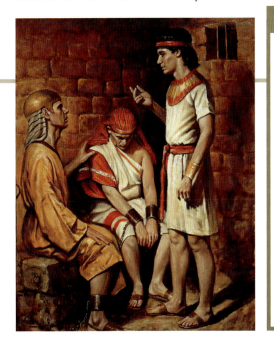

KEY INSIGHTS ABOUT THE SAVIOR

- The Lord will lead us through affliction.
- The Lord will bless us and prosper us if we will keep the commandments, but if we stray from them, we have no promise.
- As we serve Him in righteousness, the Lord will support us and will confound our enemies.
- Through our faith, the Lord will reveal great things to us.
- The Lord will give liberally to those who ask.

2 Nephi 5

"And we did observe to keep the and the commandments of the Lord law of Moses." (2 Ne. 5:10)

MAJOR CONCEPT

In our everyday lives, we need to separate ourselves from evil and focus on keeping the commandments of the Lord.

OVERVIEW Because of the continued wickedness of Laman and Lemuel, the Lord warns Nephi and his followers to flee into the wilderness and separate themselves from the Lamanites—those who follow Laman and Lemuel. Nephi heeds that warning, flees for many days, and establishes the civilization of the Nephites at a new location. Living in righteousness with his followers, Nephi builds a temple and continues to engrave on the small plates; he uses the sword of Laban as a pattern and manufactures weapons to protect his people against the Lamanites. The Lamanites are cut off from the presence of the Lord, which was the "curse."

PROMINENT PEOPLE

- Nephi
- Jacob
- Joseph

INTERESTING FACTS ABOUT THE TEMPLE Early critics of the Book of Mormon used Nephi's building of a temple as evidence, saying that no Jew would want to build a temple outside of Jerusalem. But papyri discovered in 1954 tells of a group of Jews who fled Jerusalem (perhaps when it was destroyed), settled far up the Nile, and built a temple in that location (see *Echoes*, 474). Israeli archaeologist Avraham Negev also tells of a temple built in Arad, an ancient city in the Negev, that was patterned after Solomon's temple (see *Echoes*, 130). It is only one of a group of smaller temples that were built away from Jerusalem at the time of Lehi's exodus. While Nephi certainly knew about these temples and patterned his own after them, Joseph Smith would not have known of that practice because the archaeological evidences were not discovered in his lifetime.

MAIN THEMES

- Wickedness is always the great divider.
- Keeping the commandments is the key to prosperity and brings lasting happiness to our lives.
- When we are wicked, we curse ourselves by offending the Holy Ghost and cutting ourselves off from God.
- The "curse" that came upon the Lamanites was being cut off from God's presence; the "mark" was the dark skin. Today the curse has been removed, but the mark remains.

WHO WAS SOLOMON? The son of David and Bathsheba, Solomon was the successor to David on the throne of Israel and reigned

600 BC

90 BC

588-570 BC

judgments, and the statutes, in all things, according to the

Land of Nephi

Place of first landing

for about forty years. He wrote the book of Proverbs; some believe he also wrote the book of Ecclesiastes. Solomon was most revered for his wisdom and for his building of the Lord's temple. In this chapter of 2 Nephi, we read that Nephi built a temple—the first mention of temple-building in the Book of Mormon—after the pattern of Solomon's temple, using the materials available to him in the promised land. Solomon's temple took seven years to build and was constructed of wood, stone, gold, and other precious materials. The inner sanctuary housed the ark of the covenant, and the brazen sea for ritual washing was upheld by twelve oxen. It was roughly the size of our large meetinghouses.

Middle Image: Modern-day Kaminaljuyu, thought to be the land to which Nephi and his people fled.

KEY INSIGHTS ABOUT THE SAVIOR

- The Lord warns the righteous when danger is imminent.
- The Lord appoints spokesmen to guide and direct us according to His instruction.
- As we strive to walk in obedience, the Lord provides help and direction.
- If we keep the commandments, the Lord is with us.
- Bringing people to Christ was the purpose for Nephi being commanded to make the small plates.

2 Nephi 6

" . . . those who were at Jerusalem, nevertheless, the Lord will be merciful Redeemer, they shall be gathered

MAJOR CONCEPT

Members of the Church will be instrumental in bringing the gospel to the Jews in the latter days.

OVERVIEW Jacob quotes the prophet Isaiah in telling the history of the Jews. In this chapter, Isaiah relates that the Jews were taken captive by the Babylonians but were eventually released. He prophesies of the ministry and crucifixion of the Savior and prophesies that, with help from the Gentiles, the Jews will return to their homeland and eventually accept the Savior as the Messiah in the latter days.

INTERESTING FACTS ABOUT THE JEWS RETURNING TO JERUSALEM Isaiah's prophecy that the Gentiles would help the Jews return to Jerusalem (see 2 Ne. 6:6) began to be fulfilled in November 1917, when Britain helped open Palestine as a Jewish homeland; both Britain and the United States helped the Jews return at that time. In 1946, Britain surrendered its mandate over Palestine to the United Nations, and in 1947 the land was officially opened to the Jews (see *Book of Mormon Student Manual*, 86).

PROMINENT PEOPLE

- Jacob
- Isaiah
- The Gentiles
- The Jews

MAIN THEMES

- The Jews will be scattered and smitten but will eventually be gathered as they accept Jesus Christ as their Redeemer.

- We should study the scriptures and apply them to our own circumstances.

- We are saved as we repent, refuse to fight against Zion, and resist uniting ourselves with the world.

- Those who fight against the covenant people will be smitten and afflicted.

- The gospel will be set up as a standard and will become as a nursing mother to the world.

600 BC

90 BC

from whence we came, have been slain and carried away captive . . . unto them, that when they shall come to the knowledge of their together again to the lands of their inheritance." (2 Ne. 6:9–11)

WHO WERE THE JEWS? In its most specific sense, the term *Jews* refers to people of the lineage of Judah, son of Jacob. In a broader sense, the term can be applied to those who over the generations were citizens of Jerusalem, even though they were not of Jewish lineage. Thus, Lehi was part of the Jewish community of his day, although he was by lineage from the tribe of Joseph through Manasseh. The Jews rejected Jesus Christ as the Messiah and will not accept Him as the Messiah as a nation until His Second Coming. In a poignant reference, the Lord predicts the state of mind of the Jews at the time of His Second Coming when they realize the millennial Lord is the same Jesus Christ whom their leaders had crucified (see D&C 45:51–53).

Image: One of the first ships full of Jews returning to Jerusalem.

KEY INSIGHTS ABOUT THE SAVIOR

- The Lord will always fulfill the covenants He makes with us.
- The Lord will be merciful to the Jews so that as they accept Him they will be gathered to the land of their inheritance.
- When the Jews come to a knowledge of their Redeemer they will be spiritually gathered.
- At the Lord's Second Coming, He will manifest Himself in great glory.
- When the Lord comes again, He will show the wounds in His hands and feet to the Jews, who will mourn when they realize where the wounds came from.
- The Lord will deliver His covenant people and will destroy their enemies.

2 Nephi 7

"I gave my back to the smiter, and off the hair. I hid not my face from

MAJOR CONCEPT

The Savior accepted the call to atone for our sins and was crucified for us.

OVERVIEW In this chapter, Jacob quotes Isaiah as Isaiah prophesies of the coming Messiah.

INTERESTING FACTS ABOUT ISAIAH IN THE BOOK OF MORMON No other prophet who wrote on the brass plates is referred to as extensively as Isaiah. Of those references, 234 verses of Isaiah were modified by Joseph Smith as he translated the Book of Mormon; 199 verses of Isaiah appear word-for-word as they do in the book of Isaiah in the Old Testament. Although Nephi recognized that Isaiah's words were "hard to be understood" by his people, he himself delighted in them.

MAIN THEMES

- Jesus Christ is our Savior and Redeemer.
- When we try to solve our own problems without the help of the Lord, we are doomed to walk in our own light instead of benefitting from the Light of Christ.
- It isn't possible to walk in darkness if we fear the Lord and listen to His servants.

PROMINENT PEOPLE

- Jesus Christ

WHO WAS ISAIAH? The most quoted of all prophets in the scriptures, Isaiah ministered as a prophet in Jerusalem between 740 and 701 BC. The general messages of the book of Isaiah refer to the Lord's design for His covenant children and their eventual salvation and contain rich prophecies regarding the Savior's birth, ministry, Atonement, and Second Coming. Highlights in the book of Isaiah include poignant explanations of the Lord's role in the plan of salvation, the gathering of the ten tribes, the coming forth of the Book of Mormon, and the restoration of the gospel. The books of Nephi and Jacob in the Book of Mormon include abundant excerpts from the writings of Isaiah.

my cheeks to them that plucked shame and spitting." (2 Ne. 7:6)

KEY INSIGHTS ABOUT THE SAVIOR

- The Lord has tremendous power over the elements.
- Jesus Christ was generally not accepted by the Jews as the Messiah when He ministered in mortality.
- The Savior willingly atoned for our sins.
- The Lord will never "divorce" us; we "divorce" Him through our unrighteousness and breaking of covenants.

2 Nephi 8

"But my salvation shall be forever, be abolished." (2 Ne. 8:6)

MAJOR CONCEPT

During the latter days, which is our day, the Lord's righteousness and law will prevail.

OVERVIEW In this chapter, Jacob again quotes from the book of Isaiah, taking excerpts from Isaiah 51 and 52. The main theme of this chapter focuses on the fact that the Lord will comfort Zion during the last days and will gather Israel amid great joy.

PROMINENT PEOPLE

- Jesus Christ
- Zion

INTERESTING FACTS ABOUT ISAIAH'S STYLE OF WRITING Sidney B. Sperry wrote that Isaiah "combined earthly and heavenly wisdom to a most unusual degree," and that his natural gifts were disciplined and sharpened by the best education available at that time (*The Voice of Israel's Prophets,* 14). Isaiah purposefully wrote in such a way that only those filled with the spirit of prophecy themselves could hope to fully understand his message or share his mighty vision. In order to understand Isaiah, we need to carefully and prayerfully study his writings, seeking the Spirit to assist us.

WHO OR WHAT IS ZION? *Zion* is often used as a term to indicate the place where the Lord's people dwell, or a geographical location (see LDS Bible Dictionary, 792–793). However, Isaiah also uses it as a term for the people themselves. Zion consists of a people unified in the discipleship of the Redeemer, as were the people of Enoch (see Moses 7:18)—of one heart and one mind, pure in heart, dwelling in righteousness. The name *Zion* as used to describe the people of the Lord is reinforced in latter-day scripture.

MAIN THEMES

- We must place our trust in the Lord, not in man.
- The rejection of Israel—Jerusalem and the Jews—is over, and they will not again suffer it.
- The gathering in the last days will be one of everlasting joy and great holiness.

600 BC

90 BC

559–545 BC

and my righteousness shall not

KEY INSIGHTS ABOUT THE SAVIOR

- Wherever the Lord's people are, He will comfort and sustain them.

- The Lord's righteousness and law will prevail.

- The Lord's righteousness is eternal.

- The Lord will plead the cause of His people and will serve as a great mediator for all of us at the judgment bar.

- The salvation of the Lord is forever; it will cover all generations of time and will never be abolished.

2 Nephi 9

"And he commandeth all men baptized in his name, having perfect or they cannot be saved in the

MAJOR CONCEPT

The Atonement makes it possible for all mankind to repent and be saved in the kingdom of God.

OVERVIEW In a chapter sometimes considered to be the heart of the gospel, Jacob summarizes the writings of Isaiah regarding the gathering of the Jews, then teaches about the Atonement of the Savior and the general process of judgment whereby those who repent are saved as a result of the Atonement and those who sin are condemned. Jacob bears testimony that the only way to gain salvation is through Jesus Christ.

INTERESTING FACTS ABOUT OUR OWN JUDGMENT In this chapter, Jacob alludes to the fact that we will participate in our own judgment (see 2 Ne. 9:46). President John Taylor said that a record of our acts is recorded on the tablet of

PROMINENT PEOPLE

• Jesus Christ

our own mind. Elder Bruce R. McConkie added that our acts will also be recorded in our bodies, and that every thought, word, and deed will leave their marks (see *Mormon Doctrine,* 97). At the judgment, President Taylor said, that record will stare us in the face, and if we have not repented,

MAIN THEMES

- Death is as important to the plan of salvation as is birth.

- Fundamental to our religion is a testimony of Jesus Christ and His Atonement.

- At the judgment, the wicked will have a perfect knowledge of their guilt, while the righteous will have a bright recollection of their joy and goodness.

- The Atonement takes care of those without the law as it satisfies the demands of justice, and no person in all of eternity will be denied a blessing to which he or she is entitled.

- To be carnally minded is death; to be spiritually minded is life eternal.

- Pride is a great destroyer.

- Satan's plan is to get us caught up in our learning (intellectualism) to the point that we neglect God's counsel.

- Worldly wealth cannot purchase salvation.

- We will help judge ourselves.

- Once the resurrection and judgment occur, there will be no more opportunity to repent.

- The consequences of sin are never worth the sin.

600 BC

90 BC

559–545 BC

that they must repent, and be
faith in the Holy One of Israel,
kingdom of God." (2 Ne. 9:23)

it will bear record against us as it is unfolded before God and the angels (see *Journal of Discourses,* 11:78–79).

INTERESTING FACTS ABOUT LANGUAGE PATTERNS Had Joseph Smith written the Book of Mormon instead of translating it from ancient records, he would have used the language with which he was familiar. Instead, the Book of Mormon is full of language patterns not of Joseph Smith's day, but of ancient Old Testament times. For example, a characteristic feature of Hebrew grammar is compound prepositions—such as *from before*—which are common in the Book of Mormon. Also common are "prophetic speech patterns," commonly used in the Old Testament at the beginning of a prophecy or revelation—such as *woe unto, thus saith the Lord,* and *the Lord God hath sworn.* Finally, the Book of Mormon uses numerous examples of seven types of parallelism that were not identified until 1898, long after the Book of Mormon was translated (see *Echoes,* 169–173).

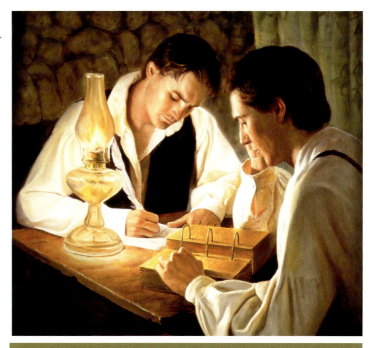

KEY INSIGHTS ABOUT THE SAVIOR

- Because Jesus Christ paid the price for us and became our Mediator, He earned the right to dictate the rules and conditions of our salvation.

- The Lord is characterized by attributes of goodness and greatness.

- Through His Atonement, Jesus saves us from both physical and spiritual death. Everyone will be resurrected (saved from physical death), and everyone will return to God's presence for judgment (saved from spiritual death).

- Without the infinite Atonement of Jesus Christ, we would be captives of Satan forever.

- The Lord is the perfect judge.

- Christ is the keeper of the gate of heaven.

2 Nephi 10

"Therefore, cheer up your hearts, and for yourselves—to choose the way of eternal life." (2 Ne. 10:23)

MAJOR CONCEPT

By reconciling ourselves to the will of the Lord and obeying His commandments, we can gain salvation through His grace.

OVERVIEW Jacob continues to prophesy about the Jews, noting in this chapter that the Jews will crucify the Savior and be scattered until they began to believe in Him. Jacob also prophesies that America will be a land of liberty and that the Gentiles will never be ruled by a king. Finally, Jacob provides the key to gaining salvation: reconciling our will to that of Christ, whose name he has just learned from an angel.

INTERESTING FACTS ABOUT AMERICA Jacob refers to himself and his people as living in the *promised land*, which he calls an "isle of the sea" (2 Ne. 10:20). This same terminology has been used in previous chapters (as an example, see 1 Ne. 22:4). To the Hebrews of that day, Asia and Africa were the entire world. Anything they could reach only by sailing across water was considered an "isle of the sea"—even if it couldn't be strictly defined as an island. The designation of America as a "choice land . . . above all other lands" is a recurring theme in the Book of Mormon, as is the obligation of those who are privileged to live on that land (see Ether 2:8–12 for the obligations of those who live in America).

PROMINENT PEOPLE

- Jacob
- Jesus Christ
- The Jews
- The Gentiles

MAIN THEMES

- Those who fight against Zion will perish.
- Those who are not for the Lord are against Him.
- Those who have the opportunity to live in a free land have the obligation to serve the Lord.
- We are commanded to reconcile ourselves to the will of the Lord and to serve Him, but have the freedom to choose how we will act.

remember that ye are free to act
everlasting death or the way of

KEY INSIGHTS ABOUT THE SAVIOR

- The Lord ministered among the Jews in mortality because no other nation on earth would have crucified Him.

- The Lord consecrated the land of America as a covenant land.

- The Lord remembers all those who were scattered or broken off.

- When the day comes that the Jews believe in Christ, they will be restored to the lands of their inheritance.

- We are saved only in and through the grace of the Savior.

- The Lord saves us from physical death through the Resurrection and from spiritual death through the Atonement.

2 Nephi 11

"For if there be no Christ there be are not, for there could have been he is Christ, and he cometh in the

MAJOR CONCEPT

Jesus Christ is the Redeemer, and all that has gone before and after Him points directly to Him.

OVERVIEW Nephi testifies that he, Jacob, and Isaiah all saw the Lord Jesus Christ. Nephi also testifies that the law of Moses is a type, or foreshadowing, of Jesus Christ, who will come in glory. Chapter 11 is Nephi's introduction to the Isaiah chapters, which include 2 Nephi 12–24; Chapter 25 then tells how to interpret Isaiah. Nephi included the Isaiah chapters because Isaiah saw Christ, Nephi delights in proving the coming of Christ, and Nephi delights in the covenants of the Lord.

INTERESTING FACTS ABOUT TYPES A rite that has a spiritual meaning attached to it is a symbol or shadow. If that symbol also points to a future reality and the associated blessing, it

PROMINENT PEOPLE

- Nephi
- Jacob
- Jesus Christ
- Isaiah

MAIN THEMES

- Covenants are the means whereby we link ourselves to the Savior in order to lay hold upon eternal life.

- The words of Isaiah can be likened unto us and unto all men.

- We should delight in the opportunity to teach and convince others of the reality of Jesus Christ.

- The law of Moses was given to testify of the coming of Jesus Christ.

becomes a type. A good example is baptism: it symbolizes our birth into Christ's family and uses the same symbols associated with birth—water, blood, and spirit. But baptism is also a type, typifying our future death and resurrection. In this chapter, Nephi points out that the law of Moses, with its constant requirement of offering sacrifice, is a type—typifying the Savior, who would offer the ultimate sacrifice through the Atonement.

WHO WAS JESUS CHRIST? The name *Jesus* is the Greek form of the name *Joshua* or *Jeshua*, meaning "God is help"—in other words, "Savior" (see *LDS Bible Dictionary*, 713). The name implies the sacred office of Redeemer, the One who brings about the Atonement through the sacrifice of the Crucifixion and the process of the Resurrection. In His capacity as Savior, Jesus is the means for rescuing all mankind from the effects of temporal death and enabling the obedient to escape spiritual death.

no God; and if there be no God we
no creation. But there is a God, and
fulness of his own time." (2 Ne. 11:7)

Image: Lehi offers sacrifice.

Key Insights about the Savior

- The Lord establishes His word in the mouth of three witnesses.
- The Lord will prove all His words.
- The Lord is the source of grace, power, justice, mercy, and deliverance from death.
- The God of the Old Testament is Jesus Christ.

2 Nephi 12

"Come ye, and let us go up to the the God of Jacob; and he will teach paths. . . ." (2 Ne. 12:3)

MAJOR CONCEPT

Those who worship anything other than God the Father and Jesus Christ will be brought low at the last day.

OVERVIEW Nephi again quotes from Isaiah, who saw in vision the temples in the latter days. Isaiah prophesies of the gathering of Israel and the judgment and peace associated with the Millennium. More than half of the verses from Isaiah 2 were altered in this chapter. During the Millennium there will be two world capitols: out of the New Jerusalem (in Jackson County) will go forth the law; out of the Old Jerusalem will go forth the will of the Lord.

INTERESTING FACTS ABOUT IDOL WORSHIPPERS Much of this chapter deals with idol worshippers—those who worship the work of their own hands. Verses 5 through 9 list the Lord's complaints against the idol worshippers.

PROMINENT PEOPLE

• Isaiah

Verses 10 through 18 discuss the Lord's judgments against such people: not only will He destroy their idols, but He will bring those who worship the idols low. Finally, verses 19 through 21 indicate the misery of idol worshippers as they face that judgment.

MAIN THEMES

- The Lord's house—the temple—will be established in the last days, and all nations will be blessed as a result.
- The Millennium will be a time of great peace.
- We practice a form of idol worship when we esteem ourselves to be of greater importance than the Lord.
- We need to put our trust in the Lord, not in man.

Bottom Image: The Philistine city of Ekron.

mountain of the Lord, to the house of
us of his ways, and we will walk in his

WHO WERE THE PHILISTINES? The
Philistines (see verse 6) were an ancient
tribe or group of tribes that contended with
the Israelites, particularly during the time
of King Saul and King David. Goliath,
the giant slain by David, was a Philistine.
Originally, the Philistines resided in
Caphtor, thought to be the island of Crete
or perhaps part of the Egyptian delta.
Eventually they established a powerful
confederacy of five cities in the territory
between Judea and Egypt. The name
Palestine, which designates the Holy Land,
derives from the name of the Philistines.

KEY INSIGHTS ABOUT THE SAVIOR

- The Lord teaches us precious truths in the temple.
- The Lord will destroy all idols in the last day.
- The Lord alone will be exalted at the last day; those who did wickedness will be made low.

2 Nephi 13

"Wo unto the wicked, for they shall shall be upon them!" (2 Ne. 13:11)

MAJOR CONCEPT

Chaos and disaster will befall those who continue in wickedness.

OVERVIEW Isaiah prophesies that Judah and Jerusalem will be punished for their wickedness but foretells that the Lord will plead for His people before passing judgment on them. The women of our day are seen in prophecy and cursed for their worldliness. The material in this chapter corresponds with Isaiah 3.

INTERESTING FACTS ABOUT THE DESTRUCTION OF JUDAH AND JERUSALEM In the first seven verses of this chapter, Isaiah prophesies about the utter chaos that will afflict Judah. He then clarifies that Judah and Jerusalem will revel in sin, which will lead to their destruction. Those prophecies were actually fulfilled twice. In 587 BC, the

PROMINENT PEOPLE

- People of Jerusalem
- People of Judah
- Daughters of Zion

Babylonians destroyed Jerusalem (an event of which Lehi was warned) and took Judah into captivity. Then in AD 70, the Romans razed Jerusalem and scattered the Jews, representing a second great destruction because of continued wickedness.

MAIN THEMES

- Those who continue in wickedness will be destroyed.
- In our day, women will assume the roles intended for men.
- In our day, politicians and government leaders will seek to destroy the family.
- We are cursed and tormented when we focus on ourselves instead of the Lord.

600 BC

90 BC

559–545 BC

WHO WERE THE DAUGHTERS OF ZION?

The "daughters of Zion" were actually the women of the house of Jacob. They were singled out by Isaiah because of their adherence to worldly standards—a problem, he stated, that would also afflict women of our day. Isaiah speaking to his day as well as ours is called "dualism." The worldly things specified by Isaiah include but are not limited to elaborate hairstyles, expensive clothing (including hats and shoes), exotic perfumes, and ornate jewelry, including piercings. Interpretations of the clothing and other elements are found in the LDS Bible footnotes for Isaiah 3.

KEY INSIGHTS ABOUT THE SAVIOR

- The Lord won't continue to protect those who cast Him aside.
- The Lord will curse those women who adhere to worldly standards.

Image: Titus destroying Jerusalem.

2 Nephi 14

"And the Lord will create upon every her assemblies, a cloud and smoke by night; for upon all the glory of Zion

MAJOR CONCEPT

In the millennial day, Zion and her daughters will be cleansed and redeemed.

OVERVIEW The final ten verses of 2 Nephi 13 prophesy of the worldly condition of the daughters of Zion and the cursing of the Lord upon them. In this chapter, which corresponds to Isaiah 4, Isaiah prophesies that the millennial day will bring about cleansing and redemption—not only for the daughters of Zion, but for all of Zion.

INTERESTING FACTS ABOUT THE RATIO OF MEN TO WOMEN

At first glance, verse 1—in which seven women will take hold of one man—might appear to be a reinstitution of polygamy, but it is not. It actually has two meanings. For the women of Jerusalem in biblical times, there were few men during this period because of the war referred to in

PROMINENT PEOPLE

• Zion

2 Ne. 13:25, during which "thy men shall fall by the sword." In 2 Nephi 14:1, "that day" refers to the day of the shortage of men because of the war. In our day, this verse refers to the fact that women are willing to do anything to marry—including support their husbands by being the primary wage earners—so they will not bear the status of being single.

MAIN THEMES

- The Millennium will be a time of restoration, cleansing, and redemption.
- Those who are a Zion people at the last day will be holy.

dwelling-place of mount Zion, and upon
day and the shining of a flaming fire by
shall be a defence." (2 Ne. 14:5)

Key Insights about the Savior

- The Lord will wash away the filth of the daughters of Zion during His millennial reign.
- The Lord is our protector.
- The Lord guides our paths.

2 Nephi 15

"Therefore, is the anger of the Lord against them, and hath smitten them; of the streets. For all this his anger is

MAJOR CONCEPT

Despite the things we do, even if our acts are wicked, the Lord will never forget or abandon us.

OVERVIEW In a chapter comparable to Isaiah 5, Isaiah prophesies of the scattering of Israel (His vineyard) and the destruction that will come upon them in their apostate condition. He then prophesies of the gathering of Israel at a time when the Lord will lift an ensign in their behalf. The ensign that will be lifted up includes the Church (see D&C 115:3–5), the covenant (see D&C 45:9), and the Book of Mormon (see 2 Ne. 29:2).

INTERESTING FACTS ABOUT ISAIAH'S PROPHECY From the descriptions Isaiah provided in this chapter, it is apparent that he saw our day and strove to describe amazing things he saw in the future with the labels and language common

PROMINENT PEOPLE

- The House of Israel
- The men of Judah

to his day. Many believe that his description, "horses' hoofs shall be counted like flint, and their wheels like a whirlwind" told of railroad trains. And "speed swiftly" and "roaring like a lion" could definitely describe airplanes—something he also described as flying "as a cloud" (Isa. 60:8). Finally, the dense housing of our day is described clearly in verse 8.

MAIN THEMES

- When, despite our best efforts, things don't turn out as we hope, we should start over and try again.
- Despite mistakes and even wickedness, it is never too late for us to come back to the Savior.
- Pride is the source of great woe.

kindled against his people, and he hath stretched forth his hand and the hills did tremble, and their carcasses were torn in the midst not turned away, but his hand is stretched out still." (2 Ne. 15:25)

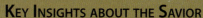

KEY INSIGHTS ABOUT THE SAVIOR

- The Lord never forgets us, even if we forget Him.
- The Lord will always prevail.
- The Lord's mercy is everlasting.
- Those who despise the Holy One of Israel will be devoured as stubble.

2 Nephi 16

"Also I heard the voice of the Lord, who will go for us? Then I said: Here

MAJOR CONCEPT

Isaiah was called to serve the Lord as His prophet and served until the end of his days as a man of great influence over his people.

OVERVIEW In this chapter, which compares to Isaiah 6, Isaiah—who lived around 750 BC—describes the miraculous event in which he received his call to serve the Lord as a prophet. Isaiah then prophesies that the Jews would reject the Savior but that a remnant of them would return.

PROMINENT PEOPLE

- Jesus Christ
- Seraphim
- Isaiah

INTERESTING FACTS ABOUT ISAIAH'S PROPHECIES Isaiah's prophecies had three main themes: 1) We should trust in the saving power of the Lord; 2) Covenant people have social and moral obligations; and 3) God's justice will prevail. Jan Valeton the Younger said of him: "Never perhaps has there been another prophet like Isaiah, who stood with his head in the clouds and his feet on the solid earth, with his heart in the things of eternity and with mouth and hand in the things of time, with his spirit in the eternal council of God and his body in a very definite moment of history."

MAIN THEMES

- Our obligation to serve the Lord never ends.
- The live coal—a symbol of the Holy Ghost—that purged Isaiah's sins can also cleanse us of sin.

WHO ARE THE SERAPHIM? The word *seraphim* is used only rarely in scripture, here in Isaiah's description of his vision of the Lord. Apparently the seraphim are angelic beings who dwell in the presence of the Lord and who give continual glory, honor, and adoration to Him. They are depicted symbolically as having the capacity to fly (which is why they are winged—see D&C 77:4) and having the commission to administer rites of purification. In this chapter, the seraph places a live coal on Isaiah's mouth, taking away his iniquity and purging him of sin. The wings in this vision (and others) symbolize the power to move and act.

saying: Whom shall I send, and am I; send me." (2 Ne. 16:8)

KEY INSIGHTS ABOUT THE SAVIOR

- The entire earth is filled with the glory of the Lord.
- Isaiah's call—"Here am I, send me"—is a type of the Savior's role and response in the pre-existence when He said, "Here am I, send me" (Abr. 3:27).

2 Nephi 17

"Therefore, the Lord himself shall shall conceive, and shall bear a son, (2 Ne. 17:14)

MAJOR CONCEPT

While Judah will be subjected to invasions, it will be delivered—but the land will be one of great emptiness following the invasion of the Assyrians.

OVERVIEW This chapter, taken from Isaiah 7, provides a description of the political conditions in Isaiah's day. The prophecies it contains predict that Ephraim and Syria will wage war against Judah. While the invasion will fail, and Israel and Syria will fall, Judah will be delivered. This chapter also prophesies that the Savior would be born to a virgin.

INTERESTING FACTS ABOUT ISRAEL The prophecy in this chapter is a prophecy against the kingdom of Israel; in it, Isaiah prophesies that the kingdom of Israel will fall and its confederacy will be broken. That prophecy was fulfilled in 721 BC—more than a hundred years before

PROMINENT PEOPLE

- Isaiah
- Ahaz
- Judah
- Syria
- Ephraim
- Shearjashub

MAIN THEMES

- The Savior would be born of a virgin.
- Though political turmoil will always exist, everlasting peace is to be found only through the Savior.
- Israel will be scattered but will eventually be delivered and gathered.

Lehi and his family left Jerusalem and fled into the wilderness—when Assyria overran Israel and captured Samaria, its capital.

WHO WAS AHAZ? Ahaz was the king of Judah in the 730s and 720s BC (see *LDS Bible Dictionary,* 738). He provides a dramatic contrast to the towering spiritual strength of his contemporary, Isaiah, for Ahaz was given over to a life of wickedness. Ahaz represented idolatry and evil, while Isaiah stood for righteousness and honor. Beginning at the age of twenty, Ahaz ruled in wickedness, corrupting the temple rites and subjecting his own son to rites of abomination. During his days, Ahaz and his nation were subjected to aggressions from the neighboring nations of Syria and Israel. In an attempt to comfort Ahaz, Isaiah prophesied that the Savior would be born and Ahaz's enemies would be confounded. Instead of taking hope in

600 BC

90 BC

559–545 BC

give you a sign—Behold, a virgin and shall call his name Immanuel."

that prophecy, Ahaz buried himself in the political turmoils of his day and continued in his misguided and evil ways until the end of his days.

Image: Assyrian army.

KEY INSIGHTS ABOUT THE SAVIOR

- The Savior was prophesied to be born of a virgin.
- The Savior is over all and directs the affairs of man.
- Mary's son will be named "Immanuel," which means "God with us."

2 Nephi 18

"Take counsel together, and it shall
and it shall not stand; for God is

MAJOR CONCEPT

We should turn to the Lord for direction, guidance, and revelation.

OVERVIEW In this chapter, which compares to Isaiah 8, Isaiah prophesies that Judah will be delivered despite its initial fall to the Assyrians. Isaiah teaches that the Lord will be a strength to the righteous and a stumbling block to the wicked. He warns the people against looking to anyone other than the Lord for revelations and prophesies that the Jews will be driven into darkness for rejecting the Lord.

WHO WAS MAHER-SHALAL-HASH-BAZ? The prophet Isaiah had two sons, one of whom was Maher-shalal-hash-baz. Each son bears a symbolic name that essentially predicts the outcome of the Lord's designs for His people,

PROMINENT PEOPLE

- Isaiah
- Maher-shalal-hash-baz

and Isaiah tells us that the names of his sons were given as a sign. *Maher-shalal-hash-baz* means in Hebrew "hurrying to the spoil hastens the plunder." His name refers to the misguided alliance of Ephraim and Syria that was defeated by the Assyrians in 721 BC—and can also be applied to the

MAIN THEMES

- We should turn to the Lord—not worldly men or sorcerers who claim to be able to see the future—for guidance and revelation.

- As we obey the Lord in righteousness, He will protect us.

eventual defeat of all earthly kingdoms that rise up in opposition to the kingdom of God. Isaiah's other son was named *Shearjashub,* which means in Hebrew "a remnant shall return." His name alludes to the fact that in the last days Israel will eventually be restored according to the design of the Lord. Isaiah's name means "Jehovah saves." In summary, then, one son's name means that Israel will be scattered; one son's name means that Israel will be gathered; and Isaiah's name means that Jehovah (Jesus) will save us.

KEY INSIGHTS ABOUT THE SAVIOR

- The Lord was in control of the battles between Judah and Assyria, so mortal armaments were useless.

- The Lord directs His people.

- The Lord is a sanctuary to the righteous and a snare to the wicked.

- The Lord is the source of all revelation.

- The Lord will gather Israel in His own due time.

- Jesus will be a stumbling block for the Jews (a statement also made by Paul [see Rom. 9:32–33] and Jacob [see Jacob 4:15–17]).

2 Nephi 19

"For unto us a child is born, unto be upon his shoulder; and his name Mighty God, The Everlasting Father,

MAJOR CONCEPT

Jesus Christ is the Messiah.

OVERVIEW In this chapter, which compares to Isaiah 9, the prophet Isaiah bears powerful testimony of the coming Messiah, who will lead His people from darkness and who will be considered the Prince of Peace.

WHO IS JESUS CHRIST? President Gordon B. Hinckley said of the Savior, "Jesus was in very deed the great Jehovah of the Old Testament, who left His Father's royal courts on high and condescended to come to earth as a babe born in the most humble of circumstances. His birth was foretold centuries earlier by Isaiah. . . . This Jesus Christ of whom we solemnly testify is, as John the Revelator declared, 'the faithful witness, and the first begotten of the dead, and the prince of the kings of the earth.' He 'loved us, and washed us from our sins in his own blood, and hath made us kings and priests unto God and his Father; to him be glory and dominion for ever and ever' (Rev. 1:5–6)" ("A Testimony of the Son of God," 2).

PROMINENT PEOPLE

• Jesus Christ

MAIN THEMES

• Jesus Christ is the Savior of all mankind, and it is to Him we must turn.

us a son is given; and the government shall
shall be called, Wonderful, Counselor, The
The Prince of Peace." (2 Ne. 19:6)

KEY INSIGHTS ABOUT THE SAVIOR

- The Messiah's coming brought justice, righteousness, and peace.
- Those who walked in darkness saw a great light at the coming of the Savior.
- Jesus breaks the yoke of our spiritual burdens.
- Jesus Christ is the Son of God.
- The Lord's anger and judgment are kindled against those who do evil.
- Despite His anger over those who are evil, the Savior's hand of mercy is continually stretched out.
- Jesus is the everlasting Father because through Him we are born again, He created this world, and He speaks as the Father through divine investiture of authority.

2 Nephi 20

"For though thy people Israel be
them shall return; the consumption
(2 Ne. 20:22)

MAJOR CONCEPT

The unrighteous and the unjust will be defeated, and the righteous will be preserved.

OVERVIEW In this chapter, which compares to Isaiah 10, Isaiah points out that the destruction of Assyria is a type or prediction of the destruction of the wicked at the Second Coming of the Lord. After the Lord comes again, says Isaiah, there will be few left, but the remnant of Jacob—the people of Zion who trust in the Lord—will return in that day.

WHO WERE THE ASSYRIANS? Many tribes and cultures interacted with Israel over the generations, often with tremendous aggression. The three major empires that fought against Israel were the Babylonians, the Egyptians, and the Assyrians. There were two major invasions by the Assyrians

PROMINENT PEOPLE

- Jesus Christ
- The people of Assyria
- The people of Zion

that had special impact on the Israelites. First was the invasion of Shalmaneser into the northern kingdom around 721 BC that resulted in the dispersion of the ten tribes northward into Assyria and beyond. The second was the defeat of Sennacherib and his hosts through divine intervention during the siege of Jerusalem in 699 BC.

MAIN THEMES

- We need to acknowledge the hand of the Lord in all things.

- We must avoid the sin of pride.

- We as Church members are the remnant of Jacob who trust in the Lord, who overflow with righteousness, and who will be delivered at the last day.

- We should not fear mortal enemies but should depend on the Lord for guidance and deliverance.

Top Image: Assyrian carving depicting the conquering of the Jews.
Bottom Image: Sennacherib's army is destroyed.

as the sand of the sea, yet a remnant of decreed shall overflow with righteousness."

KEY INSIGHTS ABOUT THE SAVIOR

- The Lord's anger is kindled against the unjust.
- Despite the transgressions of the people, the Lord's hand of mercy is forever stretched out.
- The Lord will destroy the hypocrites.
- The Lord will destroy those who take all credit for themselves in their pride and their arrogance.
- The Lord will preserve and deliver His people against their enemies.
- The Lord will punish the Assyrians following His judgments on Israel and Judah. (Immediately after the prophecy of the destruction of Israel, Isaiah gave a prophecy concerning the destiny of Assyria so people wouldn't conclude that this heathen nation was righteous [see *CES Old Testament Student Manual,* 147]).

2 Nephi 21

"And it shall come to pass in that day remnant of his people . . . And he shall and gather together the dispersed of

MAJOR CONCEPT

At the last day, the gospel will be restored and preached to all nations, playing a part in the final gathering of Israel.

OVERVIEW In this chapter, which compares to Isaiah 11, the prophet Isaiah tells of the coming of the Savior, sheds a little light on His mortal ministry, and prophesies of the peace that will signify His millennial reign. He then explains that the knowledge of the Lord will cover the earth and that the Savior will raise an ensign to the nations that will result in the gathering of Israel. This chapter is so important that it was quoted by Moroni on his visit to Joseph Smith on September 21, 1823 (see JS—H 1:40).

INTERESTING FACTS ABOUT THE STEM OF JESSE According to Elder Bruce R. McConkie, the stem of Jesse spoken of in this chapter is Jesus Christ; that designation signifies that

PROMINENT PEOPLE

- Jesus Christ
- Jesse
- Joseph Smith

the Savior descended from Jesse, a noble Israelite who sired King David (see *Mormon Doctrine*, 766). In Hebrew, the word *stem* is the stock that remains in the earth after the tree is cut down. The rod that comes forth from the stem of Jesse is the Prophet Joseph Smith; gospel scholar Sidney B. Sperry says that Joseph is both the rod discussed in verse 1 and the root referred to in verse 10. As such, Isaiah in this chapter was prophesying of the Prophet Joseph Smith, his role in erecting an ensign to the nations for the teaching of the gospel, and the fact that he would inherit exaltation (a "glorious rest"). According to Elder Bruce R. McConkie, the "branch" that will grow out of the root of Jesse is the King who will reign during the Millennium (see *The Promised Messiah*, 193). The "stem," then, is the mortal Christ, and out of the stem will grow the branch that will be the millennial Christ.

MAIN THEMES

- Joseph Smith was raised up by the Lord as a prophet in this dispensation in fulfillment of the prophecy of Isaiah.

- There will be complete peace on earth during the Millennium.

- During the Savior's millennial reign, the gospel will spread throughout the earth and the persecution of the righteous will cease.

- The dispersed of Judah will be gathered from the four corners of the earth during the Millennium.

that the Lord shall set his hand again the second time to recover the set up an ensign for the nations, and shall assemble the outcasts of Israel, Judah from the four corners of the earth." (2 Ne. 21:11–12)

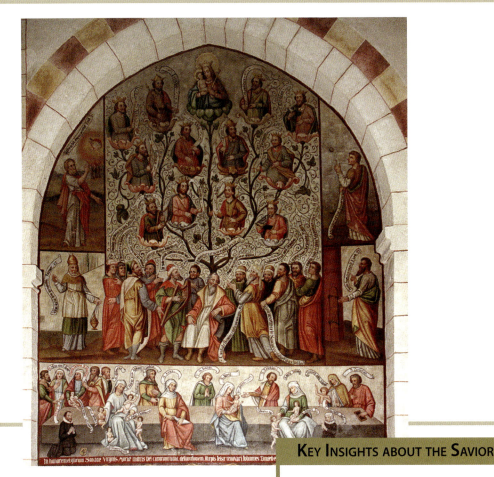

Image: Depiction of Christ's lineage.

KEY INSIGHTS ABOUT THE SAVIOR

- The first time the Lord gathered His remnant was when He led His people out of Egyptian bondage; the second time will be during the Millennium.

- The Lord will recover His people a second time when He sets up an ensign for the nations, assembles the outcasts of Israel, and gathers the dispersed of Judah from the four corners of the earth.

- The Lord raised up Joseph Smith to fulfill prophecy and erect an ensign to the nations.

2 Nephi 22

"Behold, God is my salvation; I will Lord Jehovah is my strength and salvation." (2 Ne. 22:2)

MAJOR CONCEPT

All men will praise the Lord in the millennial day, and He will dwell among them.

OVERVIEW This chapter—only six verses long—consists of a song of praise to the Lord by Isaiah, who prophesies the conditions of the Millennium and the state of mind of the Lord's people during that time. It can be compared to Isaiah 12. Among other popular LDS hymns, "The Lord Is My Light" (*Hymns*, 89) was inspired by this chapter of Isaiah.

INTERESTING FACTS ABOUT SONGS OF PRAISE These few short verses are a heartfelt song of praise by the prophet Isaiah in which he not only prophesies of the conditions of the Millennium but pours out the feelings of his own heart. Verse 2 particularly gives voice to

PROMINENT PEOPLE

- Jesus Christ (Jehovah)
- God (Eloheim)

the tender feelings of Isaiah's heart as he expresses the love of the Lord that will be felt and freely expressed during the Savior's millennial reign. Others in the scriptures have written similar songs of praise; consider especially Nephi's moving psalm in which he praises the Lord (see 2 Ne. 4:15–35). Knowing of Nephi's own psalm, it is easy to imagine that he must have been particularly moved by Isaiah's beautiful song of praise.

MAIN THEMES

- We should always trust in the Lord.
- We should develop feelings of gratitude toward the Lord for all He has done and should express our thanks often.
- We should bear witness of the goodness of the Lord.
- We should call upon the Lord in all our doings.

trust, and not be afraid; for the
my song; he also has become my

KEY INSIGHTS ABOUT THE SAVIOR

- The Lord is our salvation.
- The Lord is the source of our strength.
- The Lord's Atonement is the reason for our hope and joy.
- The Savior has been exalted.
- During the Millennium, the Lord will dwell among men.

2 Nephi 23

"Every one that is proud shall be
that is joined to the wicked shall fall

MAJOR CONCEPT

The kingdom of the devil—or "the whore of all the earth" (1 Ne. 14:10)—will be destroyed
immediately prior to the Second Coming.

OVERVIEW In this chapter, which compares to Isaiah 13, Isaiah prophesies the destruction of Babylon, seeing it as a day of wrath and vengeance. He clarifies that the destruction of Babylon is a type or symbol of the destruction that will take place at the Second Coming of the Lord.

WHAT WAS BABYLON? Babylon actually has both a literal and a figurative meaning. Its literal meaning refers to a once-great city that existed six centuries before Christ was born; the city went through a long period of decline, eventually fell, and was deserted—never again to be inhabited. The figurative meaning of the word refers to Satan's kingdom, or the world. This chapter refers to the figurative term of Babylon, or the church of the devil, which will be destroyed and come to utter desolation when the Savior comes again. Isaiah prophesied that Babylon would never be inhabited (see v. 20); it is unusual for a city that size to be left desolate. Jerusalem, Damascus, and Jericho were all destroyed, yet have been rebuilt (see *CES Old Testament Student Manual*, 134).

PROMINENT PEOPLE

- Babylon
- Jesus Christ

MAIN THEMES

- If we oppose the Lord, we will be destroyed.
- We will be able to withstand destruction and will be preserved if we are faithful in obeying the Lord.

thrust through; yea, and every one by the sword." (2 Ne. 23: 15)

Image: Babylonian ruins.

2 Nephi 24

"And it shall come to pass in that rest, from thy sorrow, and from thy wherein thou wast made to serve."

MAJOR CONCEPT

At the last day, the wicked will be destroyed, Satan will be cast out, and the righteous will find refuge in the Lord.

OVERVIEW Isaiah prophesies that at the last day Israel will be gathered and preserved and will enjoy peace and rest during the Millennium. Babylon will be destroyed, Satan will be cast out, and the wicked nations of the earth will fall and be destroyed. At the last day, Israel will triumph over Babylon—the world—and refuge will be found in Zion. This chapter can be compared to Isaiah 14.

INTERESTING FACTS ABOUT SATAN'S NAMES Verse 12 in this chapter and the corresponding verse in Isaiah 14 are the only two places in the Bible and the Book of Mormon where Satan is called *Lucifer*, a name that means "light bearer" or "son of the morning." In D&C 76, we

PROMINENT PEOPLE

- Jesus Christ
- Satan (Lucifer)
- Babylon and Assyria

learn that Lucifer was Satan's name in the premortal world; its meaning reminds us that Satan was once in a high position but fell due to his rebellion, wanting to take the glory for himself, and wanting to remove our agency. While Lucifer is a name that represents light, *Perdition*—another name by which Satan is known—means "utter loss," the condition in which Satan now finds himself.

MAIN THEMES

- In order to experience peace and rest at the last day, we must have faith and be obedient.
- Our refuge will be in Zion.
- Followers of Lucifer lose the blessings of the Abrahamic covenant (including land, authority, and posterity).

day that the Lord shall give thee fear, and from the hard bondage (2 Ne. 24:3)

KEY INSIGHTS ABOUT THE SAVIOR

- The Lord will have mercy on His righteous.
- The Lord will choose and restore Israel over all other nations.
- Babylon—the wicked nations and peoples of the world—will be smitten and destroyed by the Lord.

2 Nephi 25

MAJOR CONCEPT

The purpose of the Book of Mormon is to persuade people to come unto Christ.

OVERVIEW From here through Chapter 30, Nephi addresses three different audiences: the Jews (2 Ne. 25:10–20), the Lamanites (2 Ne. 25:21 to 2 Ne. 26:11), and the Gentiles (2 Ne. 26:12 to 2 Ne. 29:14); the audience he is addressing makes a huge difference in his approach. Here, Nephi acknowledges that the words of Isaiah that he quoted in the previous chapters can be difficult to understand—especially if we do not understand the ways in which prophecies were given in Isaiah's time—but maintains that we will understand Isaiah's words in the last days. Nephi then bears testimony of the Savior's coming and testifies that the Jews would reject Him, crucify Him, and be scattered as a result. Once they believe in the Savior, Nephi writes, the Jews will be restored. The Nephites believe Nephi's teachings, believe in Christ, and keep the law of Moses.

INTERESTING FACTS ABOUT GRACE Some in the world believe that the Savior's grace is all that is needed to obtain salvation. However, Nephi makes clear in verse 23 of

PROMINENT PEOPLE

- Nephi
- Isaiah
- The Jews
- The Messiah

MAIN THEMES

- To more fully understand Isaiah, we need to understand the manner of prophesying among the Jews; we need to be filled with the spirit of prophecy (a testimony of Jesus); we need to know the geographical regions involved. Finally, the words and prophecies of Isaiah will be widely understood when those prophecies are fulfilled.

- We better understand Isaiah if we have a testimony that he was preaching about Jesus.

- Nephi delighted in the words of Isaiah and proclaimed that they would be of great worth to us in the latter days.

- All who believe on the name of the Savior will be saved in the kingdom of God.

- The nations that possess the word of God in the Book of Mormon will be judged according to the words that are written in it.

- The purpose of Nephi's record is to persuade everyone to believe in Christ.

- The "right way" is to believe in Christ and deny Him not.

- We are saved by grace after all we can do.

- The Lord never destroys a people without first warning them through His prophets.

Christ, we preach of Christ, we prophesy of prophecies, that our children may know remission of their sins." (2 Ne. 25:26)

this chapter that we are saved by grace after all we can do. Elder Bruce R. McConkie taught, "Man cannot be saved by grace alone; as the Lord lives, man must keep the commandments . . . ; he must work the works of righteousness . . . ; he must work out his salvation with fear and trembling before the Lord . . . ; he must have faith like the ancients—the faith that brings with it gifts and signs and miracles. Does it suffice to believe and be baptized without more? The answer is no, in every language and tongue" (*Sermons and Writings,* 76–77). We are saved by grace after all we can do, and "all we can do" is defined in Alma 24:11— all we can do is to repent of our sins.

KEY INSIGHTS ABOUT THE SAVIOR

- The judgments of the Lord will come upon all nations.
- The Lord reveals all necessary things to His servants, the prophets.
- Following His crucifixion, the Lord rose from the dead and revealed Himself to as many as believed on His name.
- The Lord scourged the Jews from generation to generation, for many generations, and will continue to do so until they are persuaded to believe in Him.
- The Lord will gather His people a second time.
- The Lord is performing a marvelous work and a wonder among the children of men.
- The Savior brought forth His words to the Jews, and those words will be used to judge them at the last day.
- There is only one Messiah, and His name is Jesus Christ; He is the one who was rejected by the Jews.
- There is no name other than Jesus Christ by which men can be saved.
- The Lord promised Nephi that his record would be preserved and would come forth at the last day.

2 Nephi 26

"For none of these iniquities come of the
inviteth them all to come unto him and
white, bond and free, male and female;

MAJOR CONCEPT

The record of the Nephites was preserved and has come forth in these latter days.

OVERVIEW In this chapter, Nephi and Isaiah combine to unveil the future, and Nephi is speaking not to his people, but to those generations of the last days—our generation. After telling of the destruction of his people, Nephi prophesies that the Savior will minister to them. He also prophesies of the importance of the records kept by the Nephites and says they will speak from the dust to later generations. He decries false churches and secret combinations and teaches that the Lord forbids men to practice priestcrafts. In verses 1–11, Nephi walks through the history of his second audience, the Lamanites; beginning in verse 12, he addresses his third audience, the Gentiles.

PROMINENT PEOPLE

- The Messiah
- Nephi
- The Nephites
- The Laman-
  ites

INTERESTING FACTS ABOUT THE BOOK OF MORMON In this chapter, Nephi envisions the time when his record—and those of future record-keepers in the promised land—will be revealed and will speak to the people in the latter days as if it were a voice from the dust. Through the words

MAIN THEMES

- The righteous who follow the prophets and look toward Christ will not be destroyed.

- The Book of Mormon seems familiar to those who already believe in the Bible.

- Secret combinations will be prevalent in the last days.

- Spiritual poverty results from pride, failure to acknowledge the miracles of the Lord, reliance on self, and neglect of the poor.

- Many in the last days will stumble because of a lack of knowledge and spiritual understanding due to an imperfect Bible.

- Priestcraft—preaching for popularity and financial gain—will be prevalent in the last days.

- Satan is the source of apostasy and darkness.

- We should work to persuade all men to repentance.

- Christ denies no one (male, female, black, white) from coming unto Him.

- We must not murder, lie, steal, take the name of the Lord in vain, have envy, feel malice, contend with one another, or indulge in immoral behavior.

600 BC

90 BC

559–545 BC

Lord; for he doeth that which is good among the children of men; . . . and he partake of his goodness; and he denieth none that come unto him, black and and . . . all are alike unto God, both Jew and Gentile." (2 Ne. 26:33)

of the righteous that are written in the records, he prophesies, the prayers of the faithful will be answered, and the Lord will remember those who have dwindled in unbelief for so long. Nephi's language parallels that of Isaiah, who foresaw the same restoration when the voice of prophets would "speak out of the ground, and thy speech shall be low out of the dust" (Isa. 29:4). Over generations and at the hand of multiple translators, plain and precious truths were removed from the Bible, causing many to stumble and lack spiritual understanding. The Book of Mormon contains the fulness of the gospel, restoring truths that were lost from the Bible. The Book of Mormon will be the most important factor in bringing modern-day people to Jesus Christ and to the truth.

KEY INSIGHTS ABOUT THE SAVIOR

- The eventual victory of good over evil will be centered in Jesus Christ.
- The Spirit of the Lord will not always strive with man.
- The Lord destroys those who are wicked.
- The Lord provides salvation as a free gift to all who will repent.
- The Savior forbids the seeking of personal gain, praise, and popularity without concern for the welfare of Zion.
- The Lord forbids violation of the Ten Commandments.
- Iniquity never comes from the Lord.
- The Lord invites all to come unto Him and partake of His goodness.
- The Lord denies none who come unto Him.

2 Nephi 27

"Therefore, I will proceed to do a wisdom of their wise and learned prudent shall be hid." (2 Ne. 27:26)

MAJOR CONCEPT

The Book of Mormon came forth in our day in direct fulfillment of prophecy made by both Nephi and Isaiah.

OVERVIEW In this chapter, which compares to Isaiah 29, Nephi prophesies that darkness and apostasy will cover the earth in the last days because the people will reject the prophets. He also prophesies of the coming forth of the Book of Mormon, saying that three witnesses will testify of the book and that a learned man will say he is not able to read from a sealed book. Through this book, he says, the Lord will do a marvelous work and wonder (the restoration of the gospel) among the children of men. This is the last of the Isaiah chapters that Nephi enters into his record.

INTERESTING FACTS ABOUT WITNESSES AND DOCUMENTS
Recent archaeological discoveries have shown that many

PROMINENT PEOPLE

- Jesus Christ
- The Three and Eight Witnesses
- A learned man

Israelites—including those in Lehi's day—used doubled, sealed, and witnessed documents. When written on papyrus or parchment, a legal document was written twice on the same sheet, at the top and at the bottom. The document was then folded and sealed, leaving one part open for inspection

MAIN THEMES

- Those who stumbled before the gospel was restored did so because there was no prophet.

- The Book of Mormon came forth in our day to illuminate the world against false religions and untrue teachings.

- The sealed portion of the Book of Mormon, which contains a history of the world from the beginning to the end, will not be delivered until the own due time of the Lord.

- The Three Witnesses and Eight Witnesses of the Book of Mormon saw the plates in direct fulfillment of prophecy.

- Martin Harris showing part of the translation of the Book of Mormon to Charles Anthon—a "learned man"—was in direct fulfillment of prophecy.

- Critics who try to destroy the Book of Mormon will be cut off.

- The Book of Mormon will provide answers for those who are unable to hear the whisperings of the Spirit and who can't see the hand of the Lord in the affairs of men.

- People who murmur don't understand doctrine.

600 BC

90 BC

559–545 BC

while sealing the other part. When engraved on metal, two plates were used in a similar way. Witnesses were necessary to verify a document; for example, in the Talmud, the law required three witnesses to a sale of property. The way the Book of Mormon was put together and the way in which witnesses were provided makes complete sense in view of these ancient methods of document preservation, though these ancient practices were not known until long after the Book of Mormon was published—another evidence of its authenticity (see *Echoes,* 374–379).

Image: Charles Anthon.

KEY INSIGHTS ABOUT THE SAVIOR

- The Lord's judgments are just and come upon men because of their disobedience and iniquity.
- The judgments of the Lord upon a group of people can take many forms, including thunder, earthquake, destructive storms, tempests, and devouring fire.
- The Lord engineered the coming forth of the Book of Mormon.
- The Lord is in complete control over the release of the sealed portion of the Book of Mormon.
- When it comes forth, the sealed portion of the Book of Mormon will be read by the power of Christ.
- The Lord has brought forth a "marvelous work and wonder" in our day—including the Book of Mormon, the restoration of the Church and the priesthood, and the return of prophets to the earth—restoring all things previously lost to the children of men.

2 Nephi 28

"And others will he pacify, and lull say: All is well in Zion; yea, Zion cheateth their souls, and leadeth them

MAJOR CONCEPT

In these latter days, Satan rages in the hearts of men and attempts to destroy us.

OVERVIEW Nephi prophesies of and exposes the false philosophies of churches in our day and the careful strategies of Satan for leading the wicked to destruction. He specifically tells us that Satan will rage in the hearts of men and will teach all manner of false doctrines in his attempt to lead people astray; Nephi provides a clear analysis of Satan and his strategies. Nephi begins this chapter—which was written specifically for us in our day—by saying that the Spirit instructed him to write it.

INTERESTING FACTS ABOUT "LINE UPON LINE" The Lord is the master teacher; He endows us with truth in accordance with our capacity to receive it. He tells us in this chapter

PROMINENT PEOPLE

• Satan

(see verse 30) that He will give us "line upon line, precept upon precept, here a little and there a little"—a sentiment that is repeated various other times in the scriptures (see Isa. 28:10, 13; D&C 98:12, 128:21; and Alma 12:9–11). We grow in this way—line upon line, precept upon precept—

MAIN THEMES

• The Book of Mormon is of great worth to us in our day; Nephi lists conditions of the last days that show why we need the Book of Mormon.

• False churches that contend with one another and claim to be the true church deny the power of God.

• The Book of Mormon instructs us about the challenges of our day, including false churches that teach false doctrine, excusing sin and wickedness; teachers who are corrupted; widespread apostasy; deception; and persecution of the meek.

• Satan wants us to believe he does not exist; one of his key strategies is to pacify us into thinking all is well.

• While Satan is very real and battles for our souls, he will fall.

• If we fail to repent, we will belong to Satan, not the Lord.

• We need to trust in the Lord's revelations rather than man's reasoning and choose to follow the prophets of God rather than the precepts of man.

them away into carnal security, that they will prospereth, all is well—and thus the devil away carefully down to hell." (2 Ne. 28:21)

because growth is a process. As we listen to and follow the Lord's instructions, we gain wisdom and thereby qualify to receive more. By being patient and recognizing the Lord's way of teaching us, we will be endowed with increasing measures of truth and light.

WHO IS SATAN? Satan has a pervasive presence in the Book of Mormon—due in large part to the fact that Mormon saw the history of God's people in the New World over a two-thousand-year period of time and was able to make an accurate judgment of Satan's works and influence. The Book of Mormon confirms that Satan has been among the children of men from the beginning, spreading darkness and abominations throughout the world. In his perceptive analysis of Satan's strategies, Nephi shows that Satan has devised a meticulous system of temptations to draw men from the pathways of righteousness and into wickedness, with its inevitable downward spiral.

and we ᵃneed ᵇno more of the word of God, for we have enough!
30 For behold, thus saith the Lord God: I will give unto the children of men line upon line, precept upon ᵃprecept, here a little and there a little; and blessed are those who hearken unto my precepts, and lend an ear unto my counsel, for they shall learn ᵇwisdom; for unto him that ᶜreceiveth I will give ᵈmore; and from them that shall say, We have enough, from them shall be taken away even that which they have.
31 Cursed is he that putteth his ᵃtrust in man, or maketh flesh his

KEY INSIGHTS ABOUT THE SAVIOR

- The Lord will judge all those who do evil—including Satan.
- The Lord warns those who oppose modern-day revelation.
- The truth of the Lord is built on a solid foundation.
- The Lord will provide for us line upon line, precept upon precept; those who listen to Him will gain wisdom and will receive more truth.
- The Lord will be merciful to those who repent and come unto Him.

2 Nephi 29

"For I command all men . . . that
them; for out of the books which shall
according to their works, according

MAJOR CONCEPT

The Book of Mormon is part of a canon of scripture published after the Bible that represents the ongoing revelation of the Lord from which we will be judged.

OVERVIEW Nephi quotes the Lord, who reiterates that He will do a marvelous work in our dispensation by bringing forth the Book of Mormon. The Lord indicates that many will reject the book because they believe all truth is contained in the Bible and that revelation has ceased. Indicating the need for ongoing scripture, the Lord makes clear that He will judge us out of the books that are written.

INTERESTING FACTS ABOUT THE TIMING OF THE BOOK OF MORMON President Ezra Taft Benson gives interesting perspective on how its timing bears testimony of the importance of the Book of Mormon: "A powerful testimony to the importance of the Book of Mormon is to note where

PROMINENT PEOPLE

- Jesus Christ
- The Jews and the Nephites
- The lost tribes of Israel

the Lord placed its coming forth in the timetable of the unfolding Restoration. The only thing that preceded it was the First Vision. . . . Think of that in terms of what it implies. The coming forth of the Book of Mormon preceded the restoration of the priesthood. It was published just a few days before the Church was organized. The Saints were given the Book of Mormon to read before they were given the revelations outlining such great doctrines as the three degrees of glory, celestial marriage, or work for the dead. It came before priesthood quorums and Church organization. Doesn't this tell us something about how the Lord views this sacred work?" (*The Teachings of Ezra Taft Benson,* 49).

MAIN THEMES

- The Book of Mormon has been rejected by many who believed that the Bible contains all truth and revelation and that no more scripture is necessary.

- The Book of Mormon is a standard or ensign.

- Latter-day critics of the Book of Mormon are actually fulfilling a sign of the times.

- The Bible does not contain all the words of the Lord; there are records from many nations that will eventually testify of Him.

- In the last days three major records will testify of Christ: the Bible, the Book of Mormon, and the records of the lost tribes of Israel.

they shall write the words which I speak unto be written I will judge the world, every man to that which is written." (2 Ne. 29:11)

Key Insights about the Savior

- The restoration of the gospel and the coming forth of the Book of Mormon were accomplished by the Lord in remembrance of the covenants He had made with Nephi and Lehi.
- The Lord never forgets His people.
- The Lord created all men on the earth and continues to bring His word to all nations of the earth; as a result, those nations will eventually testify of Him.
- The Lord is the same yesterday, today, and forever.
- Revelations from the Lord have not ceased and will never cease until the end of man.
- The Lord will show all those who fight against His word that He is God.

2 Nephi 30

"And the gospel of Jesus Christ shall wherefore, they shall be restored unto knowledge of Jesus Christ, which

Major Concept

As a result of the Book of Mormon, many Gentiles, Jews, and Lamanites will be converted to the gospel.

OVERVIEW Nephi prophesies that during the last days, many Lamanites and Jews will believe the word of God as written in the Book of Mormon and will become acceptable to the Lord. He also prophesies that the converted Gentiles will be numbered with the covenant people in our day. In a message repeated many times in the Book of Mormon, he prophesies that Israel will be gathered and restored and that the wicked will be destroyed. Nephi describes the Second Coming and the conditions that will exist during the Millennium. This chapter contains several remarkable predictions that didn't seem likely or possible when the Book of Mormon was translated; for example, in 1830 there were no Lamanites in the Church and no Jews in Palestine. This

Prominent People

- Jesus Christ
- The Gentiles
- The Jews
- The Lamanites

chapter is a summary message to the three groups Nephi addressed in the previous five chapters (the Gentiles, the Lamanites, and the Jews).

INTERESTING FACTS ABOUT LINEAGE How are the Book of Mormon people descendants of the Jews? Lehi is a descendant of Manasseh, the son of Joseph; Ishmael is a descendant of Ephraim, son of Joseph. Both of their families originated in Jerusalem and came from the Jewish nation. Before they left Jerusalem, both families were Jews by citizenship (*Jew* is a national name as well as a tribal name). But there is another way in which the Book of Mormon people descend from the Jews: Mulek, the founder of the Mulekites—a people that later joined the Nephite culture—is of the tribe of Judah. There is a physical Israel and a spiritual Israel; true members of the house of Israel are those who believe in and follow Christ.

Main Themes

- Any Gentile who is not of the bloodline of Israel can become a covenant member of the house of Israel through repentance.

- The people in our day who will be spared from destruction are those who give heed to the prophets and Apostles.

- The major part of the gathering of Israel will occur during the Millennium.

- All things will be revealed during the Millennium, including things no man has known.

- During the Millennium, Satan will no longer have power over the hearts of the children of men.

600 BC

90 BC

559–545 BC

be declared among [the remnant of our seed]; the knowledge of their fathers, and also to the was had among their fathers." (2 Ne. 30:5)

KEY INSIGHTS ABOUT THE SAVIOR

- The Lord covenants with no one except those who repent and believe in Him.
- At the last day, the Lord will divide His people; He will spare the righteous and destroy the wicked.
- During the Millennium, the Lord will make all things known, including the sealed portion of the Book of Mormon.

Image: Missionaries on their way to teach the Native Americans.

2 Nephi 31

"Wherefore, ye must press forward and a love of God and of all men. Christ, and endure to the end, thus

MAJOR CONCEPT

Just as Jesus was baptized to fulfill all righteousness, we too must be baptized and must endure to the end in obedience if we hope to gain eternal life.

OVERVIEW Nephi explains why the Lord was baptized and goes on to say that all men must follow the Savior, be baptized, receive the Holy Ghost, and endure to the end if they hope to be saved. He clarifies that baptism alone is not sufficient to gain eternal life, but that we have to repent and keep the commandments after we are baptized if we hope to gain the great reward. Chapters 31 through 33 contain the final words of Nephi, describing how to gain life with God for all eternity.

INTERESTING FACTS ABOUT BAPTISM OF FIRE At Jesus' baptism, the Holy Ghost descended on Him as a dove descends; after we are baptized, we are given the gift of the Holy Ghost. We are told in verse 13 that following our baptism, we receive the baptism of fire—the gift of the Holy Ghost—so called in part because the Holy Ghost cleanses us as if by fire. Elder Bruce R. McConkie wrote that baptism by fire is the actual enjoyment of the gift of the Holy Ghost—the cleansing agent in the repentance

PROMINENT PEOPLE

- God the Father
- Jesus Christ

MAIN THEMES

- Nephi wanted his words to be plain enough for us to understand.
- We need to be baptized just as Jesus was baptized. For us, baptism provides a remission of sins, gives us membership in the Church, and opens the door to personal sanctification.
- The gate to the kingdom of God is baptism.
- The path to eternal life is strait and the gate through which we must enter is narrow.
- If we hope to follow Jesus, we must keep the commandments of the Father.
- We must guard against hypocrisy, a situation

in which we pretend to be something we are not or we assume false roles that do not reflect our true thoughts and feelings.
- In order to gain eternal life, we must endure to the end in faith and obedience.
- Eternal life comes to those who press forward—who move with complete dedication along the path to perfection despite distraction or adversity—with steadfastness, a firm determination to follow the Savior.
- We must feast on the words of Christ to remain on the straight and narrow path.

600 BC

90 BC

106   559–545 BC

with a steadfastness in Christ, having a perfect brightness of hope,
Wherefore, if ye shall press forward, feasting upon the word of
saith the Father: Ye shall have eternal life." (2 Ne. 31:20)

process. He wrote in *Mormon Doctrine* that through the power of the Holy Ghost, "dross, iniquity, carnality, sensuality, and every evil thing is burned out of the repentant soul as if by fire; the cleansed person becomes literally a new creature of the Holy Ghost" (*Mormon Doctrine*, 2nd edition, 73). Parley P. Pratt wrote that the Holy Ghost is, "as it were, marrow to the bone, joy to the heart, light to the eyes, music to the ears, and life to the whole being" (*Key to the Science of Theology*, 97).

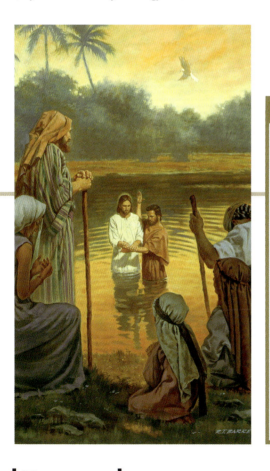

KEY INSIGHTS ABOUT THE SAVIOR

- The Lord speaks to us in our language based on our ability to understand and when needed provides additional light.

- The doctrine of Christ is to believe in Christ, repent, be baptized, receive the Holy Ghost, and keep the commandments.

- Jesus had to be baptized to fulfill all righteousness.

- At His baptism, the Lord humbled Himself before the Father and demonstrated His willingness to obey all the commandments.

- The Savior chose to be baptized in order to show us how to gain entrance into the celestial kingdom.

- In His baptism, Jesus set an example for all mankind to follow.

- The Lord condemns hypocrisy.

2 Nephi 32

MAJOR CONCEPT

The Holy Ghost will show us all things we need to do to inherit eternal life.

OVERVIEW Nephi continues his final counsel by urging us to pray so we can gain knowledge for ourselves through the Holy Ghost. In underscoring the importance of the Holy Ghost, he explains that angels speak to man by the power of the Holy Ghost.

PROMINENT PEOPLE

- Jesus Christ
- The Holy Ghost

WHO IS THE HOLY GHOST? The Holy Ghost is the third member of the Godhead, serving in unity and glory with the Father and the Son. Unlike the Father and the Son, who have glorified bodies of flesh and bones, the Holy Ghost is a personage of spirit who does not have a body of flesh and bones—something that makes it possible for Him to dwell in our hearts (see D&C 130:22). From the Creation onward, the Holy Ghost is found at work through all the generations of time, guiding, illuminating, warning, counseling, confirming, and blessing the lives of God's children. Isaiah made clear that the Holy Ghost would bless and sustain the Savior during His Atonement

MAIN THEMES

- Revelation is promised us through our faithfulness and comes through the Holy Ghost.

- We are counseled to feast upon the words of Christ.

- If we ask for help in understanding the words of Christ, the Holy Ghost can make all things clear to us.

- Those who are not brought into the light of the Spirit will perish in the darkness.

- We must pray always and seek guidance from the Lord in all situations.

- We must pray in the name of Christ.

- It is the spirit of the devil that teaches us not to pray.

- The key to spiritual power is earnest, pleading prayer combined with righteous living as we pray.

that if ye will enter in by the way, and unto you all things what ye should do."

(see Isa. 11:2; 42:1; 48:16–17). He also assures us that the Holy Ghost, or Spirit of the Lord, will be at work in the last days, gathering the Saints, preparing the world for the Second Coming, and inaugurating the Savior's millennial reign. We receive the gift of the Holy Ghost by the laying on of hands following baptism, but our ability to have His companionship and the blessings He brings depends on our faithfulness and virtue. The key to regaining the Spirit once we have lost it is earnest repentance through pleading, yearning, hungering prayer and a steadfast effort to obey the commandments.

KEY INSIGHTS ABOUT THE SAVIOR

- The words of Christ will tell us all things we should do.
- The Lord withholds information He would otherwise reveal if we are not prepared to receive it.
- When we pray in righteousness, the Lord will consecrate our performance for the welfare of our souls.

2 Nephi 33

"But I, Nephi, have written what great worth, and especially unto my

MAJOR CONCEPT

Christ commanded Nephi to write the things he did, and Christ will eventually testify that they are His words.

OVERVIEW In concluding his account, Nephi testifies that his words are true, saying that those who believe in Christ will also believe his words. Nephi finishes his record by promising that his words will stand as a witness and by bidding us farewell until he meets us before the judgment bar of God.

INTERESTING FACTS ABOUT MERISMUS A *merismus* is an ancient rhetorical device in which a topic or statement is divided into parts in such a way that the entire topic or statement can be remembered by listing only one or more of the parts. To see how it works, think of the six major points of doctrine the Savior taught: faith, repentance, baptism, the gift of the Holy Ghost, enduring to the end, and eternal life. In a merismus, naming just two points of that doctrine—for example, faith and enduring to the end—would bring to mind all six points, or the entire list. Verse 4 contains a merismus—"endure to the end, which is life eternal." By

PROMINENT PEOPLE

- Nephi
- Jesus Christ
- The Jews
- The Gentiles
- The Lamanites

MAIN THEMES

- The Book of Mormon is of great worth to us.
- By the power of the Holy Ghost we can know the truth of Nephi's words.
- When one speaks by the power of the Holy Ghost, the message is conveyed to the heart (spirit) of the listener(s).
- Believing in Christ and enduring to the end will bring us eternal life.
- Only those who are under the influence of Satan will be angry at the words Nephi has written.

- Nephi glories in plainness, in truth, and in the Savior and encourages us to do the same.
- We must enter through the narrow gate and walk in the strait path that leads to eternal life.
- Nephi prayed that the people of our day would be saved in the kingdom of God.
- The words of the Book of Mormon will condemn those who do not believe them.
- Nephi will meet us face-to-face at the judgment bar along with Jacob (see Jacob 6:13) and Moroni (see Moro. 10:27).

I have written, and I esteem it as of people." (2 Ne. 33:3)

including just those two points of doctrine, Nephi reminds us of the other four, and we go away remembering the entire list of what we need to do to gain eternal life. The merismus is frequently used in the Bible, and in the Book of Mormon there are at least 130 meristic statements about Christ's doctrine (see *Echoes,* 141–143).

KEY INSIGHTS ABOUT THE SAVIOR

- The Lord will consecrate Nephi's prayers and words for our gain.
- The Lord commanded Nephi to write the words he wrote.
- Nephi's words are the Lord's words.
- The Lord commanded Nephi to seal up the condemnation of those who would not believe the words of the Book of Mormon.

Jacob 1

"And we also had many revelations, and the wherefore, we knew of Christ and his kingdom, (Jacob 1:6)

MAJOR CONCEPT

We should believe in Christ and consecrate our service to Him with devotion and obedience.

OVERVIEW In this chapter—the first in which the plates are directly under Jacob's stewardship—he establishes the criteria he will use in recording on the plates. He and his brother Joseph intend that their writings will be used to persuade men to believe in Christ and obey His commandments. Their older brother, the prophet Nephi, dies. They appoint a man to replace Nephi as king.

INTERESTING FACTS ABOUT COLOPHONS Major sections of the Book of Mormon are introduced by or concluded with a language construction known as a *colophon*. The colophon informs the reader about the author and the source of the material. The first three verses of the Book of Mormon

PROMINENT PEOPLE

- Jacob
- Joseph
- Nephi

are an excellent example of a colophon, which typically includes the name of the author ("I, Nephi"), mentions the merits of the parents ("having been born of goodly parents"), and confirms the truth of the writing ("And I know that the record which I make is true"). The colophon—which

MAIN THEMES

- Jacob's purpose is to persuade us to come unto Christ so that we might enter His rest.

- We suffer the "cross" when we bear our own afflictions and trials while maintaining faith in Christ.

- One of our key responsibilities is to persuade others to believe in Christ and keep His commandments so they can gain exaltation.

- We "magnify" our calling when we focus in on the light of the Savior.

- If we fail to teach those within our circle of influence with all diligence, we will not be found spotless but will find their sins upon our own heads.

- Though not readily apparent, we can deduce that Nephi was a king because Jacob referred to Nephi as a king; Nephi himself spoke of his "reign"; the man who replaced Nephi was the "second king"; and subsequent kings were named Nephi after their first king.

- We are responsible for those we might have saved had we labored diligently.

600 BC

90 BC

544–421 BC

means "finishing touch" in Greek—is an Egyptian literary device that was well established and often used in ancient times. Hugh Nibley wrote that the colophon was a required part of any properly composed Egyptian autobiography of Nephi's time (see *Echoes,* 474). Here, in verse 2, Jacob uses a colophon to tell readers that he is the author and that he was given a commandment to write the things he "considered to be most precious."

WHO WAS JACOB? The brother of Nephi, Jacob was born while his parents traveled in the wilderness after fleeing from Jerusalem to escape destruction. He was the older of Lehi's two sons to be born in the wilderness; the other was Joseph. Jacob bridged the gap between the old and the new promised lands; as such, he was sensitive to both the Jews and to his own people. He was between forty-four and fifty-four years old when Nephi gave him the plates with a charge to record the things most precious to him; the fact that he received the plates is evidence that Jacob had heeded Lehi's counsel to follow Nephi and remain righteous. We are told that Jacob saw the Savior.

KEY INSIGHTS ABOUT THE SAVIOR

- The Lord calls and consecrates those who would be His servants.
- Those who serve the Lord are guided by revelation and the spirit of prophecy.

Jacob 2

"But before ye seek for riches, seek ye for the

MAJOR CONCEPT

Of primary importance in the things we do is the motivation behind our actions.

OVERVIEW In this, one of four "temple discourses" in the Book of Mormon, Jacob speaks plainly against pride, unchastity, and the love of riches. He counsels that men should use riches to help their fellow men, and emphasizes that the Lord delights in the chastity of women. (The other "temple discourses" include one by King Benjamin and two by the Savior.) The Nephites at this time were more wicked than the Lamanites because they broke the hearts of their wives through immorality and justified having more than one wife because of the lives of David and Solomon.

INTERESTING FACTS ABOUT MONEY AND WEALTH Money itself is a medium of exchange and is of itself neutral. The attitude we have toward money is what removes it from its neutral position. Brigham Young taught that a person who esteems wealth above the things of God "has no eyes to see, no ears to hear, no heart to understand" (see *Discourses of Brigham Young*, 306–307). Gold is not what corrupts

PROMINENT PEOPLE

- Jacob
- David
- Solomon
- Jesus Christ

MAIN THEMES

- The pleasing word of God heals wounded souls.

- We are responsible to God for those over whom we have stewardship.

- Prophets and those who have stewardship over us speak to us and admonish us with boldness and plainness.

- When we are blessed with wealth, our first priority is to use it righteously in blessing our fellow man.

- We should seek wealth only for the intent to do good with that wealth.

- Pride is an abomination.

- We cannot rationalize our own unrighteous behavior by leaning on examples from the scriptures.

- The only time plural marriage should be practiced is when the Lord specifically commands it.

man, but the motive for obtaining gold. In accumulating wealth, our first priority should be building the kingdom of God—and our attitude toward material things is inescapably determined by our two most basic relationships: that with God and that with our fellow men. As spelled out in verse 19, the righteous use of wealth is to serve others—and when we lose sight of the brotherhood of man, we turn to dishonesty, neglect of the poor, and selfishness as we begin to use our wealth for unrighteous purposes (as outlined in verses 13 and 14). Riches alone can never make us happy; true happiness comes from serving the Lord and having His Spirit to be with us.

KEY INSIGHTS ABOUT THE SAVIOR

- One person is as precious to the Savior as every other person.
- The cries of those who are pure and righteous will be a testimony to the Savior against those who come against them in unrighteousness.
- We were created by the Lord to keep His commandments and glorify Him forever.

Jacob 3

"O all ye that are pure in heart, lift up your word of God, and feast upon his love; for forever." (Jacob 3:2)

MAJOR CONCEPT

Those who are pure in heart will receive the choicest blessings of God.

OVERVIEW Jacob records the importance of being pure in heart; as part of that, he prophesies that the Lamanites will eventually become more pure in heart—more righteous—than the Nephites. He reminds the people that purity and righteousness require that they protect against every sin, including fornication and lasciviousness. Jacob requests that the pure in heart look to God, pray with faith, receive the Word, and feast on His love; the Lord will then console them in their afflictions, plead their cause, and send justice upon those who seek their destruction.

INTERESTING FACTS ABOUT LAND OF INHERITANCE In verse 4, Jacob refers to the "land of your inheritance,"

PROMINENT PEOPLE

- Jacob
- Jesus Christ
- Nephites
- Lamanites
- Sons of perdition ("angels to the devil")

a phrase that is repeated in the Book of Mormon—sometimes as "the land of their inheritance" or "the land of their first inheritance." According to scholar Eduard Meyer, Israel's power and authority came from the first allotments of land made by the leaders when they settled what they considered to be their land of promise. Only one who still inhabited "the land of his inheritance" could be part of the ruling body in Jerusalem. That tradition is obvious throughout the Book of Mormon—the first land the people obtain is always referred to as the land of their inheritance. The ancient idea of a permanent inheritance of land was not known until modern times, long after Joseph Smith translated the Book of Mormon (see *Echoes*, 466–467).

MAIN THEMES

- We need to exercise firmness and great faith in our dealings with the Lord.

- If we remain faithful, we will receive the pleasing word of God and feast on His love forever.

- Marital fidelity is a critical component of righteousness.

- Wickedness is often the result of how people are taught rather than an inherently wicked nature.

- We should examine our own weaknesses instead of judging those of others.

heads and receive the pleasing
ye may, if your minds are firm,

WHO ARE THE SONS OF PERDITION?
President Joseph Fielding Smith taught
that while "the vast majority of mankind
will never be privileged to come back to
dwell in the presence of the Father and
the Son," all will receive some measure
of salvation and divine benediction
except the sons of perdition. The sons of
perdition, he wrote, are "those who have
had the testimony of the Holy Ghost and
who have known the truth and then have
rejected it and put Christ to open shame"
(*Answers to Gospel Questions,* 1:76, 78).

KEY INSIGHTS ABOUT THE SAVIOR

- The Lord will console those who are pure in heart and protect them against their enemies.
- The Lord will send down justice on those who seek to destroy the pure in heart.
- The Lord is merciful unto those who keep His commandments.
- In times of great wickedness, the Lord will lead out the righteous from among the wicked.

Jacob 4

"For, for this intent have we written these
we had a hope of his glory many hundred
a hope of his glory, but also all the holy

Major Concept

All things are accomplished by the power of the Lord, and our testimonies of Him build on the testimonies of the prophets throughout the ages.

OVERVIEW Jacob begins this chapter describing his experience in writing on the plates, giving fascinating insight into the difficulty of the process, the reason for using plates, and his purpose for keeping the record—to convince his children and his brethren of Christ. He then states that all the prophets before him have testified of Christ; these include all the Old Testament prophets, and their prophecies of Christ represent the main "plain and precious truth" taken out of the Bible. Jacob then bears his own powerful testimony of the Savior.

INTERESTING FACTS ABOUT LOOKING BEYOND THE MARK
In verse 14, Jacob attributed spiritual blindness to the fact

Prominent People

- Jacob
- Jesus Christ
- The Jews

that people—in this case, the Jews— "looked beyond the mark," something that caused them to stumble and fall as the Lord removed the plainness of His gospel from them. In one fragment of the Dead Sea Scrolls the false teachers of the Jews were accused of breaking out of the boundaries set by law, thereby stepping beyond the designated mark (see *Echoes,*

Main Themes

- The records we leave for our posterity can be a tremendous blessing to them if we use them to testify of Christ.

- Our faith can enable us to do mighty things.

- The Nephites kept the law of Moses, but unlike the Jews they realized it was instituted to point them to Christ.

- We should never seek to counsel the Lord but should instead receive counsel from Him.

- We will be resurrected because of the Savior's Atonement.

- We can always rely on the whisperings of the Spirit.

- We should adhere to the simple and plain parts of the gospel instead of seeking those things that seem more mysterious.

- Abraham sacrificing his son, Isaac, was a similitude of God and His Only Begotten Son to help us understand what the Father felt in allowing the death of His Son.

600 BC

90 BC

544–421 BC

118

things, that they may know that we knew of Christ, and years before his coming; and not only we ourselves had prophets which were before us." (Jacob 4:4)

477). There continues to be much of "looking beyond the mark" in our day as well. By looking beyond the mark, we venture into unknown and dangerous territory. Elder Neal A. Maxwell explained that a good example of "looking beyond the mark" occurs when we "are more interested in the physical dimensions of the cross than in what Jesus achieved thereon" (*Not My Will, But Thine,* 26).

KEY INSIGHTS ABOUT PLATES VERSUS PARCHMENT The leading scholars of Joseph Smith's day believed that ancient manuscripts would have been written on rolls of parchment using elegant handwriting, complete with Roman letters and Latin language. If Joseph Smith had created the Book of Mormon on his own, he certainly would have used a format consistent with what was believed in that day—and would not have claimed to have found the record engraved on brass plates in reformed Egyptian, a direct contradiction to what scholars of his day would have accepted (see *Echoes,* 317–318). The first metal plates found in our day—also found in a stone box—were found in the tomb of King Darius the First and date back to 515 BC.

Image: Fragments from the Dead Sea Scrolls.

KEY INSIGHTS ABOUT THE SAVIOR

- Power and miracles are exercised in the name of Jesus Christ.
- The works of the Lord are great and marvelous.
- It is impossible for us to know all the mysteries of the Lord unless He reveals them to us.
- The Lord created the world and man by the power of His word.
- The Lord counsels in wisdom, justice, and great mercy over all His works.
- The Spirit of the Lord speaks the truth and does not lie; it speaks of things as they really are and as they really will be.
- The Lord performed the Atonement, making possible resurrection for all.
- The Jews looked beyond the mark by worshipping the law rather than the Lawgiver.
- At the last day, the Lord will become the only sure foundation upon which the Jews can build.

Jacob 5

"Behold, for this last time have we nourished diligent in laboring with me in my vineyard, the natural fruit . . . behold ye shall have

MAJOR CONCEPT

The Lord will strive with the world at least four different times; after the final gathering, the wicked will be destroyed, and the final cleansing of the earth will be by fire.

OVERVIEW In this chapter, Jacob quotes the Old Testament prophet Zenos regarding the allegory of the tame and wild olive trees. The tame olive trees represent Israel, or the Church; the wild olive trees, Gentiles or Israel in apostasy; the grafting in of branches, the gathering of Israel through baptism; and cutting off the branches, the scattering of Israel as a result of apostasy.

INTERESTING FACTS ABOUT THE ALLEGORY OF THE OL-IVE TREE An *allegory* is a story with more than one level of meaning; it uses symbols to represent spiritual ideas. The allegory of the olive tree details four different visits of the Lord to the earth, which is called His vineyard. First (see

PROMINENT PEOPLE

- Jacob
- Zenos
- The Lord
- Servants (the prophets)
- Other servants

verses 4–14) is His intimate involvement in governing the earth; He sent prophets to Israel to foretell His ministry, but only some of the people responded. In the second visit (see verses 15–28), the early Christian church flourished and several groups of scattered Israelites—including part of Lehi's

MAIN THEMES

- The gospel never changes.
- Many of the people have apostatized and fallen into wickedness, but the "main root"—the gospel and its covenants—will never be done away.
- Prophets plead with the Lord in our behalf.
- The exercise of agency can result in apostasy despite the care and attention of Church leaders and the Lord.
- Our greatest source of corruption occurs when we take upon ourselves credit for our

accomplishments—we rely upon ourselves and our own strength and dismiss or forget about the Lord.

- Sometimes when we prosper we are farthest from the Lord.
- The righteous will grow and thrive in the latter days.
- As part of the final judgment, the earth will be cleansed by fire and the wicked will be destroyed to prepare the earth to receive its celestial glory.

600 BC

544–421 BC

90 BC

my vineyard. . . . And blessed art thou; for because ye have been and have kept my commandments, and have brought unto me again joy with me because of the fruit of my vineyard." (Jacob 5:75)

posterity—produced faithful Saints. In the third visit (see verses 29–60), many of the scattered Israelites became unfaithful, and a universal, worldwide apostasy occurred; Lehi's wicked descendants overpowered his righteous posterity, and evil triumphed. Finally, prophets are to be sent to us in latter days (see verses 61–77), a great gathering will take place, the wicked will be destroyed, and the final cleansing of the earth will occur. There are three long periods between the four visits: the period of time between the Old and New Testament; the time between the great apostasy and the Restoration; and the one thousand years of the Millennium.

Image: Olive orchard.

KEY INSIGHTS ABOUT THE SAVIOR

- The Savior taught in parables and allegories to hide doctrine so that only the spiritually literate could understand it; figurative language forces us to search, ponder, and pray.

- Jesus Christ is the "master of the vineyard."

- Jesus' prophets through the ages are His "servant" with which He visits in the allegory.

- The Lord has continually worked with the inhabitants of the earth, trying to persuade them to obedience and good works.

- The Lord sends prophets and other leaders to teach the children of men.

- The Lord and His prophets have visited those who have been scattered.

- The Lord has led the righteous to a promised land.

- In the end, the Lord will prevail and evil will be defeated.

Jacob 6

"O then, my beloved brethren, repent ye, strait gate, and continue in the way which obtain eternal life." (Jacob 6:11)

MAJOR CONCEPT

At the final day, the earth will be destroyed by fire, and only those who follow Christ will be spared.

OVERVIEW Jacob provides his commentary on the prophecies of Zenos, which were given in Chapter 5, the allegory of the wild and tame olive trees. Jacob summarizes the allegory by teaching that God always remembers Israel, that we must cleave unto God as He cleaves unto us, and by warning us against rejecting the prophets.

INTERESTING FACTS ABOUT ZENOS Zenos—who was slain for testifying boldly about the things God revealed to him—was a prophet of Old Testament times who is no longer mentioned in the Old Testament, but who is mentioned twelve times in the Book of Mormon. In addition to Jacob, he is quoted by Nephi (see 1 Ne. 19), Alma (see Alma 33), Amulek (see Alma 34), Samuel the Lamanite, and Mormon

PROMINENT PEOPLE

- Jesus Christ
- Zenos

MAIN THEMES

- While the Lord's mercy is extended to all of us, we must guard against hardening our hearts and rejecting His help.

- Those who will not repent and acknowledge the goodness of the Savior will be subjected to endless torment.

- In order to gain eternal life, we must repent and follow the exacting requirements of exaltation.

- Repentance must be followed by full purpose of heart in keeping the commandments.

- Those who reject the words of the prophets, reject the words of Christ, and mock the great plan of redemption will stand with shame and awful guilt before the judgment bar.

- Those who have labored to bring souls unto Christ will be blessed at the judgment bar, while those who have rejected the Savior and His prophets will be cursed and cast out at the last day.

- Even those who have been taught the gospel and who have accepted it—who have been "nourished by the good word of God all the day long"—can become wicked, produce evil fruit, and be cast into the fire at the last day.

600 BC

544–421 BC

90 BC

and enter in at the
is narrow, until ye shall

(see 3 Ne. 10:16). Zenos ranks with Isaiah, Moses, and Jacob as one of the Old Testament prophets mentioned most often in the Book of Mormon. Elder Bruce R. McConkie said that next to Isaiah, "there was not a greater prophet than Zenos" (Millet and McConkie, *Doctrinal Commentary on the Book of Mormon,* 2:47).

KEY INSIGHTS ABOUT THE SAVIOR

- The Lord wants to save us!
- The teachings of Christ exist in tandem with the power of God and the gift of the Holy Ghost.
- The Lord's arm of mercy is extended toward all.
- The Lord will save all those who do not harden their hearts toward Him.
- Denying the words of Christ drives away the Holy Spirit.
- Jacob will meet us at the judgment bar of Christ.

Jacob 7

"And it came to pass that he said unto me: this power of the Holy Ghost, in the which (Jacob 7:13)

MAJOR CONCEPT

Jesus Christ is the author of our salvation, and all the prophets have testified of Christ and His Atonement.

OVERVIEW In this chapter, Jacob introduces Sherem, the first of the anti-Christs in the Book of Mormon, and describes the manner in which Sherem opposes the Lord. Jacob testifies that all the prophets have spoken of Christ and His Atonement, then describes the state of the Nephites as a civilization that wanders in tribulation.

INTERESTING FACTS ABOUT ANTI-CHRISTS In the simplest terms, an anti-Christ is a person who opposes the Lord. He either sets himself up as the source of power and salvation, instead of acknowledging the Savior as that source, or he sets up another person or system as the source of such and looks elsewhere for the solution

PROMINENT PEOPLE

- Jacob
- Sherem

to spiritual problems. The anti-Christ discussed in Jacob 7, Sherem, said he was willing to believe previous prophets but did not believe the living prophet, Jacob. Modern anti-Mormons accept only past revelation (the Bible) but reject modern-day prophets such as Joseph Smith and Thomas S. Monson.

WHO WAS SHEREM? Sherem was a skilled and proud orator who lived during the time of the prophet Jacob, the successor of Nephi. His message was a total denial of the being and mission of Jesus Christ, claiming that no one could know what was to come. Having drawn away many of the people of God, Sherem confronted Jacob, where he attempted to justify his untenable position. His teachings were similar to those of two later anti-Christs, Nehor and Korihor. Jacob, however, was given power by God to confound Sherem and was bold in defending the Savior. Sherem then insisted

MAIN THEMES

- Satan assists those who try to lead people away from Christ.
- Those who preach against Christ often use tremendous flattery and impressive powers of language and speech.
- Sign-seeking is not the same as seeking gifts of the Spirit through faith, humility, and devotion to righteousness.
- Signs always follow belief in the true gospel; sign-seeking is evidence of gross wickedness.

Show me a sign by ye know so much."

on a sign; through the power of the Lord, he was incapacitated for many days, after which he confessed his guilt and witnessed the truthfulness of Christ and the power of the Holy Ghost. He died admitting he had been deceived by the devil.

A WORD ABOUT *ADIEU* Critics of the Book of Mormon use the final word of Jacob 7—*adieu*—as evidence that the Book of Mormon could not have been translated, since the French language did not exist among the Nephites. The word *adieu,* as used by Joseph Smith, was probably used for the Hebrew word *Lehitra'ot,* which means not only "farewell," but is also a blessing. The word *adieu* is simply the word Joseph Smith used to come closest to the meaning of what Jacob expressed in his final blessing.

KEY INSIGHTS ABOUT THE SAVIOR

- The Lord defends and helps those who testify of Him.

Enos

"Whatsoever thing ye shall ask in faith, believing the name of Christ, ye shall receive it." (Enos 1:2)

MAJOR CONCEPT

We must be willing to pay whatever price is exacted if we hope to have a truly dynamic relationship with the Lord.

OVERVIEW Having been taught the gospel by his father, Jacob, Enos desires a remission of his sins. He travels into the forest to hunt, and in that place, free from distraction and with his thoughts turned to spiritual things, he kneels in repentant prayer to ask forgiveness. Describing his experience as a "wrestle" with himself before God, Enos prays all day and all night before hearing the voice of the Lord proclaim that his sins have been forgiven because of his faith in Christ. Enos then pleads on behalf of his people, the Nephites; for his brethren, the Lamanites; and for the preservation of the Nephite records.

PROMINENT PEOPLE

• Enos

INTERESTING FACTS ABOUT PRAYER President Spencer W. Kimball taught, "To those of us who would pay pennies toward our unfathomable debt, may we remember Enos, who, like many of us, had great need. . . . Here is no casual prayer; no trite, worn phrases; here no momentary appeal. All

MAIN THEMES

• Wrestling with ourselves before God requires deep thought, meditation, and concentration as we go beyond the clichés of prayer, pour out our souls, feel deep yearning, and allow ourselves to be guided by the Spirit.

• Forgiveness is possible only through Jesus Christ, Who atoned for our sins; the key to forgiveness is faith in the Atonement.

• It's important for us to know the Lord's attributes; because Enos knew that God cannot lie, he had full trust that his sins had been forgiven.

• The righteous experience an expanding sphere of concern—first for themselves, then for their own people, and finally for their enemies.

• Both the Bible and the Book of Mormon were preserved by the Lord to come forth at a later time.

• Even though the effort we must make to have a relationship with the Lord is great, the reward is even greater.

600 BC   90 BC

544–421 BC

the day long, with seconds turning into minutes, and minutes into hours, and hours into an 'all day long.' But when the sun had set, relief had still not come, for repentance is not a single act nor forgiveness an unearned gift. So precious to him was communication with, and approval of, his Redeemer that his determined soul pressed on without ceasing. . . . As you struggle in the spirit and cry mightily and covenant sincerely, the voice of the Lord God will come into your mind, as it did to that of Enos, 'Thy sins are forgiven thee, and thou shalt be blest'" ("Prayer," 8–10). We learn from various accounts of the First Vision that Joseph Smith entered the Sacred Grove not only to ask which church to join, but also to ask for forgiveness of his sins.

WHO WAS ENOS? Enos was the son of Jacob, brother of Nephi. His well-known experience with prayer took place sometime between 544 BC and 421 BC. Following his spiritual rejuvenation, Enos served his people in righteousness throughout the remainder of his life.

KEY INSIGHTS ABOUT THE SAVIOR

- The Lord grants answers to our prayers in His due time, not according to our timetable. Our faith in Him needs to include faith not only in His overall timetable, but in His will and timetable for us as individuals.

- Christ is our Advocate; He bought us. Only through His infinite Atonement are repentance and forgiveness possible. That applies not only to us who have lived since Christ, but to all who have ever lived—including Enos, who had faith in Christ many hundreds of years before He came to dwell in the flesh.

- One of our rewards for a life of righteousness is that we, like Enos, can look forward with eagerness to meeting the Savior face-to-face—and that He will invite us to dwell in the mansion that He has prepared for us.

Jarom

"Behold, it is expedient that much should be the deafness of their ears, and the blindness of exceedingly merciful unto them, and has not

MAJOR CONCEPT

Prophets of God labor diligently to teach people of Christ and to lead them to salvation.

OVERVIEW Jarom, the son of Enos, records the growing apostasy among many of the Nephites but emphasizes that many are also devoted to keeping the law of Moses. He says those who are not stiffnecked commune with the Holy Spirit and look forward to the coming of Christ; he also uses the phrase "plan of salvation," a phrase that does not occur even once in the Bible.

WHO WAS JAROM? Jarom, the son of Enos, continued the process of record-keeping on the small plates of Nephi from around 420 to 361 BC. His contribution is brief, comprising the shortest book in the Book of Mormon—likely because the plates, which Nephi had made almost 150 years earlier,

PROMINENT PEOPLE

- Jarom
- The Nephites and Lamanites
- Omni

were almost full. Jarom comments that those who have kept the records before him have already revealed the plan of salvation, and concludes that any efforts on his part would be redundant. He states that his purpose for writing what he has is to continue his family's genealogy (see verse 1) and to benefit

MAIN THEMES

- Apostasy was rampant among the Nephites, though there was a strong core of faithful believers.

- The Nephite laws were strict.

- The Nephites had been able to advance beyond a simple agricultural form of society; the industry depicted in the book of Jarom contrasts with the rural, pastoral society described by Enos.

- Key qualities among spiritual people is strong faith and humility.

- Righteous leaders provide protection to their people.

- An effective teaching method of prophets is to ask people to believe in something as though it already exists.

- We need to be continually stirred up to repentance.

- The intent of keeping the law of Moses was to persuade the people to look forward to the coming Messiah.

600 BC

90 BC

420–361 BC

done among this people, because of the hardness of their hearts, and their minds, and the stiffness of their necks; nevertheless, God is as yet swept them off the face of the land." (Jarom 1:3)

the Lamanites (see verse 2). In his few verses, Jarom describes the prevailing tendency among many of his countrymen (see verse 3), offers insights concerning the work of the Lord during his time (see verse 4), and describes the efforts of the prophets of God to ward off pride (see verses 11–12).

KEY INSIGHTS ABOUT THE SAVIOR

- The Savior's mercy is continually extended toward all, even those who have cast aside His commandments.
- The Savior reveals much to His followers.
- The Lord prospers those who obey the commandments and follow Him in faith.
- The Lord uses prophets and other leaders to deliver His messages to His people.

Omni

"Inasmuch as ye will not keep my commandments

MAJOR CONCEPT

Regardless of the time in which we live, we should offer our souls as an offering to Christ.

OVERVIEW The book of Omni is written prior to the reigns of Mosiah and Benjamin. Four generations of scribes—including Omni, Omni's son Amaron, Amaron's brother Chemish, Chemish's son Abinadom, and Abinadi's son Amaleki—keep the records found in this chapter. Though all but Amaleki write very little, they preserve important records—records that paint a picture of growing Nephite apostasy and wickedness. Mosiah discovers the people of Zarahemla and is made king over them; the Mulekites had discovered a survivor of the Jaredites named Coriantumr. They learn from Mosiah's interpretation of the writing on a stone they had carried with them that the Jaredites had departed from the Tower of Babel and traveled in barges to

PROMINENT PEOPLE

- Omni
- Amaron
- Chemish
- Abinadom
- Amaleki
- Mosiah
- Coriantumr
- Benjamin

the promised land. King Benjamin succeeds Mosiah. Amaleki writes only a small portion but provides important historical information that links three major colonies. Amaleki gives the small plates to King Benjamin; from that point (130 BC) on, the prophet/king keeps both sets of records.

ABOUT MULEKITES Mulek was the only surviving son of King Zedekiah, the last king of Judah at the time of the Babylonian conquest of Jerusalem in 587 BC. While Lehi had been brought by the Lord to "the land south," Mulek and his followers fled Jerusalem and were led by the Lord across the ocean to "the land north" (Hel. 6:10), also known as Zarahemla. As such, the Mulekites were the second colony of Jews who escaped to the promised land from Jerusalem. The seed of Manasseh came through Lehi; the seed of Ephraim came through Ishmael; and the seed of Judah came through the Mulekites.

MAIN THEMES

- Written records are extremely valuable for all generations. Because the Mulekites had brought no scriptures with them, they had lost their belief in God, and their language had been corrupted.

ye shall not prosper in the land." (Omni 1:6)

WHO WAS OMNI? Omni received the sacred records from his father, Jarom, around 361 BC with the commission to keep them according to the commandments of their fathers. Omni wrote only a few verses but did record the genealogy of his family. Despite his confession that he was "a wicked man, and [had] not kept the statutes and the commandments of the Lord as I ought to have done," he was a strong defender of his people and fought courageously to keep the Nephites from falling into the hands of the Lamanites. He also faithfully guarded and preserved the records for some forty-four years during a time of considerable turmoil and warfare. Around 317 BC, he delegated to his son Amaron the task of maintaining the records.

KEY INSIGHTS ABOUT THE SAVIOR

- The Lord does not make idle threats.
  - Even when forced to visit great judgment upon a people, the Lord spares the righteous and delivers them out of the hands of their enemies.
  - The Lord delivers His people according to His will.
  - All good comes from the Lord, and all evil comes from Satan.

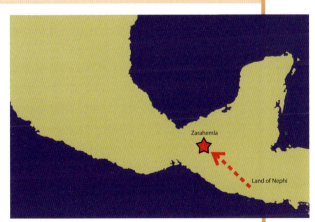

Top Image: Mosiah interprets a Jaredite stone.

Words of Mormon

MAJOR CONCEPT

Mormon and others who wrote and abridged the records in the Book of Mormon did so with guidance and inspiration from the Lord.

OVERVIEW Mormon, who has seen the literal fulfillment of prophecy, writes this book after abridging the other plates in the Book of Mormon with both a prayer that his records will be preserved and a warning that we will be judged according to the truths written in the Book of Mormon. He then introduces King Benjamin as a person who ruled over his people in righteousness.

INTERESTING FACTS ABOUT THE WORDS OF MORMON Mormon was called to serve as chief administrator in finalizing the ultimate structure and content of the Book of Mormon; with the help of his son, Moroni, he completed his assigned mission. The Words of Mormon

PROMINENT PEOPLE

- Mormon
- King Benjamin

is approximately 500 years out of context and was written around AD 385, near the end of Mormon's life, for the purpose of connecting the two major records—the small plates of Nephi and Mormon's abridgement of Mosiah through 4 Nephi. Mormon found the plates of Nephi after he had finished his work on the book of Mosiah.

WHO WAS MORMON? Born around AD 310, Mormon received revelation from the Lord at the age of fifteen (see Morm. 1:15), and at the age of sixteen he was appointed commander of the armies of the Nephites (see Morm. 2:1–2). He commanded the Nephite forces until the final battle at Cumorah, in which he witnessed the destruction of at least a half million of his people. He remained faithful to the end, eventually turning the records over to his son Moroni. The 116 pages of manuscript that Martin Harris lost consisted of

MAIN THEMES

- We will be judged by what is in the Book of Mormon; it will be the rod against which we will be measured.
- A knowledge of God and of the redemption of Christ influences us toward righteousness.
- Righteous leaders are key to establishing peace in any nation.

pray to God that [these plates] may be preserved from this time henceforth. will be preserved; for there are great things written upon them, out of which brethren shall be judged at the great and last day. . . ." (W of M 1:11)

Mormon's abridgement of Lehi through King Benjamin; when those pages were lost, the small plates of Nephi—containing the spiritual account of the same period—were used instead. The large and small plates were handed down from generation to generation until they came into the hands of Mormon.

Key Insights about the Savior

- The Lord, Who knows all things from the beginning, directs His servants to accomplish His will. The Lord, knowing the future, had Nephi create the small plates in 570 BC (twenty years after the large plates were made) for the specific purpose of using them to replace the lost 116 pages. Mormon attached the small plates to the gold plates for a "wise purpose" that he himself did not know. The "wise purpose," of course, was to replace the 116 pages that the Lord knew were going to be lost.

Mosiah 1

"And now, my sons, I would that ye profit thereby; and I would that ye the land according to the promises

MAJOR CONCEPT

The scriptures have great importance to us in preserving the saving principles of the gospel and in providing us a way to teach our children the things they need for exaltation.

OVERVIEW The book of Mosiah—named after King Benjamin's son, who kept the records—picks up where the book of Omni leaves off, approximately 130 BC. It begins Mormon's abridgement of the large plates of Nephi, which contain the historical chronicles of Mosiah, Alma, Helaman, 3 Nephi, and 4 Nephi; the abridgement is called the plates of Mormon. 1 Nephi through Omni are all written in first person. This and following chapters are written in third person because someone else—Mormon—is relating the events. In this first chapter, King Benjamin teaches his sons the language and prophecies of their fathers, which have been preserved in the records—the standard works of their day. Mosiah becomes king and is given stewardship over the records.

PROMINENT PEOPLE

- King Benjamin
- Mosiah
- Helorum
- Helaman

INTERESTING FACTS ABOUT THE MYSTERIES OF GOD We often hear the phrase *the mysteries of God* in the scriptures and other writings. The mysteries of God actually refer to the saving principles of the gospel. They are not called mysteries because they are mysterious or difficult to understand.

MAIN THEMES

- The mysteries of God—in other words, the saving principles of the gospel learned through divine revelation—are contained in the scriptures.

- We should teach our children and grandchildren from the scriptures.

- We need the scriptures because none of us can remember on our own all the things contained in them.

- The corruption of civil law always precedes the corruption of spiritual law.

- As members of His Church, we carry the name of Jesus Christ, which distinguishes us above all others.

600 BC

90 BC

130–124 BC

should remember to search [the scriptures] diligently, that ye may should keep the commandments of God, that ye may prosper in which the Lord made unto our fathers." (Mosiah 1:7)

Instead, they are called mysteries because they are truths made known through divine revelation and, as such, are unavailable to the natural man. King Benjamin's people were spiritually literate and were able to understand the teachings as recorded in the brass plates.

INTERESTING FACTS ABOUT WORDPRINTS

Each author has a wordprint—a unique style of writing that leaves a distinct stamp and differentiates his text from that of other writers—a concept that would have been unknown to Joseph Smith. The small plates of the Book of Mormon were written by Nephi and Jacob, with large sections quoted from Isaiah. Beginning with Mosiah 1, the text is written in third person by Mormon. California scientist John L. Hilton, who developed a computer program that detects wordprints, verified that the Book of Mormon could not have been written by Joseph Smith because it does not contain his wordprints. Hilton also verified that statistical analysis of the book shows that the parts of the book claimed to be written by different prophets do have distinguishable wordprints that confirm Joseph Smith's explanation of the origin of the book. The statistical odds that Joseph Smith is the single author of the Book of Mormon are less than 1 in 100 billion (see Reynolds, *Book of Mormon Authorship Revisited,* 156–188).

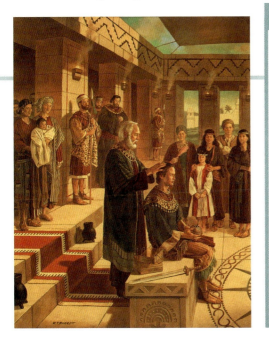

KEY INSIGHTS ABOUT THE SAVIOR

- The Lord has promised that we will prosper in the land if we remain righteous.

- Prophecies come from the Lord.

- Jesus Christ is the only name that brings salvation. There is no other name through which men can be saved.

- If we become wicked and adulterous, we will become weak and will no longer be preserved by the Lord through His matchless power.

- Had it not been for the Lord preserving the Nephites, they would have fallen into the hands of the Lamanites and become victims of their hatred.

MAJOR CONCEPT

Humility—true recognition of our actual position in relationship to the Lord—is a hallmark of greatness and is essential to exaltation.

OVERVIEW Knowing he is about to die, King Benjamin confers the kingship on his son Mosiah. In this chapter King Benjamin gathers his people to the temple and addresses them from atop a tower; his address begins in this chapter and continues through the beginning of Mosiah 6. King Benjamin follows tradition by beginning his remarks with an accounting of his stewardship, acknowledging his dependence on the Lord, and emphasizing that his reign was one of service. His remarks in this chapter constitute one of the greatest discourses on humility. He then teaches the importance of following the Lord.

PROMINENT PEOPLE

- King Benjamin
- Mosiah

INTERESTING FACTS ABOUT HUMILITY AND OUR INDEBTEDNESS TO THE LORD Anyone who lacks humility needs only to look at our relationship to the Lord. The Lord gives all men birth, life, agency, and all the blessings of existence; therefore, man is indebted to Him. Through our efforts to

MAIN THEMES

- It is important that we keep our families united.
- We should not exalt ourselves over those we serve.
- A key element of great leadership is service.
- As we serve and lead others, we should help them focus on the Lord, not on us as leaders.
- We can never do as much for the Lord as He has done for us.

- We will not be held accountable for the wrongdoing of those under our stewardship if we have made every effort to teach them the truth.
- Sin leads to misery, suffering, and a loss of agency for the one who commits the sin.
- Obedience leads to everlasting happiness.

ye may learn wisdom; that ye may learn that when ye are in the
in the service of your God." (Mosiah 2:17)

repay or serve the Lord, we are immediately blessed, which increases our indebtedness. The Savior gave His atoning sacrifice for all men that they might live, and all who properly repent and faithfully endure to the end will have exalted life. The resultant debt is too great to comprehend. Evidence of the Lord's great love for us is found in the fact that He could require anything of us—but asks only that we keep His commandments. We are totally dependent on Him, and our debt to Him is completely beyond our ability to repay . . . a truth that inspires deep humility.

WHO WAS KING BENJAMIN? King Benjamin is one of the most beloved and oft-quoted personalities in the Book of Mormon. His valedictory discourse to his people—contained in Mosiah 1–6—is one of the most celebrated gospel sermons ever recorded and describes a Christ-centered life of service and spiritual integrity. Benjamin was the son of the first Mosiah, who was commanded of the Lord to depart from the land of Nephi with his followers to preserve their lives and the records of their ancestors. They traveled north and settled in Zarahemla, where they joined the descendants of Mulek. In King Benjamin's day, civil and religious law and authority were united under the king in a form of government some call theocratic monarchy.

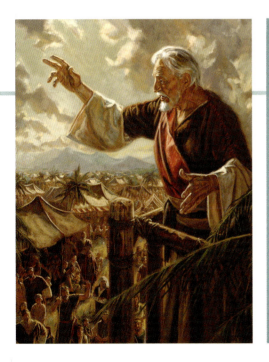

KEY INSIGHTS ABOUT THE SAVIOR

- We can do nothing to put the Lord in our debt; we are completely indebted to Him.

- Everlasting punishment means that the Lord's punishment is fixed: the same punishment always follows the same offense; when we pay the penalty, we are released.

- "Everlasting punishment" and "never-ending torment" do eventually end. They are referred to as "endless" because they are God's punishment, and His name is "Endless" (this mystery is further understood through D&C 19).

- Those who do not repent are ineligible for mercy.

- Sin places us in open rebellion and opposition against the Lord.

Mosiah 3

MAJOR CONCEPT

The Savior, Jesus Christ, lived and ministered among us and performed the infinite Atonement, which is the only means whereby we can attain salvation.

OVERVIEW In a continuation of King Benjamin's majestic discourse, he prophesies of the Savior's birth, ministry, and Atonement, teaching that the only way to salvation is through the Savior. He also distinguishes between the reward for the righteous and the wicked. This segment of the discourse presents a clear prophecy and testimony of the coming Savior. King Benjamin received the material for his discourse from an angel.

INTERESTING FACTS ABOUT THE NATURAL MAN In verse 19, King Benjamin discusses the "natural man," who is an "enemy to God" unless he "yields to the enticings of the Holy Spirit, and putteth off the natural man and becometh a saint." The natural man referred to by King Benjamin is fallen or sinful, having been born into a fallen world as a result of the Fall. He is in a state of spiritual death and is an enemy to God—akin to Satan, because he doesn't know the mind of God. Each person born into the world

PROMINENT PEOPLE

- King Benjamin
- Jesus Christ

MAIN THEMES

- We must repent and exercise faith in the Savior in order to gain exaltation.

- We must become as little children—submissive, meek, humble, patient, full of love, and willing to submit to all the Lord asks of us.

- Once we repent and keep the commandments, we are born again and become friends of God.

- The time will come when knowledge of the Savior will spread throughout the entire world.

- Those who are evil will be brought to a view of their own sins, will shrink from the presence of the Lord, and will enter a state of endless torment.

is, in fact, a natural man. The change from that state occurs when we accept Christ, access the Atonement through repentance, strive to live the commandments, and are sanctified by the Holy Ghost. We then become Saints, justified and sanctified heirs of the celestial kingdom. The only way in which that change occurs, and the only way in which we become Saints, is through the Atonement of Jesus Christ. He, then, is the only means by which we can attain salvation and exaltation.

KEY INSIGHTS ABOUT THE SAVIOR

- Jesus Christ is the Lord Omnipotent, meaning that as the Lord of all He has all power.

- Jesus is the creator of the world and all things on it.

- Jesus was born to Mary.

- The anguish of the Savior in Gethsemane was so great that He bled from every pore, enduring more than any mortal could ever endure.

- Even after all the Savior did for us in providing for our salvation, he was ridiculed, scourged, and crucified.

- The Savior rose the third day, providing resurrection for all who have ever lived or will ever live.

- The Savior's Atonement pays the price for those who die without knowing the will of God and for those who sin in ignorance.

- The Savior's Atonement provides for the exaltation of infants and young children.

- Salvation comes to none except through repentance and faith in Jesus Christ; there is no other name nor means by which we can attain salvation.

- The Savior's judgment is just.

Mosiah 4

MAJOR CONCEPT

We are totally dependent on the Lord for our salvation and eternal life; without Him, we are nothing.

OVERVIEW In a further continuation of his final discourse, King Benjamin again emphasizes that salvation comes only through the Atonement of the Savior and that we retain a remission of our sins through faith in Him. He also counsels the people to impart of their substance to the poor and to do all things in wisdom and order.

INTERESTING FACTS ABOUT OUR "NOTHINGNESS" Several verses in this chapter talk about our "nothingness," one asking us to always "retain in remembrance" our "own nothingness" (verse 11). We are also told that we are unworthy and "even less than the dust of the earth" (verse 2). Such language may at first seem contradictory to the declaration that all souls are great in the sight of God and that each being is of inestimable worth. So which sentiment is true? Both are. We are told we are less than the dust of the earth because the dust is always obedient to the commandments of its Creator; as mortals, however, we

PROMINENT PEOPLE

- King Benjamin
- Jesus Christ
- Angel of the Lord

MAIN THEMES

- Following our repentance, the Holy Ghost brings us a knowledge that our sins have been forgiven through peace of conscience.

- We must watch our thoughts, words, and deeds as we prepare for the Second Coming of the Lord

- As we are righteous, we have no desire to injure others, but wish only to live peaceably.

- We must teach our children to walk in the ways of truth and to love and serve one another.

- We should serve and give in wisdom and order to those less fortunate.

- Coveting is an attitude toward material things; it is possible to covet our own possessions.

- It is for God to judge and be just; it is up to us to be merciful.

- Worldly wealth is an illusion; all we have—including our very lives—belongs to the Lord.

- The highest spirituality comes to us as we conquer the flesh.

600 BC

90 BC

124 BC

that he created all things, both in heaven and in earth; believe that in heaven and in earth; believe that man doth not comprehend comprehend." (Mosiah 4:9)

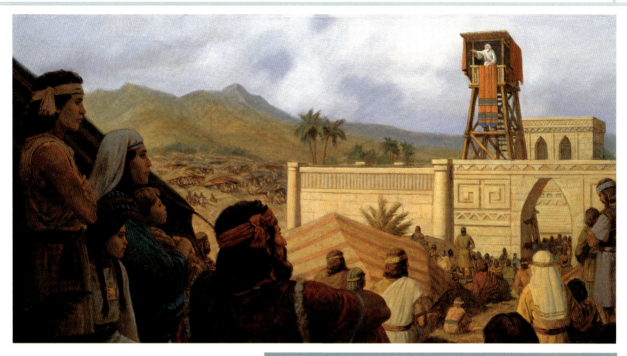

have a tendency to rebel against His will. And in these scriptural passages, our "nothingness" refers to the fact that we are totally dependent on God—the Lord—for salvation and eternal life, which we gain through His Atonement and no other way. In other words, without Him we are nothing; it is not possible for us to gain salvation on our own, regardless of our abilities and strengths. At our best and brightest, we are but a pale reflection of our Creator.

KEY INSIGHTS ABOUT THE SAVIOR

- Jesus Christ is the only way and means by which man can attain salvation.
- The Savior has all knowledge and power, both in heaven and in earth.
- We cannot comprehend the things the Lord comprehends.
- The Atonement was prepared from the foundation of the world and is infinite, without time limitations; it covers everyone since the Fall of Adam, including those living in the past, present, and future.

Mosiah 5

MAJOR CONCEPT

Because He atoned for us, Jesus Christ is our Father and we are His sons and daughters.

OVERVIEW Nearing the conclusion of his mighty discourse, King Benjamin explains to his people that as Saints they are sons and daughters of Christ through the faith they have in Him. As such, they are called by His name. King Benjamin then counsels his people to be steadfast and immovable in doing good works.

INTERESTING FACTS ABOUT BECOMING SONS AND DAUGHTERS In verse 7, King Benjamin explains that because they entered into a covenant to keep the commandments through the remainder of their days, the people had become the sons and daughters—the children—of Christ. President Joseph Fielding Smith explained that a child is one who is begotten, or is given life by another. Because of the Atonement, Christ has given us life—eternal life, the power to overcome the grave. Because He has given us immortality and through Him we are "born again," He becomes a father to us. And as a child takes on the name of its father,

PROMINENT PEOPLE

- King Benjamin
- Jesus Christ
- The Nephites

MAIN THEMES

- A mighty change of heart involves the core of our life and strength—our character, mind, spirit, and soul; our entire emotional nature and understanding; and the seat of our affection.

- A mighty change of heart can come to anyone who repents and humbles himself before God.

- We must be willing to enter into a covenant with the Lord to do His will.

- Those on the right hand of God enjoy mercy, righteousness, power, and salvation; those on the left hand suffer uncleanness and damnation.

- As part of our taking upon ourselves Christ's name, His name is written on our hearts—and we must retain it there forever.

- We can come to a knowledge of the Lord by serving others.

- We must be steadfast and immovable, abounding in good works, that the Lord may seal us His.

thou hast spoken unto us; and also, we know of their surety and Omnipotent, which has wrought a mighty change in us, or in disposition to do evil, but to do good continually." (Mosiah 5:2)

we take upon us the name of Jesus Christ. It is then up to us to develop a relationship with Him. President James E. Faust said that to develop such a relationship requires daily prayer, daily study of the scriptures, daily selfless service to others, daily striving for increased obedience and perfection, and daily acknowledgment of Christ's divinity. If we succeed in developing a powerful relationship as His sons and daughters, says President Faust, "he will unveil his face unto you" (D&C 88:67). Each of us needs to ask ourselves if we are willing to pay the price to become a son or daughter of Christ and to develop that kind of relationship with Him.

KEY INSIGHTS ABOUT THE SAVIOR

- Jesus Christ has spiritually begotten—or given birth to—us.
- All of God's authority has been conferred on Jesus Christ.
- Jesus Christ is the only name by which salvation is given.
- When we are baptized and strive to keep the commandments, the Savior's name is written on our hearts.
- No man knows the master he has not served; if we have not served the Lord, we are a stranger to Him.

"And it came to pass that there was not the covenant and had taken upon them

MAJOR CONCEPT

Righteous leaders exert a powerful influence upon the people they serve.

OVERVIEW After concluding his discourse, King Benjamin causes to be recorded the names of each person who has entered the covenant to take upon themselves the name of Christ. He then consecrates his son Mosiah as king and appoints priests to teach the people and help them remember the covenants they have made; he dismisses the people, who return to their homes. Mosiah II begins his reign, following the righteous example of his father. King Benjamin dies three years later.

INTERESTING FACTS ABOUT THE TREATY/COVENANT PATTERN King Benjamin's farewell address reflects a literary pattern used by the ancient Israelites, the treaty/

PROMINENT PEOPLE

- King Benjamin
- Mosiah

MAIN THEMES

- Covenants are solemn agreements between God and man that lift us and make us free, keeping the channels open between us and the Lord.

- Righteous leadership has a powerful saving influence.

- The most powerful and influential leaders are those who serve the people and work for their own sustenance.

covenant pattern, that contains six specific elements: (1) God is acknowledged as the one making the covenant; (2) the Lord's past dealings with Israel are reviewed; (3) the terms of the covenant are listed; (4) the people are acknowledged as formally accepting the covenant; (5) blessings for obeying and cursings for disobeying the covenant are listed; and (6) arrangements are made for safekeeping a copy of the covenant. This pattern—which was not studied until the 1930s—was completely unknown when the Book of Mormon was published in 1830 (see *Echoes,* 389–394).

WHO WAS THE ORIGINAL MOSIAH? The Mosiah who is appointed king in this chapter is the son of King Benjamin; he was named after King Benjamin's father, who was commanded to flee into the wilderness to escape the wicked Nephites. Mosiah I, the father of King Benjamin, was a descendant of Lehi who lived in

one soul, except it were little children, but who had entered into the name of Christ." (Mosiah 6:2)

the southern area of the country where Lehi and his family had first settled in the promised land. In those early days, Nephi and his righteous followers, having been warned of the Lord, separated themselves from Laman and Lemuel for reasons of safety (see 2 Ne. 5:5–7). The animosity of the Lamanites against the Nephites had continued for many generations by Mosiah's time—and, because of his obedience, Mosiah was also warned by the Lord to flee into the wilderness to preserve his life from his enemies (see Omni 1:13). Mosiah and his followers fled to the north, where they settled in the land of Zarahemla among people who were the descendants of Mulek, the lone surviving son of King Zedekiah of Judah, who had traveled to this land similar to—but separate from—Lehi. Mosiah thus encountered a colony of people whose history closely paralleled that of Lehi and his family, with one important exception: the Mulekites had brought with them no records containing their genealogy or their spiritual foundations. Mosiah, however, had brought with him the sacred records that preserved not only the language of their fathers, but a record of God's dealings with His people. Mosiah taught the people of Mulek his language and the principles of the gospel; he was so revered and loved that he was appointed king over the people of Zarahemla. His was a reign of righteous leadership. King Benjamin carried on his father's righteous leadership and became one of the greatest prophet-rulers in the Book of Mormon.

KEY INSIGHTS ABOUT THE SAVIOR

- The Lord blesses those who keep the covenants they have made with Him.

Mosiah 7

"Therefore, lift up your heads, and rejoice, God. . . ." (Mosiah 7:33)

MAJOR CONCEPT

Deliverance does not come to those who are in iniquity but only to those who have turned to the Lord and serve Him with full diligence.

OVERVIEW King Mosiah sends sixteen men, led by Ammon, to the land of Lehi-Nephi to find the people who have left Zarahemla and gone northward. As Ammon enters the land, he is arrested by King Limhi, a Nephite—but instead of killing Ammon, Limhi asks what his purpose is. Once he learns that Ammon is from Zarahemla, he rejoices; he gathers the people to hear what Ammon has to say. The Nephites are in terrible bondage to the Lamanites that surround them, and Ammon tells them that deliverance will come only through righteousness and serving the Lord.

INTERESTING FACTS ABOUT BEING DELIVERED In addition to enduring periodic attacks and fairly constant threats

from the Lamanites, Zeniff and his people lived in virtual slavery: among other things, they were required to pay one-half of all their crops, all their grain of every kind, all the increase of their flocks and herds, and all they had or possessed to the Lamanites. The people of Limhi prayed repeatedly to

PROMINENT PEOPLE

- Mosiah
- Ammon
- Limhi
- Zeniff

MAIN THEMES

- We find ourselves in bondage—physical and spiritual—when we depart from the Lord and become steeped in sin.

- If we work iniquity, we will reap the results of it, which lead to destruction.

- If we are to be preserved and delivered, we must trust in the Lord.

- In order to be delivered, we must turn to the Lord with full purpose of heart and serve Him.

600 BC   90 BC

121 BC

MOSIAH

be delivered from the Lamanites, but their prayers went unanswered because they were not walking in the ways of righteousness. Their plight was similar to that of the Saints in Jackson County, Missouri, who were not faithful in keeping their covenants (see D&C 101:7–8). As spelled out in verse 33, deliverance comes only when we turn to the Lord with full purpose of heart, put our trust in Him, and serve Him with full diligence of mind.

WHO WAS ZENIFF? Zeniff, a Nephite from Zarahemla, was a member of an expeditionary army around 200 BC intent on returning southward to reclaim the land of Nephi from whence their ancestors—led by Mosiah I—had fled according to the command of God (see Omni 1:12–13, 27–30). Zeniff was a principled person who refused to participate in the destruction of the Lamanites that had been ordered by his leader (see Mosiah 9:1). Though ordered to be executed as a result of his refusal to destroy the Lamanites, he survived and returned to Zarahemla for a time before setting out again to attain the land of Nephi, which was then controlled by the Lamanites. He made a treaty with Laman, king of the Lamanites, to occupy part of the land, not knowing that Laman's intent was to enslave the Nephites. Over a period of several decades, Zeniff and his people labored to preserve and sustain their families while at the same time defending themselves against periodic attacks from the Lamanites. (Learn more about Zeniff in Mosiah 9.)

KEY INSIGHTS ABOUT THE SAVIOR

- The Lord suffers evil to come upon people who fall into transgression.
- The Lord will not succor His people while they are in transgression, but will cause their ways to become a stumbling block before them.
- The Lord delivers us out of bondage as we turn to Him, trust in Him, and serve Him.
- The Lord was born into mortality and took upon Himself a mortal body and ministered among men in the flesh.
- A prophet named Abinadi was slain by the Nephites because he testified of Christ.

Mosiah 8

"And . . . a seer is a revelator and a should possess the power of God, which (Mosiah 8:16)

MAJOR CONCEPT

We are enormously blessed by those who are prophets and seers.

OVERVIEW After he finishes preaching to the people of Limhi, Ammon is given the plates that contain the record of the people from the time they left Zarahemla, which he reads. He then learns that a group of Limhi's people had tried to find Zarahemla, but instead wandered in the wilderness and found the land of the Jaredites; they returned with twenty-four gold plates written in an unknown language. Limhi asks Ammon if he can interpret the plates; Ammon cannot but says that Mosiah II—who is a seer—can not only interpret the plates using the interpreters, but is also a prophet and a revelator. Elder John A. Widtsoe defined a prophet, seer, and revelator this way: "A prophet is a teacher of known truth. A seer is a perceiver of hidden

MAIN THEMES

- The scriptures—the record of the Lord's dealing with His people—are of great value to us.

- A seer is greater than a prophet because a seer is also a revelator and a prophet.

- A seer can know of things that are past and things that are to come and can bring to light hidden things for the benefit of man.

- Without the Lord and our own desires for wisdom and righteousness, we are as a wild flock that flees from the shepherd and is scattered and devoured.

PROMINENT PEOPLE

- Limhi
- Ammon
- Zeniff

truth. A revelator is a bearer of new truth" (*Evidences and Reconciliations*, 258–259).

INTERESTING FACTS ABOUT THE TWENTY-FOUR GOLD PLATES The forty-three men dispatched by Limhi to find the land of Zarahemla got lost in the wilderness and wandered for many days before discovering a land covered with bones of men and beasts and with the ruins of buildings. They returned to Limhi with twenty-four plates of pure gold, engraved in a language they could not read, as well as intact brass and copper breastplates. The plates they found comprise the book of Ether; their discovery was not an accident, as Ether hid the plates in a way so they could be found by the people of Limhi (see Ether 15:33). The plates contained visions given to the brother of Jared, who was commanded to not make them public in his lifetime but to record them in the language used before the Tower of Babel (which was no longer

600 BC

90 BC

121 BC

prophet also; and a gift which is greater no man can have, except he no man can; yet a man may have great power given him from God."

known) and to seal them until a future people would find them.

WHO WAS AMMON? Ammon, a strong and mighty man, was a descendant of Zarahemla and of Mulekite lineage. He was the leader of a group sent out around 121 BC by King Mosiah II—the son of King Benjamin—to determine the circumstances of a group of colonists led by Zeniff who had left Zarahemla about 200 BC bound for the land of Nephi. Successful in his mission, Ammon found Limhi and his followers, who were in bondage to the Lamanites. Through the assistance of Ammon and Gideon, a strong soldier in Limhi's army, the colony was able to escape the Lamanites and return safely to Zarahemla. There, they were baptized by Alma the Elder.

KEY INSIGHTS ABOUT THE SAVIOR

- The Lord has provided seers so that man, through faith, might work mighty miracles.
  - The works of the Lord are marvelous and are done for the benefit of man.

Image: Ruins found in Central America.

MAJOR CONCEPT

Only by remembering the Lord and following Him in righteousness are we protected and delivered by Him.

OVERVIEW With this chapter (a flashback in time to 200 BC) begins the record of Zeniff; Mosiah 9–10 are a direct quote from Zeniff, and his record continues through Mosiah 22. His complete account is a record of his people from the time they left Zarahemla until the time they were delivered out of bondage to the Lamanites. In this chapter, Zeniff leads a group from Zarahemla to the land of Lehi-Nephi, where after fighting and slaying each other, most of the group is destroyed. Zeniff and the few remaining followers return to Zarahemla to inform the wives and children of those who have died. Zeniff then enlists a new group and reaches the land of Lehi-Nephi, where they persuade the king to let them settle; they are unaware of the king's intent to take them into bondage. Zeniff relates some detail about the battles between his people and the Lamanites.

PROMINENT PEOPLE

- Zeniff
- Laman

INTERESTING FACTS ABOUT SHEUM In verse 9, Zeniff lists the crops that he and his people began to cultivate as they

MAIN THEMES

- We often encounter more harm by fighting among ourselves than from outside influences.

- When we are slow to remember the Lord, blessings are withheld.

- We need to remember that agreements made with unrighteous people will likely not be honored.

MOSIAH

craftiness of king Laman, to bring my people into bondage, that possess it." (Mosiah 9:10)

tilled the ground in their new settlement in Lehi-Nephi. Most are familiar to us—corn, wheat, and barley—but he also mentions *sheum*. In the last four decades, *she'um* has been identified as the most important grain among the Babylonians of Mesopotamia. Depending on the language used, it could have two distinct meanings: in Old Assyrian it means *wheat*, while in Akkadian (the language used in Babylonia) it means *barley*. Therefore, many scholars believe that the Nephites gave the name *sheum* to a different crop they cultivated (see *Echoes,* 288).

WHO WAS ZENIFF? Zeniff (also discussed in Mosiah 7) was the leader of the southern group of Nephites from around 200 BC until around 160 BC, when Noah took over leadership as the second of the colonial kings. Zeniff was able to bring the people back to the knowledge and discipleship of the Lord, where previously they had not understood the ways of the Lord. Under this banner of truth, Zeniff—as king in the Nephite colony—was able to lead the people to victory over the Lamanites and preserve at least a semblance of stability and peace for a period of time. That delicate balance between the Nephites and Lamanites ended to the disadvantage of the colonists soon after Zeniff conferred the kingdom on his son Noah. Throughout his days of service, Zeniff remembered the Lord and attempted to guide his people in righteousness. Zeniff and his people are examples of those who seek happiness and security in the things of heaven.

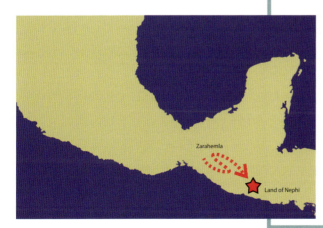

KEY INSIGHTS ABOUT THE SAVIOR

- The Lord will deliver those who call upon Him in righteousness.

  - The Lord answers the prayers of those who obey Him.

  - The Lord does not pour blessings out upon those who are slow to remember Him.

Mosiah 10

"Now, the Lamanites knew nothing depended upon their own strength."

MAJOR CONCEPT

Many of the beliefs that cause one people to act in vengeful anger against another—in nations as well as in families—are the result of false ideas passed from one generation to another.

OVERVIEW King Laman—he who allowed Zeniff and his people to settle in Lehi-Nephi with the intent of enslaving them—dies; Zeniff leads his people in righteousness, and they enjoy a twenty-two-year period of peace. Then the Lamanites, a wild and ferocious people, come to battle against the people of Zeniff because of false traditions passed down from their fathers. Zeniff and his people succeed in driving the Lamanites out of their lands. Zeniff confers the kingdom on Noah, one of his sons.

INTERESTING FACTS ABOUT FALSE TRADITIONS As used in the Book of Mormon, *false traditions* describe inaccurate beliefs that are perpetuated and handed down from one

PROMINENT PEOPLE

- Zeniff
- The Lamanites
- Nephi

generation to another until, over time, they are accepted as truth. This chapter details some of the false beliefs about Lehi and his family that had been taught by generations of Lamanites over a period of almost five hundred years—among them that Lehi was driven out of Jerusalem because of

MAIN THEMES

- Righteous leadership is a critical factor in establishing peace.

- False ideas and beliefs can be handed down from one generation to another until they are eventually accepted as truth.

- It is critical that we teach our children in truth and righteousness, setting a proper example for them.

- Those who do not understand the ways of the Lord are often angry with those who obey Him.

his iniquity; that Laman and Lemuel were wronged by their brothers in the wilderness and again while crossing the sea; that Nephi had wrongly usurped power by leading the family after they arrived in the promised land; and that Nephi robbed Laman and Lemuel and their followers by departing into the wilderness and taking with him the plates of brass. In reality, as we know, Lehi was warned to flee Jerusalem to avoid destruction; it was Laman and Lemuel who committed wrongs in the wilderness and while crossing the sea; the Lord gave leadership to Nephi because of his righteousness; and Nephi, as the designated religious leader, was entitled to take the plates with him when he was warned by the Lord to separate himself from his wicked brothers. As is detailed in verse 17, these false traditions, repeated over hundreds of years, caused such great hatred among the Lamanites that they wanted to completely destroy the Nephites.

KEY INSIGHTS ABOUT THE SAVIOR

- The Lord protects and delivers those who put their trust in Him.
- The Lord favored Nephi as the leader of his family because of Nephi's faithfulness in keeping the commandments.

Mosiah 11

"And it shall come to pass that except be brought into bondage; and none (Mosiah 11:23)

MAJOR CONCEPT

Prophets of God who teach the truth are typically rejected by those who do iniquity.

OVERVIEW King Noah rules in wickedness, rejecting the message of the prophet Abinadi to repent. Noah has wives and concubines—in this case, he was living with women outside of marriage without the Lord's approval. Noah seeks Abinadi's life when he prophesies that the people will be taken into bondage; Abinadi flees from the land to preserve his life.

INTERESTING FACTS ABOUT WINE Some discount the mention of wine in verse 15, pointing out that wine produced from grapes was not made or used in ancient America. In actuality, grapes are not mentioned, though they could have been used—grape plants were recently identified near ancient ruins in the Mexican state of Chiapas. Regardless, the term *wine* was used to describe many other fermented drinks by Europeans hundreds of years ago. Among other things, they were made by fermenting the juice of bananas, pineapples, hearts of palm, or the agave plant. Spaniards

PROMINENT PEOPLE

- Noah
- Abinadi

MAIN THEMES

- A wicked government causes the people it governs to become wicked.
- False prophets and corrupt leaders initially flourish because they salve the wicked and approve their wicked acts as acceptable to God.
- Unrighteous governments in all ages have maintained power by appealing to the vanity of the people over whom they rule; victory at war is one of the ways unrighteous leaders appeal to vanity.

- The natural man—he who is not influenced by the Atonement—is a war-like person, a state that is repugnant to the Lord.
- Getting caught up in the things of the world readily distracts us from our righteous pursuits.

600 BC

90 BC

160–150 BC

this people repent and turn unto the Lord their God, they shall shall deliver them, except it be the Lord the Almighty God."

who came to Mesoamerica hundreds of years ago made a variety of native "wines," including an intoxicating beverage made from water, honey, and bark from a specific type of tree (see *Echoes*, 288–289).

WHO WAS NOAH? When Zeniff grew old, he conferred the kingdom on his son Noah, who in sharp contrast to Zeniff ruled the kingdom in wickedness and refused to honor the covenants that had been made with the Lord. Noah's example of greed and lasciviousness led the people into a state of godlessness early in his reign, which led to bondage and oppression at the hands of their Lamanite hosts. Noah walked in darkness and sin, luring the people away from God and removing righteous people from office;

his reign was marked by crime and cruelty, in direct contrast to that of his father, Zeniff. After rejecting the warnings of Abinadi and putting him to death, Noah fled into the wilderness before the invading Lamanites and commanded his men to abandon their wives and families to the mercy of the enemy. Noah's son Limhi and others remained with their families; the Lamanites did have mercy on them but ordered them to deliver Noah and made them pay a tax of one-half of all they possessed. Gideon sent a search party to find Noah in the wilderness. Instead, the search party found a group of people who had begged to return to their families; when Noah had denied them that right, they had burned him to death.

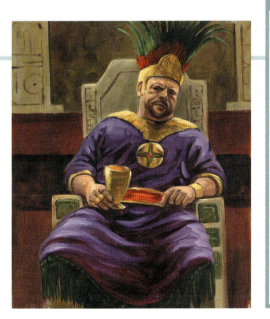

KEY INSIGHTS ABOUT THE SAVIOR

- The Lord offers two clear choices: we can repent, or we can be taken into bondage (usually spiritual bondage).
- The Lord is the only one who can deliver us from bondage.
- If we cast aside the commandments and our covenants, the Lord will be slow to hear and answer our cries.
- Unless we are repentant, the Lord will not hear our prayers or deliver us from our afflictions.

Mosiah 12

"And it shall come to pass that except they shall leave a record behind them, and I even this will I do that I may discover

Major Concept

Prophets are accepted and obeyed by the righteous but are rejected and sometimes destroyed by the wicked.

OVERVIEW Abinadi disguises himself and returns after two years to the land of Lehi-Nephi. Seeing that the people still refuse to repent, he delivers a much harsher message, prophesying that they will be destroyed and that King Noah will die. Confronted by the false priests in much the same way as the Sanhedrin approached the Savior, Abinadi begins to teach the priests the Ten Commandments. The three charges brought against Abinadi were actually from the law of Moses. (1) He reviled the king, which violates Ex. 22:28. (2) He was believed to be a false prophet, and the law of Moses states that false prophets must die. (3) He was accused of blasphemy; the law of Moses states that blasphemy is punishable by death.

Prominent People

- Abinadi
- Noah
- The priests of Noah's court

INTERESTING FACTS ABOUT SIMILE CURSES A *simile* is a comparison between two objects and is often expressed using the words *like* or *as*. *Simile curses* express the way harm will come upon someone, comparing the cursed person to an object that incurs harm. Simile curses appear only

Main Themes

- Those who are wicked often try to confuse and make light of those who are righteous.
- Filled with hypocrisy, the wicked may try to appear righteous.
- Lack of understanding of spiritual truths is often the result of sin.
- The wicked pervert the ways of the Lord.

MOSIAH

repent I will utterly destroy them from off the face of the earth; yet they will preserve them for other nations which shall possess the land; yea, the abominations of this people to other nations." (Mosiah 12:8)

a few times in the Old Testament, so Joseph Smith would likely not have been aware of such a concept, even though simile curses are found in many ancient Near Eastern writings, including prophecies, religious texts, and treaties (see *Echoes,* 156–159). In this chapter, Abinadi uses two simile curses against King Noah: that his life will be valued as a garment in a hot furnace (see verse 3) and that he will be as a dry stalk in the field that is trampled by beasts and trodden underfoot (see verse 11).

WHO WAS ABINADI? The name *Abinadi* is Hebrew in origin. *Ab* means "father"; *Abi* means "my father"; and *Nadi* means "is present before you." The name *Abinadi,* then, means "my Father is present before you," which is the actual charge used in Mosiah 17:8: that God Himself would come down to put Abinadi to death. Around 150 BC, the Lord sent the prophet Abinadi to the land of Lehi-Nephi to preach repentance and warn the people that they would be brought into bondage if they did not repent. His teachings were rejected, and he was driven from the land; two years later he returned in disguise to repeat his message and warn the people of their complete destruction. Bound and brought before the king, he was interrogated in an attempt to cross him. He boldly proclaimed the truth, which caused the priests to petition Noah to execute Abinadi. Proclaiming that his death would stand as a testimony against Noah at the last day and that Noah would suffer the same fate, Abinadi was executed by being burned at the stake. In fulfillment of Abinadi's prophecy, King Noah was later burned to death by his own people.

KEY INSIGHTS ABOUT THE SAVIOR

- The Lord is the author of salvation.
- Salvation comes from no other source than the Lord.
- All punishment from the Lord is meted out as a result of wickedness and sin on the part of those who receive it.
- The Lord will destroy the wicked and cause great afflictions to come upon them.
- The Lord will comfort and redeem His people but will cause the wicked to endure great burdens.
- Noah's priests pretended to understand the spirit of prophecy but could not, because the spirit of prophecy is the testimony of Jesus.

Mosiah 13

"I say unto you, that salvation doth which God himself shall make for the . . ." (Mosiah 13:28)

MAJOR CONCEPT

The Lord is the only pathway to salvation and is the fulfillment of the law of Moses.

OVERVIEW Abinadi, who has been thrown in prison, is again brought before the king, despite Noah's order that Abinadi be executed. After teaching the Ten Commandments, Abinadi teaches that the Lord will atone for the sins of all mankind and is the only source of redemption.

INTERESTING FACTS ABOUT PORTRAYALS OF MOSES Traditionally, art portraying Moses on Mt. Sinai—such as the magnificent sculpture done by Michaelangelo—shows Moses with horns on his head. That's because Catholic translators thought the word meaning *shone* actually meant *horned*, giving rise to generations of

PROMINENT PEOPLE

- Noah
- Abinadi
- The priests of Noah's court

Biblical scholars who agreed that the prophet had horns. Verse 5 in this chapter clearly states that Abinadi's face "shone with exceeding luster" because the Spirit of the Lord was upon him—just as was the case with Moses "while in the mount of Sinai, while speaking with the Lord."

MAIN THEMES

- No righteous man is taken before his time.
- We are preserved and protected until we have accomplished the mission the Lord has in store for us.
- A solid knowledge of the gospel and the scriptures allows us to testify with power.
- The Ten Commandments still apply to us in our day.
- We are responsible for teaching the truth to those within our stewardship.

600 BC

90 BC

148 BC

not come by the law alone; and were it not for the atonement, sins and iniquities of his people, . . . they must unavoidably perish.

INTERESTING FACTS ABOUT THE LAW OF MOSES The law of Moses—consisting of a complex and detailed set of 613 laws and requirements—was given to the people as a preparatory law, leading to the coming of the Savior and the higher law that He gave. It consisted of a number of symbols, or types, that looked forward to the coming of the Savior and taught of the Atonement; as such, the law of Moses was actually a great prophecy, and Jesus was its fulfillment. While it helped prepare the people, the law of Moses on its own was insufficient: it required the Savior and His Atonement for its fulfillment. The people of King Noah's time were spiritually unprepared to accept the higher law of the Atonement; Noah and his people had falsely attributed salvation to the law of Moses and did not recognize it as a symbol of Christ's atoning sacrifice.

KEY INSIGHTS ABOUT THE SAVIOR

- The Lord came to earth, experienced mortality, and went forth in great power upon the face of the earth.
- The Lord Himself was oppressed and afflicted.
- The Lord brought forth resurrection from the dead.
- The law of Moses was a great prophecy, a provisional pathway pointing to something more important to come; the Lord was the fulfillment of that prophecy.
- Without the Atonement of the Lord, all are lost.
- What the court of King Noah did to Abinadi was a type of the trials of Jesus.
- All prophets who ever lived testified of Christ.

Mosiah 14

Major Concept

The Savior made Himself an offering for our sins and made intercession for all transgressors.

OVERVIEW Isaiah—who had a clear understanding of the Savior seven hundred years before His birth—wrote in Isaiah 53 that the Savior would suffer for our sins and would offer up His soul for our transgressions. In this chapter of Mosiah, Abinadi bears testimony of the Savior by quoting the words of Isaiah.

Prominent People

• Jesus Christ

INTERESTING FACTS ABOUT "DECLARING HIS GENERATION"
In verse 8, we are asked, "who shall declare his generation?" The root of *generation* is "genesis," or origin; Isaiah, then, is asking, "Who will declare Jesus' origin?" The prophets declare His origin: they testify that He is the Son of God. What does Isaiah's question mean to us? The things we must ask ourselves as a result of that question are profound. What it asks us is this: Do we consider ourselves to be of the seed of Christ? Do we accept His offering—and do we demonstrate our acceptance by valiantly obeying His commandments? If we do consider ourselves to be His seed and we respond with obedience, He will declare us to be of His generation—His sons and daughters and joint-heirs with Him in the kingdom of His Father. We will join the others of His seed: all the holy prophets since the world began and those who have believed on the Savior and have repented.

Main Themes

• We owe all of our opportunity for salvation to Jesus Christ.

MOSIAH

transgressions, he was bruised for our iniquities; the chastisement of stripes we are healed." (Mosiah 14:5)

KEY INSIGHTS ABOUT THE SAVIOR

- The Lord came to earth in a body of flesh and blood, just as all mortals do; He did not appear to be divine or immortal.

- Jesus was despised and rejected, acquainted with grief.

- The Savior bore our griefs and carried our sorrows; as such, He is in a unique position to succor us.

- Despite His affliction, the Lord did not complain or protest.

- The Lord was a sinless sacrifice.

- Jesus went through exquisite agony in the Garden of Gethsemane to pay for our sins and transgressions; as a result of His infinite Atonement, we are healed.

- The Lord made intercession for the transgressors—He paid the price for every sin that would ever be committed and made repentance possible.

"And because he dwelleth in the flesh subjected the flesh to the will of the Eternal Father of heaven and of

MAJOR CONCEPT

As our Savior, Jesus Christ has borne our transgressions and made intercession for us and makes possible our resurrection.

OVERVIEW In this chapter, Abinadi continues to answer the priests' questions. He explains that the Father and the Son are one in unity and purpose. He bears powerful testimony of the Savior, teaching that He will pay the price for our sins, make intercession for us, and make possible the resurrection. He also teaches that because of the Atonement, little children will inherit eternal life.

PROMINENT PEOPLE

- Abinadi
- Jesus Christ

INTERESTING FACTS ABOUT THE FATHER AND THE SON
As this chapter opens, Abinadi is trying to teach that Jesus will inherit the Father's power and characteristics, so He will be a manifestation of the Father in the flesh. Abinadi teaches that empowered by the Father, Christ is to manifest the will and the power of the Father. The divine investiture of authority in the Son makes it possible for Him to literally become the Father and the Son, or one God. On June 30, 1916, the First Presidency and the Quorum of the Twelve issued a detailed statement

MAIN THEMES

- We are the seed of Jesus Christ if we hear the words of the prophets and look toward the Savior for a remission of our sins.

- All the prophets since the beginning of the world have taught of the Savior.

- Those who believe and obey the prophets will be resurrected in the first resurrection.

- Under the Atonement, little children who die will inherit eternal life.

- The first resurrection will include prophets and people who died before Jesus and who were resurrected immediately after His resurrection.

600 BC

90 BC

148 BC

he shall be called the Son of God, and having Father . . . And they are one God, yea, the very earth." (Mosiah 15:2–4)

about this principle; the entire statement is found in Elder James E. Talmage's *The Articles of Faith* (see 465–473). In short, they stated that Jesus Christ is represented as the Father in three ways: (1) He created all things; (2) He is the Father of all who accept His atoning sacrifice; and (3) He is the fully authorized and commissioned representative of the Father. Mosiah 15 is an explanation of Jesus' roles as Father and Son; it is to help explain Mosiah 14:10, which says that Jesus (as Jehovah) sent Himself as the Son to earth. When Abinadi uses the terms *man, flesh,* or *Son,* he is describing Jesus' role as Son. When he uses the terms *God, Spirit,* or *Father,* he is describing Jesus' role as Father.

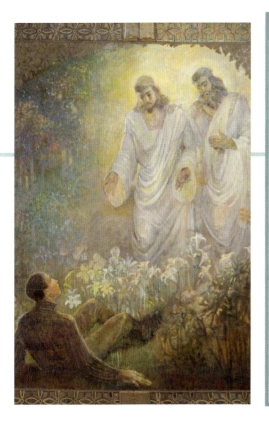

KEY INSIGHTS ABOUT THE SAVIOR

- The Lord is one with the Father in will and purpose.
- The Lord was subjected to temptation in the flesh but resisted that temptation.
- During His mortal ministry, Jesus was mocked, scourged, disowned, and cast out by His own people.
- Jesus wrought many miracles during His ministry.
- The Lord was crucified without complaint or protest.
- The Savior gained victory over death through the empowerment of the Father, bringing to all mankind the resurrection.
- Jesus took upon Himself our sins and redeems us by satisfying the demands of justice.
- The Savior becomes the spiritual Father of all who believe on His name.
- Because of its infinite nature, the Atonement was in force before the world was formed.

Mosiah 16

MAJOR CONCEPT

The Lord's Atonement stands ready to bless and redeem all mankind; our exaltation depends on our repentance and obedience.

OVERVIEW Abinadi continues to teach the false priests, bearing testimony of the Savior and His atoning sacrifice. He explains that the Atonement redeems men from their fallen state if they repent but that those who are wicked are not redeemed. He also bears testimony of the resurrection that will be wrought by the Savior.

INTERESTING FACTS ABOUT RESURRECTION We know that because of the Atonement of Christ, all who are born to this earth with a physical body will receive the gift of the resurrection. The infinite Atonement was required to overcome the Fall and to bring about the Savior's Resurrection in fulfillment of the merciful plan

PROMINENT PEOPLE

- Jesus Christ
- Satan

of redemption. Through the Atonement, then, all are liberated from the bands of death—"For as in Adam all die, even so in Christ shall all be made alive" (1 Cor. 15:22). Elder Bruce R. McConkie taught that many of the righteous dead who lived before Christ were resurrected with Him

MAIN THEMES

- The time will come when all will see and recognize the Savior and will admit that His judgments are just.

- Satan has power over those who persist in their sins and they will be cast out.

- Those who persist in their sins and refuse to repent are enemies to God.

- We will all be brought to the judgment after we are resurrected; we are resurrected with one of three types of bodies—celestial, terrestrial, or telestial. If judged to be celestial, we will be resurrected to eternal life and

happiness, but if judged to be telestial, we will be resurrected to damnation and delivered to Satan.

- The law of Moses was a type or shadow of things to come; without the Savior, its precepts were empty.

see the salvation of the Lord; when every shall see eye to eye and shall confess before (Mosiah 16:1)

(see D&C 133:54–55). Elder McConkie also taught that for those who have lived after the resurrection of Christ took place, their resurrection is still in the future and will take place at the time of the Second Coming (see *Mormon Doctrine*, 639).

KEY INSIGHTS ABOUT THE SAVIOR

- Without the Savior, there would have been no redemption and all mankind would have been endlessly lost.
- The Lord will not redeem those who are wicked and carnal.
- Without Christ there would have been no resurrection.
- Jesus Christ is the light and life of the world; His light can never be darkened.
- The Lord continually stretches forth His arm of mercy, even to the wicked.
- We can be saved only in and through Jesus Christ.

Mosiah 17

"Yea, I will suffer even until death, and stand as a testimony against you. And and this shall also stand as a testimony

MAJOR CONCEPT

Martyrdom is the supreme earthly sacrifice one can make.

OVERVIEW Abinadi has finished testifying to the priests; one of the priests, Alma, believes Abinadi and pleads with Noah to spare Abinadi's life. Noah is enraged, casts Alma out, and sends his servants after Alma to slay him. Alma hides from those seeking his life and writes all the words of Abinadi. Noah orders Abinadi's execution; the reason he cites is Abinadi's claim that God will come to earth and dwell among men—but the real reason is that Abinadi has spoken evil of Noah and his people. Abinadi prophesies that if he himself is executed, the same fate will befall Noah and the descendants of his priests. Abinadi is burned to death.

PROMINENT PEOPLE

- Abinadi
- Alma
- Noah
- The priests of Noah

INTERESTING FACTS ABOUT "JUST ONE CONVERT" Elder Joseph B. Wirthlin wrote, "Abinadi may have felt that he failed as a missionary because he had only one convert, so far as the record shows. However, that one convert, Alma, and his descendants were spiritual leaders among the Nephites and

MAIN THEMES

- One of the tactics of the guilty is to destroy those who expose their guilt.

- True martyrs of religion—those who could escape death by denying the truth—receive eternal life, and their murderers are condemned.

- Martyrs seal their words with their death.

- We are prompted to ask ourselves, Is my commitment such that I will remain faithful regardless of the circumstances in which I find myself?

> I will not recall my words, and they shall if ye slay me ye will shed innocent blood, against you at the last day." (Mosiah 17:10)

Lamanites for about three hundred years. His son Alma became the first chief judge of the Nephite people and the high priest over the Church. Alma's other descendants who became prominent religious leaders include his grandson Helaman; his great-grandson Nephi; and his great-great-great-grandson Nephi, who was the chief disciple of the resurrected Jesus Christ. All of this resulted from Abinadi's lone convert" (*Finding Peace in Our Lives*, 220). Much of the religious history of the Nephite nation over the ensuing three hundred years is concerned with Alma and his descendants; Alma himself initiated a religious revival and because of his influence churches were established throughout the land of Zarahemla.

INTERESTING FACTS ABOUT NOAH AS A TYPE   Noah is a type of Pontius Pilate. Just as Pilate was willing to release Jesus but was persuaded by the priests of his day to kill Jesus, so also was Noah about to release Abinadi when he was persuaded by the priests to kill Noah. Both Jesus and Abinadi were subjected to a "mock" trial. Both were bound, taken before an illegal court, tried according to the law of Moses, accused of blasphemy, tortured, and executed.

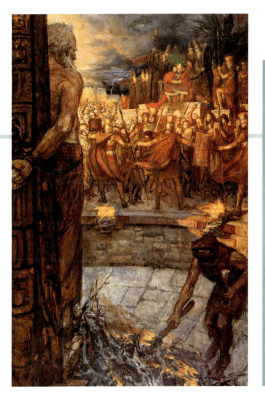

Key Insights about the Savior

- The Lord executes vengeance on those who destroy His people.

Mosiah 18

MAJOR CONCEPT

Baptism, a covenant consisting of a two-way promise, is our admission into the Church and kingdom of God and symbolizes the rebirth of a new spiritual person.

OVERVIEW Having fled from King Noah and hidden to spare his own life, Alma begins to teach the words of Abinadi in private. Setting forth the covenant of baptism, he baptizes several hundred people at a fountain of clear water known as the Waters of Mormon. He then organizes the Church of Christ and ordains priests who begin to teach the people. Alma and his people desire to practice their religion and they flee into the wilderness to escape King Noah.

INTERESTING FACTS ABOUT THE BAPTISMAL COVENANT
Every person who is baptized a member of The Church of Jesus Christ of Latter-day Saints takes upon himself or herself the baptismal covenant, which is spelled out in plainness in

PROMINENT PEOPLE

- Alma
- Noah
- Helam
- A "goodly" number of Nephites

Mosiah 18. Covenants are two-way promises between us and the Lord. As our part of the baptismal covenant, we promise that we are willing to be called the Savior's people; to bear one another's burdens, that they may be light; to mourn with those that mourn; to comfort those that stand in need of comfort; and to

MAIN THEMES

- Membership in the Church and kingdom of God comes through baptism.

- When we are baptized, we are numbered among the people of God.

- At baptism, we are filled with the grace of God.

- Baptism involves us in a promise to mourn with those who mourn, comfort those who stand in need of comfort, and stand as witnesses of God at all times and in all places throughout the rest of our lives.

- Our baptism is a witness that we have entered into a covenant with the Lord.

- Once we are baptized, we must keep the commandments—including living in unity without contention, keeping the Sabbath day holy, and imparting of our substance to the poor.

- We should be of one faith, one baptism, having our hearts knit together in unity.

- We should teach nothing except those things spoken of by the prophets.

MOSIAH

600 BC

90 BC

147 BC

desire of your hearts, what have you against Lord . . . ?" (Mosiah 18:10)

stand as witnesses of God at all times and in all things and in all places, even until death and to serve Him and keep His commandments. As we are faithful to that covenant, we receive His promise: that He will pour out His Spirit abundantly upon us and that we will be redeemed of God, numbered among those of the first resurrection, and receive eternal life.

WHO WAS ALMA? A member of wicked King Noah's court, Alma the Elder had, by his own admission, done many things that were abominable to the Lord. After hearing Abinadi's words around 150 BC, however, Alma experienced a mighty change of heart. He pled unsuccessfully for Abinadi's life and was cast out and hunted down by Noah's servants. He secretly gathered those who wanted to be baptized at the Waters of Mormon; Alma states that he had authority to baptize, and immersing himself in the water with Helam (see verse 12) was a sign of Alma's humility and repentance (see *Answers to Gospel Questions,* 3:203, 204). The truths Alma taught are the same as those that have been taught in the Church throughout all time; they were new teachings for his people, however, who had been living in apostasy under King Noah. Alma founded the Church of Christ among the faithful who had been baptized and led them into the wilderness to escape persecution. He estab-

lished the city of Helam, a refuge from King Noah's priests and his band of Nephites. Alma was finally able to guide his followers to the land of Zarahemla around 120 BC. More information about Alma is provided in later chapters.

Image: Lake Atitlan, thought to be the location of the Waters of Mormon.

KEY INSIGHTS ABOUT THE SAVIOR

- The Lord counts as His people those who have been baptized in His name.

Mosiah 19

"And the king commanded them that angry with the king, and caused that (Mosiah 19:20)

MAJOR CONCEPT

The prophecies of God's servants are fulfilled.

OVERVIEW This and the next three chapters are taken from the record of Zeniff's colony; part of the account in these records is also included in the final chapters of Mosiah. When Noah's army returns without having found Alma and his people, a small part of the army begins to rebel against the king; one of the soldiers, Gideon, draws his sword and swears he will kill the king. They fight, and just as he is about to be overcome, Noah climbs to the top of a tower. He sees the Lamanite armies approaching, and pleads with Gideon to spare him so Noah's people can defend themselves. Noah orders his men to leave their wives and children and flee from the Lamanites; some do as they are commanded, but many stay behind with their families. The Lamanites have mercy on them because of the

PROMINENT PEOPLE

- Noah
- Gideon
- Limhi

beauty of the Nephite daughters and take them to the land of Nephi, where they are given land on which to live in exchange for half of all they possess. Those who went with the king want to return to their families; when the king forbids them, they burn him to death, thus fulfilling Abinadi's prophecy, but

MAIN THEMES

- Those who are righteous encourage family unity.
- Those things that are spoken in prophecy by God's servants are fulfilled.
- Righteousness inspires peace.
- Bondage always follows rejection of the prophet's words.

they should not return; and they were he should suffer, even unto death by fire."

his priests escape. The kingdom is conferred upon Limhi, the righteous son of Noah.

INTERESTING FACTS ABOUT JUSTICE Abinadi had warned the rebellious and prideful King Noah that the same fate he chose to inflict upon Abinadi would, in turn, be inflicted on him. Not long after Abinadi suffered death by fire, Noah was burned to death by his companions when he refused to allow them to return to their families. The justice of God is immovable. Just as God will fulfill His promised blessings to the righteous without fail, He will also execute judgment upon those who reject His word. President Spencer W. Kimball taught, "Remember, God is in his heavens. He knew what he was doing when he organized the earth. He knows what he is doing now. Those of us who break his commandments will regret and suffer in remorse and pain. God will not be mocked" ("God Will Not Be Mocked," 4).

WHO WAS GIDEON? A soldier in the army of King Noah, Gideon led a revolt against the abuses of the king and attempted to slay him; his plan was interrupted when the Lamanites invaded and Noah escaped. Gideon consistently stood firm against those who acted contrary to God's laws and violated the rights of God's people. He rose up to take action on three separate occasions: (1) in opposition to the abuses of wicked King Noah; (2) in devising a successful plan to liberate the people of Limhi from Lamanite bondage; and (3) in defying the false doctrines preached by Nehor in Zarahemla. In Zarahemla, Gideon became a teacher in the Church of Christ, the position he held when he challenged Nehor. Old and weak, Gideon was unable to withstand the lethal blows of Nehor's sword, and he died. Nehor was subsequently found guilty of priestcraft and murder and was put to death.

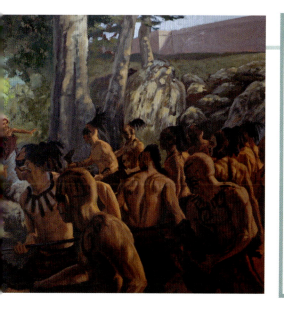

KEY INSIGHTS ABOUT THE SAVIOR

- The Lord counts as His people those who have been baptized in His name.

Mosiah 20

MAJOR CONCEPT

Prophecies regarding the Lord's judgment against the wicked are fulfilled as the wicked fail to repent and turn away from iniquity.

OVERVIEW The priests of Noah, who fled into the wilderness when Noah was burned to death, find a group of Lamanite daughters who are singing and dancing in Shemlon; the priests abduct twenty-four of the women and take them into the wilderness. The Lamanites, assuming Limhi's people are responsible, break their oath of peace and attack. Limhi promises to find the responsible parties and kill them. Gideon reminds Limhi that Noah's priests fled into the wilderness and are likely responsible for abducting the Lamanite women; peace is restored between the Lamanites and Limhi's people.

INTERESTING FACTS ABOUT ROMANCE IN THE BOOK OF MORMON During the period when Joseph Smith was

PROMINENT PEOPLE

- Daughters of the Lamanites
- Priests of King Noah
- Limhi
- Gideon

translating the Book of Mormon, many literary works of the day revolved around themes of courtship and romance; examples include the novels of Jane Austen, icons of traditional romance that appeared in the same time period as the Book of Mormon. But while courtship and romance do take place in the Book of Mormon—examples being the marriages of Lehi's sons to Ishmael's daughters and the marriages of the daughters of the Lamanites to King Noah's priests—the details are related in a very matter-of-fact way, in sharp contrast to popular nineteenth-century notions of romantic love (see *Echoes*, 311–312).

MAIN THEMES

- Serious disagreement can be the result of simple misunderstanding.
- It's important to get all the facts before making judgments or decisions.
- The warnings and words of prophets are always fulfilled.

WHO WERE THE DAUGHTERS OF THE LAMANITES? The daughters of the Lamanites discussed in this chapter were twenty-four young women who gathered together in an isolated area outside Shemlon "to sing, and to dance, and to

MOSIAH

fulfilled, which he prophesied against us—hearken unto the words of the Lord, and turn

make themselves merry" (Mosiah 20:1). They were discovered and subsequently abducted by the priests of King Noah who had fled into the wilderness when Noah was killed by his people. These priests were used to an immoral lifestyle and had been celibate in the wilderness for two years. Fearing for their own lives, they had remained hidden in the wilderness and had not dared return to their wives and families. We know that the priests of Noah at some point married the daughters of the Lamanites, because an army of Lamanites later discovered them (see Mosiah 23:30–34), and the daughters of the Lamanites pleaded with the army to spare the lives of their Nephite husbands.

KEY INSIGHTS ABOUT THE SAVIOR

- The Lord metes out judgment upon those who remain in iniquity and sin.

Mosiah 21

"And they did humble themselves to God; yea, even all the day long did of their afflictions." (Mosiah 21:14)

MAJOR CONCEPT

Despite our fervent prayers for help, the Lord delivers us according to His own will and due time, allowing us to learn the lessons essential to exaltation.

OVERVIEW Though peace prevails for a time in the city of Nephi, Lamanite oppression increases, causing the people of Limhi to murmur against the king. He allows his armies to go to battle against the Lamanites, resulting in tremendous loss of life. The Lamanites beat the Nephites back three times. Humbled, the people of Limhi pray for deliverance; the Lord softens the hearts of the Lamanites, and the Nephites' burdens are lightened. Ammon and his party arrive with the Jaredite plates they discovered as they searched for Zarahemla. Limhi and his people are converted by Ammon and covenant to serve the Lord; they want to be baptized.

MAIN THEMES

- Our prayers are not always immediately answered in the way we expect or hope, but the Lord always hears our cries.

- Iniquity leads to destruction.

- Ordinances like baptism must be performed by those having proper authority and keys.

PROMINENT PEOPLE

- Limhi
- Ammon

INTERESTING FACTS ABOUT ANSWERS TO PRAYER In this chapter, the Nephites under the leadership of Limhi were subjected to tremendous burdens at the hands of the Lamanites. At first the Lamanites reluctantly refused to go to battle against the Nephites, despite their hatred, because they had sworn an oath not to—instead, they increased the burdens placed on Limhi and his people. But after going to battle three times and suffering terrific loss, the Nephites pleaded with the Lord to deliver them out of their afflictions. The Lord's response is instructive: while He did not see fit to lift their burdens—because they needed to pay the price for their iniquities—He did lighten their burdens out of mercy so that their suffering would not be as sore.

WHO WAS LIMHI? Limhi was the last of the Nephite kings in the colony established by Zeniff among the Lamanites in the even in the depths of humility; and they did cry mightily they cry unto their God that he would deliver them out

land of Nephi beginning around 200 BC. When wicked King Noah was burned to death by his people, they conferred the kingdom upon Noah's righteous son Limhi around 145 BC. He ruled for a number of years in an atmosphere of bondage by the Lamanites and constant fear of Lamanite attack or retribution—initially fueled when twenty-four Lamanite daughters were abducted. Ammon and his group from Zarahemla discovered Limhi's people around 121 BC, and they were eventually freed from Lamanite bondage. Limhi, who served as a spiritual guide for his people, had three basic goals: (1) to remind the people continuously that wickedness leads to spiritual and physical enslavement; (2) to preserve peace, order, and a prevailing attitude of trust in God; and (3) to find an effective way to escape from the Lamanites and return to their homeland of Zarahemla.

Image: Carrying large loads on one's back is still common in the modern Mayan culture.

KEY INSIGHTS ABOUT THE SAVIOR

- There is no way we can deliver ourselves from bondage; the only deliverance comes through Jesus Christ.
- The Father always hears our prayers, and we pray to the Father through the Son.
- The Lord is slow to hear the cries of those who do iniquity.
- Though the Lord is mindful of our situation, sometimes we must wait to be delivered from bondage we bring upon ourselves.
- The Lord demonstrates great mercy even to those who have forgotten Him.
- The Lord delivers His people after imperative lessons have been learned.

Mosiah 22

"And it came to pass that Mosiah received their records, and also the people of Limhi." (Mosiah 22:14)

MAJOR CONCEPT

Escape from bondage requires full dependence on the Lord and a willingness to completely obey and follow Him.

OVERVIEW Gideon comes up with an inspired plan to help Limhi and his people escape from the Lamanites. The people gather all their goods and their flocks and prepare to flee; Limhi provides extra wine to the Lamanite guards, who become drunk. In the cover of night, Limhi and his people escape and are led through the wilderness by Ammon and his brethren. After being lost in the wilderness for a time, they arrive in Zarahemla and are received with joy by Mosiah. Efforts by the Lamanite guards to pursue Limhi and his people are unsuccessful.

INTERESTING FACTS ABOUT DELIVERANCE FROM BONDAGE
The story of Limhi and his people offers some unique insights

PROMINENT PEOPLE

- Gideon
- Limhi
- Ammon
- Mosiah

MAIN THEMES

- We may experience bondage until we repent and have a mighty change of heart.
- In times of need, we should rely on those who are righteous to guide and direct us.

about the steps that lead people out of bondage. Scholars Monte S. Nyman and Charles D. Tate, Jr., identified four steps that combine to deliver people from bondage. First is for the oppressed to be humbled before the Lord; such humility involves turning to the Lord with full purpose of heart. Second is for them to engage in mighty prayer with complete trust in the Lord. Third is for them to exhibit a willingness to covenant with the Lord to keep His commandments, followed by strict obedience. The last step is for them to serve the Lord with all diligence (Nyman and Tate, 269–270).

WHO WAS AMMON? A descendant of the Mulekites, Ammon was a strong and mighty explorer who was sent by Mosiah around 121 BC to find out what happened to a group of colonists who had left Zarahemla approximately eighty years earlier. Ammon was successful: he discovered Limhi and his people, who were then in bondage to

MOSIAH

received them with joy; and he also records which had been found by the

Image: The escape of the people of Limhi.

the Lamanites. Ammon taught Limhi and his people and brought them up to date on what had happened in Zarahemla since they had left—including telling them of King Benjamin's great final discourse. Ammon then worked with Gideon, a powerful soldier in Limhi's army, to help Limhi and his people escape from the Lamanites and return to Zarahemla, where they were baptized by Alma.

Key Insights about the Savior

- The Lord pours out His Spirit most abundantly upon those who serve Him and keep His commandments.

- In His own due time and according to His will, the Lord delivers us.

- The Lord will obstruct the path of our enemies if we are humble and follow His counsel.

MAJOR CONCEPT

We should strive for righteous leadership and should trust no one to teach us except those who are men and women of God.

OVERVIEW After fleeing from the Lamanite army, Alma and his people settle in the land of Helam, where they begin to grow crops and build homes. They try to make Alma their king, but he refuses, instead serving as their high priest. As they prosper in the land, they are invaded by a Lamanite army that takes possession of the land. The Lamanites also find the priests of King Noah who had abducted and married the daughters of the Lamanites; their leader, Amulon, pleads for their safety and joins the Lamanite army. Amulon rules the land under the Lamanite king.

INTERESTING FACTS ABOUT RIGHTEOUS LEADERSHIP The people of Alma loved and trusted him and naturally wanted

PROMINENT PEOPLE

- Alma
- Amulon

MAIN THEMES

- Liberty is a gift from the Lord that should be safeguarded and protected.

- We should do whatever we can to avoid leaders who choose iniquity over righteousness.

- All authority to act in behalf of the Lord comes from Him.

- Even when we are sorely tried, the Lord will deliver us in His own time if we have faith.

- We should always remember the Lord and trust in Him but should not place our trust in the arm of flesh.

him to be their king. However, Alma was reluctant for two reasons: he remembered the iniquity and oppressions of King Noah and his priests, and he saw beyond the present moment and understood the potential danger of another unrighteous king. Having seen firsthand the destruction that can be caused by an unrighteous king, Alma counseled his people to accept no one as their leader except he be a man of God who walked in the ways of righteousness. Alma then served his people as their high priest. That same philosophy applies to us today—we have a right to expect honesty and integrity from our leaders and must stand up for truth and righteousness in our interactions with our government leaders.

WHO WAS AMULON? Amulon was the leader of the priests of King Noah from about 150 to 121 BC; having escaped into the wilderness following King Noah's death, he and the other priests abducted

teacher nor your minister, except he be a man keeping his commandments." (Mosiah 23:14)

and subsequently married twenty-four daughters of the Lamanites and remained in the wilderness until they discovered Alma and his people in Helam. The Lamanites promised Alma's people liberty if they would reveal the way back to the land of Nephi. Alma complied, but the Lamanites did not keep their promise; they placed guards around Helam and appointed Amulon the ruler of the land. Having served in Noah's court with Alma, Amulon hated Alma for his conversion to righteousness. Amulon placed tremendous burdens on the people in order to punish Alma for his betrayal.

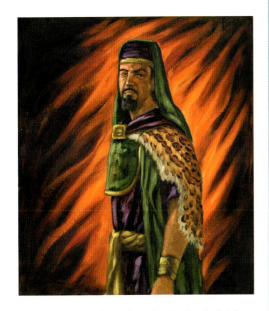

Top Image: Area thought to be the land of Helam.

KEY INSIGHTS ABOUT THE SAVIOR

- The Lord strengthens His people against their enemies.
- Jesus Christ does not esteem one person above another.
- The Lord gives authority to His servants to teach and preach and administer in the ordinances of the gospel; that authority comes from no other.
- The Lord is the only one who can deliver His people from bondage.
- The Lord sometimes chastens good and righteous people to try their patience and faith.

Mosiah 24

"And I will also ease the burdens which backs, even while you are in bondage; that ye may know of a surety that I,

MAJOR CONCEPT

The Lord will deliver His people out of bondage and will exact judgment upon those who persecute His people.

OVERVIEW In this chapter—likely inserted by Mormon because of the lessons it holds for us today—we read the final account of Alma's deliverance. The wicked ruler Amulon increases his persecution of Alma and his people; it becomes so intense that Alma and his people are threatened with death if they are caught praying. In answer to their fervent prayers, the Lord first lightens their burdens and then delivers them from bondage by causing the Lamanites to fall into a deep sleep, enabling Alma and his people to escape. They return to Zarahemla.

INTERESTING FACTS ABOUT BONDAGE We learn in Mosiah of two separate groups of people who were subjected to bondage: Limhi and his people, who negotiated with the Lamanites to

PROMINENT PEOPLE

- Amulon
- Alma
- Laman

settle on part of their land and who were subsequently taken captive and heavily taxed; and Alma and his people, who were taken into bondage when the Lamanite armies conquered Helam. In both these cases, the people petitioned the Lord for help, and in both cases He delivered them. However, there are instructive differences between the two. Because Alma and his people humbled themselves out of love for the Lord instead of being compelled to be humble, the Lord eased the burdens of Alma's people even before they were delivered; in essence, their burdens were significantly easier to bear. The people of Limhi persisted in their sins and waited longer to repent than did Alma and his people, who repented more swiftly. The message for us is to correct those things in our lives that need to be addressed as soon as we recognize them. Sin itself places us in bondage, and the slower we are to repent and return to the Lord, the more difficult and lengthy will be our bondage (see Nyman and Tate, 272).

MAIN THEMES

- We can petition the Lord by praying silently in situations when we are not able to pray aloud.
- Our efforts to be delivered from bondage of any kind must be accompanied by faith and patience.
- We need to constantly prepare for deliverance so when the time comes we are ready to follow.
- We must always remember to thank the Lord for His mercy toward us.

600 BC

90 BC

180

145-121 BC

are put upon your shoulders, that even you cannot feel them upon your
and this will I do that ye may stand as witnesses for me hereafter, and
the Lord God, do visit my people in their afflictions." (Mosiah 24:14)

KEY INSIGHTS ABOUT THE SAVIOR

- The Lord knows the thoughts and intents of our hearts.
- The Lord will ease our burdens by making them lighter even before He removes those burdens from us.
- The Lord can bless us with strength to endure even while we are being tested.
- The Lord has the power to make even the most unlikely things happen if it is His will to do so.
- Covenants are extremely important to the Lord.

Top Image: The escape of Alma's people.
Bottom Image: An example of how burdens are still carried on the backs of the people.

Mosiah 25

"And thus, notwithstanding there being even the church of God; for there was it were repentance and faith in God."

MAJOR CONCEPT

The kingdom of God is built by righteous and faithful people who teach repentance and administer the ordinances of the gospel with proper authority.

OVERVIEW As Alma and his people arrive in Zarahemla, King Mosiah rejoices; he reads the records of Zeniff and the account of Alma and his people, and the inhabitants of Zarahemla marvel and express great joy over the release of their brethren from bondage. Alma baptizes Limhi and his people, and Mosiah authorizes Alma to organize the Church of God. Churches—each with their priests and teachers—are established throughout the land, all being part of the single Church of God.

INTERESTING FACTS ABOUT ZARAHEMLA In their book *Echoes and Evidences of the Book of Mormon*, Donald W. Parry, Daniel C. Peterson, and John W. Welch point out that next

PROMINENT PEOPLE

- King Mosiah
- Alma
- Limhi

to the Grijalva River in the Mexican state of Chiapas lies an archaeological site that meets all the geographical requirements for the Nephite city of Zarahemla. The ruin—known half a century ago as Santa Rosa—now sits underwater, but the evidences are clear. Excavations around

MAIN THEMES

- The scriptures and our own personal histories have tremendous value in converting others to the truth.

- Knowledge is an important factor and must be added to faith in the process of being born again.

- Whenever we are delivered from difficult circumstances, we need to remember that it is the Lord who delivered us.

- The gospel changes behavior.

- The steps that Book of Mormon people went through to repent and effect a mighty change of heart are the same steps we all need to go through.

- We can learn much of value from the experiences of others.

MOSIAH

600 BC

90 BC

120 BC

many churches they were all one church, yea, nothing preached in all the churches except (Mosiah 25:22)

the site show that a great deal of building and activity took place there around the first century BC. A huge platform was built in the center of the city, suggesting that the people of the city were divided into two social groups. We remember that during the time of King Mosiah I the people of Zarahemla spoke two different languages, and when they gathered to hear him, they did so in two separate groups. The archaeological evidence also shows that large earthen mounds were formed, typical of the people of King Mosiah (see *Echoes,* 296–298). From Mosiah 24:25 we learn that it was a twelve-day journey from Helam to Zarahemla. From Mosiah 23:3 we learn that it was an eight-day journey from the waters of Mormon to Helam. Therefore, it was an approximate twenty-day journey from Nephi to Zarahemla.

Key Insights about the Savior

- The Lord delivers His people.
- The Lord pours out His Spirit on His righteous people.

Image: The Grijalva River, which now covers the Santa Rosa ruins.

Mosiah 26

"Yea, blessed is this people who are they be called; and they are mine."

MAJOR CONCEPT

The faithful and repentant are to be received into the Church and forgiven as often as they repent, while those who refuse to repent are not numbered among Church members.

OVERVIEW Those who were too young to remember the words of King Benjamin begin to drift away from the Church; refusing to be baptized, they begin to lead many away. Alma turns to the Lord for help, is promised eternal life, and preaches repentance to the people. Those who confess their sins and repent are forgiven, and those who refuse to repent are excommunicated.

INTERESTING FACTS ABOUT THE CYCLE OF UNBELIEF In this chapter, we learn that the rising generation—those who could not remember the great discourse of King Benjamin and who did not believe the teachings of their parents—began to lead away many members

PROMINENT PEOPLE

- King Mosiah
- Alma

of the church. We may wonder how something as simple as unbelief leads to such dramatic results. There is a specific cycle that follows unbelief: first there is apathy—the absence of emotion, passion, or excitement—which causes people to stop trying. As the cycle

MAIN THEMES

- When righteousness predominates the lives of parents, their children are more likely to follow the same pattern.

- Violations of the commandments of God are to be handled by religious authorities, not civic authorities.

- We are blessed as we bring others to the truth.

- As we learn to know the Lord and continue in faith and obedience, we secure a place with Him in eternity.

- Knowing the Father and the Son requires that we go through a spiritual rebirth and

assume the Savior's countenance.

- Confession of sin must involve the heart and mind in addition to the lips.

- There must be two confessions of serious sin: to the Lord and to our priesthood leader.

- Perfection doesn't happen overnight; the Lord will continue to forgive those who are diligently trying to do better.

- Those who repent are assured of continued fellowship and good standing in the Church; those who continue in serious iniquity without a desire to repent are excommunicated.

continues, obedience wanes, the heart hardens, and the Spirit is lost. When the Spirit is lost, sin is the result. Eventually, very serious sin may be committed. Rebirth from serious sin results only when a person hears the word of God, passes through trial and affliction, recognizes the shock of falling into sin, and suffers the rebuke of a Church court. In this chapter of Mosiah, the rising generation would not believe in Christ's coming or in His resurrection because they wouldn't exercise faith (see verse 3), they hardened their hearts (see verse 3), and they refused to pray (see verse 4).

KEY INSIGHTS ABOUT THE SAVIOR

- The Lord requires great effort on our part.
- The Lord blesses those who are called by His name and who continue in righteousness.
- The Lord freely forgives those who repent and are baptized in His name.
- Those who know the Lord will come forth in the first resurrection, or the resurrection of life.
- The Lord took upon Himself the sins of the world, and His Atonement makes repentance possible.
- The Lord will continue to forgive those who continue to repent.
- Those who continue in transgression and iniquity without a desire to repent are not recognized by the Lord.

Mosiah 27

"Marvel not that all mankind, yea, men and people, must be born again; . . . And they do this, they can in nowise inherit

MAJOR CONCEPT

True repentance is a powerful tool that enables us to be born again.

OVERVIEW Persecution of church members becomes so severe that Mosiah intervenes and issues a proclamation forbidding such persecution. Following a period of peace, the sons of Alma and Mosiah work diligently to lead people from the Church, causing a great deal of dissension. Finally an angel appears to them, commanding that they stop their efforts to destroy the church; they fall to the ground in astonishment and are struck dumb. Subsequently they go throughout the church preaching truth and trying to repair the damage they caused. They became instruments in the hand of God.

INTERESTING FACTS ABOUT THE APPEARANCE OF THE ANGEL We know that Alma the Younger and the sons of

PROMINENT PEOPLE

- King Mosiah
- Alma the Younger
- The sons of Mosiah

Mosiah had been creating major dissension among the people and exerting great effort to lead away members of the church when the angel appeared to them and called them to repentance. We know, too, that Alma the Elder had been praying fervently as a father that his son might be brought to

MAIN THEMES

- We should esteem our neighbors as ourselves.
- True contrition consists of godly sorrow.
- As parents, we can enlist the Lord to help our children through our own diligence, humility, and faithful prayers.
- Angels are sent from God.
- Alma the Younger experienced a mighty change of heart quickly in response to the angel; more often, such a change requires time, determination, and hard work.
- As righteous people, we feel joy when someone repents.

- Those who become "new creatures" are born again and can then inherit the kingdom of God.
- A broken heart is one that can be led by the Lord.
- A covenant with the Lord involves a promise to do, not merely to refrain from doing—to work righteousness, not just to avoid evil.
- Genuine and complete rebirth is always accompanied by great concern for the salvation of others.

600 BC

90 BC

100– 92 BC

and women, all nations, kindreds, tongues, thus they become new creatures; and unless the kingdom of God." (Mosiah 27:25–26)

a knowledge of the truth. So why don't we have more experiences like this in our day? President Wilford Woodruff answered that question by teaching that the Lord sends an angel only to perform a work that cannot be performed in any way other than by the administration of an angel; He never sends angels just because someone desires it or has prayed for it (see *Deseret Weekly*, 641). In almost all cases, the Holy Ghost is able to accomplish the things we need or desire. It wasn't the appearance of the angel alone that converted Alma; we learn later that his conversion included many days of fasting and prayer (see Alma 5:46).

WHO WAS OMNER? Initially, Omner—one of the sons of Mosiah—was among the very vilest of sinners (see Mosiah 28:4) and was numbered among the unbelievers (see Mosiah 27:8) who went about trying to lead people away from the Church. But after an angel appeared to him, his brothers, and Alma the Younger, he became a stalwart missionary beginning in 90 BC and served with his brothers a fourteen-year mission to reclaim thousands of Lamanites. He later helped Ammon secure an area south of Bountiful where those Lamanites—then known as the Anti-Nephi-Lehies—could live safely, free from the assaults of their former countrymen.

KEY INSIGHTS ABOUT THE SAVIOR

- The Lord has established His church, and nothing will overthrow it.
- The Lord gives to every person conscience—a celestial spark that spurs us to repentance—for the purpose of saving our souls.
- The Lord has all power.
- The Lord hears and answers the prayers of the righteous in behalf of those who are struggling.
- The Lord has redeemed us and through repentance enables us to become new creatures.
- At the last day, all will stand to be judged by the Lord, and all will confess that He is God.

Mosiah 28

"Now they were desirous that salvation could not bear that any human soul

MAJOR CONCEPT

Those who have received the truth and believe on it are desirous that others should be saved.

OVERVIEW The sons of Mosiah, having seen an angel and desiring to preach the gospel, ask their father for permission to go to the land of Nephi and teach their enemies, the Lamanites. The Lord promises He will "deliver" them on their missions (meaning He will deliver them out of the hands of the Lamanites). Mosiah takes their request to the Lord, who approves it. They depart into the wilderness. Mosiah uses the Urim and Thummim to translate the Jaredite plates of gold. Since all of his sons are gone, he confers the plates of brass, the plates of gold, the Urim and Thummim, and all other pertinent things on Alma the Younger. With that act, the rule of the kings ends.

PROMINENT PEOPLE

- King Mosiah
- The sons of Mosiah
- Alma the Younger

INTERESTING FACTS ABOUT THE INTERPRETERS We are told in this chapter that King Mosiah used "those two stones which were fastened into the two rims of a bow" (verse 13) to translate the twenty-four plates of gold that had been found by the people of Limhi. We

MAIN THEMES

- Christianity is the solution to political, social, and economic problems.
- Once we are converted, we desire to teach others the truthfulness of the gospel.
- We serve formal missions as we are called by the Lord to do so.
- When facing the unknown, we should ask the Lord for guidance.

should be declared to every creature, for they should perish. . . ." (Mosiah 28:3)

know those plates of gold to be the book of Ether, a record of the Jaredites from the time the language was confounded at the Tower of Babel until their destruction in the promised land. The interpreter used by King Mosiah was the Urim and Thummim—the same one used by the brother of Jared and by Joseph Smith—and is the same instrument "prepared from the beginning" and "handed down from generation to generation, for the purpose of interpreting languages" (verse 14). We are further told that whoever uses the interpreters is considered to be a seer.

WHO WERE THE SONS OF MOSIAH? The sons of Mosiah—Ammon, Aaron, Omner, and Himni—were initially numbered among the unbelievers who perpetrated crimes against the church. When an angel appeared to them they, along with Alma the Younger, experienced a mighty change of heart and turned from their evil ways to become powerful forces for good in the kingdom of God. Together, they served a fourteen-year mission to the Lamanites, during which time they brought thousands of people unto the Lord.

KEY INSIGHTS ABOUT THE SAVIOR

- The Lord preserves and protects His missionaries.
- The Lord has preserved the Urim and Thummim from the beginning of recorded history so that everyone who possesses it will know of the iniquities and abominations of His people.
- The Lord has held back the complete record of the brother of Jared; we will receive it at a future time (see Ether 4:5–6).

Mosiah 29

"Now it is better that a man should judgments of God are always just, but (Mosiah 29:12)

MAJOR CONCEPT

We have a responsibility to do everything possible to elect good people as our leaders.

OVERVIEW Knowing he is near the end of his reign, King Mosiah asks who the people want as their next king; they choose Mosiah's son Aaron, who is on a mission to the Lamanites in the land of Nephi. None of Mosiah's sons will accept the kingship. Mosiah proposes instead that judges be chosen in place of a king, because he has seen the devastating effects unrighteous kings can have on the people. He has also just completed the translation of the Jaredite record, so he knows that an entire nation ruled by kings was destroyed on this continent. Alma the Younger, who is also the high priest over the church, is chosen by the people as chief judge. This change in government is considered so significant that from this point on, the

PROMINENT PEOPLE

- King Mosiah
- Aaron
- Alma the Younger

Nephites record time from the beginning of the reign of judges (instead of from the time of Lehi leaving Jerusalem). Alma the Elder dies at the age of eighty-two, and King Mosiah dies at the age of sixty-three.

MAIN THEMES

- We should establish correct laws and then choose leaders who rule according to the law.
- Men are not always just; they allow ignorance and love of power to interfere with their being righteous leaders.
- A single evil leader can cause tremendous iniquity and great destruction and can pervert the ways of all righteousness.
- It is extremely difficult to get rid of an evil leader, and the attempt often results in much bloodshed.

- Only the righteous and responsible can be truly free.
- With free agency comes great responsibility.

MOSIAH

600 BC

90 BC

92–91 BC

be judged of God than of man, for the the judgments of man are not always just."

INTERESTING FACTS ABOUT BOOK OF MORMON POLITICS Even though Book of Mormon leaders—some of them kings themselves—are uncomfortable about monarchs and warn the people against the harm that occurs when an unrighteous king takes the throne, the people in general are repeatedly desirous of having a king and living under a monarchy. Such an attitude is in direct contrast to the prevailing attitude at the time Joseph Smith translated the Book of Mormon: people of his time generally viewed monarchs as oppressive. Joseph Smith, in particular, was not that far removed from the American Revolutionary War, in which the colonists fought for freedom from the tyranny of a monarchy. The people of his day considered the Revolutionary War soldiers to be heroes who resisted living under a monarchy. If Joseph Smith had written the Book of Mormon instead of translating it, one would expect the views of the people in the Book of Mormon to more closely reflect the attitudes of the Prophet's times (see *Echoes,* 146–148).

WHO WAS MOSIAH II? The last king on this continent, Mosiah II taught the evils of wicked men as kings and instead suggested that the people be ruled by judges. He taught that it is uncommon for the voice of the people to desire that which is not right, and taught that when the majority chooses wrong they will face destruction. As a result of his influence, judges were appointed by a vote of the people.

> **KEY INSIGHTS ABOUT THE SAVIOR**
>
> - The judgments of the Lord are always just.
> - The Lord will deliver us when we are sufficiently humble and obedient.
> - By giving us agency, the Lord rewards us for our righteousness and punishes us for our transgressions.

Alma 1

"For the hearts of many were hardened . . . a great trial to those that did stand fast in the commandments of God, and they bore with

MAJOR CONCEPT

Priestcraft—the concept of preaching false doctrine for one's own popularity and monetary gain—is against the laws of God and has the capability of destroying a people.

OVERVIEW During Alma's first year in the judgment seat, Nehor practices priestcraft and establishes his own church by luring away the people of God. When Gideon opposes him, Nehor slays Gideon with the sword. Nehor is brought before Alma, sentenced to death for murdering Gideon, and executed despite his confession. After his death, priestcraft still flourishes among the people, but those of the church of God remain steadfast, and the Church prospers.

INTERESTING FACTS ABOUT THE JUDGMENT SEAT In the time of King Zedekiah of Judah, a centuries-old institution called the council of elders was overthrown. In its place, proud and aspiring men assumed the powerful judgment seats—then systematically abused their power, oppressed the nation of Israel, and suppressed criticism of their own unrighteous actions. As a result, the idea of ruling judges was not new—though, sadly, there was not a tradition of righteous men serving in those positions. The judgment

PROMINENT PEOPLE

- Alma the Younger
- Gideon
- Nehor

MAIN THEMES

- We should trust no one to be our teacher or leader unless he is a man of God.

- The important quality in a religious leader is not popularity but reliance on the Spirit and the ability to instill faith in others.

- Capital punishment was a component of the law of Moses.

- Removing a wicked leader does not always eliminate the wicked practices he taught.

- Persecution of the righteous by the wicked has always existed.

- The Church prospers when its members live in righteousness and obey the law.

- Those who fail to obey the laws of the land are disloyal to the Church and to the Lord.

- We are expected to care for the poor and to impart of our goods to those less fortunate.

- We are not to consider ourselves above others; the preacher or teacher is not any better than the learner.

[and] also many withdrew themselves from among them. Now this was faith; nevertheless, they were steadfast and immovable in keeping the patience the persecution which was heaped upon them." (Alma 1:24–25)

seat also existed outside Israel; as one example, Ammon's chief priest, Korihor, seized the Egyptian throne in 1085 BC, after which Ammon's priests ran the country as judges. Because of this history, Lehi and his descendants would have been familiar with the concepts of judges and judgment seats, so the smooth transition from kings to judges in the Book of Mormon makes complete sense (see *Echoes,* 467–468).

WHO WAS NEHOR? Nehor, a man who was extremely strong and large in stature, began preaching among the Nephites around 91 BC; his agenda was that the religious ministry should be professional and should be paid from the public coffers—a system known as priestcraft, which the Lord condemned and which was against the law earlier established by Mosiah. Captivated by his own success and pride, he began to build up a church of his own consisting of followers he was able to lure away from the people of God. When Gideon opposed him, Nehor slew him with the sword. He was brought before Alma and sentenced to death. Even though Nehor confessed that what he had taught was against the word of God (see verse 15), he was executed. Despite his death, his teachings lived on and were subsequently evidenced from time to time among the people.

KEY INSIGHTS ABOUT THE SAVIOR

- The Lord regards priestcraft as an abomination.
- A major false doctrine taught by the purveyors of priestcraft is that all will be saved regardless of what they do; those involved in priestcraft do not believe in repentance for their sins. This discounts the need for a Savior and Redeemer—when in reality it is only through the Atonement of the Savior and through our access of that Atonement as we repent that we can be saved.

"Nevertheless, the Nephites being
prayed mightily to him that he would deliver
therefore the Lord did hear their cries, and

MAJOR CONCEPT

Dissensions will always arise, but those who are on the Lord's side are sustained and strengthened.

OVERVIEW In the first major challenge to the system of judges, Amlici seeks to be king. The people by vote reject Amlici's bid and instead support Alma as chief judge. Bitter over his rejection, Amlici gathers his followers, and they come to battle against the Nephites. When they are defeated, they garner the support of the Lamanites, again come to battle against the Nephites, and are again defeated. Alma slays Amlici.

INTERESTING FACTS ABOUT HERMOUNTS In verse 37, the name *Hermounts* is used to describe the part of the wilderness that was infested by wild and ravenous beasts—in other words, it was the wild country used as hunting grounds. Scholars have found the name very peculiar because it has neither classical

PROMINENT PEOPLE

- Alma the Younger
- Amlici

nor oriental roots. Hugh Nibley pointed out that a similar area existed in Egypt in the land of Month in the Egyptian Pan; it was called Hermonthis after the god of wild places and things—and is linguistically close enough to Hermounts to explain the name (see *Echoes*, 474–475).

MAIN THEMES

- There is safety in following the law.
- We must guard against those who would deprive us of our rights and work to destroy the Church.
- When united against evil, the righteous have power.
- Righteous people must sometimes take up arms to defend their liberty.
- When involved in conflict, we are victorious because of our reliance on the Lord, who will strengthen us against our enemies.

WHO WAS AMLICI? A Nephite dissenter in the land during the time of Alma the Younger, Amlici was a follower of Nehor, who had introduced priestcrafts to the land. Amlici managed to attract a large group of followers who helped him campaign to become king over the people. When the majority of the people rejected his bid to become king, he gathered his followers in battle against the Nephites. Amlici and his forces were defeated, primarily because the Nephites fought with the strength of the Lord. Still determined to defeat his enemies, Amlici entered into an alliance with the Lamanites and came to battle against the Nephites again.

ALMA

strengthened by the hand of the Lord, having them out of the hands of their enemies, did strengthen them. . . ." (Alma 2:28)

Alma himself led the Nephites in battle; they were able to defeat the Amlicites and the Lamanites, and Alma killed Amlici during the battle. As a result of Amlici's rebellion, 12,532 Amlicites died and 6,562 Nephites died—a total of more than 19,000 people died as the result of a wicked king fulfilling Mosiah's words that only through much bloodshed can the people dethrone an iniquitous king (see Mosiah 29:21).

KEY INSIGHTS ABOUT THE SAVIOR

- The Lord goes with His people into battle and strengthens them against their enemies.
- Men of God serve as instruments in the hands of the Lord to save and preserve His people.

Alma 3

> "Now I would that ye should see that [the curse; and even so doth every man that condemnation." (Alma 3:19)

MAJOR CONCEPT

When we choose to follow Satan, we soon find ourselves caught in our own snare; we hurt ourselves through our rebellion.

OVERVIEW Following the defeat of the Amlicites at the hand of the Nephites, the Amlicites join with the Lamanites and, in a desire to distinguish themselves, they paint their foreheads with red paint—unknowingly fulfilling a prophecy that those who rebel against the word of God will be cursed and separated from the people of the Lord (see also 2 Ne. 5:20–21). The Lamanites continue to be cursed for their rebellion and are defeated in battle by the Nephites.

INTERESTING FACTS ABOUT THE TOLL OF BATTLE
Through a single unrighteous act—Amlici's desire to be king—a ripple effect occurred that ended up taking the lives of tens of thousands of people, many of them righteous men, women, and children. Beasts were also killed and fields of crops destroyed, impacting livelihood of the Nephite civilization. In just one battle initiated by Amlici and his people, more than 19,000 people were slain (see

PROMINENT PEOPLE

- Alma
- The Amlicites
- The Lamanites

MAIN THEMES

- Those who are rebellious often distinguish themselves physically.
- When we use our agency to violate the commandments of God, we bring upon ourselves "the curse," meaning the judgment of God.
- We are rewarded by the Lord when we obey Him, but sin brings its own condemnation.
- We hurt ourselves when we rebel against God.
- Every person who is cursed brings that curse upon himself/herself.

Alma 2:19). Over the course of a year, as the Nephites defended themselves from the fallout of Amlici's wicked desires, tens of thousands of people were killed in battle. In this chapter, we learn that the Lamanites who came to battle were naked other than loincloths and armor, and that their heads were shorn; the Amlicites who battled with them painted their foreheads red so they would not be killed by the Lamanites, a direct fulfillment of prophecy (see verse 14) and something Daniel Ludlow theorized could have been the origin of war paint among the Native Americans.

WHAT IS THE DIFFERENCE BETWEEN THE MARK AND THE CURSE ASSOCIATED WITH THE LAMANITES? The *mark* set upon the Lamanites was dark skin, something that was done so that their seed might be distinguished from that of the Nephites. The intent was that the Lamanites and Nephites would not mix, saving the Nephites from believing in incorrect traditions. The *curse* was being cut off from the presence of God (see 2 Ne. 5:20); the Lamanites brought that curse upon themselves, as do all who are cursed. Today, the mark (dark skin) remains upon the descendants of the Lamanites, but the curse does not.

Image: The rebellious often distinguish themselves physically in some way.

KEY INSIGHTS ABOUT THE SAVIOR

- From time to time the Lord separates His people for the purpose of blessing them according to their faithfulness and judging them according to their transgressions.

- The Lord separated the Lamanites from the Nephites so the Nephites would be protected from the false traditions of the Lamanites.

- The Lord rewards the righteous with eternal happiness and curses the wicked with eternal misery, each according to their works and the spirit they obey.

Alma 4

"The people of the church began to be lifted and upon the vain things of the world, that to persecute those that did not believe

MAJOR CONCEPT

We need to constantly guard against pride, which can lead to apostasy.

OVERVIEW Peace returns to the land, and Alma baptizes thousands of converts. Sadly, wickedness and pride again creep into the hearts of the people, and the progress of the church is hindered. As the high priest, Alma desires to devote himself fully to the ministry, so Nephihah is appointed as chief judge to govern the temporal affairs of the people.

INTERESTING FACTS ABOUT THE PRIDE CYCLE In the Book of Mormon, we see a repeated cycle among the people in response to affliction, known as the pride cycle: The people are righteous → The Lord blesses the people → The people prosper → Prosperity leads to pride and

PROMINENT PEOPLE

- Alma the Younger
- Nephihah

apostasy as people lean on themselves → The people lose spiritual power → The people lose the Lord's protection → The people are subjected to war and suffering → The people are humbled → The people turn once again to the Lord → The people become righteous. At that point, the cycle starts all over again. When the people become so wicked that their sufferings no longer humble them, they become ripe for destruction.

WHO WAS NEPHIHAH? Nephihah was the second chief judge in Zarahemla, succeeding Alma the Younger around 83 BC. Alma had become increasingly concerned about the declining spirituality of the people and was inspired by the Spirit to devote himself full-time to the ministry. In order to do that, he chose Nephihah—a wise man who was also an elder in the church (see verse 16)—to govern in a political capacity, a choice that the people approved. Alma

MAIN THEMES

- Affliction often leads to repentance and humility.
- Unless we guard against it, prosperity can lead to pride and a loss of humility, which can eventually lead to apostasy.
- A hallmark of the proud is their failure to assist the poor and needy.
- We can experience hope and joy even in the midst of affliction if we put our faith in the Lord.
- Alma had great political power but used it righteously.

up in the pride of their eyes, and to set their hearts upon riches they began to be scornful, one towards another, and they began according to their own will and pleasure." (Alma 4:8)

delivered up the judgment seat so he could preach the word of God, stir the Nephites to a remembrance of their duty, pull down pride and craftiness, and bear down in pure testimony. Important events during Nephihah's tenure included the destruction of Ammonihah by the Lamanites, the establishment of the protectorate at Jershon for the Lamanites who were converted by the sons of Mosiah, the Zoramite dissension, and the insurrection of Amalickiah. During Nephihah's years of service, the people increased in both commercial ventures and prosperity. Nephihah served righteously as chief judge until his death around 67 BC, when he was replaced by Pahoran.

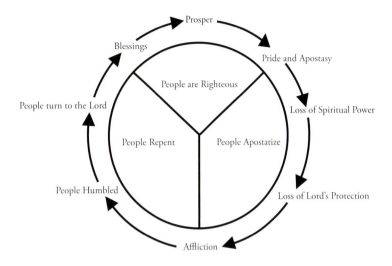

KEY INSIGHTS ABOUT THE SAVIOR

- The Lord knows the impact of pride in our lives and allows affliction to humble us so we will return to an attitude of humility.

- The Lord strengthens and supports His leaders in their efforts to help us.

- The Lord provides remission of our sins when we succor those in need and impart of our substance to the poor.

"And now behold, I ask of you, my brethren been born of God? Have ye received his ye experienced this mighty change in your

MAJOR CONCEPT

The truthfulness of the gospel and its doctrine spells out the things we need to do to gain salvation; unless we repent, we cannot inherit the kingdom of heaven.

OVERVIEW The second-longest chapter in the Book of Mormon, Alma 5 contains more than forty questions (not unlike the temple recommend questions) we should ask ourselves and is much like a conference address—while it touches on many subjects, its overall focus is to bring us back to Christ. In his great discourse to the people of Zarahemla, Alma spells out the things we need to do to gain salvation, testifies of the truth of Christ's doctrine, and calls upon his people to repent. He explains that the names of the righteous will be written in the book of life.

INTERESTING FACTS ABOUT CONVERSION President Marion G. Romney taught that conversion involves a

PROMINENT PEOPLE

- Alma
- Jesus Christ
- The people of Zarahemla

spiritual and moral change that comes along with a change of belief. It involves being "born again," which is a condition of a "newness of life" (Rom. 6:3–4) (see *Look to God and Live,* 109). A person who walks in a newness of life is converted and becomes a partaker of the divine nature. Once we

MAIN THEMES

- Only those who have been born again and have experienced a mighty change of heart will live in the celestial kingdom.

- The Spirit actually transforms a person whose heart is changed, causing him or her to be more like Christ.

- We cannot hope for salvation if we have yielded ourselves to Satan and fail to repent of our transgressions.

- It is a serious offense to experience a mighty change and then relapse into apathy and sin.

- When we sin, we serve Satan.

- To receive the spirit of revelation, we must be as little children.

- Through fasting and prayer, we may know the truth of all things.

- Our birth into the kingdom of heaven takes place when we become alive to the things of the Spirit and have the companionship of the Holy Ghost.

- We must separate ourselves from the wicked and not touch their unclean things.

- We must continually and consistently repent if we are to gain salvation and exaltation.

of the church, have ye spiritually image in your countenance? Have hearts?" (Alma 5:14)

KEY INSIGHTS ABOUT THE SAVIOR

- If we repent, the Lord will receive us.
- All that is good comes from the Lord; all that is evil comes from Satan.
- The things of the Lord are not known or received by the natural man but only through repeated witnesses of the Holy Ghost.
- Jesus Christ came to take away the sins of the world—to take away the sins of every person who steadfastly believes on His name.
- The Lord calls out to us—if we hear His voice and follow Him, He will bring us into His fold.
- If we are not stripped of pride, we are not prepared to meet the Lord.

are converted, that conversion becomes a motivating force that causes a change in our understanding of life's meaning and a change in our allegiance to the Savior and our Heavenly Father. We can know if we have been born again: we will know light from darkness, will recognize the things of God and heaven, and will have no more disposition to do evil.

Alma 6

> "And now it came to pass that [Alma] . . . laying on his hands according to the order of the church." (Alma 6:1)

MAJOR CONCEPT

God's house is a house of order, and maintaining order is one of the great responsibilities of the presiding prophet.

OVERVIEW Following his landmark discourse to the people of Zarahemla, in which he outlined the way to gain salvation, Alma goes about cleansing the church and setting it in order by baptizing those who qualify and excommunicating those who refuse to repent and abandon their wickedness. He then leaves for Gideon, where he begins to preach the gospel.

INTERESTING FACTS ABOUT ORDER The Church is a house of order governed by the spirit of prophecy and revelation. God has ordained that prophets will regulate the affairs of His Church and kingdom according to eternal principles. Alma's extraordinary discourse to the people of Zarahemla helped them have a clear vision of their covenant duties and was instrumental in establishing order in the church in Zarahemla. In our time, President David O. McKay defined the "order of the Church" as the process of "regular arrangements, rules, regulations,

PROMINENT PEOPLE

• Alma the Younger

MAIN THEMES

- Church leaders—beginning with the prophet—are responsible for maintaining order in the Church.

- Leaders of the Church are called by authority and ordained by the laying on of hands.

- Those who repent are to be baptized and received into the Church.

- Church members who are wicked, prideful, and refuse to repent will have their names blotted out from the Church.

- No one should be denied from hearing the word of God.

- We are commanded to gather together often and to join in mighty prayer and fasting for those who do not know God.

- Missionaries and others who preach the gospel do so by revelation.

ordained priests and elders, by God, to preside and watch over

and operations so that everything is in its proper place and working well . . . being directed by the priesthood" (*Gospel Ideals,* 85). President John Taylor explained the concept of order in the Church when he wrote, "The order of the church is for us to fulfil and magnify the calling to which we are called, and do it with an eye single to the glory of God, each man fulfilling the various duties and responsibilities of his office" (*The Gospel Kingdom,* 150–151).

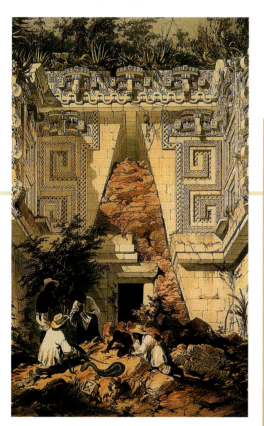

Image: Central American ruins.

KEY INSIGHTS ABOUT THE SAVIOR

- The Lord will redeem us from our sins.
- Prophets knew of the Lord long before He was born; Alma declared the word of God according to the revelations of prophets, the spirit of prophecy, and his testimony of Jesus even before Jesus was born into the world.

Alma 7

"And he shall go forth, suffering pains and every kind; and this that the word might be upon him the pains and the sicknesses of

MAJOR CONCEPT

Jesus Christ came to earth and suffered for our pains, sicknesses, afflictions, and sins, and the way to eternal life is to repent and obey His commandments.

OVERVIEW While Alma had to preach repentance to the people of Zarahemla, he commends the people of Gideon for their righteousness. In this discourse to the people of Gideon, Alma bears testimony of the Savior and prophesies of Christ's coming. He testifies that those who are wicked cannot inherit the kingdom of God and explains that those who repent, are baptized, and keep the commandments with humility, faith, hope, and charity will gain eternal life.

INTERESTING FACTS ABOUT CHRIST BEING BORN AT JERUSALEM In his discourse to the people of Gideon, Alma says that the Savior will be born of Mary "at Jerusalem" (verse 10). Alma's prophecy that Jesus would be

PROMINENT PEOPLE

- Alma the Younger
- Jesus Christ

born "at Jerusalem" has drawn significant criticism since the initial publication of the Book of Mormon in 1830, because as all Christians know, Jesus was born in the town of Bethlehem. There are two ways to answer that criticism. First, the discovery of the Dead Sea Scrolls and other ancient

MAIN THEMES

- Prophets feel great joy over our righteousness.
- Nothing that is filthy can be received into the kingdom of God.
- Though repentance is possible, it is always preferable for us to remain righteous and not commit transgression.
- When we repent, our sins are blotted out as a result of the Atonement.
- We cannot inherit the kingdom of heaven unless we are born again.
- When we are baptized, we witness to the Lord that we are willing to repent and to covenant to keep His commandments.
- Whoever keeps the commandments of the Lord until the end will have eternal life.
- As followers of Christ, we are required to be humble, submissive, gentle, patient, long-suffering, temperate, diligent in keeping the commandments, and quick to thank the Lord for the things we are given.
- If we have faith, hope, and charity, we will always abound in good works.

afflictions and temptations of fulfilled which saith he will take his people." (Alma 7:11)

documents shows that Bethlehem was anciently considered part of the "land of Jerusalem" (see *Echoes,* 211). Second, the Bible Dictionary defines *at* as meaning close to, by, or within; since Bethlehem is only six miles from Jerusalem, it would certainly qualify under that definition. Alma was likely simply thinking of a geographical point when he said Christ would be born "at Jerusalem." Also, the angel told the shepherds, "For unto you is born this day in the city of David a Saviour, which is Christ the Lord" (Luke 2:11). Both 2 Kings 14:20 and 2 Samuel 5:6–7 identify the City of David as Jerusalem (see *Answers to Gospel Questions,* 1:174, 175).

KEY INSIGHTS ABOUT THE SAVIOR

- The Savior was born of Mary near Jerusalem.
- Mary conceived the Savior by the power of the Holy Ghost; God is His Father.
- The Lord did not minister among the Nephites while He was in mortality.
- The Lord suffered pain, afflictions, and temptations of every kind so He would be uniquely qualified to succor us in our suffering. The Atonement covers all our pains, sicknesses, and infirmities, whether physical, mental, emotional, or spiritual. Anything brought upon us by the Fall can be removed through the Atonement.
- The Savior took upon Himself all our sins.
- Jesus Christ loosed the bands of death.

Alma 8

> "And behold, I am sent to command thee preach again unto the people of the city; . . . the Lord he returned speedily to the land of

MAJOR CONCEPT

The Lord always provides a second witness for those who are proclaiming the truth.

OVERVIEW Continuing on his mission to preach the gospel, Alma preaches and baptizes in Melek. He then goes to Ammonihah but is rejected of the people; leaving the city, he goes toward the city of Aaron. The Lord through His angel commands Alma to return to Ammonihah and cry repentance to the people; he speedily obeys and is received by Amulek, who had been told by an angel that Alma is coming. Amulek takes care of Alma and then becomes his companion in preaching the gospel.

INTERESTING FACTS ABOUT THE LAW OF WITNESSES When Alma was commanded by the Lord to return to Ammonihah, he was received by Amulek, who recognized

PROMINENT PEOPLE

- Alma the Younger
- Amulek

MAIN THEMES

- Those under evil influence are not touched by the Spirit.
- Alma's speed in returning to Ammonihah is an example of the way in which we should speedily obey.
- Those who preach the gospel worthily are filled with the Spirit and protected by the Lord.
- We are called by the Lord to preach; we do not appoint ourselves.

Alma as a prophet of God and subsequently served alongside him as a second witness of the truth, something that led many to accept the gospel. Elder Bruce R. McConkie wrote, "Never does one man stand alone in establishing a new dispensation of revealed truth, or in carrying the burden of such a message and warning to the world. In every dispensation from Adam to the present, two or more witnesses have always joined their testimonies, thus leaving their hearers without excuse in the day of judgment should the testimony be rejected" (*Mormon Doctrine*, 436). The Lord's law of witnesses is found in both the Old Testament (see Deut. 19:15) and the New Testament (see 2 Cor. 13:1).

WHO WAS AMULEK? Amulek was a prominent citizen of the city of Ammonihah, which was steeped in full-scale apostasy when Alma arrived there to preach the gospel around 82 BC. When

ALMA

that thou return to the city of Ammonihah, and after Alma had received his message from the angel of Ammonihah." (Alma 8:16–18)

Alma returned a second time to the city, Amulek received him into his home and cared for him; the two then went forth to declare repentance to the people. Amulek was Alma's missionary companion during many of Alma's travels to preach the gospel to the Nephites, and he taught powerfully that prayer is a force for good, that the Lord would come to redeem the people from their sins, that the people needed to follow the Spirit in all things, that the Resurrection was a certainty, and that the infinite Atonement was essential for the salvation of mankind. When Alma and Amulek were thrown into prison, they were delivered by the hand of the Lord, who commanded that they leave Ammonihah; several years later, the city was attacked by the Lamanites and was completely destroyed and left desolate.

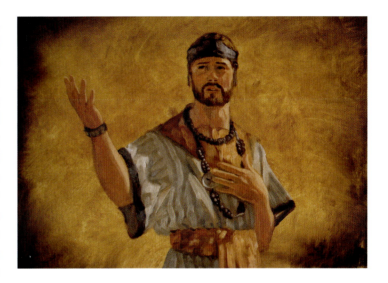

Key Insights about the Savior

- The Lord sent Alma back to Ammonihah because He knew the people there were so wicked that they would eventually destroy the liberty of the few who were righteous.
- The Lord will visit in anger those who refuse to repent.
- The Lord can protect His servants even to the point that they cannot be slain.
- The Lord sometimes allows things to happen so that He can demonstrate His power; Alma and Amulek were allowed to be cast into prison that the Lord might show forth His power in releasing them.

Alma 9

"[The] Lamanites have been cut off from [the
Nevertheless I say unto you, that it shall be more
in your sins, yea, and even more tolerable for

MAJOR CONCEPT

Where much is given, much is required; those who know nothing of the Lord are far better off than we unless we live our religion.

OVERVIEW This and the next chapter are the account of Alma's second missionary journey to the city of Ammonihah; an account of his experiences continues in Chapters 12 through 14.

INTERESTING FACTS ABOUT NAMES IN THE BOOK OF MORMON In the Old Testament, not a single surname is given; each person is simply known by one name. And when those names are translated into English, no biblical name contains the letters *q, x,* or *w,* and no name begins with *f.* Similarly, of the hundreds of characters in the Book of Mormon, none contains the letters *q, x,* or *w*; none begins with the letter *f*; and no surnames are given. Had Joseph Smith fabricated the Book of Mormon, he would have likely given at least some of the characters surnames, since that was a strongly established tradition in his day—and would also have almost certainly included names that began with *f* or contained the letters *q, x,* or *w* (see *Echoes,* 159–160).

PROMINENT PEOPLE

- Alma the Younger
- Amulek
- The people of Ammonihah

MAIN THEMES

- Those with hardened hearts do not understand the works and potential of the Lord.

- Those who keep the Lord's commandments will prosper, but those who refuse to keep the commandments will be cut off from the presence of the Lord.

- Those who have never known the truth will be under less condemnation than those of us who know the truth but refuse to repent and obey.

- If we fail to repent, we remain in our sins.

- In our day, many of the Lamanites will be converted to the gospel, will recognize that the traditions of their fathers are incorrect, and will be saved.

- Each of us will reap a reward according to our works—if we are righteous, we will reap salvation; if we are wicked, we will reap damnation and will be captive to the devil.

- Hardhearted and stiffnecked people are often angered by the words of prophets.

Lord's] presence, from the beginning of their transgressions in the land. tolerable for them in the day of judgment than for you, if ye remain them in this life than for you, except ye repent." (Alma 9:14–15)

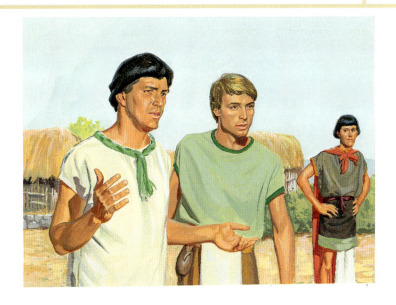

KEY INSIGHTS ABOUT THE SAVIOR

- The Lord will destroy those who refuse to repent.
- The Lord will be merciful to all who call on His name.
- The promises of the Lord are extended to the Lamanites.
- The Lord has firmly decreed that if those who have been given light and knowledge then rebel against Him, He will utterly destroy them from off the face of the earth.
- The Lord would rather have His people destroyed than allow them to live in sin.
- The Lord is the Only Begotten of the Father, full of grace, equity, and truth, full of patience, mercy, and long-suffering.
- Under most conditions, the Lord is quick to hear the cries of His people and to answer their prayers.

Image: Amulek and Alma preaching.

Alma 10

MAJOR CONCEPT

Our own testimonies are strengthened as we listen to those to whom the truth has been given.

OVERVIEW After Alma finishes teaching the people of Ammonihah, Amulek begins teaching them. He starts by stating his lineage and background—giving his credentials, so to speak—and then relates the angelic visitation he had in which he was commissioned to care for Alma and work with him in the ministry. He calls the people to repentance and says that they have been preserved only because of the prayers of the righteous. He denounces the unrighteousness of the lawyers and judges.

INTERESTING FACTS ABOUT AMULEK'S LINEAGE In his discourse Amulek provides his lineage and says he is a descendant of Lehi, who was a descendant of Manasseh.

MAIN THEMES

- Even those whose hearts have been hardened can be changed.
- Like Amulek, we reap tremendous blessings through obedience.
- Those who enter into transgression and do not repent are ripe for destruction.
- The prayers of the righteous in a land of otherwise wicked people have the power to stay the destruction of that land.
- Those who are doing iniquity become angry when their sins are pointed out to them.

PROMINENT PEOPLE

- Alma the Younger
- Amulek

This is the first clarification in the Book of Mormon that Lehi descended from Manasseh. It is well known that the tribes of Ephraim and Manasseh were taken into captivity in 721 BC when the Babylonians overthrew Jerusalem. It is less well known that in 941 BC King Asa gathered Judah and Benjamin and "strangers" (see 2 Chron. 15:9) out of Ephraim and Manasseh. According to Daniel Ludlow, those "strangers" included the forefathers of Lehi and Ishmael (see *A Companion to Your Study of the Book of Mormon,* 199). Amulek was the perfect companion for Alma—he had a known reputation, he was related to several people in Ammonihah and had many friends there, he was a successful businessman who was influential and wealthy, he had witnessed God's power before he became inactive, and he had seen an angel and had been called by God.

600 BC

90 BC

whereof [Alma] hath testified are the Lord liveth, even so has he sent unto me. . . ." (Alma 10:10)

WHO WAS AMINADI? As Alma 10 opens, Amulek is addressing the people of Ammonihah; he gives his background and lineage so he can establish credibility with the people to whom he is preaching. He says that he is a descendant of Aminadi, "who interpreted the writing which was upon the wall of the temple, which was written by the finger of God" (verse 2). Amulek's discourse is the only mention of Aminadi in the Book of Mormon, and is the only reference we have to the writing on the wall of the temple. From Amulek we know that Aminadi was a descendant of Lehi through Nephi; we assume he was a righteous man if he was given the ability to interpret writing done by the finger of God.

Image: The prophet Daniel also read the writing on the temple wall.

KEY INSIGHTS ABOUT THE SAVIOR

- The Lord often blesses us through others.
- The Lord uses the law of witnesses, always providing a second (and sometimes third) witness to the preaching of truth.
- The Lord will help us perceive the motives and thoughts of those we are teaching when they are trying to contradict or trick us.
- Those who pervert the ways of the righteous will bring down the wrath of the Lord upon their heads.
- The Savior will come among us with equity and justice.
- If all the righteous are cast out of the land, the Lord will smite the wicked of that land.

"Yea, he is the very Eternal Father of he is the beginning and the end, the first his people. . . ." (Alma 11:39–40)

MAJOR CONCEPT

While the Lord performed the magnificent Atonement to save all mankind, He will not save those who refuse to repent.

OVERVIEW As this chapter begins, the Nephite money system is explained in context of the unrighteous lawyers, whose sole purpose is to get gain. One reason for that explanation is to show how huge the bribe was that Zeezrom offered Amulek—as much as $80,000 in today's money (see *Book of Mormon Reference Companion,* 609). Amulek contends with the lawyer Zeezrom and bears powerful testimony of the Savior, His Atonement, and His Resurrection, telling Zeezrom that men will not be saved in their sins. Zeezrom begins to tremble as he becomes conscious of his guilt.

INTERESTING FACTS ABOUT THE MONETARY SYSTEM In its money, as in so many other ways, the Book of Mormon corresponds closely to other ancient cultures. A collection of Babylonian inscriptions called the Code of Eshnunna includes an elaborate description of weights and measures that resembles the system of weights and measures described in the Book of Mormon. In addition, the primary

PROMINENT PEOPLE

• Amulek
• Zeezrom

MAIN THEMES

• The time may come when we are tempted to deny our faith for worldly goods or popularity.

• Those who refuse to repent remain as though there had been no Atonement.

• Every person will be resurrected and restored to his or her perfect frame—the condition that existed before coming to earth.

• When we stand at the judgment bar, we will have a bright recollection of all our guilt.

• There will be no death after the resurrection; the physical body will be united with the spirit, becoming a spiritual body.

600 BC

90 BC

conversion in Babylon was between silver and barley—the value of precious metal was determined by how much grain it could buy. The law in the Book of Mormon (see Alma 11:15) was based on the same factor—the basic measure for silver or gold was equal to "a measure of barley" (see *Echoes,* 348–350). In Guatemala today, they still use a system of weights and measures called a *markos,* which consists of a series of brass cups inside one another. It uses the same system outlined in verses 9–13.

WHO WAS ZEEZROM? Zeezrom was a lawyer in the city of Ammonihah during the time that Alma and Amulek were preaching repentance; the tactic of the lawyers in that city was to stir the people up against each other and cause all kinds of disturbances so they might get more business. Zeezrom was one of the most expert of the lawyers in Ammonihah, and was the most aggressive in accusing Alma and Amulek. He engaged Amulek in a lengthy argument, attempting to trip him up, but ended up becoming increasingly fearful as he became more aware that his position was completely wrong. When Alma explained the principles of repentance, Zeezrom recognized the truth and later repented. See more about Zeezrom in the next chapter.

Top Image: A senine, seon, shum, and limnah.

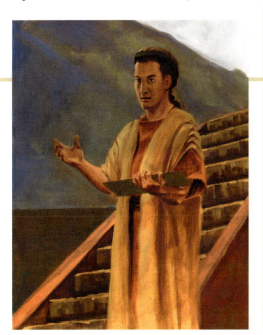

KEY INSIGHTS ABOUT THE SAVIOR

- Jesus Christ is the Son of the living God.
- Jesus Christ will not save us in our sins—in other words, His Atonement does not cover those who refuse to repent.
- The Savior is the Eternal Father of heaven and earth, the beginning and the end, the first and the last.
- Jesus Christ took upon Himself the transgressions of those who believe on His name; those who exercise faith in the Atonement by repenting are those who will receive salvation.
- Because of the Savior, everyone who ever lived will be resurrected; His gift of resurrection is universal and unconditional.
- The Savior will be joined at the judgment by the Father and the Holy Ghost.

Alma 12

"We must come forth and stand before him and acknowledge . . . that he is just in all his all power to save every man that believeth on

MAJOR CONCEPT

This life is the time to repent and prepare in all ways to meet the Lord.

OVERVIEW After Amulek catches Zeezrom in his lies, Alma contends further with Zeezrom—but soon Zeezrom's questions become an effort to gain knowledge instead of an attempt to set a snare. Alma defines the chains of hell as being taken captive by the devil and led to destruction because we do not know the word of God. Alma explains that men are judged by their thoughts, words, and deeds and that mortality is a probationary time in which men must repent. He explains the plan of redemption, teaches of the resurrection, and testifies that only those who repent have a claim on the Savior's mercy.

PROMINENT PEOPLE

- Alma
- Amulek
- Zeezrom
- Antionah

INTERESTING FACTS ABOUT THOUGHTS AND INTENTS All of us are familiar with the notion that our motives reveal our true character and that our thoughts dictate our actions. In this chapter, Alma teaches that not only will our words and works condemn us, but also our thoughts (see

MAIN THEMES

- The mysteries of God are given only to those sensitive enough to the Spirit to know when they can or cannot be shared with others.

- An adversary is one who acts contrary to someone else's purposes; by being intent on thwarting God's plan, Lucifer became "the adversary," and he seeks to bring us into his captivity and everlasting destruction.

- We cannot obey the commandments unless we know them.

- Those who harden their hearts receive a lesser portion of the word of God until they know nothing; when we do not harden our hearts, we receive increasingly more knowledge until our knowledge is full.

- We will be condemned if our hearts are hardened.

- We will be condemned by our words, works, and thoughts as well as by the intents of our hearts.

- This life is a probationary state in which we prepare to meet God.

- We will face the Savior at the judgment bar and know that He is just.

- Those who do not repent cannot be redeemed and will suffer the second death.

ALMA

in his glory, and in his power, and in his might, majesty, and dominion, works, and that he is merciful unto the children of men, and that he has his name and bringeth forth fruit meet for repentance." (Alma 12:15)

verse 14). President Spencer W. Kimball taught, "It is well for all of us to realize that our thought sins as well as all other sins are recorded in heaven. . . . There will be no omissions in the heavenly records, and they will all be available at the day of judgment" (see *The Miracle of Forgiveness,* 103–115).

WHO WAS ZEEZROM? As explained in the previous chapter, Zeezrom was a lawyer in Ammonihah who, after contending with Amulek, was taught the principle of repentance, repented of his sins, and was consequently cast out. When Alma and Amulek were seized and imprisoned, many innocent believers were martyred; the Lord destroyed the prison in an earthquake and commanded Alma and Amulek to depart to Sidom. There they learned that Zeezrom was incapacitated with a burning fever, the result of his belief that Alma and Amulek had died as a result of his wickedness. Alma and Amulek went to Zeezrom to comfort him; Alma gave him a blessing, in which Zeezrom was healed, and Alma subsequently baptized Zeezrom. This was possibly included in the record to show a principle of repentance: no matter how corrupt a person is (even a lawyer who would try to bribe a prophet to deny God), repentance is still available and possible. The new convert began from that time forward to preach the gospel; several years later he became one of Alma's missionary companions in Antionum.

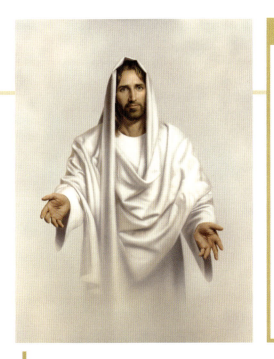

KEY INSIGHTS ABOUT THE SAVIOR

- The Lord knows our thoughts and the intents of our hearts.
- All the judgments of the Lord are just.
- The Savior executed the plan of redemption, which was prepared before the world was created.
- The Lord's mercy extends to all those who repent; they will receive a remission of their sins as a result of the Lord's Atonement.

Alma 13

"Humble yourselves before the Lord, and pray continually, that ye may not bear. . . . " (Alma 13:28)

MAJOR CONCEPT

We need to humble ourselves and repent so that we can be sanctified and made pure.

OVERVIEW Alma continues preaching to the people of Ammonihah. He explains the office of high priest and teaches of Melchizedek. He testifies that angels are declaring glad tidings throughout the land and that they will reveal the coming of the Savior.

PROMINENT PEOPLE

- Alma
- Melchizedek

INTERESTING FACTS ABOUT FOREORDINATION Foreordination is the premortal selection of individuals to come forth in mortality at specified times, under certain conditions, to fulfill predesignated responsibilities. The Prophet Joseph Smith taught that every man who "has a calling to minister to the inhabitants of the world was ordained to that very purpose in the Grand Council of Heaven before this world was" (Smith, *Teachings of the Prophet Joseph Smith,* 365). Foreordination is not the same as predetermination, which involves no choice; instead, foreordination is the outcome of voluntary choice. Foreordination comes as a blessing or reward for premortal righteousness and

MAIN THEMES

- Faithful men held priesthood power and authority in their premortal life.

- In our premortal life, we all had equal opportunity to progress through righteousness.

- We all had agency to choose good or evil in our premortal life; some were more valiant and earned a greater reward.

- When sin becomes so distasteful to us that we purge it completely from our lives, we become sanctified and pure in heart.

- Those who reject the scriptures do so to their own destruction.

- We need to humble ourselves and watch and pray continually that we won't be tempted above what we can bear and that we will be led by the Spirit.

valiant commitment to Jesus Christ; through righteousness in mortality, we can be "adopted" into certain lineages that are foreordained to certain blessings. It is also possible that those who are foreordained may fail their foreordination and give up the associated blessings through sin and rebellion (see Brent L. Top in *Encyclopedia of Mormonism*, 521–522). Elder Neal A. Maxwell said that whether it is foreordination for men or foredesignation for women, those called must prove faithful (see Conference Report, Oct. 1985, 21).

WHO WAS MELCHIZEDEK? Melchizedek, the king of Salem, was the great high priest and prophet who lived at the time of Abraham, approximately 2,000 years before Christ. When Melchizedek became prophet, Salem was under a veil of spiritual darkness and rebellion, but his faith and righteousness had such an impact on the people that they were all brought back into the fold. He was placed in charge of the Lord's kingdom as the keeper of the storehouse and the person to receive tithes; Abraham paid tithing to Melchizedek. His righteousness was so unmatched and he magnified his office so well that the higher priesthood was named after him. Many people believe that Melchizedek was without father or mother because of Hebrews 7:3. The Book of Mormon makes clear that it is the *priesthood* named after Melchizedek that is without father or mother (see Alma 13:8, 9).

KEY INSIGHTS ABOUT THE SAVIOR

- The Lord declares glad tidings through the voice of angels.
- The "rest of the Lord" involves the fullness of God's glory.
- The Savior's Atonement gives us the opportunity to repent and be made pure, thus escaping the chains of hell.
- The ordinances of the Melchizedek Priesthood (the temple ordinances) are types of the Son of God.

Alma 14

MAJOR CONCEPT

The way in which we deal with our trials and afflictions will determine in part the reward we receive.

OVERVIEW When Alma finishes testifying to the people, some believe his words and repent; most, however, are angry and want to destroy Alma and Amulek. Many of the righteous are cast into a fire along with their scriptures and are received by the Lord as martyrs; Alma and Amulek are cast into prison. The Lord destroys the prison in an earthquake and frees Alma and Amulek. Those who persecuted Alma and Amulek are slain.

INTERESTING FACTS ABOUT THE SUFFERING OF THE INNOCENT The righteous often suffer persecution for the sake of the gospel. Most of the people taught by Alma and Amulek refused to believe and condemned those who did believe to a fiery martyrdom. The Spirit constrained Alma from intervening to stop the persecution so that the impending judgments against the wicked would be just. Why are the righteous persecuted? President Harold B. Lee wrote that "To be persecuted for righteousness sake in a great cause where truth and virtue and honor are at stake is god-like" (*Decisions for Successful Living,* 61). President Spencer W. Kimball taught that if righteous people were never allowed to suffer, "there would be no test of strength, no development of character, no growth of powers, no free agency. . . . There would also be an absence of joy, success, resurrection, eternal life, and godhood" (*The Teachings of Spencer W. Kimball,* 77).

PROMINENT PEOPLE

- Alma
- Amulek
- Zeezrom

MAIN THEMES

- The wicked become angry when their wickedness is revealed.
- Once we repent, we feel great sorrow over those we influenced in our wickedness.
- The blood of righteous martyrs stands as a witness against those who persecuted them.
- Wicked people seek physical signs to prove the reality of God.

ALMA

600 BC

90 BC

constraineth me that I must not stretch
receiveth [the martyrs] up unto himself, in
do this thing. . . ." (Alma 14:11)

KEY INSIGHTS ABOUT THE SAVIOR

- The Lord sometimes permits the righteous to suffer or die, both for their experience and for His own reasons.
- The Lord sometimes allows the wicked to hurt the righteous so that His wrath and punishment are justified.
- The Lord receives martyrs to righteousness in glory.
- The Lord does not allow people to be taken in death before their mission is accomplished.
- The Lord hears the cries and prayers of the righteous.
- The Lord grants power to the righteous.

Alma 15

MAJOR CONCEPT

Those who believe in the Lord and follow Him experience both physical and spiritual healing.

OVERVIEW After escaping from prison, Alma and Amulek are commanded by the Lord to go to Sidom, where the righteous have fled; there they establish a church. Zeezrom, who had been burning with fever because he thought his wickedness had led to the deaths of Alma and Amulek, learns they are alive and sends for them. Alma gives Zeezrom a blessing; he is healed and baptized and teaches the gospel to the people in Sidom. The Church prospers, and Alma and Amulek return to Zarahemla.

INTERESTING FACTS ABOUT INFLUENCE OF THE SPIRIT ON THE BODY As it becomes clear to Zeezrom that his beliefs and behavior were wrong, we are told that he was

PROMINENT PEOPLE

- Alma
- Amulek
- Zeezrom

"harrowed up" (Alma 14:6). To harrow is to break up earth that has been hardened through disuse and neglect so that seeds can be planted and grow in the earth. The same kind of process needs to take place in hearts that have been hardened so that the seed of the gospel and the desire for repentance can be planted there. Zeezrom did experience a change of heart. When word of the destruction of the prison in Ammonihah reached him, Zeezrom mistakenly thought Alma and Amulek had been killed. His mind was again harrowed up (see verse 3) as he realized that his previous behavior contributed to their deaths. As he pondered this, he became incapacitated and began burning up with fever. This is just one example of how vital spiritual well-being is to physical health. Two decades of landmark medical research have recently shown that negative spiritual conditions—such as hostility, hate, envy, and anger—lead to

MAIN THEMES

- Sin and its effects can negatively impact physical health.
- There is great power in sacrificing the things of the world for the things of eternity.
- Praying continually helps deliver us from Satan.
- Those involved in priestcraft do not believe in repentance; they put their faith in money and popularity instead of in the Atonement. Priest-craft on earth is basically the alternative Satan proposed in our premortal existence: salvation without regard to works.

ALMA

600 BC

90 BC

220

Christ thou canst be healed." (Alma 15:8)

actual physical changes that harm health. On the other side, the same research has shown that positive spiritual conditions—such as love, forgiveness, prayer, worship, and service—lead to positive changes in the immune system that protect health. President Boyd K. Packer testified that body and spirit are bound together, and quoted a physician who said that only 20 percent of the maladies he treats are actual physical disorders (see "The Balm of Gilead," *Ensign*, Nov. 1977, 59).

KEY INSIGHTS ABOUT THE SAVIOR

- The Lord is the one who makes possible salvation.
- The Lord redeems those who believe in and obey Him.
- Faith in Christ has powerful potential to heal.

Image: A farmer harrowing his fields.

Alma 16

"And many of the people did inquire God should come; and they were taught resurrection; and this the people did hear

Major Concept

We need to assess our spiritual readiness to meet the Savior and make corrections as they are needed.

OVERVIEW In fulfillment of Alma's prophecy (see Alma 9:4), the city of Ammonihah is destroyed in a single day by the Lamanites, who take some people from the city captive into the wilderness. Zoram, chief of the Nephite army, seeks direction from Alma and engages the Lamanites in battle, scattering them into the wilderness and freeing the captives. Alma, Amulek, and many others preach the gospel; they testify that Christ will appear to the Lamanites after His resurrection.

INTERESTING FACTS ABOUT AMMONIHAH AS A TYPE "Ammonihah, a city pretending religion, a religion perfectly tolerant of any action save it be the preaching of

Prominent People

- Alma
- Amulek
- Zoram

the gospel of repentance! To preach repentance, to testify of Christ, to speak of the necessity of good works—these were sins too grievous to be borne. Their effect was to unite in wrath and bitterness the diversified factions within the congregations of this purportedly "ever-tolerant" religion. These missionaries of righteousness must be mocked, ridiculed, beaten, and imprisoned. Their adherents must be stoned, driven from the community, or burned at the stake. Such were the seeds they planted and such was the harvest they reaped in the desolation of Nehors. We are left to wonder to what extent Ammonihah is a prophetic foreshadowing of . . . events that will precede and attend the coming of our Lord and Master that will bring again that peace once known to the faithful of the Nephite nation" (McConkie and Millet, *Doctrinal Commentary on the Book of Mormon,* 3:119).

Main Themes

- Despite powerful preaching, people may still reject the truth.
- Those who receive the Lord are privileged to enter His rest, overcoming physical and spiritual death to enter the presence of the Lord.

concerning the place where the Son of that he would appear unto them after his with great joy and gladness." (Alma 16:20)

WHO WAS ZORAM? Zoram—mentioned only twice in the Book of Mormon—was chief captain over the Nephite armies at the time the Lamanites attacked and destroyed the city of Ammonihah in 81 BC in fulfillment of prophecy. Some of the people of Ammonihah were taken captive by the Lamanites. Zoram asked Alma, the high priest, where he should take his armies to recover the captives; Alma received direction from the Lord, which he passed on to Zoram. Zoram took his two sons—Aha and Lehi—and his armies and engaged the Lamanites in battle. As a result, the Lamanites were scattered and driven into the wilderness, and Zoram was able to return the Nephite prisoners to their homes unhurt. He is not the Zoram who was Laban's servant or the Zoram who founded the Zoramites.

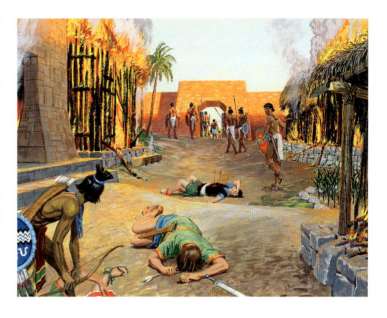

KEY INSIGHTS ABOUT THE SAVIOR

- Where there is no inequality, the Lord pours out His Spirit on people to prepare them to hear His word.
- The Lord blesses true Saints with the ability to enter into His rest.
- The Lord visited the Nephites following His mortal ministry and Resurrection.

Alma 17

MAJOR CONCEPT

In order to be effective missionaries we must show forth love, be patient in long-suffering, and be examples of righteousness.

OVERVIEW As Alma continues his missionary labors, he encounters the sons of Mosiah, who have been preaching with the spirit of prophecy and revelation for fourteen years. They had gone their separate ways to do missionary work among the Lamanites. One of the sons of Mosiah, Ammon, goes to the land of Ishmael and becomes the servant of King Lamoni so that he can remain in the land and overcome the Lamanite hatred. While guarding the king's sheep at the Waters of Sebus, Ammon saves the king's flocks and slays those who attempt to steal them.

INTERESTING POSSIBILITIES ABOUT PLUNDER AT THE WATERS OF SEBUS The "practice of plunder" among the Lamanites at the Waters of Sebus was probably much like a game that followed specific rules. Ammon's slaying of several men and smiting off the arms of others appears harsh, but archaeological evidence shows that in many such ceremonial games the loser was killed. Examples of such

PROMINENT PEOPLE

- Alma
- King Lamoni
- Ammon
- The sons of Mosiah

MAIN THEMES

- We can gain the spirit of prophecy and revelation by searching the scriptures, praying and fasting often, and serving the Lord even under the most trying of circumstances.

- The most effective teaching is that done by the power and authority of God.

- The key to being effective in missionary work is to love those we teach.

- We can seek the help of the Lord in touching the hearts of those we want to teach.

afflictions, that ye may show forth
will make an instrument of thee in my
(Alma 17:11)

deadly games include Aztec duels, chariot races of the princes, the ancient game of Nemi, and others. The most dramatic example of this phenomenon may be the ball games played in ancient Mesoamerica, in which members of the losing team were often beheaded (see *Echoes,* 478–479).

WHO WAS AMMON? Ammon was one of the sons of Mosiah who, with Alma the Younger, were visited by an angel and called to repentance. Following his miraculous conversion, Ammon desired more than anything else to declare the gospel of Jesus Christ to every creature. He and his brothers embarked on a missionary journey among the Lamanites that lasted fourteen years. At one point they separated in order to teach greater numbers, and Ammon journeyed to the land of Ishmael around 90 BC. When the Lamanites discovered him, he was bound and taken to King Lamoni; expressing his desire to serve the king, Ammon saved the king's flocks and destroyed the king's enemies. Lamoni was converted by Ammon and overcome by the Spirit; he later joined with Ammon in preaching to his people. When Ammon's brothers were imprisoned in Middoni, Ammon and King Lamoni succeeded in freeing them. While on that journey, Ammon's example prepared the father of King Lamoni—king over all the Lamanite people—to respond to the missionary message of Aaron and come into the fold with much of his nation. Later, Ammon and his brothers helped the converted Lamanites distinguish themselves from their hard-hearted brethren and gather in the land of Jershon, where they became known by the Nephites as the people of Ammon.

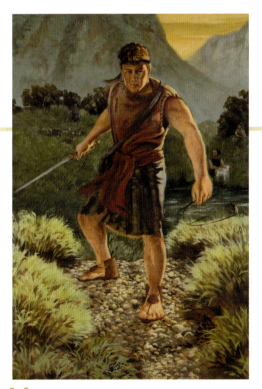

KEY INSIGHTS ABOUT THE SAVIOR

- The Lord prepares people to hear and receive the gospel.
- The Lord protects and strengthens those who serve Him.

Alma 18

> "And Ammon said: Yea, and [God] men; and he knows all the thoughts and they all created from the beginning."

MAJOR CONCEPT

The proper motivation for missionary work is a love of people and the desire to bring them peace and joy.

OVERVIEW After saving King Lamoni's flocks, Ammon is brought before the king, who believes that Ammon is the Great Spirit. His belief in a Great Spirit is evidence that the Lamanites had retained a fragment of the truth. Ammon teaches him correct doctrine regarding the existence of God, the Creation, the redemption that comes through the Savior, and God's dealings with His children. Lamoni believes Alma and is overcome with the Spirit. He falls to the ground as if dead, and his family mourns.

INTERESTING FACTS ABOUT "WISE AND HARMLESS" In verse 22, we are told that Ammon was "wise, yet harmless." There is only one other place in the scriptures where these words are used in counterposition to each other— Matthew 10:16, where the Savior instructs the Twelve, "Behold I send you forth as sheep in the midst of wolves: be ye therefore wise as serpents, and harmless as

PROMINENT PEOPLE

- Ammon
- King Lamoni

MAIN THEMES

- When we live so that we reflect the Spirit of the Lord, others will want to listen to us.

- We demonstrate our spirituality by how we live and how we treat others.

- A key to effective missionary work is to establish a relationship with and serve those we want to teach.

- The power to discern thoughts is given by the Holy Spirit to servants of the Lord.

- When teaching others, we need to teach at the level they are prepared to comprehend.

- We gain knowledge through the Holy Ghost.

- The Spirit can overcome the natural body, as demonstrated not only by King Lamoni, but by Alma the Younger (see Mosiah 27), Zeezrom (see Alma 11–12), King Lamoni's father (see Alma 22), Moses (see Moses 1:9–10), Paul (see Acts 9:1–10), and Joseph Smith (see JS—H 1:20, 48).

looketh down upon all the children of
intents of the heart; for by his hand were
(Alma 18:32)

doves." Ammon was harmless—without guile, pure, with an eye single to the glory of God. He was also wise—skillful in establishing a framework of operation where his listeners would be guided into a state in which they would be receptive to the Spirit.

WHO WAS RABBANAH? *Rabbanah* was the title given to Ammon by one of the king's servants (see verse 13). In this verse, we are told that *rabbanah* means "powerful or great king." This provides evidence that the language of the Nephites and Lamanites had originally derived from Hebrew, in which *rabboni* means "one who is a leader" (see John 20:16) and *rabbi* means "one who teaches or leads." In Mormon 9:33, further evidence is given that the Nephites knew Hebrew— Mormon states that if the plates had been large enough, they would have written their record in Hebrew instead of in the reformed Egyptian, which was a much more condensed form of "shorthand."

KEY INSIGHTS ABOUT THE SAVIOR

- When we have His Spirit, the Lord enables us to perceive the thoughts of others.
- The Lord and all His holy angels dwell in heaven.
- The Lord knows the thoughts and intents of our hearts.
- The Lord created man in His image.
- The Lord is the centerpiece of the plan of redemption.

Alma 19

> "And . . . all the servants of Lamoni . . . same thing—that their hearts had been to do evil." (Alma 19:33)

MAJOR CONCEPT

The Spirit of the Lord is the key element in bringing souls to Christ.

OVERVIEW After hearing Ammon preach, King Lamoni receives light and sees the Lord; overcome by the Spirit, he and most of his household fall into a trance and are believed to be dead. The queen sends for Ammon, who assures the queen that her husband will arise the next day. She believes him. The king arises the next day and bears witness of the Atonement, saying he has seen the Redeemer; he, the queen, and Ammon are all overcome by the Spirit and fall to the ground. Abish—a Lamanite woman who, unknown to others, was a convert—witnesses the miracle and runs to tell others. Dissension follows, a man who tries to kill Ammon is struck dead by the power of God, and after reviving the king goes forth to help teach the gospel to the Lamanites. Many are baptized.

MAIN THEMES

- Faith can work miracles.
- We experience great joy when we convert souls to Christ.
- When we ourselves are converted, we are filled with the desire to convert others.
- Those whose hearts are hardened are not receptive to the Spirit.
- The greatest way to demonstrate love for others is to proclaim the gospel of Jesus Christ to them.
- The clear definition of conversion is a mighty change of heart with no more desire to do evil.

PROMINENT PEOPLE

- Ammon
- King Lamoni
- Abish
- King Lamoni's queen

INTERESTING FACTS ABOUT THE FAITH OF THE QUEEN Consider the implications of what has occurred in this account. A stranger has come onto the scene whom the queen has never before seen. He is respected and even held in awe by the servants because of how he protected the king's flocks—but the queen was not an eyewitness to his miraculous power. Now, under the administration of this stranger, her husband is comatose, considered by many to be dead. And yet she believes the words of Ammon. That is the power of her "great faith," a faith greater than any among the Nephites—and evidence of the operation of the Spirit in this situation. The queen's commitment and support becomes an important part of the foundation being laid for the work of the gospel among the Lamanites.

WHO WAS ABISH? Abish was a Lamanite woman in the household of King Lamoni; she was the only one not overcome by the

did all declare unto the people the self-changed; that they had no more desire

Spirit when Ammon taught the gospel—she had already been converted to the Lord as a result of a vision her father had experienced years earlier. (We have no information on the specifics of her father's vision.) She had kept her conversion a secret, but after seeing the impact of the Spirit on the members of the household and being touched by the Spirit herself, she shared her conversion. Abish's testimony had unexpected results, creating dissension—and even a desire to slay Ammon—among those who heard it. Filled with sorrow as a result of their unbelief, she wept, then took the queen—who had been overcome by the Spirit—by the hand, and she stood on her feet. The queen then took the king by the hand, and he regained consciousness; he went forward and preached the gospel to his people, resulting in the baptisms of many. Abish was instrumental in converting hundreds of Lamanites. Other than Eve and Mary, she is one of only three women mentioned by name in the Book of Mormon; the other two are Sariah, Lehi's wife (see 1 Ne. 2:5), and Isabel, the harlot (see Alma 39:3).

KEY INSIGHTS ABOUT THE SAVIOR

- The Spirit of the Lord may have a very dramatic effect on people who have been especially wicked.
- The Lord will redeem all those who believe in Him.
- The Lord protects and spares His servants.
- The Lord's arm is extended to all who will repent and believe on His name.
- The Lord keeps His promises; Ammon could not be slain because the Lord had promised his father (King Mosiah II) that He would protect his sons on their missions.

Alma 20

> "Behold, thou shalt not slay thy son; fall than thee, for behold, he has repented this time, in thine anger, thy soul could

MAJOR CONCEPT

Miracles are wrought and hearts softened by the power of love and righteousness.

OVERVIEW The Lord commands Ammon to go to Middoni and free Aaron and his missionary companions from prison. On their way to Middoni, Ammon and King Lamoni run into King Lamoni's father, who is king over all the Lamanites. He tries to slay Ammon, but Ammon subdues him and agrees to spare his life if he will release Aaron and his companions. The father is touched by Ammon's love of King Lamoni, and he gives Lamoni independence to run the affairs of his own kingdom. They arrive in Middoni and are able to secure the release of the missionaries from prison.

PROMINENT PEOPLE

- Ammon
- King Lamoni
- Aaron
- The father of Lamoni

INTERESTING FACTS ABOUT LOVE Love, felt and expressed, becomes a great motivator for righteousness. This is demonstrated when Ammon and King Lamoni encounter Lamoni's father on the way to Middoni. At first angry and determined to kill Ammon, the old king's heart is softened

MAIN THEMES

- As we seek the Lord's guidance, we become instruments in His hands.
- We can set a powerful example for others by the way we react in a crisis.
- Seemingly small or isolated acts can have tremendous impact.
- We make a favorable impression on others when our motives are not selfish or mercenary.

600 BC

90 BC

nevertheless, it were better that he should of his sins; but if thou shouldst fall at not be saved." (Alma 20:17)

when he sees the great love that Ammon feels for Lamoni. The pure love of Christ is especially powerful; it is the motivating energy within every righteous act. When love is felt, lives are changed, and gratitude is realized, leading to the kind of action later taken by Lamoni's father.

WHO WAS THE FATHER OF LAMONI? The king over all the Lamanite territories at the time of the fourteen-year mission of the sons of Mosiah is not named in the Book of Mormon; he is referred to simply as "the father of Lamoni." He maintains power over King Lamoni, a "lesser king" who, along with his wife and members of his court, is converted by Ammon. When King Lamoni

and Ammon encounter Lamoni's father on their way to Middoni, he initially resists them—but their love and dedication impress him, and the stage is set for the father's eventual conversion when he is later taught by Aaron. Following his conversion, the father of Lamoni is the one who makes possible the establishment of the Church throughout the entire land of the Lamanites.

Image: King Lamoni's father.

KEY INSIGHTS ABOUT THE SAVIOR

- The Lord directs and inspires us as we work to accomplish His purposes.
- The Lord strengthens and protects His servants.

Alma 21

"And it came to pass that the Lord began many to the knowledge of the truth; yea, of the traditions of their fathers, which

Major Concept

Missionary work, while often very difficult, brings the reward of conversion to those who are diligent.

OVERVIEW When the sons of Mosiah go their separate ways to preach the gospel, Aaron goes to a city called Jerusalem, inhabited by Lamanites whose hearts are hardened. The Lamanites reject Aaron's message, and he goes to Ani-Anti, where he encounters fellow missionaries Muloki and Ammah. The three preach but are rejected. They then go to Middoni, where they are cast into prison. They are freed as a result of Ammon's efforts and continue to preach, converting many. Lamoni grants religious freedom to the people in the land of Ishmael.

INTERESTING FACTS ABOUT THE AMALEKITES AND AMULONITES We learn in Alma 21 that the Amalekites and

Prominent People

- Aaron
- Muloki
- Ammah
- The Amulonites and Amalekites

Amulonites worked with the Lamanites to establish a city they called Jerusalem. The Amalekites were a sect of Nephite apostates who had affiliated with the Lamanites; they were often chosen to lead Lamanite armies because of their strong character and intense hatred of the Nephites. They

Main Themes

- We have the responsibility to testify with courage.
- We have been commanded to teach the gospel, even when those we teach do not accept the message.
- Often the worst enemies of the Church are those who have left the Church.
- Diligent and continual missionary efforts are often rewarded with conversion.
- One of the purposes of government is to allow the exercise of religious worship.
- We can learn about the Lord by listening to those who truly serve Him.

600 BC

90 BC

to bless them, insomuch that they brought they did convince many of their sins, and were not correct." (Alma 21:17)

are the ones who led the massacre of the Christian Lamanites of Anti-Nephi-Lehi. The Amulonites were Nephites on their fathers' side and Lamanites on their mothers' side, though they were considered to be Lamanites. Many became wicked and followed the order of Nehor—they denied Christ, believing that God would save all men and that no one could know the future; they were subsequently scattered. Some of the Amulonites later became displeased with the conduct of the majority and assumed the identity of Nephites; thereafter they were forever considered Nephites.

WHO WAS MULOKI? Muloki was a participant in the missionary excursion to the Lamanites, led by the sons of Mosiah—Ammon, Aaron, Omner, and Himni—that began around 90 BC. The first reference to Muloki is when the Lord commands Ammon to go to Middoni and help free Aaron and his companions—including Muloki and Ammah. Aaron had been teaching in the city of Jerusalem, but his message was soundly rejected. He had then gone to Ani-Anti, a village where Muloki and Ammah were attempting to preach the gospel. When the people of that village also rejected the gospel, the three of them went to Middoni, where they were cast into prison and suffered great hardship. After being freed from prison as a result of Ammon's intervention, Muloki and his companions went wherever they were led by the Lord and continued preaching the gospel.

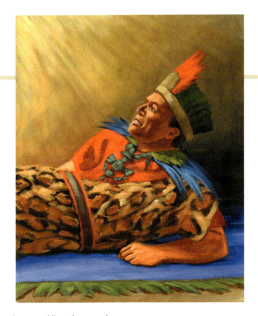

Image: King Lamoni.

KEY INSIGHTS ABOUT THE SAVIOR

- The Lord provides direction to those who serve Him.
- The Lord achieves His will on earth through those He directs to accomplish His work.

"If thou wilt bow down before God, yea,
will bow down before God, and call on
receive, then shalt thou receive [eternal

MAJOR CONCEPT

The principles Aaron used in his teaching are fundamental principles that pertain to all missionary labors today.

OVERVIEW After being freed from prison, Aaron is led by the Spirit to the land of Nephi, where he teaches the father of King Lamoni. Aaron testifies of the Creation and the plan of redemption through Christ. The father of Lamoni and all his household are converted, and the king divides the land between the Lamanites and the Nephites.

PROMINENT PEOPLE

- Aaron
- The father of Lamoni
- The mother of Lamoni

INTERESTING FACTS ABOUT BOOK OF MORMON LANDS
The last section of Alma 22 describes how the land was divided between the Lamanites and the Nephites. Because of its references to geography (see verses 27, 28, 31, and 32), this chapter is used more than any other in the Book of Mormon to develop theories about the location of Book of Mormon lands. But the more important message in these verses is that the more righteous and the less righteous—even wicked—needed to be separated. Elder George Q. Cannon emphasized that the Book of Mormon is not a geography primer and was not written to teach

MAIN THEMES

- The fundamental principles of missionary work are to be led to people by the Spirit, to teach by the Spirit, respect those we teach, serve those we teach, and be honest and straightforward in all we teach.

- True conversion occurs when we are willing to pay the price to have eternal life.

- Powerful conversion occurs when we are willing to give away all our sins to know the Savior.

- Led by the Spirit, servants of the Lord can work miracles.

- The conversion of just one person can have a tremendous influence on the conversion of many.

600 BC

90 BC

if thou wilt repent of all thy sins, and his name in faith, believing that ye shall life]." (Alma 22:16)

geographical truths (see *Juvenile Instructor*). He counseled that we are to focus on the spiritual truths contained in the book and not to attempt to tie Nephite and Lamanite cities to current geographical locations.

WHO WAS AARON? Aaron, one of the great missionary figures of the Book of Mormon, was one of the sons of Mosiah who were initially numbered among the unbelievers. After an angel was sent to call Alma the Younger, Aaron, and the other sons of Mosiah to repentance, Aaron embarked on a fourteen-year mission to the Lamanites. At first rejected, persecuted, and even imprisoned, Aaron was eventually led by the Spirit to the land of Nephi, where he had the remarkable opportunity to preach the

gospel to the king over all the Lamanites. The king's subsequent conversion led to the conversion of thousands. Aaron continued to faithfully serve the Lord throughout his life. Aaron's method of teaching Lamoni's father followed the same pattern that Ammon used to teach Lamoni: simplicity, testimony, scriptures, and prayer. Aaron also taught the same doctrine as did Ammon: the Creation, the Fall, and the Atonement.

KEY INSIGHTS ABOUT THE SAVIOR

- Jesus Christ is the God of the Old Testament.
- The sufferings and death of Jesus Christ atone for all our sins as we exercise faith and repentance.
- The Savior broke the bands of death so that death and the grave could have no victory over us.
- The Lord grants eternal life to all those who repent, bow down before Him, and call on His name, believing that they will receive eternal life.

Alma 23

MAJOR CONCEPT

Religious freedom is a divinely inspired principle that allows for conversion to the truth.

OVERVIEW Following his conversion, the king of all the Lamanites grants religious freedom to his people and sends forth a proclamation that there will be no persecution of those who are teaching the gospel. As a result of the efforts of the sons of Mosiah, the Lamanites in seven lands are converted to the gospel of Christ. Part of their preparation was being taught the Nephite language years earlier by the priests of King Noah (see Mosiah 24:2–5). Those who are converted begin to call themselves Anti-Nephi-Lehies, and the curse is removed from them. Only one Amalekite is converted, and all of the Amulonites reject the truth.

MAIN THEMES

- Where religious freedom exists, the work of the Lord can flourish.

- Those nations that open their doors to the preaching of the gospel are blessed temporally and spiritually.

- Those who embrace righteousness generally hope to distinguish themselves from those who do not.

PROMINENT PEOPLE

- The sons of Mosiah
- The king of the Lamanites

INTERESTING FACTS ABOUT ANTI-NEPHI-LEHIES Gospel scholar Daniel H. Ludlow gave the following insight about the name *Anti-Nephi-Lehies:* "The 'Nephi-Lehi' part of the title probably had reference to the lands of Nephi and Lehi (or the people then living in those lands) rather than to the descendants of Nephi or Lehi." He points out that Hugh Nibley found a Semitic root corresponding to *anti* that means "in the face of" or "facing a mirror," by extension meaning "one who imitates." Therefore, says Ludlow, "the term 'Anti-Nephi-Lehies' might refer to those who imitate the teachings of the descendants of Nephi and Lehi" (*A Companion to Your Study of the Book of Mormon,* 209). The conversion of these people was so powerful that they never fell away (see verse 6).

WHO WAS OMNER? Omner was one of the sons of Mosiah who had been one of the "very vilest of sinners" (Mosiah 28:4).

proclamation throughout the land unto his people, that the word of God
forth throughout all the land, that his people might be convinced concerning
they might be convinced that they were all brethren. . . ." (Alma 23:3)

When an angel of the Lord visited Alma
the Younger as well as Omner and his
brothers—Ammon, Aaron, and Himni—
and called them to repentance, they were
filled with a desire to preach the gospel and
embarked on a fourteen-year mission to the
Lamanites. Omner later helped Ammon
secure an area south of Bountiful where the
Lamanites who had been converted—the
Anti-Nephi-Lehies—could be safe from the
assaults of their former countrymen.

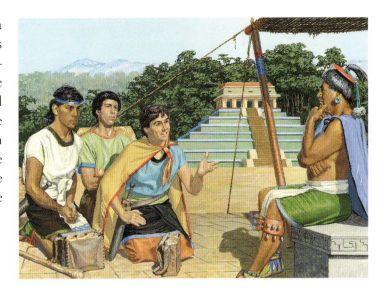

KEY INSIGHTS ABOUT THE SAVIOR

- The Lord prepares the way for the gospel to be preached.
- The Savior enlists the help of His servants in opening the nations for the preaching of the gospel.
- True conversion is conversion to the Lord—not to the Church, its programs, or its missionaries.

Alma 24

Major Concept

We are blessed when we honor and obey the covenants into which we have entered.

OVERVIEW Before he dies, the aging king of the Lamanites confers the kingdom upon one of his sons, whom he names Anti-Nephi-Lehi. The Lamanites who have not been converted to the gospel begin to be stirred up in anger against those who have; their hatred causes them to rebel against the king, and they attack the Anti-Nephi-Lehies. The Anti-Nephi-Lehies, who have covenanted to forsake any form of aggression, bury their weapons and refuse to take up arms to defend themselves. They rejoice in Christ and are visited by angels, and additional Lamanites are converted.

INTERESTING FACTS ABOUT EXEMPTION FROM MILITARY SERVICE The Anti-Nephi-Lehies—Ammon's converts who had

Prominent People

- Anti-Nephi-Lehi
- Ammon

repented of their previous shedding of blood and buried their weapons—were the only people in the Book of Mormon exempted from military service. These righteous Lamanites were spared having to go to battle if they would help supply their Nephite protectors with provisions. In ancient times, every able-bodied man was

Main Themes

- When we become a Zion people, we go to war only when directed to do so by inspiration.

- Even those who have committed serious sins can be forgiven if they repent.

- An important part of repentance is to forsake the sin.

- Our repentance and forsaking of our previous sins is a testimony to the Savior that we will follow Him.

- A depth of conversion is manifest when we are willing to suffer death rather than violate our covenants or commit sin.

- Once we join the Church, we are enlisted to serve the Lord.

- If we fall away after having great knowledge and being enlightened by the Spirit of God, we are worse off than if we had never known about the gospel.

ALMA

God, that he hath granted unto us that we might repent of us of our many sins and murders which we have committed, through the merits of his Son." (Alma 24:10)

obligated by law to defend his nation or tribe; this was also the case in Nephite society. Certain exceptions were allowed under the law of Moses—one of those was that the duty of military service applied only when fighting an enemy, not when fighting against one's brethren. In the Nephite army, the Anti-Nephi-Lehies would have been forced to slay their own brethren, the Lamanites, so they would have been exempted. Under the law of Moses, the humanitarian exemptions were also given to those who had recently married, built a new house, planted a new vineyard, or were "fearful and fainthearted" (see Deut. 20:5–9). The Anti-Nephi-Lehies also qualified under this exemption, since they certainly would have been "fearful and fainthearted" at the thought of breaking an oath with God by taking up arms. According to the Mosaic law, the men who did not fight because of exemption were required to provide behind-the-lines support, which the Anti-Nephi-Lehies did by providing provisions to the Nephite army (see *Echoes*, 357–361).

WHO WAS ANTI-NEPHI-LEHI? We know very little about the background of Anti-Nephi-Lehi except that he was a son of the great king over all the Lamanites; when that king decided to confer the kingdom upon one of his sons, he gave that son the name of Anti-Nephi-Lehi. When Ammon and the new king meet with the people to determine how they will answer the aggression of the Lamanites, Anti-Nephi-Lehi reminds them of their covenant to forsake their former warlike behavior and to embrace the gospel with total commitment. His impact as a leader must have been tremendous, since Mormon preserved in Alma 24 the text of Anti-Nephi-Lehi's speech to his people.

KEY INSIGHTS ABOUT THE SAVIOR

- The Lord shed His blood to redeem us from our sins.
- The Savior's Atonement enables us to be redeemed even from serious sins.
- Because of His great love for us, the Lord provides for the plan of salvation to be taught to us in each generation when the priesthood is on the earth.
- The Lord is merciful.
- Through the Lord, we become clean, able to return to Him and be saved.
- Those who repent have guilt taken away from their hearts through the merits of Christ.
- We are saved by the grace of Christ after all we can do to repent of all our sins.

Alma 25

MAJOR CONCEPT

The Lord always keeps His promises.

OVERVIEW The Lamanites destroy the city of Ammonihah. The Amulonites who escape kill many Lamanite converts by fire. After these battles, many Lamanites become righteous, join the Anti-Nephi-Lehies, keep the law of Moses, and look forward in faith to the coming of the Savior. The sons of Mosiah rejoice in the success of their missionary labors.

INTERESTING FACTS ABOUT FULFILLMENT OF PROPHECY

Many of the things that happen to the people in this chapter are not a matter of mere consequence—as the adversary would have us believe—but are in direct fulfillment of prophecy. The Lamanites descend on and destroy the city of Ammonihah in a single day, a direct fulfillment of the prophecy uttered by Alma, who prophesied that the city would be destroyed in a day if the people failed to repent (see Alma 8:16). The wicked priests of Noah kill many of the Lamanite converts by fire, in direct fulfillment of the prophecy of Abinadi (see Mosiah 13:10). The Lamanites also hunt down and kill the descendants of Amulon, again in fulfillment of the prophecy of Abinadi (again, see Mosiah 13:10). In this complex series of events, we see fulfillment of the words of Alma, who said that "the word of God must be fulfilled" (Alma 5:58).

PROMINENT PEOPLE

• The sons of Mosiah

MAIN THEMES

• Prophecy is always fulfilled—sometimes soon after it is uttered, and sometimes centuries or millennia later.

• Affliction has a natural tendency to humble people and cause them to remember the Lord.

• We are blessed for our obedience.

came by the law of Moses; but the law of Moses did serve to they did retain a hope through faith, unto eternal salvation, which spake of those things to come." (Alma 25:16)

KEY INSIGHTS ABOUT THE SAVIOR

- The law of Moses was given as a precursor to the Savior's greater law.
- The Lord fulfilled the law of Moses.
- The Savior provided the way to eternal salvation.
- The Lord answers the prayers of His servants and blesses them with success in their labors.
- The Lord delivers His servants.
- The law of Moses was a type of Christ's coming.
- Salvation did not come through the law of Moses, but the law of Moses served to strengthen the Nephites' faith in Christ.

Alma 26

> "Yea, I know that I am nothing; as to my boast of myself, but I will boast of my things. . . ." (Alma 26:12)

Major Concept

With the Lord's help, all things are possible.

OVERVIEW The sons of Mosiah rejoice as they reflect on their missionary labors, which have resulted in the conversion of thousands of Lamanites. Aaron grows uncomfortable and warns Ammon not to boast; Ammon clarifies that he is not boasting of his own strength, but boasting of the strength of the Lord—he attributes all his success to the Lord. Those who have been converted and remain faithful are given increased knowledge. Ammon testifies that the Lord has all power and comprehends all things.

INTERESTING FACTS ABOUT TEACHING THE GOSPEL There have been many well-trained and skilled teachers, but those are not the qualities that make someone effective when teaching the gospel. Anyone can teach and convince, but it is the Spirit of the Lord that brings about true conversion. President Brigham Young once said that he would rather hear five words spoken by the Spirit than an entire sermon preached without it. The truths of the gospel are

Prominent People

- Ammon
- Aaron

Main Themes

- We are blessed for our role in converting others to the gospel, as we become instruments in the Lord's hands.
- The number of people we are able to teach and convert depends on our strength and diligence in the work.
- Those who accept the gospel and remain faithful will be gathered and protected from the destruction of the last day.
- We should remain humble and give the credit for our accomplishments to the Lord.
- We can teach and convince, but true conversion comes only through the power and Spirit of the Lord.
- We can know all things if we pray fervently, exercise faith, and remain obedient.
- Even people who initially persecute the Church can change, repent, and be very successful missionaries through the mercies of Christ.

600 BC

90 BC

strength I am weak; therefore I will not
God, for in his strength I can do all

actually plain and simple to understand to those who have the Spirit—but, as Joseph Fielding Smith said, the best scholars in the world may not be able to comprehend even the simplest gospel truths if they are not in tune with the Spirit. If we are to teach with power to the convincing of souls, we must first seek the Spirit by repenting, exercising faith, and praying without ceasing.

KEY INSIGHTS ABOUT THE SAVIOR

- The Lord uses faithful and dedicated servants as instruments in His hands to bring His marvelous light—the gospel of Christ—to men.

- The Lord will gather up and protect His people at the last day.

- The Lord will work righteousness forever.

- The Lord is not dependent on us; we are dependent on Him.

- The Lord can do all things; without Him, we can do nothing.

- The Savior's love and salvation are everlasting.

- The Lord has great power, mercy, and long-suffering toward the children of men.

- The Lord reveals the fulness of His word—the mysteries of God—to those who repent, exercise faith, and pray without ceasing.

- The Lord promises success to those who bear their afflictions with patience.

- The Lord has all power, all wisdom, and all understanding.

- The Savior is merciful, offering salvation to those who repent and believe on His name.

- The Lord is mindful of every person, no matter where he or she is, and He pours out His mercy on all the earth.

Alma 27

"And they did look upon shedding the abhorrence; and they never could be their brethren. . . ." (Alma 27:28)

MAJOR CONCEPT

True conversion brings about a mighty change of heart and blesses both the converts and those who teach them the gospel.

OVERVIEW The Lamanites who had come to battle against the Nephites and the people of Anti-Nephi-Lehi become exceedingly angry and continue to come to battle, destroying the faithful who refuse to take up arms in their own defense. Ammon inquires of the Lord as to what he should do to help protect the converts. He is directed to return to the land of Zarahemla; on the way he and his brothers encounter Alma, who is overjoyed to see them. Alma takes the sons of Mosiah to his own home and they tell the chief judge what has happened to the people. They vote as to whether to allow the converted Lamanites to stay. The chief judge gives the Anti-Nephi-Lehies the land of Jershon as an inheritance and vows to station armies around the land for their protection.

MAIN THEMES

- True missionaries are concerned with both the spiritual and temporal well-being of those they teach.

- We should seek the Lord's will in all our doing.

- Satan stirs up the hearts of people with anger, contention, and hatred.

- True conversion results in lasting righteousness even in difficult circumstances.

PROMINENT PEOPLE

- Ammon
- Alma
- Aaron
- Sons of Mosiah
- Anti-Nephi-Lehi

The converted Lamanites occupy the land of Jershon, are called the people of Ammon, and become a highly favored people of the Lord.

INTERESTING FACTS ABOUT ASYLUM As part of the law of Moses, a person who committed inadvertent manslaughter could seek asylum, which involved escaping to a city of refuge. Moses established at least six of these cities where people guilty of inadvertent manslaughter could live until the death of the current high priest. By residing in such a place of asylum, the person—if found innocent of murder by a council of elders—could escape the blood vengeance of the victim's family. The Nephites would have been aware of the seriousness of premeditated murder and would also have been aware of the provisions in the law of Moses that dealt

blood of their brethren with the greatest
prevailed upon to take up arms against

with inadvertent manslaughter. Many scholars consider Jershon—the Nephite land that was given to the Anti-Nephi-Lehies—to be a city of refuge. Though we don't have proof that such is the case, Jershon certainly could have qualified as such a place. As converted Lamanites, the Anti-Nephi-Lehies were judged by the congregation at Zarahemla and were then given the land of Jershon, where they could seek refuge from the Lamanites. The Nephites then protected the Anti-Nephi-Lehies with their armies, thus fulfilling another provision of the law of Moses in regard to asylum (see *Echoes,* 425–430). As another evidence that Jershon might have been a place of asylum, the Hebrew word *Jer* means "land of asylum," and words ending in *on* designate cities.

WHO WAS AMMON? In this chapter, we are told that the sons of Mosiah encounter Alma on their way to Zarahemla—a reunion that brings much joy to all of them. Each person sees for himself that his brethren who were visited by the angel are still faithful and serving the Lord. We learn (see verse 17) that Ammon was overcome with such joy that he lost his strength and collapsed. This reunion was first described in Alma 17:1–2. Describing a similar type of reunion, Joseph Smith wrote, "The expectation of seeing my friends in the morning of the resurrection cheers my soul

and makes me bear up against the evils of life. It is like their taking a long journey, and on their return we meet them with increased joy" (*History of the Church,* 5:362).

Image: Ruins in Central America.

KEY INSIGHTS ABOUT THE SAVIOR

- The Lord intervenes in behalf of those who believe in Him and seek Him.
- The Savior highly favors those who love Him, obey Him, and exercise faith in Him.
- Faith in the Savior can overcome the fear of death; the people of Ammon never feared death because of their testimony of Christ and His victory over death.

Alma 28

MAJOR CONCEPT

Wickedness brings everlasting misery and woe, while righteousness brings everlasting happiness.

OVERVIEW As the people of Anti-Nephi-Lehi—the converted Lamanites—are led to and situated in the land of Jershon, the wicked Lamanites follow them and come against them in the most ferocious battle since Lehi left Jerusalem; tens of thousands are slain. The Lamanites are defeated and scattered. Many thousands come into the fold of Christ.

WHO WERE THE ANTI-NEPHI-LEHIES? The missionary journeys of the sons of Mosiah among the Lamanites between approximately 90 and 77 BC brought many thousands into the fold of Christ, including the households of King Lamoni in the land of Ishmael and of his father, king over all the Lamanite lands. Those who were converted were so strong that they never fell away. So firm was their resolve to place their wicked deeds behind them that they buried their weapons in the earth and swore an oath to never again take them up. Assuming

PROMINENT PEOPLE

- Ammon
- The Anti-Nephi-Lehies
- The Lamanites

MAIN THEMES

- While we mourn over the loss of those we love, we know that the righteous are in a state of everlasting happiness.

- Sin and transgression come from the devil.

- Satan tempts us so he can ensnare us and prevent us from achieving eternal life.

- We have great reason to hope because of a promised reward in Christ.

ALMA

of men to labor in the vineyards of the Lord; and thus we of rejoicing—sorrow because of death and destruction among Christ unto life." (Alma 28:14)

the new name of Anti-Nephi-Lehies to distinguish themselves from their former brethren, they became industrious and prosperous. When the Lamanites came up against them to slay them, they remained firm in their commitment to the Lord and chose to die rather than fight; as a result, their ranks were increased by a thousand new converts—more than the number killed in the attack. For their protection, the Lord commanded Ammon to lead them out of the Lamanite territories; they were received by the Nephites by the voice of the people (through a vote) and given the land of Jershon in which to live. There, they became known as the people of Ammon. Despite continued severe attacks by the Lamanites, they remained true to their covenant to not take up arms. Their sons—who had not made such an oath—did eventually take up arms in defense of their liberties and were known as the "stripling warriors." Mormon summarizes what we learn from the experience of the Anti-Nephi-Lehies: how great the inequality of man because of sin; the great call of man is to labor in the vineyard; the reasons for sorrow are death and destruction; and the reasons for joy revolve around the Savior Jesus Christ. (Whenever the text reads "and thus we see," Mormon is adding his commentary as he abridges the record.)

Image: Mayan warriors.

KEY INSIGHTS ABOUT THE SAVIOR

- The Lord will not redeem those who die in sin.
- The Lord has a promised reward for those who die in righteousness, and theirs will be a state of great joy and everlasting happiness.

Alma 29

"O that I were an angel, and could have and speak with the trump of God, with unto every people!" (Alma 29:1)

MAJOR CONCEPT

One of the greatest possible sources of joy is converting others to the truth.

OVERVIEW Alma expresses an overwhelming desire to preach repentance and to be an instrument in bringing others to the Lord. He feels great joy in those he has been able to convert and also expresses joy over the success of his brethren in those they have been able to bring to the Lord. He invokes a blessing on his brethren and their converts.

INTERESTING FACTS ABOUT BEING CALLED OF GOD

According to the Lord's infinite wisdom, He determines the measure of truth dispensed to each nation. It is our opportunity in this life to serve as instruments in His hands to bring people unto Him. The Prophet Joseph Smith was specifically called to be an instrument in the hands of God:

MAIN THEMES

- Those who love the gospel have the desire to teach it to others.

- Repentance alleviates sorrow.

- We are the ones who determine our course by causing salvation or destruction through our acts.

- Those who cannot know good from evil are blameless before the Lord.

- Seeing others repent and accept the truth brings us great joy.

- It is a sign of our true discipleship when we rejoice in the progress of others.

- We are called by the Lord to teach the gospel.

PROMINENT PEOPLE

- Alma

"This messenger [Moroni] proclaimed himself to be an angel of God, sent to bring the joyful tidings that the covenant which God made with ancient Israel was at hand to be fulfilled, that the preparatory work for the second coming of the Messiah was speedily to commence; that the time was at hand for the Gospel in all its fullness to be preached in power, unto all nations that a people might be prepared for the Millennial reign. I was informed that I was chosen to be an instrument in the hands of God to bring about some of His purposes in this glorious dispensation" (*History of the Church,* 4:536–537).

600 BC

90 BC

the wish of mine heart, that I might go forth a voice to shake the earth, and cry repentance

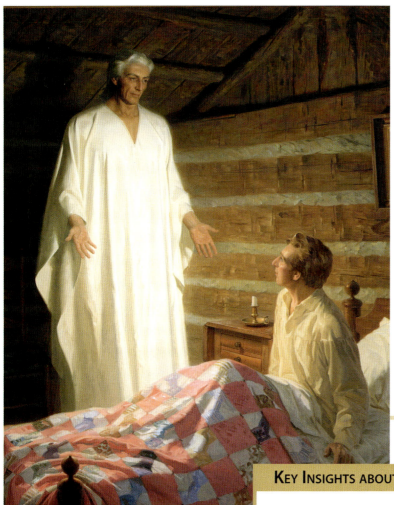

KEY INSIGHTS ABOUT THE SAVIOR

- The Savior grants us according to our desire—whether we desire death or everlasting life.
- The Lord makes it possible for all to be taught His word.
- The Lord—the God of Abraham, Isaac, and Jacob—delivers His people out of bondage.
- The same God that delivered Israel from the Egyptians (the Lord) also delivered the Nephites from bondage.

"Thou hast had signs enough; will ye
ye have the testimony of all these thy
before thee, yea, and all things denote

Major Concept

There will always be those who preach against Christ and try to offer salvation on terms other than those laid down by Christ.

OVERVIEW Korihor comes among the people and teaches that there is no Christ, no God, no penalty for sin, and no fall of man. He is bound and brought before Alma, the high priest, who testifies to Korihor that all things denote there is a God and that Christ will come. Korihor demands a sign and is struck dumb; he realizes that he was deceived by the devil, who told him what to say. He is trampled and dies.

INTERESTING FACTS ABOUT THE ANTI-CHRIST An anti-Christ is a person who opposes the true gospel, opposes the true church, denies the existence of Christ, and offers salvation to men on some other terms than those laid down by Christ. Those who abridged the Book of Mormon preserved the accounts of the anti-Christs because they knew we would face them in our day. It is anyone or anything that counterfeits the true gospel or plan of salvation (see *LDS Bible Dictionary,* 609). President Ezra Taft Benson wrote, "The Book of Mormon exposes the enemies of

Prominent People

- Alma
- Korihor

Main Themes

- Mourning is negative only when the mourner refuses to find comfort in the gospel.

- Free agency is a divine right that enables us to believe what we will.

- Those who preach against the truth accuse believers of having "a frenzied mind."

- Those who preach against truth claim that men manage themselves, prosper according to their own strength, and are not accountable or punished for wrongdoing.

- As we teach, we should carefully follow the revealed word of God.

- A clear evidence of the truthfulness of the gospel is that it brings joy.

- Sign-seekers want to gain faith and knowledge without paying the price of humility, earnest seeking for truth, and obedience to gospel principles; they are adulterous.

- Evidence of God's existence comes from our own testimony, the testimonies of the prophets, the testimonies of others, the earth and all on it, and the order of the universe.

- Satan can appear as an angel to deceive us.

- The devil will not support his people at the last day.

600 BC

90 BC

tempt your God? Will ye say, Show unto me a sign, when brethren, and also all the holy prophets? The scriptures are laid there is a God. . . ." (Alma 30:44)

Christ. . . . The type of apostates in the Book of Mormon are similar to the type we have today. God, with His infinite foreknowledge, so molded the Book of Mormon that we might see the error and know how to combat false educational, political, religious, and philosophical concepts of our time" ("Rely on the Book of Mormon").

WHO WAS KORIHOR? Korihor was a radical dissenter who came into the land of Zarahemla around 74 BC and began preaching against the prophecies about the coming Messiah. He preached that there was no life after death and that all men managed themselves and prospered according to their own genius, conquered because of their own strength, and were not punished for any wrongdoing. He also claimed that the priests were holding the people in bondage for their own monetary gain. Because he was preaching blasphemies, he was brought before Alma, the chief judge, who countered Korihor's claims and bore testimony of the Savior. Korihor remained unconvinced and demanded that Alma give him a sign. In the name of God, Alma struck Korihor dumb. Korihor wrote out a message confessing that he had always known there was a God, but that he had been deceived by the devil, who had allegedly appeared as an angel to Korihor and had filled him with hatred. Korihor begged for relief, but Alma perceived that his repentance was insincere and that he would soon return to his wicked

ways. He was reduced to begging for food until he was trampled to death by Zoramites (Nephite dissenters), causing Mormon to say the devil won't support his own children (the dissenters).

KEY INSIGHTS ABOUT THE SAVIOR

- Christ came to earth, suffered for our sins, and offers salvation to those who repent and follow Him.
- All the prophets from the beginning of time have testified of the Savior.
- Korihor's assertion that "no man can know of things to come" denies the principle of revelation from the Savior.
- Korihor's assertion that you can't know what you can't see denies the existence of Jesus.
- Korihor's assertion that remission of sin is the sign of a deranged mind denies the Savior's Atonement.
- Korihor's statement that death signals the end of existence denies the Savior's Resurrection.

"Behold, O Lord, their souls are precious, therefore, give unto us, O Lord, power these, our brethren, again unto thee."

MAJOR CONCEPT

Those steeped in apostasy have withdrawn from the Spirit of the Lord.

OVERVIEW Having heard that the Zoramites were falling into apostasy, Alma heads up a mission to reclaim them; he takes with him Ammon, Aaron, Omner, Amulek, Zeezrom, Melek, Shiblon, and Corianton. They find that the Zoramites deny Christ and worship with set prayers, among other things, offering their prayers on the Rameumptom ("holy stand"). Alma offers a stirring prayer for the success of their missionary labors, and he and his brethren are filled with the Holy Spirit.

INTERESTING FACTS ABOUT APOSTASY In this chapter, we learn about the apostate condition of the Zoramites: they refused to obey the commandments, refused to observe the performances of the Church, focused on building wealth, built synagogues in which they observed their own form of worship, used set prayers, taught that God existed only in spirit form, and said there would be no Christ. They also had a false concept of the doctrine of election,

PROMINENT PEOPLE

- Alma
- Zoram

MAIN THEMES

- The righteous sorrow in the iniquities of others.

- The preaching of the word of God is more powerful than the sword or anything else.

- Universal signs of apostasy include refusal to accept the truth, denial of Christ, and creation of new religions or religious practices.

- Set, established prayers recited by rote are not pleasing to the Lord.

- People often invent their own forms of worship so they can assure themselves of reward despite their behavior.

- A prophet's prayers for his people are earnest and pleading.

and many of them are our brethren; and wisdom that we may bring (Alma 31:35)

they often separated themselves from the Church (by gathering in Antionum), and their prayers focused on themselves (while Alma's prayers focused on others). These same signs of apostasy exist in our day. We can discern truth from error by following the counsel in D&C 50:22–24: those things that do not edify are not from God, and that which is of God brings increasing light. President J. Reuben Clark said that for members of the Church, two things can never be forgotten, shaded, or discarded: Jesus Christ is the Son of God, and the Father and Son appeared to Joseph Smith (see "The Charted Course").

WHO WAS ZORAM? Zoram was a Nephite dissenter who led a group called the Zoramites away to a community called Antionum. Alma, the high priest, was distressed to hear that Zoram was perverting the ways of the Lord by teaching his people to worship their worldly possessions; he then led a mission in 74 BC to preach the truth to the Zoramites. Only a few were converted, and they joined the people in the land of Jershon. Zoram threatened those in Jershon with destruction if they did not reject the converts and began to work with the Lamanites to try to destroy those who lived in righteousness.

KEY INSIGHTS ABOUT THE SAVIOR

- The Lord pours His spirit out upon His righteous servants.
- The Lord provides for and protects those who serve Him.
- The Lord gives strength to those who endeavor to serve Him.
- The Savior uses us as instruments in His hands to bring about His will.
- The Lord hears and answers the prayers of His people.

"Faith is not to have a perfect knowledge ye hope for things which are not seen,

MAJOR CONCEPT

Faith, like a seed, must be planted in the heart and constantly nurtured; its reward is eternal life.

OVERVIEW In his magnificent discourse on faith, Alma is preaching to the poor among the Zoramites; because they have been exposed only to false doctrine, he does not try to give them the entire doctrine of faith all at once but begins with a pure and simple explanation. He testifies that faith is like a seed that must be planted and nourished; as it grows it becomes like a tree from which the fruit of eternal life can be picked.

INTERESTING FACTS ABOUT THE EXPERIMENT OF FAITH In his mighty sermon on faith, Alma describes an experiment that shows the process of developing faith. It's a laboratory we can all enter—and, by applying proper principles, we can gain spiritual evidence of the truth. We are advised to test the truths of the gospel (see John 7:16–17; John 10:37–38; 1 Thes. 5:21; Matt. 5:16; 1 Pet. 2:12; and James 1:5). This chapter provides elegant instructions for such a test. The experiment Alma describes consists of the following:

PROMINENT PEOPLE

• Alma
• The Zoramites

MAIN THEMES

• Afflictions often humble people and prepare them to hear the word.

• Faith is a gift of God to those who serve Him.

• Angels minister to men, women, and children.

• In order to develop powerful faith, we must begin with the desire to do so.

• Faith is hope in the truth, not a perfect knowledge; it is things hoped for but not seen that are true.

• Blessed are people who are humble without being compelled to be humble.

• We cannot know anything of a surety at first; we must plant and nourish the seed of faith properly and diligently.

• The seed of faith flourishes only if it is not cast out by unbelief or resistance to the Spirit.

• Those things that are good enlarge the soul and cause a swelling in the bosom.

• If our faith is neglected, it will wither.

• Eternal life is the most precious gift of God.

• Faith provides trust, hope, and confidence.

of things; therefore if ye have faith which are true." (Alma 32:21)

(1) Compare the word of God to a seed (verse 28). (2) Plant the seed in your heart, not your head (verse 28). (3) Don't cast the seed out by unbelief or by resisting the Spirit of the Lord (verse 28). (4) If the seed starts to swell, it is good; if not, cast it away (verses 28–32). Alma continues with hypotheses about his experiment (see verses 21, 26, and 27) and conclusions about his experiment, outlined in verses 33–42.

Images: Photo and drawing from Pacal's sarcophagus at Palenque—a "tree of life" growing from the king's chest.

KEY INSIGHTS ABOUT THE SAVIOR

- The Lord blesses those who are humble and believe the word of God.

- The Lord is merciful to all who believe on His name.

- The Savior desires that we cultivate and nourish faith.

- The Lord will reward faith, diligence, patience, and long-suffering.

- Alma speaks of planting a seed in one's heart; the seed is "the word," and the "word" is Christ. Therefore, the experiment involves planting Christ in one's heart.

Alma 33

"Cast about your eyes and begin to believe in
suffer and die to atone for their sins; and that he
all men shall stand before him, to be judged at

MAJOR CONCEPT

Jesus Christ is the Son of God and came to earth to atone for our sins and bring to pass
the resurrection of the dead.

OVERVIEW Alma continues to preach to the poor among
the Zoramites. He refers to Zenos, who taught that men
should pray and worship in all places. He then refers to
Zenock, who taught that mercy is provided as a result
of the Savior. Finally, he refers to Moses, whose dealings
with the children of Israel in the wilderness represented
the coming Messiah.

**INTERESTING FACTS ABOUT PRAYER AS A FORM OF
WORSHIP** We worship God in many places, including our
homes, our offices, the outdoors, in private places, and in
congregations. We also worship God in many ways—some
of them include worshiping through love and obedience

PROMINENT PEOPLE

- Alma
- Zenos
- Zenock
- Moses

(see John 14:15), through reverence and
devoted service (see 3 Ne. 13:24), and
through prayer. Prayer is the very essence of
worship; it is through prayer that we show
respect and veneration for the Almighty. It
is divine communication between God and
all mankind. We submit to Heavenly Father
when we call upon Him in gratitude and
reverence for all things (see Alma 33:4–11;
34:17–28).

WHO WAS ZENOCK? Zenock was a
Hebrew prophet whose writings were
included in the brass plates—and, as
a result, were available to the Book of
Mormon prophets. Zenock bore solemn
witness of the mission of the Son of
God (see Alma 33:15), that the Messiah
would yield Himself into the hands of
wicked men to be crucified (see 1 Ne.
19:10), and that He would be the source
of redemption for all mankind (see Alma
34:7). Mormon referred to Zenock when

MAIN THEMES

- The judgments of God are turned away from us
  because of the mercy and Atonement of the Savior.
- All the prophets of old testified of the Savior and
  His atoning mission.
- Salvation is offered to those who do not harden
  their hearts and perish in unbelief.
- Our burdens can become light through our faith
  in the Savior.
- Those who fail to look to Christ will not be healed.

ALMA

600 BC

90 BC

256

the Son of God, that he will come to redeem his people, and that he shall shall rise again from the dead, which shall bring to pass the resurrection, that the last and judgment day, according to their works." (Alma 33:22)

he spoke about the universal destruction across the land at the time of the death of the Savior (see 3 Ne. 10:15–17). While we know that Zenock was of the lineage of Joseph, nothing is known of his parentage or the time of his service, except that it must have been prior to 600 BC when Lehi left Jerusalem. In verse 17 of this chapter, Alma testifies that Zenock was a martyr, as was Zenos (see Hel. 8:19). Zenock's words have been preserved in the Book of Mormon as an added confirmation of the divine mission of the Savior.

KEY INSIGHTS ABOUT THE SAVIOR

- The Lord is merciful to those who call upon His name.
- The Lord hears the cries of His people.
- The Savior is our Mediator and tempers the judgments of God in our behalf.
- The Lord came to redeem His people.
- The Savior suffered and died to atone for our sins.
- The Savior rose from the dead to bring to pass the Resurrection.
- We will stand before the Savior at the judgment day, and He will judge us according to our works.
- Moses lifting up the brass serpent in the wilderness was a type of Jesus being lifted up on the cross (see John 3:14).

Alma 34

MAJOR CONCEPT

As the Son of God, Jesus Christ is the infinite and eternal sacrifice who atoned for our sins.

OVERVIEW After Alma finishes his discourse to the Zoramites, Amulek delivers a powerful sermon in which he testifies of the coming Savior and His atoning sacrifice. He testifies that the entire law of Moses points toward the sacrifice of the Messiah, the Son of God, and that the eternal plan of redemption is based on faith and repentance. He teaches that this life is the time to prepare to meet God and counsels the people to work out their salvation with fear and trembling.

INTERESTING FACTS ABOUT GARMENTS MADE WHITE Many passages in the Book of Mormon refer to white garments; Alma declares that a man's garments must

PROMINENT PEOPLE

- Amulek
- Jesus Christ

be washed white or he cannot be saved, and Amulek in this chapter writes that a man's garments must be made white through the blood of the Lamb. Modern scholars, such as Erwin Goodenough, have identified the white garment as being of particular importance to the

MAIN THEMES

- We are responsible for our own sins and cannot atone for the sins of others.

- Those who exercise faith and repentance are encircled in the arms of mercy; those who don't will be subject to the demands of justice.

- We can call upon God at all times and in all places, both for ourselves and others.

- Mercy can only satisfy justice if there is faith unto repentance. Those who do not exercise faith unto repentance are exposed to the whole law of the demands of justice.

- Prayer is the way we begin to exercise faith unto repentance.

- We must repent now; if we procrastinate our repentance until we die, we will subject ourselves to the devil.

- The miracle of forgiveness is available to all who turn from evil and return to it no more.

- If we don't prepare now for eternity, darkness will overcome us.

- If we neglect the needy, naked, sick, and afflicted, our prayers will avail us nothing.

ALMA

a great and last sacrifice; yea, not a sacrifice manner of fowl; for it shall not be a human eternal sacrifice." (Alma 34:10)

Jews. Paraphrasing Goodenough, Hugh Nibley stated that "God himself may be represented in the earliest Jewish art as one of three men clothed in white. . . . This image [from the Dura Europos synagogue] wasn't even known to exist until 1958 . . . there are three men in white, or a single figure, the prophet in white. The symbol for the chosen prophet, an emissary from God, is always the white robe, which is reserved for heavenly beings." This coincides perfectly with testimonies in the Book of Mormon that the righteous will be "clothed with purity, yea, even with the robe of righteousness" (2 Ne. 9:14) (see *Echoes,* 485).

Bottom Image: One of the murals from the Dura Europos synagogue.

KEY INSIGHTS ABOUT THE SAVIOR

- The Lord always uses at least two witnesses of His truth—in this case, Alma and Amulek.
- The Lord's Atonement was made for the sins of all mankind; without it, all mankind would perish.
- Every whit of the law of Moses pointed to or symbolized Christ or His gospel in some way.
- As the Son of God, the Savior is infinite and eternal, and His sacrifice was infinite and eternal—it covers all mankind, the earth itself, and all forms of life on the earth.
- The Savior's sacrifice fulfilled the law of Moses.
- Christ's sacrifice brings about mercy, which satisfies the demands of justice.
- The Lord does not dwell in unholy temples but only in the hearts of the righteous.

Alma 35

Major Concept

Abandoning evil ways and converting to the truth can result in persecution, but the Lord blesses those who follow Him.

OVERVIEW This chapter begins one of the longest periods of war between the Nephites and the Lamanites. After Amulek finished his powerful testimony of the Savior, the Zoramites are angry because it destroyed their priestcraft. They cast out those who have become converted by the words of Alma and Amulek; the converts are brought to the land of Jershon, where the people of Ammon welcome them, give them land for their inheritance, and minister to their needs. Alma sorrows over the wickedness of the people. When the Zoramites and Lamanites prepare to come to war against the people of Ammon, they depart from Jershon and go to the land of Melek so the Nephite armies can inhabit the land of Jershon. The final verse

Main Themes

- We are blessed when we demonstrate true Christianity toward others.
- The iniquity of our loved ones causes us sorrow.
- The hardened hearts and iniquity of those we teach causes us sorrow.
- Parents should teach their children in righteousness.
- People with hardened hearts are offended by the strictures of the word of the Lord.

Prominent People

- Alma
- Amulek
- Zoram

of Alma 34 refers to the commandments Alma gives his sons; these consist of the next seven chapters, which are inserted into the record before the subsequent forty-four chapters, which deal with war.

INTERESTING FACTS ABOUT COUNSELING OUR CHILDREN In verse 16, Alma gathers his sons so he can give them individualized instruction and his blessing as a righteous father and priesthood holder. It is the intention of the Lord that fathers have the responsibility to bless and counsel their children. Fathers and mothers should sit together in council on how best to nurture and teach their children—a sacred responsibility that is not transferable (see Mosiah 4:14–15; D&C 68:25–28). Giving correction is one of the most difficult things parents do, but it is their duty to correct, as moved upon by the Holy Ghost, early on and with clarity, and always with love. Teaching moments

ALMA

receive all the poor of the Zoramites that came over unto did clothe them, and did give unto them lands for their unto them according to their wants." (Alma 35:9)

emerge as parents plan and ponder about counseling and blessing their children. There are also scheduled times such as family home evening, family scripture reading, and family council. Mealtimes often present ideal opportunities to discuss the events of the day, build relationships of trust, and teach or discuss principles of the gospel.

Image: Central American ruins.

KEY INSIGHTS ABOUT THE SAVIOR

- The Lord watches over and blesses those who follow Him in righteousness.
- The Savior bears up the righteous in their afflictions.

Alma 36

"I could remember my pains no more; yea, oh, what joy, and what marvelous light as was my pain!" (Alma 36:18–19)

MAJOR CONCEPT

We find relief and joy through sincere repentance.

OVERVIEW Alma testifies to his son Helaman about the experience of being converted by an angel of God and bears powerful testimony of what it is like to be born again. The "murders" to which he refers describe spiritual death, not physical death. He testifies of seeing concourses of angels praising God. He tells Helaman of the souls he has converted and testifies that they too have experienced being born again.

INTERESTING FACTS ABOUT CHIASMUS A distinct writing style employed by many ancient writers, *chiasmus* involves arranging a series of words or ideas in one order and then repeating them in reverse order. In Alma 36:1–27, at least

PROMINENT PEOPLE

- Alma
- Helaman

seventeen key elements are mentioned and then repeated in the opposite order. A repeated declaration that Jesus Christ is the Son of God appears in the exact center of the chapter, and the symbolism of this placement cannot be missed. Scholar John W. Welch, who discovered chiasmus in the

MAIN THEMES

- Example is powerful when bearing testimony: those who live according to what they preach teach with greater impact.

- Righteous parents hope to help their children live righteously and avoid repeating the mistakes they themselves made.

- We demonstrate humility when we acknowledge God's help.

- Great sorrow over sin inspires the desire to repent.

- The thought of being in God's presence fills the wicked with inexpressible horror.

- Until we cry unto the Lord in sincere repentance, we will not be born again.

- Sincere repentance brings profound relief.

- True conversion inspires the desire to preach the gospel and bring others to the truth.

- We must stand on higher spiritual ground in order to lift others up.

- When we keep the commandments we prosper; when we do not keep the commandments, we are cut off.

600 BC

90 BC

I was harrowed up by the memory of my sins no more. And did I behold; yea, my soul was filled with joy as exceeding

Book of Mormon in 1967, maintains that Alma 36 is the best chiasm in the entire Book of Mormon, if not in all of world literature (see "Chiamus in Alma 36" and "Alma 36: A Masterpiece").

WHO WAS HELAMAN? Helaman, the eldest son of Alma the Younger, was both the leading high priest of his generation and a military hero; he lived from around 100 to 57 BC. Alma entrusted Helaman with the sacred things of the Lord (see Alma 37:47), including the brass plates, the sacred Nephite records, the twenty-four Jaredite plates, the interpreters (the Urim and Thummim), and the Liahona. Alma then commanded him to become the spiritual leader of the people. Helaman not only exercised great care over the church but supported Captain Moroni in withstanding the attacks of traitors and enemies. At the request of the legendary 2,000 stripling warriors, he became their leader in the struggle to defend the liberty of the people. See more about Helaman in later chapters.

KEY INSIGHTS ABOUT THE SAVIOR

- The Lord rewards our righteous works.
- The Lord supports those who are righteous through even the most difficult afflictions.
- The Savior will deliver those who trust in Him.
- The Lord is the one who delivered Lehi and his family out of Jerusalem, sparing them from destruction.

Alma 37

"Counsel with the Lord in all thy doings,

MAJOR CONCEPT

Regardless of our circumstances in life, we should counsel with the Lord in all our doings and permit Him to direct us in every way.

OVERVIEW Alma continues counseling his son Helaman; Alma entrusts the records to Helaman and commands him to continue making a record of his people. He testifies that the records are preserved to bring souls to salvation and explains that the Jaredites were destroyed because of their wickedness. He commands Helaman not to use the interpreters to bring to light the secret oaths and covenants because the Lord does not want us to read them and learn how to use them. He advises Helaman to always counsel with the Lord in all his doings.

WHO WAS GAZELEM? When Alma counsels his son Helaman concerning the care and management of the sacred records and associated objects, he gives him the "interpreters" (the Urim and Thummim) as the divine means for revealing the history of past peoples. The name *Gazelem* appears to refer to a seer, or servant of God, commissioned to use the Urim and Thummim to expose the

PROMINENT PEOPLE

- Alma
- Helaman

MAIN THEMES

- By small and simple things, great things are brought to pass.
- The scriptures help convince us of the error of our ways and bring us to a knowledge of the Lord.
- Those who keep the commandments of the Lord will prosper; those who do not will be cut off.
- Destruction comes to all who work darkness.
- We should stay focused on the Savior and preach repentance and faith on the Lord.

- We should counsel with the Lord in all our doings.
- We should give heed to the words of the Lord just as Lehi looked to the Liahona for direction; the words of Christ, if followed, lead us to the ultimate "promised land," the celestial kingdom.
- When we forget to look to God, we lose our sense of moral and spiritual direction.
- We should not expose ourselves to works of darkness (such as the occult, Ouija boards, and Satan worship) lest they lead us to sin.

600 BC

90 BC

wickedness of past nations and thus warn future generations to live according to the principles of the gospel. In some of the early revelations, Joseph Smith was referred to by the names "Gazelam" or "Enoch" in order to keep his identity secret from his enemies. Elder Bruce R. McConkie postulated that Alma's Gazelem may be a variant of Gazelam and may actually refer to the Prophet Joseph Smith (see *Mormon Doctrine*, 307–308).

KEY INSIGHTS ABOUT THE SAVIOR

- The Lord preserved and kept the sacred records—the scriptures—until it was time for them to go forth among men.
- The Lord protects sacred records against all the powers of earth and hell.
- The Lord has not yet revealed all holy writ.
- The Lord prepared the Urim and Thummim.
- The Lord prepared the Liahona to show Lehi the course he should travel in the wilderness.
- The Lord reveals sacred records for His own wise purpose and to demonstrate His power.
- The Lord is wise, His paths are straight, and His course is one eternal round.
- The Lord's commandments are strict.
- The Lord fulfills all His promises.

Image: Central American ruins.

89 BC   MERIDIAN   421 AD

Alma 38

"There is no other way or means whereby is the life and light of the world. Behold,

Major Concept

We should bear all things in patience and put our trust in the Lord.

OVERVIEW Alma counsels his son Shiblon, who had been persecuted for his righteousness. Alma testifies to Shiblon about his own experience with the angel and his subsequent conversion and testifies that salvation comes only through Christ, who is the light and life of the world. He counsels Shiblon to bridle his passions so that he can be filled with love.

WHO WAS SHIBLON? Shiblon, the son of Alma, was described by Mormon as a just man who walked uprightly before God, continually did good, and kept the commandments (see Alma 63:2). Shiblon accompanied Alma on his mission to the Zoramites around 74 BC,

Prominent People

• Alma
• Shiblon

along with Corianton, Amulek, Zeezrom, Ammon, Aaron, and Omner. Shiblon performed his labors with honor. Alma counseled Shiblon to put his trust in God and to continue teaching the word; Shiblon obeyed his father and was later mentioned by Mormon as being a valiant disciple of

Main Themes

- We should follow the example of Alma in counseling our children often and steadily.

- The righteousness of children brings great joy to their parents.

- Those who endure to the end are blessed.

- We should put our trust in the Lord, and He will deliver us from our trials, troubles, and afflictions.

- Those who serve full-time missions should continue to teach after returning home.

- Returned missionaries should not boast in their wisdom and must refrain from idleness.

- Those who trust in the Lord will be lifted at the last day.

- We should be diligent and temperate in all things and should govern our passions.

- We should pray continually for forgiveness and mercy.

- We should acknowledge our unworthiness before God at all times.

man can be saved, only in and through Christ. Behold, he he is the word of truth and righteousness." (Alma 38:9)

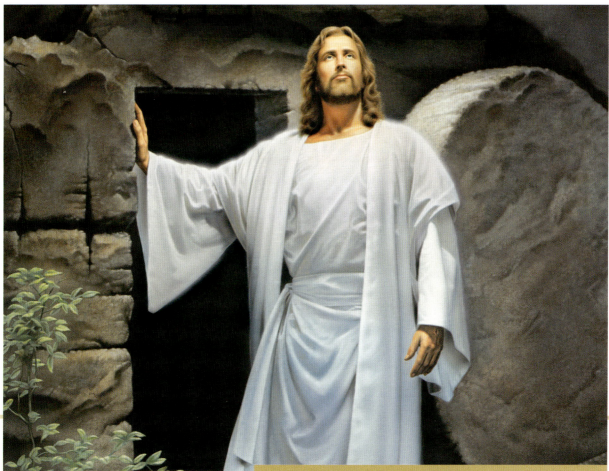

KEY INSIGHTS ABOUT THE SAVIOR

the Lord responsible for bringing great blessings to the people. In the year 56 BC, Shiblon received the sacred records from his older brother, Helaman, and he succeeded Helaman as keeper of the records. Three years later, Shiblon conveyed the records to his nephew, Helaman (son of Helaman), and he died shortly thereafter.

- The Savior enables us to bear persecution and afflictions.
- The Lord delivers those who put their trust in Him.
- The Savior's Atonement makes possible a remission of sins.
- Jesus Christ is the only way and means by which we can gain salvation.
- The Savior is the word of truth and righteousness.

Alma 39

MAJOR CONCEPT

We must repent of our sins and make restitution where we can, which is the only way to gain lasting happiness.

OVERVIEW Alma gives counsel to his son Corianton, who had boasted in his own strength and had left the mission in violation of the law of chastity. Alma testifies that sexual sin is an abomination to the Lord and tells Corianton that his sins were a main reason why the Zoramites did not receive the word of the Lord. Alma testifies that redemption comes through Christ, and that those who repent and follow the commandments will be forgiven and redeemed, even if they live before the Savior performs His atoning sacrifice.

INTERESTING FACTS ABOUT THE HARLOT ISABEL According to Hugh Nibley, Isabel was the name of

PROMINENT PEOPLE

- Alma
- Corianton

the Patroness of Harlots among the Phoenicians. The Book of Mormon, Nibley wrote, distinctly hinted of a pagan mother goddess in the account of Corianton, who had committed immoral acts with the harlot Isabel and who had to go to the land of Siron to do so. The

MAIN THEMES

- Those who boast of their own strength believe they can do everything without the need of guidance or advice.

- Sexual sin is an abomination before the Lord and more serious than all other sins except murder and denying the Holy Ghost.

- Denying the Holy Ghost is an unpardonable sin.

- Murder is called "the unforgivable sin" because a person must make his own payment for it.

- We cannot hide our sins from the Lord;

when we sin, we are making the record from which we will be judged.

- The only way to lasting happiness is through repentance.

- If we do not repent and forsake our sins, we cannot inherit the kingdom of God.

- The sins we commit can influence and harm others.

- In forsaking sin, we must turn to the Lord with all our mind, might, and strength.

- Part of restitution is acknowledging our wrongdoing.

ALMA

600 BC

90 BC

from God; and except ye repent they will last day." (Alma 39:8)

"Great Mother" is the so-called mother of the gods, an ancient fertility goddess worshipped by various pagan religions—including, but not limited to, Ishtar (Babylon), Isis (Egypt), Ceres (Rome), and Demeter (Greece). Nibley explains that the Book of Mormon does not specifically mention the Great Mother but does describe all non-Nephite people as involving idol worship (see *Echoes*, 480).

WHO WAS CORIANTON? Corianton, son of Alma, was a member of the group that accompanied Alma on his mission to the Zoramites around 74 BC. Others on the mission were Shiblon, Ammon, Aaron, Omner, Amulek, and Zeezrom, providing the opportunity for Corianton to serve in a circle of tremendous spiritual power. But instead of serving honorably, Corianton abandoned his ministry, went into the land of Siron, and had sexual relations with the harlot Isabel. When Alma took the opportunity to counsel all his sons individually, he gave loving reproof and counsel to Corianton. As they spoke, Corianton asked many questions of Alma, who answered his concerns and counseled him to embark again on his missionary travels. Corianton humbly repented and resumed his missionary service, this time with the highest standards of humility and devotion. By the year 72 BC, Corianton had achieved a place of recognition among the leading brethren of the church. The last reference to Corianton (see Alma 63:9–10) indicates that he sailed into the north countries around 56–54 BC to carry provisions to the large numbers of people who had emigrated northward.

Image: Central American ruins.

KEY INSIGHTS ABOUT THE SAVIOR

- The Savior came to take away the sins of the world.
  - The Lord is the way to salvation.
  - The Savior revealed the plan of redemption to prophets from the beginning of time.

Alma 40

"The soul shall be restored to the body, and joint shall be restored to its body; but all things shall be restored to their

MAJOR CONCEPT

Because of the Savior's Atonement, we will all be resurrected.

OVERVIEW Alma continues teaching Corianton. Now that he has called Corianton to repentance, Alma answers a number of questions Corianton has about gospel principles. Alma testifies of the Resurrection and explains the outcome of both the righteous and the wicked after they die.

INTERESTING FACTS ABOUT THE RESURRECTION Elder Bruce R. McConkie taught that those who lived before the Resurrection of Christ considered the day of His coming forth from the dead as the first resurrection. Abinadi and Alma, for example, taught this principle (see Mosiah 15:21–25; Alma 40). To those who have lived since that day, the first resurrection is yet future and will take place at the time of the Second Coming (see D&C 88:96–102). We don't have any knowledge of an ongoing resurrection that is currently taking place or of people who have been resurrected since the Resurrection of Christ other than a select

MAIN THEMES

- The resurrection is absolutely universal.

- There is a space of time between the time we die and the time we are resurrected; during that time, the spirits of all men, whether they are good or evil, return to the world of spirits.

- After death, the spirits of those who are righteous are received into paradise, a state of rest and peace; the spirits of those who are evil will be cast out into misery and will be captive to the devil.

- There was an initial resurrection of the righteous who lived before Christ was resurrected; they were resurrected when He ascended into heaven.

- During resurrection, the soul will be reunited with the body, and all will be restored to their proper and perfect frame.

- Following the resurrection, the righteous will inherit the kingdom of God, and the wicked will be cast out and will not be able to partake of the things of righteousness.

ALMA

and the body to the soul; yea, and every limb yea, even a hair of the head shall not be lost; proper and perfect frame." (Alma 40:23)

few. Though all are assured of a resurrection, all will not be resurrected at the same time, because there will be varying degrees of glory to which each is resurrected (see *Mormon Doctrine*, 638–639). According to President Joseph Fielding Smith, we will meet at the resurrection the same body we laid down; it will then progress to perfection. Those who died as children will come forth as children and will gain full stature after the resurrection (see *Doctrines of Salvation*, 2:293).

KEY INSIGHTS ABOUT THE SAVIOR

- The atoning sacrifice of the Savior provides for the resurrection of all of mankind who ever live, regardless of whether they are righteous or wicked.
- The Savior overcame death and the grave.

Alma 41

MAJOR CONCEPT

Heavenly Father's plan requires that all things be restored to their proper order.

OVERVIEW Knowing Corianton's heart, Alma continues to instruct him, providing further teachings and details about resurrection and the state of people after they die—things about which Corianton is troubled. Alma teaches that we will each be restored to the qualities and characteristics we had in mortality, testifies that wickedness never was happiness, and defines the state of those who are carnal.

INTERESTING FACTS ABOUT RESTORATION There is no discontinuity in one's spiritual makeup in the transition from this world to the next. Goodness translates to goodness, evil to evil. If we align ourselves in this life with that which is evil and refuse to repent, that same disposition will continue with us into the next sphere of existence. The law of the harvest is the principle by which we progress and are blessed (see D&C 130:20–21). We are judged according to our desires, the thoughts of our hearts, and

PROMINENT PEOPLE

- Alma
- Corianton

MAIN THEMES

- In the resurrection, the soul will be reunited with, or restored to, the body.
- We will be judged according to our works. If they were righteous, we will be restored to endless happiness in the kingdom of God.
- If our works were evil, we will be restored to endless misery in the kingdom of the devil.
- Our reward will be based in large part on our own desires.
- In a sense we are our own judges, because we decide, based on our conduct and desires, where it is we will spend eternity.

- We cannot be restored from wickedness to righteousness.
- Wickedness never was happiness.
- The word *restoration* means to bring back everything to its previous state: good for good, evil for evil, righteous for righteous.
- If we repent and do good continually, we will have mercy restored to us and will be given a righteous judgment.
- The word *restoration* more fully condemns the sinner, who cannot be justified.

ALMA

spoken concerning restoration, that ye
Behold, I say unto you, wickedness never was

our works. If they be righteous, then we will be restored to a state of righteousness and will be received into the kingdom of God. This is spelled out in Paul's discourse in 1 Corinthians 15:20–42. The type of body we receive will depend on the "seeds" we plant. If we live on a telestial level (sow telestial seeds), we will inherit a telestial body. Paul compares the resurrection to agriculture—we reap what we plant.

Key Insights about the Savior

- The Lord requires that all things be restored to their proper order.
- The Lord is merciful and just; we will receive those things to which we are entitled as a result of our works and the desires of our heart.
- The Savior's atoning sacrifice makes possible the resurrection and restoration of all things.

Alma 42

MAJOR CONCEPT

Sin and righteousness bring their own consequences.

OVERVIEW Alma continues to teach his son Corianton, focusing now on the Fall and the Atonement. In one of the best treatises on justice and mercy, Alma testifies that redemption comes through Christ to those who repent. Alma teaches that mercy is given to those who repent, but those who do not repent are subject to God's justice. He teaches that repentance and mercy come through the Atonement, and that only the truly penitent are saved. Alma counsels Corianton to repent and resume his missionary labors.

INTERESTING FACTS ABOUT HOPE Young Corianton received a blessing of hope from his father—hope that he can overcome the burden of sin and dispel the feelings of guilt in his heart by repenting sincerely and coming back into the fold of Christ. Hope is a precious doctrine that gives optimism to life. It helps us carry on when we are downhearted and discouraged. It helps us repent. Hope is the doctrine that is expressly connected to faith and charity.

PROMINENT PEOPLE

- Alma
- Corianton

MAIN THEMES

- This life is a probationary time in which we are given time to repent and serve the Lord.

- Death is part of the plan of salvation.

- The body dies, but the soul can never die, so the plan of redemption had to allow for a reuniting of the soul and the body.

- If it were not for the Atonement and the plan of redemption, we would be plunged into immediate and everlasting misery as soon as we die.

- Under the principle of justice, there is blessing for every obedience and punishment for every violation; the plan of redemption brought about by the Savior allows us to repent without destroying the conditions of justice.

- Law is essential to the plan of redemption.

- Only the truly penitent will be saved.

- The Atonement overcomes the spiritual death brought about by Adam's Fall by bringing everyone back to God's presence.

- We should not try to excuse or rationalize our sin but should fully and sincerely repent.

600 BC

90 BC

rob justice? I say unto you, Nay; not one (Alma 42:25)

We cannot live without hope. If hope is gone, sin is at the door. Thus when we realize that there is life after death and that our reward is directly connected to our actions here on earth, we look to God and seek to keep His commandments. Hope is continually activated when we understand and appreciate any doctrine or principle of the gospel. Our understanding then becomes a key to hope.

KEY INSIGHTS ABOUT THE SAVIOR

- The Lord saves us; through His Atonement we are redeemed.
- God's plan meets the demands of perfect justice through the infinite mercy of a loving Savior.
- The Lord pours out His mercy on those who exercise faith, repent, are baptized, receive the Holy Ghost, and endure in righteousness to the end.
- The plan of mercy could not exist without the Atonement.
- Without the Lord's Atonement, mercy could not appease the demands of justice.
- The Savior's Atonement brings to pass the resurrection of the dead.

Alma 43

"Nevertheless, the Nephites were for monarchy nor power but they were children, and their all, yea, for their rites

MAJOR CONCEPT

We are justified in war when there is no other way to preserve our rights and freedoms or to protect our homes and families.

OVERVIEW Following his individual counsel to his three sons, Alma and his sons preach the gospel to the Zoramites; rejecting the word, the Zoramites and a group of Nephite dissenters—the Amalekites and the Amlicites—join the Lamanites. The Anti-Nephi-Lehies have fled to the land of Melek, leaving Jershon open for occupation by the Nephite armies. The Lamanites come to war against the Nephite armies in the land of Jershon. The Lord reveals the Lamanite strategy to Alma; Moroni equips the Nephite armies with defensive armor. The Nephites fight to defend their homes, families, liberty, and religion. The armies of Lehi and Moroni surround the armies of the Lamanites.

MAIN THEMES

- Hatred is a key element in unrighteous war.
- Satan uses the power of confusion, bitterness, and class distinction, and he has great influence over those who declare unrighteous war.
- We should seek direction from our Church leaders in time of special concern to us.
- The prophet can seek the Lord's direction in our behalf.
- Our diligently following the prophet results in our protection.
- We should pray constantly for help.

PROMINENT PEOPLE

- Alma
- The sons of Alma
- Zerahemnah
- Moroni
- Lehi

INTERESTING FACTS ABOUT WAR Of the 522 pages in the Book of Mormon, 170—comprising 68 chapters—are devoted to war between the Nephites and the Lamanites. Nearly one-third of the entire Book of Mormon is devoted to warfare—whether preparing for war, conducting war, or dealing with war's effects. Modern scholars have discovered that even though Joseph Smith lived in modern times, the warfare described in the Book of Mormon reflects patterns of ancient warfare. Furthermore, Book of Mormon armies did not use horses or other animals during war, and Mesoamerican archaeological studies back this up. Scholars have also confirmed that weaponry used in the Book of Mormon is similar to weapons used in other ancient locations (see *Echoes*, 143–145). President Harold B. Lee stated that the parts of the body protected by physical armor have spiritual symbolism: the loins typify chastity, the heart typifies conduct, the feet represent goals, and the head represents

inspired by a better cause, for they were not fighting fighting for their liberties, their wives and their of worship and their church." (Alma 43:45)

our thoughts (see *BYU Speeches of the Year,* Nov. 9, 1954).

WHO WAS ZERAHEMNAH? Zerahemnah was a Lamanite general against whom Moroni, supreme commander of the Nephites, won a decisive victory around 74 BC. Because of Moroni's superior armaments and positioning strategy, he surrounded Zerahemnah and offered him an ultimatum: surrender and enter into a covenant to desist from warfare, or be killed. Zerahemnah agreed to offer up their arms but refused to enter a covenant to desist from war, saying he knew his people could not keep such an oath. Moroni insisted on both. As Zerahemnah rushed toward Moroni with his sword raised, one of Moroni's men knocked the sword to the ground, breaking it; he scalped Zerahemnah and lifted the scalp on the point of his sword, saying that the Lamanites would fall if they did not deliver their weapons and make a covenant of peace (see Alma 44:14). Many of the Lamanites surrendered and entered a covenant of peace; they were allowed to depart into the wilderness. Those who did not surrender their weapons or enter the covenant of peace raged forward in battle but quickly were overcome. Seeing that his fractured troops could not prevail, Zerahemnah swore an oath of peace. Moroni disarmed the Lamanites and sent them back into the wilderness.

KEY INSIGHTS ABOUT THE SAVIOR

- The Lord reveals the truth to His servants who preach His gospel.
- The Lord directs us through His prophets.
- The Lord knows all things and can detect the intents of our hearts.
- The Lord hears the prayers of the righteous.
- It is not improper to inquire of the Lord through His prophets about what to do during wartime.

"But now, ye behold that the Lord is
hands. And now I would that ye should
and our faith in Christ. And now ye see

MAJOR CONCEPT

We are expected to live a Christ-centered life and to adhere to the principles of righteousness—
even under extremely trying conditions, such as war—and to respect the lives of our enemies.

OVERVIEW The Nephite army has surrounded Zerahemnah's
army; instead of destroying them, the Nephites make a
proposal: Moroni offers to spare the Lamanites if Zerahemnah
will surrender his army's weapons and make a covenant that
his men will not come to war again against the Nephites.
Zerahemnah agrees to surrender their weapons but refuses to
make the covenant. Moroni insists on both, and Zerahemnah
refuses. The battle continues; Zerahemnah is scalped by one
of Moroni's soldiers, causing many of the Lamanites to enter
the covenant out of fear. The Nephites defeat the Lamanites.
Those Lamanites who surrender their weapons and take an
oath of peace are allowed to flee into the wilderness. This
chapter is the last of the records written by Alma.

PROMINENT PEOPLE

- Moroni
- Zerahemnah

WHO WAS MORONI? From a historical
perspective, Moroni was the chief commander of the Nephite armies from around
74 BC until his retirement, not long before
his death in 56 BC. He was only twenty-
five years old when he was appointed chief
captain; his contemporaries included Alma,
from whom he sought the Lord's advice
about how he should conduct the Nephite
campaigns; Alma's son Helaman, a powerful
ally in the war for liberty and leader of the
2,000 stripling warriors; and Pahoran, the
governor of Zarahemla to whom Moroni
sent a scathing correspondence when the
government failed to support his armies.
After a series of successful campaigns lasting
about eighteen years, Moroni gave command
of the armies to his son, Moronihah, and
retired so he could spend the rest of his
days in peace. He died shortly thereafter. A
spiritual perspective of Moroni is provided in
later chapters.

MAIN THEMES

- God defends those who fight for righteousness.

- War is often waged over religion.

- During war, we need to keep the best interests of
  our enemies at heart.

- We need to "draw our battle lines," determine
  what we will accept, and not deviate from that,
  even if the battle becomes sore.

- Every war is a continuation of the war in heaven,
  and we cannot deviate from our commitment to
  stay on the Lord's side.

- Happiness results when we maintain the sacred
  word of God.

with us; and ye behold that he has delivered you into our understand that this is done unto us because of our religion that ye cannot destroy this our faith." (Alma 44:3)

KEY INSIGHTS ABOUT THE SAVIOR

- The Lord defends His people in fighting the enemies of righteousness.
- The Lord will not suffer His people to be destroyed unless they fall into transgression.

"Behold, I perceive that this very people, is in me, in four hundred years from the shall dwindle in unbelief." (Alma 45:10)

MAJOR CONCEPT

Wickedness and unbelief can lead to the destruction of people.

OVERVIEW Alma has finished his record and hands the plates over to his son Helaman, who continues recording the affairs of the Nephites. Alma verifies that Helaman believes all he has been taught and then prophesies powerfully of the destruction of the Nephite civilization because of unbelief. He prophesies that the few who remain of the Nephite nation will be numbered among the Lamanites. Alma then both blesses and curses the land—blessing it because it is a land of promise and cursing it because the wicked will be cast out. Alma is then translated. The church is reestablished in the land, but dissension grows in the church as the people become prideful.

PROMINENT PEOPLE

- Alma
- Helaman

INTERESTING FACTS ABOUT TRANSLATION

In this chapter, we learn that Alma was translated—"taken up by the Spirit, or buried by the hand of the Lord, even as Moses" (verse 19). Joseph Smith said that Alma was translated because his body was needed for a future mission. In the

MAIN THEMES

- The Nephites would dwindle and eventually be destroyed because of their wickedness and unbelief.

- The Americas are a land of promise from which the wicked will be cast out.

- The proud do not listen to the voice of righteousness.

600 BC

90 BC

the Nephites, according to the spirit of revelation which time that Jesus Christ shall manifest himself unto them,

Book of Mormon, we read that both the Apostle John and the prophet Moses were translated. Though these events are not mentioned in the Bible, other ancient documents support the Book of Mormon assertions. In fact, the Talmud and many other Jewish texts relate that Moses never died but was alive and serving God in heaven. A fourth-century Christian writing—*The Discourse on Abbatôn*—states that John the Beloved was translated. This document was first published in 1914, and no English translation of the Talmud was available to Joseph Smith—offering further evidence of the Book of Mormon's divine origin (see *Echoes*, 247–249). Those in the city of Enoch were translated (see JST Gen.

14:25–40) and were resurrected at the time of Jesus' Resurrection (see D&C 133:54–55). Translated beings need no repentance (see D&C 49:8); they are also not subject to pain, sorrow, fire, or wild beasts (see 3 Ne. 28:7–9, 20–22). Translated beings are not in God's presence but are of a terrestrial order (see *Teachings of the Prophet Joseph Smith,* 170); they cannot enter God's presence until they undergo a change equivalent to death (see *Teachings of the Prophet Joseph Smith,* 171). Those who are translated are ministering angels to people on other planets (see *Teachings of the Prophet Joseph Smith,* 170).

KEY INSIGHTS ABOUT THE SAVIOR

- The Lord blesses those who keep His commandments.
- The Lord makes future events known to His prophets.
- The Lord sometimes makes the future known to His prophets but commands that they not reveal it until after the prophecy is fulfilled.
- The Lord cannot look upon sin with the least degree of allowance.
- The Lord occasionally takes up the very righteous to Himself without causing them to taste of death.

Alma 46

> "And it came to pass that [Moroni] rent In memory of our God, our religion, and he fastened it upon the end of a pole."

MAJOR CONCEPT

Liberty is a magnificent gift that we should fight for and covenant to keep.

OVERVIEW Amalickiah, the leader of the Nephite dissenters, wants to be king; he has many followers who have left the Church, and he begins to stir them up in anger as part of his campaign to be king. Moroni, who is chief commander of the armies, is angry over Amalickiah's tactics and raises the title of liberty, rallying his people to defend their religion. Those who believe in Christ are called Christians. Moroni and his armies enter a covenant to keep the peace. When many of Amalickiah's men begin to doubt that his cause is just, Amalickiah takes some of his followers and flees into the land of Nephi. Moroni executes those remaining Amalickiahites who will not covenant to defend freedom and maintain a free government. Order is established, and the people live in peace for four years.

INTERESTING FACTS ABOUT THE TITLE OF LIBERTY From the Dead Sea Scrolls we learn that ancient Israelite armies wrote

PROMINENT PEOPLE

- Moroni
- Amalickiah

MAIN THEMES

- The objective of those who make secret combinations is often to gain control of the government.
- Men are quick to forget the Lord and His blessings and are easily led away by those who are evil.
- One very wicked person can cause great wickedness to take place among an entire group or civilization.
- We must be aggressive and rapid in our defense of righteousness.

- We should pray for the preservation of liberty and be willing to covenant for it.
- Once we commit to the Lord, we leave neutral ground. We are either for Him or against Him.
- We can rejoice at our own death if we believe in the Lord's redemption.
- If we fall into transgression, we are subject to destruction, just as the Jaredites were destroyed.

his coat; and he took a piece thereof, and wrote upon it—freedom, and our peace, our wives, and our children—and (Alma 46:12)

slogans on their trumpets and banners—slogans that emphasized the preservation of liberty and the people's desire to be delivered from bondage. The legendary founder of the Magi and liberator of Persia, a blacksmith named Kawe, tied his leather apron around the end of a pole and used it to rally his people—and this "Flag of Kawe," says Hugh Nibley, was used for centuries as the national banner of the Persians and the sacred emblem of the Magi. Such a tradition would have very understandably influenced Captain Moroni to tear a piece from his coat, write on it, tie it to a pole, and use it as a symbol to muster his troops (see *Echoes*, 469). The rending of the people's garments when they made their covenant with Moroni was an ancient Biblical tradition designating intensity of feeling (just as the high priest rent his garment at Jesus' trial).

WHO WAS AMALICKIAH? Amalickiah was a Nephite dissenter who wanted power and control over the Nephites. Beginning in about 73 BC, he directed all his efforts at destroying the church of God and the government of the people so he could rule over all. When Moroni hoisted the title of liberty and thwarted Amalickiah's designs to take over Zarahemla, Amalickiah fled to the Lamanite armies. There he used deceit to gain control of the armies, the throne itself, and even the wife of the Lamanite king he had murdered. He then unleashed a massive assault against the Nephite strongholds but was ultimately defeated by Moroni and his forces. Around 65 BC, the Nephite general Teancum plunged a javelin into Amalickiah's heart as he slept, killing him.

KEY INSIGHTS ABOUT THE SAVIOR

- The Lord blesses those who covenant with Him.
- The Lord will cause those who do not obey the commandments and keep their covenants to perish.
- The Savior redeems His people.

Alma 47

MAJOR CONCEPT

We should trust in the Lord, not in men—we have no way of knowing their thoughts, desires, and motives.

OVERVIEW Amalickiah flees to the Lamanites, where he uses treachery, intrigue, and murder to become their king, to gain control over the Lamanite armies, and to take the wife of the murdered Lamanite king as his own. Amalickiah and all the Nephite dissenters are described as being more wicked and ferocious than the Lamanites.

INTERESTING FACTS ABOUT NAME-GIVING IN THE BOOK OF MORMON According to Jennifer Clark Lane, names in the Book of Mormon have importance and significance consistent with Israelite practices recorded in the Old Testament. The concept that a name can also be a memorial is demonstrated when Helaman talks to his sons Nephi

PROMINENT PEOPLE

- Amalickiah
- Lehonti
- Amalickiah's wife, the queen

MAIN THEMES

- Those who apostatize from the truth are generally more wicked and ferocious than they who never had it to begin with.
- Apostasy is spread when the apostate gains a little power, develops a detailed plan, and seduces others with promises.
- The wicked use fraud to gain power.
- Wicked leaders will plot against their own troops if it works to their advantage.
- Those who apostatize from the truth become hardened and entirely forget the Lord.

and Lehi about their names (see Hel. 5:6–7). The Israelite idea that a change of name shows a change of character is demonstrated by the Lamanites who covert to Christ and are desirous that they have a new name, that they may thereby be distinguished from their brethren (see Alma 23:16). As in the Old Testament, renaming is also understood to be part of a covenant. When the Lord made covenants with Abram, he was given a new name (see Gen. 17:4–7), as was his wife (see Gen. 17:15); and when the Lord made His covenant with Jacob, he was also given a new name (see Gen. 32:28). When Moroni rallies the people of Nephi with the title of liberty, those who were true believers in Christ gladly took upon them His name (see Alma 46:15). They knew that if they fell into transgression, they would then be ashamed to take upon themselves His name (see Alma 46:21). In the Book of Mormon, the making of covenants is usually connected

600 BC

90 BC

Amalickiah; for he being a very subtle man to do evil dethrone the king of the Lamanites." (Alma 47:4)

with taking upon oneself the name of Christ—a practice that connects renaming with adoption, which was done in the ancient Near East (see "The Lord Will Redeem His People: Adoptive Covenant and Redemption in the Old Testament and Book of Mormon," 47).

WHO WAS LEHONTI? Around 72 BC part of the Lamanite army resisted the command of the king to go to war against the Nephites; their leader was Lehonti. Amalickiah, now an emissary of the king, came against Lehonti and lured him down from his mountain stronghold to a conference, in which he offered to turn over himself and the king's army to Lehonti if he could be made second in command. Lehonti readily agreed. During the night, Lehonti led his forces to the valley and surrounded the king's forces, who the next morning pled with Amalickiah to spare them destruction if they would unite with the forces of Lehonti. That had been Amalickiah's plan all along. He then ordered one of his servants to poison Lehonti. Since he was second in command, Amalickiah assumed full control of all the Lamanite forces in the wake of Lehonti's demise.

KEY INSIGHTS ABOUT THE SAVIOR

- Because He grants men their agency, the Lord cannot prevent some from turning against the truth and leading others away.

Alma 48

"Yea, verily, verily I say unto you, if all Moroni, behold, the very powers of hell never have power over the hearts of the

MAJOR CONCEPT

The works and influence of just one righteous man can inspire an entire nation.

OVERVIEW As soon as Amalickiah gains control of the kingdom, he begins to inspire the hearts of the people against the Nephites. As Amalickiah gains increasing power through fraud and deceit, Moroni inspires his people to be faithful to the Lord and strengthens his armies so they can defend themselves against the Lamanites. Moroni is shown to be a determined defender of freedom and a mighty man of God and is compared to Alma the Younger and the sons of Mosiah. The Lamanites come to war against the Nephites in battles that last many years.

WHO WAS MORONI? In this chapter, Mormon maintains that if all of us were like Moroni, the devil never would have

PROMINENT PEOPLE

- Amalickiah
- Moroni

power over the hearts of men (see verse 17). This chapter specifies personality traits that contributed to Moroni's greatness which, combined with information about him in other chapters, give us a sense of why he was so favored by the Lord: he sought for and heeded the word of the Lord from prophets;

MAIN THEMES

- The wicked use fraud and deceit to achieve their purposes.
- Safety comes through faithfully following the Lord.
- We are justified in fighting for our liberty, lands, families, and religion.
- Those who are righteous strive for peace.
- We should follow Moroni's example of love for our liberty and country.
- We should be firm in the faith of Christ.
- While we may not delight in bloodshed and should not initiate battle, we should be

willing to give our own blood to defend the things that are truly important.

- Righteous men and women sorrow when they kill others even in righteous defense of liberty and truth.

90 BC

men had been, and were, and ever would be, like unto would have been shaken forever; yea, the devil would children of men." (Alma 48:17)

he was concerned about those under his command and made sure they were prepared for any situation; he was ready to forgive but firm for the right; he was patriotic and defended the liberty of his people; he held forth a standard of righteousness to follow and provided a powerful example; he was a man of God. Other traits of Moroni included that he was strong and mighty; he was a man of perfect understanding; he did not delight in bloodshed; his soul found joy in liberty and freedom; he was grateful for his blessings; he labored for the welfare of his people; he was firm in the faith of Christ; and he swore with an oath to defend his people, rights, country, and religion, even to the loss of blood.

KEY INSIGHTS ABOUT THE SAVIOR

- The Lord delivers those faithful to Him.
- When we seek His guidance in righteousness and faith, the Lord will direct our paths.
- Humble seekers of peace are highly favored of the Lord.

Alma 49

Major Concept

When we are righteous, the Lord will help us fight our battles.

OVERVIEW Moroni prepares the Nephites against the Lamanites, who use stones and arrows in battle, by building mounds of earth around the cities so high that they cannot be penetrated by the Lamanite weaponry—a type of defense never before used. The Lamanites are astonished, and Amalickiah is so angry that he swears he will drink Moroni's blood. Moroni perfectly predicts the reaction of the Lamanite leaders and prepares his people in every way to withstand the attacks. Helaman continues to strengthen the church.

INTERESTING FACTS ABOUT WARS AND WARFARE
Considering how difficult it was to engrave on the plates,

Prominent People

- Amalickiah
- Moroni
- Lehi
- Helaman
- Shiblon
- Corianton
- Ammon

Main Themes

- Wise strategy can overcome numbers in battle.
- We are better able to defend ourselves if we can predict the movements and tactics of our enemies.

we should seriously ponder what Mormon saw in our day and in these accounts of war that caused him to preserve them in his abridgement. The Book of Mormon abounds with lengthy descriptions of warfare, including the goals of military leaders, types of weapons employed, and the specific tactics used in battle. At the time the Book of Mormon was published, experts claimed that war did not play an important role in the history of Mesoamerica. But data collected in the last three decades shows that armed conflict was a major part of life in ancient Mesoamerica—scholarly information that matches the Book of Mormon record of frequent wars (see Echoes, 292–296).

WHO WAS LEHI? When Moroni was chief commander of the Nephite forces, he surrounded himself with associates of the highest character, including field

ALMA

enemies; and thus the Lamanites did attempt to destroy the slain; yea, and more than a thousand of the Lamanites were a single soul of the Nephites which was slain." (Alma 49:23)

general Lehi, who was instrumental in the Nephite victories under Moroni. In a later commission around 72 BC, Lehi was appointed chief captain over the city of Noah, which had a reputation for being weak. He successfully defended the city. In a subsequent encounter around 64 BC, Lehi and his forces assisted in the defeat of the Lamanites near Bountiful. That same year, Lehi was placed in charge of the city of Mulek, one of the chief cities of the Lamanites in the land of Nephi. Lehi was also instrumental in reclaiming the capital and in various battles in the land of Moroni, helping to restore peace around 60 BC.

Top Image: Ruins of earthen walls surrounding the ancient city of Becan in Mexico.
Bottom Image: Diagram showing a map of Becan, including the city wall.

KEY INSIGHTS ABOUT THE SAVIOR

- The Lord protects those who keep His commandments and assists them in battle against their enemies.

Alma 50-51

"And those who were faithful in
at all times, whilst thousands of
or to perish by the sword, or to

MAJOR CONCEPT

The greatest protection we can have is righteousness.

OVERVIEW Moroni carries out a strategy to fortify the Nephite lands and builds many new cities in preparation for war. Internal wars and destruction afflict the Nephites, who have become wicked. Teancum defeats Morianton and his dissenters; Nephihah dies, and his son Pahoran becomes the chief judge. When the king-men try to legally overthrow Pahoran and establish a king, the people support Pahoran, and Moroni requires the king-men to defend the country or be put to death. Many of the fortified cities are captured by Amalickiah and his Lamanite armies until Teancum slays Amalickiah in his tent.

PROMINENT PEOPLE

- Moroni
- Morianton
- Teancum
- Nephihah
- Pahoran
- Amalickiah

WHO WAS TEANCUM? Teancum was one of the great leaders who fought under Captain Moroni and was put in charge of quelling a rebellion between two Nephite groups—one led by Morianton—around 67 BC. Soon after, Teancum engaged the forces of the Lamanite army under Amalickiah, a Nephite dissenter, and killed him one night in his battle tent. Teancum was also instrumental in helping regain the city of Mulek around 64 BC. The final act of Teancum's distinguished military career involved Ammoron, Amalickiah's brother, who played a major role in the lengthy conflict between the Nephites and the Lamanites and who had been responsible for much of the bloodshed in those battles; for that reason, Teancum stole into Ammoron's tent one night and thrust a javelin into his heart. The king alerted his guards, who pursued Teancum and killed him.

MAIN THEMES

- Just as the Nephites did in battle, we need to fortify ourselves against the forces of evil.

- We are blessed in righteousness but cut off when we fail to obey the commandments.

- We increase our assurance of protection by cutting off the strength of our enemies.

- Circumstances need not determine our happiness.

ALMA

keeping the commandments of the Lord were delivered their wicked brethren have been consigned to bondage, dwindle in unbelief. . . ." (Alma 50:22)

INTERESTING FACTS ABOUT THE ROLE OF GOVERNMENT The swearing-in ceremony of Pahoran to replace Nephihah indicates what the role of government should be: to judge righteously; to keep the peace and freedom of the people; to grant sacred privileges of worship; to support and maintain the cause of God; and to bring the wicked to justice.

KEY INSIGHTS ABOUT THE SAVIOR

- The Lord is merciful and just to the fulfilling of all His words.
- The Lord blesses those who keep His commandments, but cuts off those who do not.
- The Lord delivers His righteous and consigns the wicked to bondage.

Alma 52

MAJOR CONCEPT

All those who take the sword will perish by the sword (see Matt. 26:52).

OVERVIEW Teancum and his armies continue to prepare for war, taking all necessary steps to defend themselves against the Lamanites. Ammoron, the brother of Amalickiah, is appointed king over the Lamanites, and orders his armies to maintain the cities they had taken by the shedding of blood. Moroni, Teancum, and Lehi lead the Nephite armies in a victorious war against the Lamanites; they recapture the city of Mulek, and Jacob the Lamanite is slain.

WHO WAS JACOB? Jacob was the leader of the Lamanite occupation force in the city of Mulek during the Nephite/Lamanite confrontation around 64 BC. Moroni had attempted to entice Jacob out of his position inside the city, but Jacob refused to move. Moroni then arranged for Teancum to march by the city with a small force, and Jacob couldn't resist following them. While Jacob and his army were in pursuit of Teancum, Moroni and his forces retook the city of Mulek. When Jacob realized his error and tried to retreat, he learned he was surrounded on all sides by the Nephite armies; in the furious battle that ensued, Moroni was wounded and Jacob was killed.

PROMINENT PEOPLE

- Moroni
- Amalickiah
- Ammoron
- Teancum
- Lehi
- Jacob

MAIN THEMES

- Even though we are sometimes forced to go to war to defend our liberties and our families, we should always be reluctant to engage in war.
- We should use wise strategies in defending ourselves against evil.
- We should do whatever we can to strengthen ourselves.
- War is always the result of sin and disobedience on someone's part.
- Our wrestle may not be in a war of nations but in an individual wrestle against spiritual wickedness.

ALMA

arrive with his army at the land of

KEY INSIGHTS ABOUT THE SAVIOR

- The Lord rejoices in righteousness and sorrows over the disobedience and sin that lead to war.

Alma 53

MAJOR CONCEPT

As covenant people, we are protected when we keep our covenants.

OVERVIEW In the ongoing battles between the Nephites and the Lamanites, the Lamanite prisoners are used to fortify the city of Bountiful. The Lamanites win several battles. When the Ammonites want to help defend the Nephites, they face violating the oath they took to never again take up weapons of war. Instead, their sons—who have never taken such an oath—volunteer to fight and are led by Helaman.

INTERESTING FACTS ABOUT CHIVALRY IN WAR According to Hugh Nibley, warriors in the Book of Mormon—from the Jaredites to the final battle between the Nephites and the Lamanites—consistently conformed to rules of chivalry

PROMINENT PEOPLE

- Moroni
- Helaman
- Two thousand stripling warriors

in battle. Enemies agreed to the time and place of battles, chiefs challenged each other to single combat for the kingdom, and so on. The War Scroll of the Dead Sea Scrolls gives other rules of chivalry, including that warriors were to be clean and blameless so the angels of God could provide divine

MAIN THEMES

- Sin and iniquity place us in perilous circumstances.

- Our covenants are sacred promises between us and the Lord and are not to be taken lightly or broken.

- We need to be true at all times, not just when it is easy or convenient.

- We can feel confident and safe being led by a prophet.

ALMA

soberness, for they had been taught to keep the uprightly before him." (Alma 53:21)

assistance in battle. Righteous armies in the Book of Mormon followed these criteria, especially when it came to the two thousand stripling warriors (see *Echoes*, 479–480).

WHO WERE THE 2,000 STRIPLING WARRIORS?

During the second quarter of the last century BC, Moroni and Helaman defended their land relentlessly from Lamanite invasions. Around 64 BC, a serious military situation required reinforcements on the Nephite side. The people of Ammon—Lamanite converts who had been relocated among the Nephites for safety—were grieved because of the afflictions the Nephites endured on their behalf. They were about to suspend the oath they had sworn to never again use weapons of war when Helaman dissuaded them, fearing they would imperil their salvation. The solution was in the spirit and courage of the sons of the people of Ammon who had not taken an oath against bearing arms. Two thousand of these young men—called the stripling warriors—were a decisive factor in many battles, fighting with faith, trust, courage, and obedience. They fought like lions, soundly defeating the Lamanites, and while all were injured, not a single one was slain. While their military activity was relatively brief, they remain to this day an example of great faith.

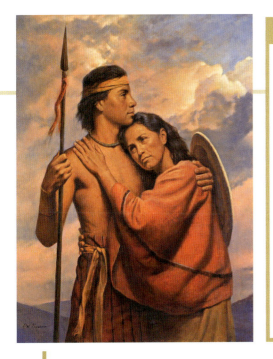

KEY INSIGHTS ABOUT THE SAVIOR

- The Savior protects the righteous in battle.
- The Lord supports us when we obey the commandments and keep our covenants.
- The Lord expects us to exercise great care in observing our vows (in this chapter, Helaman fears that breaking a vow would cost the Ammonites their souls).

Alma 54-55

"[Moroni] did not delight in delighted in the saving of his (Alma 55:19)

MAJOR CONCEPT

Those with righteous desires are protected by the Lord.

OVERVIEW These two chapters begin a word-for-word account of an epistle sent from Moroni to Ammoron, negotiating for an exchange of prisoners and demanding that the Lamanites withdraw and cease their attacks. In answer, Ammoron demands that the Nephites lay down their weapons and become subject to the Lamanites. Moroni refuses these terms. He entices the Lamanite guards to become drunk, and the Nephite prisoners are freed. The city of Gid is captured without any bloodshed.

WHO WAS LAMAN? Laman was a servant of the king of the Lamanites, the same king who was murdered by servants of the dissenter Amalickiah around 72 BC. Laman had fled

to the Nephite side and soon thereafter joined the military under the command of Captain Moroni. Over a decade later—during which time the war between the Nephites and the Lamanites continued to rage—Moroni devised a plan to disable the Lamanite guards through drunkenness. He needed a person of Lamanite descent to enact his plan, and Laman was his man. Laman and a small group of men were dispatched to the Lamanite encampment at Gid. When the guards challenged Laman, he proclaimed that he was a Lamanite who had escaped from the Nephites and that he and his men had brought wine. The strategy worked. The Lamanite guards fell into a drunken stupor, and Moroni and his army freed the Nephite prisoners and captured the city without bloodshed. The next morning when the Lamanite guards awakened, they were taken prisoner.

PROMINENT PEOPLE

- Moroni
- Ammoron
- Laman

MAIN THEMES

- Those who are steeped in iniquity generally continue in their wicked behavior.
- The righteous should not attack but should defend themselves against the attack of evil forces.
- Vengeance is an unrighteous response to affliction.
- We should always remember the Lord in our affliction.
- Prophets warn the wicked of the consequences that await them if they fail to repent.

ALMA

murder or bloodshed, but he
people from destruction. . . ."

KEY INSIGHTS ABOUT THE SAVIOR

- The Lord cuts off those who do not believe in His name.
- The Lord does not protect and defend those who are slow to remember Him in their affliction.

Alma 56-57

MAJOR CONCEPT

Faith gives us hope, calms our fears, and protects us.

OVERVIEW The battles between the Nephites and the Lamanites continue as Moroni receives an epistle from Helaman stating the affairs of his army, particularly his 2,000 stripling warriors, in regaining several captured cities. They defeat a Lamanite army several times their size. Ammoron reacts by sending Helaman an epistle offering the city of Antiparah in exchange for Lamanite prisoners, which Helaman refuses. Helaman and his army succeed in capturing Antiparah and Cumeni, due in large part to the heroic fighting of the 2,000 stripling warriors. Many of these young men are wounded, but none are slain.

MAIN THEMES

- When we are prepared, we need not fear.
- Faith results in great courage.
- If we do not doubt, the Lord will deliver us.
- We need to obey every commandment with exactness.
- We should trust in God continually.
- When the righteous are slain in battle, they are then happy in a state of paradise where they can rest from care and sorrow.
- The influence of righteous mothers on their sons cannot be underestimated.

PROMINENT PEOPLE

- Moroni
- Ammoron
- Helaman
- Antipus
- Gid

WHO WAS ANTIPUS? Antipus served as a general in the Nephite army during the time Moroni was commander and Helaman was leading his 2,000 stripling warriors. In the year 66 BC, Helaman and his army marched to the city of Judea to assist Antipus, the leader in that part of the land. The Lamanites had occupied many Nephite cities and were determined to capture Judea. Antipus and his armies had fought valiantly and were worn out from their struggles; Helaman's army restored hope to Antipus and his troops, and they were able to protect Judea from being overtaken. When the Lamanites began to vigorously pursue Helaman's army, Antipus and his troops overtook the Lamanites from the rear. Helaman and his men circled back and assisted in the battle, which the Nephites eventually won. Antipus was slain in the battle.

ALMA

they did not fear death; and they did think more upon they did upon their lives; yea, they had been taught not doubt, God would deliver them." (Alma 56:47)

KEY INSIGHTS ABOUT THE SAVIOR

- The Lord brings proper perspective to all things in His due time.
- The Lord preserves and delivers His righteous people.
- The Savior is just and powerful and protects those who are righteous.

Alma 58-60

"We did pour out our souls
deliver us out of the hands of our
God did visit us with assurances

MAJOR CONCEPT

We must be prepared as a nation; intangible defenses are the most critical.

OVERVIEW The Nephite armies under Helaman, Gid, and Teomner use strategy to capture the city of Manti; the Lamanites withdraw, and the 2,000 stripling warriors are preserved because of their great faith. The Lamanites capture the city of Nephihah, and Moroni petitions Pahoran, the governor and chief judge, for help and sustenance for the Nephite armies. No response comes, and the Nephites use all their strength and means to defend themselves against the Lamanites. Despite their efforts, they lose the city of Nephihah to the Lamanites. Moroni threatens to fight the government unless he receives help.

PROMINENT PEOPLE

- Helaman
- Gid
- Teomner
- Moroni
- Pahoran

WHO WERE TEOMNER AND GID?

Teomner—a Nephite soldier—fought along with Gid to help Helaman lure the Lamanites from the city of Manti. Teomner and a small group of soldiers lay in wait for the Lamanites on one side of the city, while Gid and another group lay in wait on the other side. Helaman marched forth and drew the Lamanites out of the city; they pursued Helaman, thinking he and his men would be easy prey. As Helaman led the army away in pursuit, Teomner and Gid moved into Manti, which had been left with only a few guards, and easily took the city. Helaman circled around during the night and reached Manti ahead of the Lamanites, who fled into the wilderness in defeat.

MAIN THEMES

- We should petition the Lord in our times of affliction.

- Our greatest source of peace is righteousness in the Lord.

- It is easier to prevent ourselves from falling into sin than to repent afterwards.

- Contending among ourselves and causing lack of unity allows the enemy to gain advantage over us.

- Righteous defenders of liberty seek not honor but the glory of God.

ALMA

in prayer to God, that he would strengthen us and enemies. . . . Yea, and it came to pass that the Lord our that he would deliver us. . . ." (Alma 57:10–11)

KEY INSIGHTS ABOUT THE SAVIOR

- The Lord delivers His people.
- The Lord speaks peace to our souls with assurances and hope as we petition Him for help.
- The Lord supports the righteous in battle.
- The Lord sometimes allows the righteous to be slain so that his judgments against the wicked can be justified.
- The righteous who die are received by the Lord and enter His rest.
- The Savior expects us to clean the inner vessel first, then the outer.

Alma 61-62

"Therefore, my beloved brother, words, . . . let us resist them with the great privilege of our church,

MAJOR CONCEPT

We should fight to resist and conquer evil in all its forms.

OVERVIEW Chapter 61—a classic in scriptural literature—unravels the misunderstanding between Pahoran and Moroni, both great men. Pahoran tells Moroni that the king-men have taken Zarahemla and are in league with the Lamanites; he asks for and receives aid from Moroni against the rebels. The king-men who refuse to defend their country are put to death. Pahoran and Moroni work together to recapture Nephihah, and many of the Lamanites join the people of Ammon. Teancum slays Ammoron and is in turn slain himself. The Lamanites are driven from the land, and peace is restored. Helaman dies.

PROMINENT PEOPLE

- Moroni
- Pahoran
- Pachus
- Teancum
- Ammoron

WHO WAS PAHORAN? Pahoran, the son of Nephihah, succeeded his father as chief judge and governor in Zarahemla around 67 BC with an oath to judge righteously, preserve the right of the people to worship the Lord, help support the cause of God, and bring the wicked to justice. He lived up

MAIN THEMES

- The righteous rejoice in the protection of the faithful and mourn over the iniquity of their enemies.

- We should be a peace-loving people.

- The word of God has the power to convince people of their wickedness.

- Regardless of our circumstances, we should humble ourselves before the Lord and pray to Him continually.

- We should "stand fast" when inaccurately accused of doing wrong and should refuse to take offense instead of becoming angry.

Moroni, let us resist evil, and whatsoever evil we cannot resist with our our swords, that we may retain our freedom, that we may rejoice in and in the cause of our Redeemer and our God." (Alma 61:14)

to that solemn oath of office throughout his sixteen-year tenure, working with Moroni to restore peace to the land in the wake of the rebellion of the king-men (those who wanted to overthrow the democratic government and reinstate a king). Pahoran is probably best known for his correspondence with Moroni, who accused him of failing to support the armies. Moroni did not know that Pahoran had been deposed by enemies and forced to flee for his life; when Pahoran finally received word of Moroni's desperate condition, Pahoran apologized profusely and did all in his power to provide aid. Moroni, on his part, rushed to the assistance of Pahoran; the two collaborated in a successful effort to rid the capital of the king-men, repel the invading Lamanites, and restore peace to the land.

KEY INSIGHTS ABOUT THE SAVIOR

- The Lord delivers His people.
- The Lord strengthens the righteous in battle.
- The Savior helps all those who stand in defense of liberty.
- Those who fight against the Lord are considered by Him to be treasonous.

Alma 63

"And [Shiblon] was a just man, and he observe to do good continually, to keep (Alma 63:2)

MAJOR CONCEPT

We should pass on our love of the scriptures to our children and grandchildren.

OVERVIEW After Helaman dies, Shiblon assumes responsibility for the sacred records; his nephew Helaman takes the records when Shiblon dies. Both are righteous men. Copies of the records other than those forbidden by Alma are made and distributed among the people of the land. Moroni dies. Approximately 5,400 Nephite men, along with their wives and children, leave the land of Zarahemla and go into the land to the north. Hagoth builds a huge ship and launches it into the sea at Bountiful, carrying many Nephite men, women, and children. Moronihah defeats the Lamanites in battle.

PROMINENT PEOPLE

- Shiblon
- Helaman
- Hagoth
- Moronihah

MAIN THEMES

- Most of those who kept the records were righteous men who tried to do good continually and obey the commandments of the Lord.

INTERESTING FACTS ABOUT HAGOTH'S SHIPS Shortly before the Savior's birth, Hagoth built ships and sent explorers northward from the "narrow neck of land" on the west coast of the Nephites' promised land. On the Pacific side of the Isthmus of Tehuantepec—which qualifies by multiple criteria as the "narrow neck of land"— lie two lagoons that are more than thirty miles long. These sheltered bodies of water would have been ideal for the building and testing of Hagoth's ships. Many centuries later in the mountains overlooking the lagoons, Spaniards found timber suitable for shipbuilding (see *Echoes*, 298).

WHO WAS HAGOTH? When the church was reestablished and the people began to prosper around 56 BC, an industry based on shipbuilding began to prosper. An "exceedingly curious man" named Hagoth built a huge ship on which many Nephites

600 BC

90 BC

did walk uprightly before God; and he did the commandments of the Lord his God. . . ."

sailed northward. The following year, Hagoth built additional ships. The original ship returned, was launched again carrying many Nephites, and was never heard from again. The people of Hagoth's day believed the passengers were drowned at sea. A second ship also set sail toward unknown destinations. Other than the fact that he was curious and built ships, little is known of Hagoth. We don't know whether he was a passenger on any of the ships he built. Elder Mark E. Petersen stated that the people of New Zealand were descendants of Hagoth's people (see Conference Report, Apr. 1962, 112).

KEY INSIGHTS ABOUT THE SAVIOR

• The Lord preserves the sacred records of His dealings with His children.

Helaman 1

"[Paanchi] was taken, and was tried for he had raised up in rebellion

MAJOR CONCEPT

The righteous who seek to preserve liberty must guard against the wicked who enter into secret oaths in order to gain power.

OVERVIEW The book of Helaman was abridged by Mormon from the large plates, which detailed the wars and contentions of the Nephites and the prophecies of those who lived just prior to the birth of the Savior. In this brief chapter, three prominent leaders are slain: Pahoran II, Pacumeni, and Coriantumr. Pahoran's son—Pahoran II—takes the judgment seat but is slain by Kishkumen. Pacumeni then fills the judgment seat but is slain by Coriantumr, the leader of the Lamanite armies, when he conquers Zarahemla. Coriantumr is then slain by Moronihah, who defeats the Lamanites and recaptures Zarahemla.

PROMINENT PEOPLE

- Pahoran II
- Paanchi
- Pacumeni
- Kishkumen
- Coriantumr
- Moronihah

WHO WAS PAHORAN II? In the year 52 BC, a heated dispute arose in Zarahemla regarding who should succeed Pahoran, the chief judge who had just died. All three of his sons—Pahoran II, Paanchi, and Pacumeni—contended for the position. The people elected Pahoran II. Pacumeni acquiesced

MAIN THEMES

- Secret combinations continued to exist just prior to the Savior's birth.

- Those who circumvent the law will resort to violence to gain power.

- Dissenters from the truth often harbor the greatest hatred for the truth and for the righteous followers of truth.

- Internal contention distracts us from protecting ourselves against outside enemies.

- The oaths sworn in connection with secret combinations are Satan's counterfeits to the covenants we make in sacred temples.

according to the voice of the people, and condemned unto death; and sought to destroy the liberty of the people." (Hel. 1:8)

to the democratic vote, but Paanchi and his followers, furious to have lost, were about to incite a revolution when Paanchi was arrested, tried, and condemned to death (see verse 8). Paanchi's followers arranged for Pahoran II to be assassinated by a wicked man named Kishkumen. Pacumeni then became chief judge and governor, a position he held until he was killed the following year by invading Lamanites.

Image: Central American ruins.

Helaman 2

MAJOR CONCEPT

The wicked who desire to gain power will make secret oaths to conspire against the righteous.

OVERVIEW Helaman, the son of Helaman, becomes chief judge in Zarahemla following the assassination of Pacumeni. Gadianton leads the band of Kishkumen, who was responsible for killing Pahoran II. Kishkumen conspires to kill Helaman, but one of Helaman's servants succeeds in killing Kishkumen. The Gadianton robbers flee into the wilderness and cannot be found.

WHO WAS KISHKUMEN? The era of peace established by Captain Moroni was shattered with the election of Pahoran II, who succeeded his father as chief judge and governor. His brother Paanchi revolted and was sentenced to death—but his faction arranged for a man named Kishkumen to murder Pahoran II as he sat on his judgment seat. Kishkumen then joined the band of dissenters, who took an oath that they would never reveal Kishkumen as the murderer. He and his band went back to Zarahemla in disguise. A man named Gadianton had assumed power of the

PROMINENT PEOPLE

- Helaman
- Kishkumen
- Gadianton

MAIN THEMES

- Those who are wicked try to trick the righteous by flattery.
- People will do almost anything to gain power.
- The wicked who enter secret combinations can cause widespread destruction.
- The main characteristics of secret combinations are that they are secret, involve murder, and revolve around getting gain.

dissenters, and he persuaded Kishkumen to also murder Helaman, the son of Helaman, who was the current chief judge. One of Helaman's servants had disguised himself and infiltrated the band of dissenters; he learned of the assassination plot, pretended to be a co-conspirator of Kishkumen, and stabbed Kishkumen in the heart on their way to murder Helaman.

ARE THERE MODERN-DAY SECRET COMBINATIONS? We have examples in our day of groups that work wickedness and oppose righteousness, just as some did in the days of the Book of Mormon. Elder M. Russell Ballard said that gangs, drug cartels, and organized crime families function today much like the secret combinations in the Book of Mormon. These all have secret signs and code words, secret rites, and secret initiation ceremonies, just as the secret combinations of old (see Conference Report, Oct. 1997, 51, 52).

KEY INSIGHTS ABOUT THE SAVIOR

- The Lord despises the wicked who conspire against the righteous.

"Yea, we see that the gate of heaven
Jesus Christ, who is the Son of

MAJOR CONCEPT

In order to become pure and holy, we must yield our hearts to the Savior.

OVERVIEW Helaman pauses in his record to tell about the large group of Nephites who left Zarahemla and migrated to the north. They establish a thriving civilization that covers the entire land and build houses of cement, cities, temples, and synagogues. He verifies that many records were kept during this period, chiefly by the Nephites. He returns to his record to say that Helaman is filling the judgment seat with justice and equity, walking in righteousness. Tens of thousands are converted to the church and are baptized, and the church prospers exceedingly. Helaman dies, and his son Nephi assumes the judgment seat.

PROMINENT PEOPLE

- Helaman
- Nephi
- Lehi
- Gadianton

MAIN THEMES

- Even a little pride can cause dissension.
- The word of God is quick and powerful in dividing asunder the snares of the devil.
- The word of God leads the man of Christ in a strait and narrow course to the right hand of God.
- Righteousness brings peace and rejoicing.
- To become sanctified—pure and holy—we must fast and pray often, become humble, and become firm in our faith of Christ.

INTERESTING FACTS ABOUT CEMENT BUILDING MATERIALS In this chapter, we read that the Nephites became expert in using cement to construct not only their houses, but entire cities. In fact, cement began to be used extensively in Mesoamerica around this time (46 BC). Found in the Valley of Mexico, the oldest-known concrete has been dated at approximately 200 BC, after which it was used on a large scale, as exemplified in the immense ruins of Teotihuacán, near Mexico City (*Echoes*, 287–288). In Guatemala, archaeologists have unearthed 2,000-year-old cement tombs and burial vaults.

WHO WAS HELAMAN? Helaman—the son of Helaman and the grandson of Alma the Younger—enjoyed the blessing of a distinguished family legacy of spiritual values upon which to build his service as chief judge in Zarahemla slightly more than a century before the resurrected Savior visited America. Having survived an assassination attempt, he presided

600 BC

90 BC

is open unto all, even to those who will believe on the name of God." (Hel. 3:28)

over a period of great economic development and exceptional growth in the church. His tenure as chief judge lasted from approximately 50 to 39 BC. His righteous leadership offered a stark contrast to the intrigues and secret combinations of Gadianton, who rose to power at the same time. Helaman named his two sons after two of their ancestors, Nephi and Lehi, and bestowed upon them inspired patriarchal blessings. Upon Helaman's death, his son Nephi assumed the judgment seat.

Image: Ruins of Teotihuacán.

Key Insights about the Savior

- The Lord is merciful to all those who call on His name with sincerity of heart.
- Jesus Christ is the Son of God.
- The Lord sanctifies those who yield their hearts unto Him.

Helaman 4

"Now this great loss of the Nephites and their abomination which was

MAJOR CONCEPT

We do not prosper spiritually if we fail to follow the commandments.

OVERVIEW The Nephites become a prideful and wicked people. Dissenters from the Nephites join with the Lamanites, who attack and gain control of the land of Zarahemla. The church dwindles, and the people become weak like the Lamanites.

WHO WAS MORONIHAH? Moronihah succeeded his father as commander of the Nephite armed forces around 60 BC. As the son of Moroni, he received superior training from his father in strategy, leadership, and love of God and liberty. Moronihah's initial battle occurred when the Lamanites launched a massive invasion and overpowered the capital city of Zarahemla in 51 BC. The Lamanites again conquered Zarahemla over a two-year period with the help of Nephite dissenters in 34 BC, driving the forces of Moronihah north toward Bountiful. Even after several years of battle, the Nephites were able to gain back only about half of their lands. Moronihah and the sons of Helaman (Nephi and Lehi)

PROMINENT PEOPLE

- Moronihah
- Nephi
- Lehi

MAIN THEMES

- Those who are wicked do not enjoy the strength of the Lord.
- Wicked practices that can lead to our defeat include pride, oppression of the poor, failure to serve, mockery of that which is sacred, denial of the spirit of prophecy and revelation, and gross sin.
- Dissension hinders spiritual growth.
- When we boast in our own strength, we are left to our own strength.
- When we turn from the Lord, our source of strength withdraws.

- When covenant people are righteous, faithful, and obedient, even the mighty cannot overthrow them.
- Our transgressions make us weak.

. . . would not have happened had it not been for their wickedness among them. . . .” (Hel. 4:11)

preached repentance to the people, and they began to respond. But Moronihah's subsequent efforts to regain the rest of the Nephite land were in vain because of the decline in spirituality among the Nephites.

Image: Stela dated to December 9, 36 BC, found in Chiapa de Corzo in Mexico—thought to be the city Sidon.

KEY INSIGHTS ABOUT THE SAVIOR

- The Lord strengthens those who turn to Him in humility.
- The Spirit of the Lord cannot dwell in unholy temples.
- The Lord preserves the righteous through His miraculous and matchless power.
- Those within the Church engaged in iniquity have the judgments of God staring them in the face.
- The Lord does not preserve those who fall into a state of unbelief and wickedness.
- When we fail to cleave unto God, we will unavoidably perish.

Helaman 5

> "And now, my sons, remember, our Redeemer, who is Christ, the foundation . . ." (Hel. 5:12)

MAJOR CONCEPT

The Lord protects His servants as they preach truth and repentance.

OVERVIEW Nephi and Lehi, hoping to honor their names, devote themselves to preaching the gospel. They have great success among the Lamanites and convert approximately eight thousand before being imprisoned for preaching the truth. As their Lamanite captors try to destroy them, Nephi and Lehi are surrounded by fire; a cloud of darkness descends on the group of three hundred Lamanites and dissenters; the earth quakes and a voice from heaven calls upon men to repent. Nephi and Lehi talk with angels, and the entire multitude is encircled by fire. Samuel the Lamanite later preaches to these three hundred.

PROMINENT PEOPLE

- Nephi
- Lehi
- Cezoram
- Aminadab
- Angels of God

WHO WAS CEZORAM? In the year 30 BC when Nephi, son of Helaman, yielded up his seat as chief judge to devote himself full-time to the ministry, he was replaced by Cezoram. It was a time of considerable political unease, because those who were evil outnumbered those who were good. Nephi and his brother Lehi had great success as missionaries, bringing about a spiritual reformation. But the peace was short-lived, and Cezoram was murdered by an unknown assailant in 26 BC. His son, who was appointed his successor by the people, suffered the same fate; the perpetrators were members of Gadianton's band.

MAIN THEMES

- A nation that pays no heed to the principles of truth will be destroyed.
- We can be forgiven of our sins through repentance.
- We cannot fall if we build ourselves on the foundation of Jesus Christ.
- Our faith in the Savior is our source of peace.

remember that it is upon the rock of
Son of God, that ye must build your

KEY INSIGHTS ABOUT THE SAVIOR

- Jesus Christ is the only source of our salvation.
- The Lord redeems us *from* our sins, not *in* our sins.
- The Savior has power to redeem us from our sins, but only if we repent.
- The Savior is our sure foundation; the devil will have no power over those built on the foundation of Christ.
- The Lord will inspire us with what we should say as we teach the truth.
- The Savior protects His servants against destruction.
- Those who seek to destroy God's servants have need to repent.
- The Lord was from the foundation of the world.

Helaman 6

> "Now behold, those secret oaths same being who did entice our first forth from the beginning of man

MAJOR CONCEPT

Satan is the author of all secret oaths and combinations, and they have existed since the beginning.

OVERVIEW As this chapter opens, the righteous Lamanites preach to the wicked Nephites in Zarahemla, converting many. For a time the Nephites and Lamanites live together in peace and prosperity. The Gadianton robbers, guided by Satan, commit murders and all manner of wickedness and take over the Nephite government. This chapter provides important insights about secret combinations.

INTERESTING FACTS ABOUT SATAN AND SECRET COMBINATIONS IN THE BOOK OF MORMON Satan is a pervasive presence in the Book of Mormon. The Book of Mormon confirms that Satan enticed Adam and Eve to partake of the forbidden fruit, conspired with

PROMINENT PEOPLE

- Cezoram
- Gadianton
- Satan

Cain to commit murder, motivated the building of the Tower of Babel, spread darkness across the globe, and put wicked designs into the heart of Gadianton. As we are told in this chapter, Satan is truly "the author of all sin" (verse 30). The Book of Mormon identifies a number

MAIN THEMES

- Repentance requires humility.
- Righteousness brings prosperity and refinement to a people.
- Those who become wealthy with the riches of the world tend to become prideful, seeking to get gain and lifting themselves above others.
- Satan is the source and inspiration for all secret oaths and combinations.

and covenants . . . were put into the heart of Gadianton by that parents to partake of the forbidden fruit . . . and he has brought it even down to this time." (Hel. 6:26, 29)

of characteristics of secret combinations, all of which are authored by Satan: they caused the destruction of both the Nephite and Jaredite civilizations; they seek to control the government; their objectives are power and gain; they are established in the more settled parts of the land; they require wickedness to survive; they thrive on secrecy, and violation of secrecy is a capital offense; they involve formal covenant-making; they include violence, plunder, vice, whoredoms, and flattery; they have secret signs, words, and codes to distinguish their members; and they seduce the more righteous people and then partake of their spoils. The only way to destroy secret combinations is through preaching the word (see Hel. 6:37).

WHO WAS GADIANTON? In approximately 50 bc, Gadianton became the leader of a band that had supported Kishkumen in his assassination and treachery. He was a destroyer who used secret combinations to obliterate righteousness. It was Gadianton's band that murdered the chief judge Cezoram and, later, his son. Members of the band continued their violence until they gained control of the government, advancing on cities and then retreating to their mountain hideouts. The "Gadianton pattern" did not originate with Gadianton, however; it began with Satan and was launched from the beginning of the world to thwart the plan of salvation through secret oaths and combinations of murder and mayhem. Eventually Gadianton's band, along with all the wicked, were destroyed in the upheavals that occurred at the death of the Savior. However, his doctrine arose again in the third century AD and continued for several generations, ultimately leading to the destruction of the Nephite civilization.

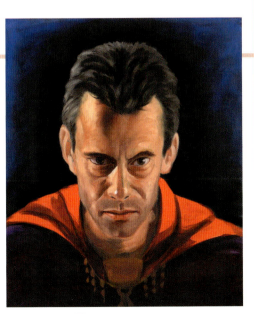

Key Insights about the Savior

- The Lord views secret combinations as above all the wickedness on the earth (see 3 Ne. 9:9).
- The Spirit of the Lord withdraws from those who become wicked.

Helaman 7

"O repent ye, repent ye! Why will the Lord your God." (Hel. 7:17)

MAJOR CONCEPT

We must repent or be destroyed.

OVERVIEW Nephi, the son of Helaman, responds to God's warning that He will destroy the people unless they repent. He preaches in the north, where his message is rejected, then returns to Zarahemla. He prays atop a garden tower, attracting a crowd of people and calling on them to repent or perish.

INTERESTING FACTS ABOUT REPENTANCE The words *repent* and *turn* both come from the same Hebrew word—*shûwb*—which means to "go back home" or "turn away."

WHO WAS NEPHI? Nephi, the son of Helaman, was taught righteousness by his father; he eventually succeeded Helaman as chief judge and served in that office in Zarahemla from approximately 39 BC to 30 BC. He then devoted himself to preaching the gospel full-time with his brother, Lehi; they went from one city to another preaching repentance. Through their efforts, some eight thousand Lamanites were converted

PROMINENT PEOPLE

• Nephi

MAIN THEMES

- The righteous sorrow over the wicked.
- Wickedness often begins with the desire to get gain and be praised by men.
- Pride stands in the way of sincere repentance.
- If we do not repent, we are in a worse circumstance than those who never knew the truth.
- Unless we repent, we will perish.
- When those involved in secret combinations participate in government, great iniquity comes upon the people.

ye die? Turn ye, turn ye unto

in Zarahemla and its vicinity. After preaching in the north for six years, they returned to Zarahemla and found that pride had consumed the people and that secret combinations were thriving. It was then that Nephi poured out his heart in sorrow from his garden tower and called the people to repentance. Nephi was still actively pursuing his ministry during the preaching of Samuel the Lamanite around 6 BC; those who were converted came to Nephi to be baptized. His ministry was completed around AD 1, and he turned the sacred records over to his eldest son, Nephi. He then departed into the land and was not heard from again.

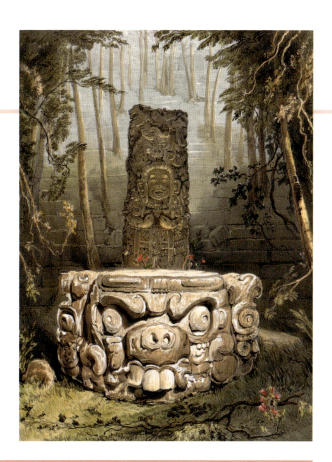

Image: Central American ruins.

KEY INSIGHTS ABOUT THE SAVIOR

- The Lord forsakes those who harden their hearts and refuse to hear His words; they provoke His anger, and He scatters them.
- The Lord does not strengthen or protect those who have turned away from Him.
- The Lord is merciful to those who repent.
- The Lord destroys the wicked.
- Prophets do not speak of themselves; their messages come from the Lord.
- Prophets always declare repentance, as opposed to the messages of priestcraft.

Helaman 8

MAJOR CONCEPT

The preeminent responsibility of a prophet is to testify and bear witness of Christ.

OVERVIEW Nephi continues preaching repentance to the people of Zarahemla; the corrupt judges try to incite the people against Nephi. He reminds the people that every holy prophet from the beginning testified of the Savior. By inspiration, he reveals both the murder of the chief judge and the identity of the murderer.

INTERESTING FACTS ABOUT THE BRAZEN SERPENT Centuries earlier, Nephi had referred to the brazen serpent raised by Moses as an emblem of the Messiah to come (see 2 Ne. 25:20). Alma also taught that this symbol pointed to Christ (see Alma 33:19–22). Through the brass plates of Laban, all the Nephite prophets had access to the account of Moses lifting the brazen serpent. Now Nephi commands the people of his day to open their eyes and look upon the Savior as the Israelites looked upon the serpent for healing (see verse 15).

PROMINENT PEOPLE

- Nephi
- Abraham
- Moses
- Zenos
- Zenock
- Ezias
- Isaiah
- Jeremiah
- Lehi
- Nephi, son of Lehi

MAIN THEMES

- True prophets are not popular with the wicked.
- When we reject the current prophet, we reject all who came before him.
- Those who accept and follow the Savior will gain eternal life.
- All true prophets of all dispensations have testified of Christ.
- Evidences in heaven and on earth witness the truth of prophets' teachings.

WHO WAS EZIAS? Ezias was an ancient prophet whose prophecies were cited by Nephi, son of Helaman, as evidence of the coming of the Son of God (see verse 19). He is named by Nephi as one of those whose testimonies confirm the mission of the Lord. We are not informed about the particulars of the life and times of Ezias but only of his firm testimony of the Savior. His writings were most likely contained in the brass plates of Laban and were familiar to those who had access to those records. The Doctrine and Covenants mentions a prophet named Esias who lived in the time of Abraham (see D&C 84:13), but we don't know whether that prophet is the same as Ezias.

600 BC

90 BC

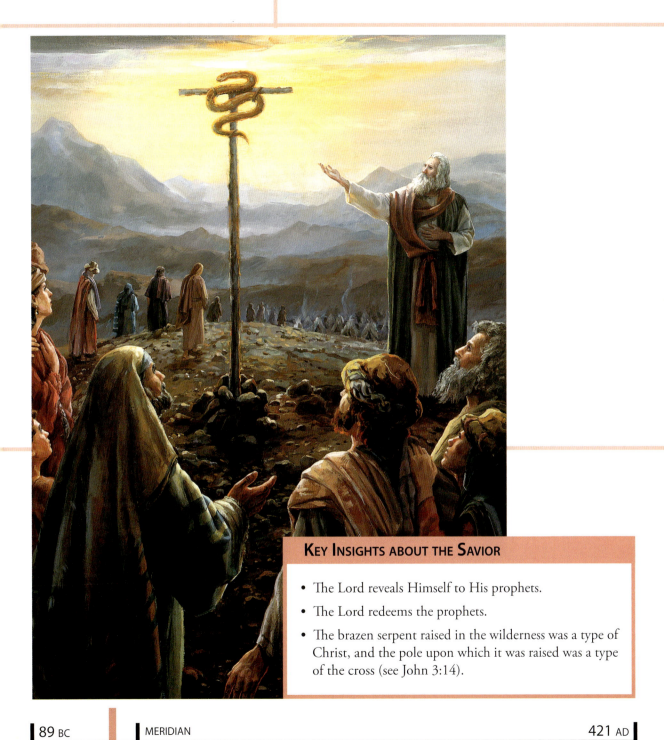

KEY INSIGHTS ABOUT THE SAVIOR

- The Lord reveals Himself to His prophets.
- The Lord redeems the prophets.
- The brazen serpent raised in the wilderness was a type of Christ, and the pole upon which it was raised was a type of the cross (see John 3:14).

"O ye fools, . . . ye blind, and ye suffer you that ye shall go on in this of the great destruction which at

MAJOR CONCEPT

A prophet can tell of all things.

OVERVIEW After Nephi discloses that the chief judge, Seezoram, has been murdered, five messengers find him lying in his own blood; they are initially arrested as suspects but are soon released. Nephi again identifies Seezoram's brother Seantum as the murderer; at first the people suspect Nephi of agreeing with someone to commit the murder, but he tells them they will find blood on the skirts of Seantum's cloak, which they do. Some accept Nephi as a prophet.

INTERESTING FACTS ABOUT RULES IN UNOBSERVED MURDERS Seantum's trial brings up some fascinating issues of Israelite (and therefore Nephite) law. Under the law of Moses, unwitnessed murders posed great difficulties, because

PROMINENT PEOPLE

- Nephi
- Seezoram
- Seantum

in order for a suspect to be convicted, every fact had to be backed up by the testimony of two witnesses. In fact, if a murderer could not be found after an unwitnessed slaying, all of the men in the village had to be purified, and solemn rituals and oaths of innocence were required (see Deut.

MAIN THEMES

- Our safety lies in following the prophet.
- True prophets give prophecies that are eventually fulfilled and validated.
- Prophets give signs when needed.

stiffnecked people, do ye know how long the Lord your God will your way of sin? O ye ought to begin to howl and mourn, because this time doth await you, except ye repent." (Hel. 9:21–22)

21:1–9). Even Seantum's confession to the murder would not generally be accepted in a court of law, as the Talmud forbids a man to be put to death by his own testimony. However, the law does include specific exceptions for convicting someone based on his own testimony, all of which Seantum's case meets. First, the confession must occur before the trial rather during it. Second, the suspect's testimony against himself must be corroborated, such as by divine inspiration (which Nephi fulfilled). Third, physical evidence of the crime must be provided, such as the blood found on Seantum's cloak (see *Echoes*, 361–364).

time of the ministry of Nephi, son of Helaman, around 23 to 20 BC. He was murdered by his brother Seantum. The murder was announced by Nephi after he preached to a wicked multitude from his garden tower; the people who had gathered around heard Nephi's announcement of both the murder and the murderer, and rushed to find Seezoram lying in his own blood. As a result of Nephi's announcement from the garden tower, some began to accept him as a prophet.

WHO WERE SEEZORAM AND SEANTUM?

Seezoram was the chief judge during the

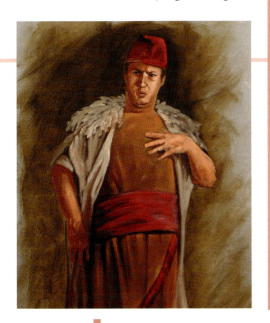

<table>
<tr><td colspan="2">KEY INSIGHTS ABOUT THE SAVIOR</td></tr>
<tr><td>

- The Lord reveals all things to His prophets.
- The Lord will destroy those who do not repent.

</td></tr>
</table>

Helaman 10

> "Behold, I give unto you power, sealed in heaven; and whatsoever heaven. . . ." (Hel. 10:7)

MAJOR CONCEPT

The sealing power, which was restored in our dispensation by the prophet Elijah, has the power to bind or loose all things on earth and in heaven.

OVERVIEW Nephi is given the sealing power and is empowered to bind or loose all things on earth and in heaven. He commands all the people to repent and tells them they will perish if they fail to do so. The people refuse and start warring with each other.

INTERESTING FACTS ABOUT THE SEALING POWER In this chapter, the Lord gives Nephi the authority to act on behalf of the Lord in a way that his priesthood administration extends beyond the boundaries of this mortal world. His actions on the basis of his priesthood calling will be recognized and accepted by the Lord in heaven as well as on earth. This is the same power given to Peter (see Matt.

PROMINENT PEOPLE

• Nephi

16:19). What is the sealing power? It is, first of all, to have merited the complete trust of the Lord in all things through the demonstration of strict obedience and unshakable faith. Next, it is to be commissioned of the Lord to serve as His messenger and agent on the earth in all things pertaining to the instruction and salvation of the Lord's children. The scope of the sealing powers of God also includes the keys of temple sealings in the spirit of Malachi's commission (see Mal. 4:5–6; D&C 2; D&C 42:69; 124:143).

MAIN THEMES

- Pondering gives us the chance to be impressed by the Spirit.

- We should ask for things from the Lord only according to His will; prophets are granted power that all things will be done according to their word because they request nothing that is contrary to the Lord's will.

- The sealing power comes from the Lord.

- Prompt obedience is important; procrastination can cause us to miss the harvest.

- If we don't repent, we will be destroyed; prophets always warn people of destruction.

HELAMAN

that whatsoever ye shall seal on earth shall be
ye shall loose on earth shall be loosed in

Image: Central American ruins.

KEY INSIGHTS ABOUT THE SAVIOR

- The Lord stands ready to bless forever those who obey Him steadfastly and without becoming weary.

- The Lord blesses those who do not ask for things that are contrary to His will.

- The Lord gives His prophets power over the inhabitants of the earth and the ability to smite the earth with famine, pestilence, and destruction.

- The Lord gives His prophets power to seal or loose on earth and in heaven.

- The Lord smites and destroys those who refuse to repent.

- The Lord protects His prophets.

Helaman 11

MAJOR CONCEPT

During times of prosperity, people tend to be slow to remember the Lord.

OVERVIEW Nephi pleads with the Lord to replace the war with a famine; many perish in the famine, and the survivors begin to repent. Nephi asks the Lord for rain to recognize the repentance of the people. The rain falls and the crops grow in their season. Nephi and Lehi receive many revelations on a daily basis. The Gadianton robbers reappear and entrench themselves in the land.

INTERESTING FACTS ABOUT THE PRIDE CYCLE The pride cycle—a well-known and oft-repeated cycle in the Book of Mormon—occurs when righteousness causes the people to prosper. In their prosperity, they forget the Lord. When they become hardened against the Lord, He withdraws His

PROMINENT PEOPLE

• Nephi

blessings, and they cease to prosper. They become humble and again return to Him. In this single chapter, the people rotate from righteousness to wickedness, and the pride cycle is repeated two and a half times: first, in verses 1–21; second, in verses 22–34; and finally, it begins again in verses 36–37.

MAIN THEMES

• Prophets plead to the Lord for the salvation of their people; they become established in the eyes of the people as their prophecies are fulfilled.

• We are prone to remember the Lord only in times of adversity.

• People tend to recognize the prophet and follow him when he tells them what they want to hear.

• Pride often leads to wickedness and occurs when we fear man's judgment more than God's judgment.

• A prophet's role is to establish true points of doctrine.

HELAMAN

people saw that they were about to perish remember the Lord their God; and they of Nephi." (Hel. 11:7)

Image: Nephi and Lehi, who "was not a a whit behind him as to things pertaining to righteousness."

KEY INSIGHTS ABOUT THE SAVIOR

- The Lord listens to the pleadings of His prophets.
- The Lord continues to give people the chance to repent and come unto Him.
- The Lord gives revelations to His prophets.

Helaman 12

MAJOR CONCEPT

By nature we are quick to do iniquity and slow to remember the Lord.

OVERVIEW In this chapter, Mormon pauses in his historical narrative to deliver one of the most powerful prophetic insights into the nature of man. He teaches of the instability of man and that men are foolish and quick to do evil. He testifies that men are nothing compared to God. He explains that the Lord chastens His children and that in the day of judgment we will gain either everlasting life or everlasting damnation.

INTERESTING FACTS ABOUT BURIED TREASURE This chapter refers to buried treasure (see verses 18–20), something early mockers of the Book of Mormon used to try to discredit the book. Because Joseph Smith had once been hired to dig for buried treasure, many of the satires published in his time dealt with his digging for treasure or hidden treasure. But references in the Book of Mormon to hidden treasure take up no more than 0.3 percent of the book, and most of those references—such as this one—are contained in prophecy rather than in historical accounts.

PROMINENT PEOPLE

- The Lord
- Mormon

MAIN THEMES

- In their natural states, our hearts are unsteady and foolish.

- When the Lord helps us by prospering us and softening the hearts of our enemies we often forget Him and even harden our hearts against Him.

- Unless we are chastened, we tend to forget the Lord.

- We are slow to remember the Lord; we forget Him because of our ease and prosperity.

- We are less than the dust of the earth, because the dust is always obedient to the Lord's commands.

600 BC

90 BC

and how evil, and devilish, and how quick to do iniquity, and children of men . . . and how slow are they to remember the Lord counsels, yea, how slow to walk in wisdom's paths!" (Hel. 12:4–5)

KEY INSIGHTS ABOUT THE SAVIOR

- The Lord, in His infinite goodness, blesses and prospers those who put their trust in Him.
- The Lord commands all the elements, and they obey Him.
- The Lord cuts off from His presence those who do iniquity.
- The Savior provided repentance so men might be saved.
- The Lord will save those who repent.
- In the Lord's plan, those who are righteous will have everlasting life, and those who will not repent from evil will have everlasting damnation.

Image: *The Last Judgment.*

"But blessed are they who will were not for the righteous who fire should come down out of

MAJOR CONCEPT

Unless we repent, we will be destroyed.

OVERVIEW Samuel the Lamanite preaches in the land of Zarahemla and prophesies that the Nephites will be destroyed unless they repent. He curses them and their riches. He testifies that they have rejected and stoned the prophets and that they seek happiness in iniquity.

WHO WAS SAMUEL THE LAMANITE? Samuel the Lamanite was sent by the Lord in 6 BC to call the people of Zarahemla to repentance. Even though Nephi had labored diligently among the people, they had quickly forgotten their promises and had returned to their wicked ways. Speaking from on top of a city wall, Samuel testified of the truth, called the people to repentance, and gave a very specific prophecy of the Savior's birth and the signs that would be manifest in Zarahemla at that time. Many believed Samuel's words and were baptized by Nephi, but the majority did not believe Samuel. Though he had been protected from stones and arrows while on the wall, he was forced to flee back to his own land. He was never heard of again among the Nephites. All of his prophecies were fulfilled. Although Samuel's appearance was fairly brief, his influence and message endured long after his ministry.

PROMINENT PEOPLE

• Samuel the Lamanite

MAIN THEMES

• The only safety we have is following the living prophet.

• We should regard the words of prophets as though they are being spoken by the Lord.

• We often pay more attention to men than we do to the prophet.

• Sometimes it is easier to heed the word of prophets of old than of the living prophet.

• If we procrastinate the day of our repentance, our efforts to repent will be in vain.

• When we abound in iniquity, we are surrounded by the devil's angels.

HELAMAN

600 BC

90 BC

repent, for them will I spare. But behold if it are in this great city, behold, I would cause that heaven and destroy it." (Hel. 13:13)

KEY INSIGHTS ABOUT THE SAVIOR

- The Lord sends prophets to warn the people of impending destruction if they do not repent.

- The Lord destroys those who refuse to repent.

- The Savior sometimes spares an entire city from destruction for the sake of a few righteous people.

- The Lord will curse the land if its inhabitants refuse to repent.

- The Lord will curse the riches of people who refuse to repent.

- The Lord saves those who repent, but withdraws His Spirit from those who refuse to repent.

- Prophets preach what the Lord or His angels put into their hearts; a prophet's message is the Lord's message.

"And also that ye might know of of earth, the Creator of all things of all your sins, that thereby ye

MAJOR CONCEPT

The Savior came to earth to redeem mankind from both temporal and spiritual death.

OVERVIEW In one of the most specific prophecies in all of scripture, Samuel the Lamanite declares that the Savior will be born in five years and prophesies of the signs that will be given in Zarahemla at the Savior's birth. He testifies that Christ will redeem men from both temporal and spiritual death. He then prophesies of the signs that will be given at the Savior's death, including three days of darkness.

INTERESTING FACTS ABOUT SPIRITUAL DEATH Those who suffer spiritual death—the second death—are dead to God, light, and truth. Their communication with God has been cut off, and they are cast out from the presence of God. According to President Joseph F. Smith, spiritual death is

PROMINENT PEOPLE

• Samuel the Lamanite

more terrible than physical death (see *Gospel Doctrine,* 14–16), and most of the world is spiritually dead in the sense that they are without both God the truth of the gospel. In order to reverse that condition, they need to repent and be baptized, which is why missionary work is so critical in our day.

MAIN THEMES

• Whoever believes on the Son of God will have everlasting life.

• We must repent and prepare for the Second Coming of the Lord.

• Prophets sacrifice and sometimes risk their lives to deliver the message the Lord has given them.

• Our sins can be forgiven because of the Savior.

• Those who will not repent are cut off, condemned, and experience a spiritual death.

• Signs that fulfill prophecy are given so that people will believe and be saved.

• Those who will not believe bring upon themselves their own condemnation.

• The choice to do good or evil is completely up to us.

• Samuel came that the people might know the judgments of God and the conditions of repentance, and that they might know of the coming of Christ and the signs of His coming.

600 BC

90 BC

the coming of Jesus Christ, the Son of God, the Father of heaven and from the beginning; . . . And if ye believe on his name ye will repent may have a remission of them through his merits." (Hel. 14:12–13)

KEY INSIGHTS ABOUT THE SAVIOR

- The Savior will redeem all those who believe on His name.
- The Lord tells His prophets what they should say.
- Jesus Christ is the Son of God, the Father of heaven and earth, and the Creator of all things from the beginning.
- The Savior provides a remission of sins through His merits for those who believe in Him and follow Him.
- The Savior had to die in order to conquer spiritual death and make salvation possible.
- The Savior had to die in order to bring resurrection to all mankind.
- The Lord has granted us the ability to know good from evil and to choose for ourselves.

Helaman 15

"And now behold, saith the repent, and observe to do my notwithstanding the many mighty

MAJOR CONCEPT

Those who are steadfast in their faith can call upon the Lord's mercy, while those who refuse to repent will be destroyed.

OVERVIEW Samuel continues preaching and prophesying to the people of Zarahemla. He testifies that they have been chastened by the Lord because of the great love of the Lord for them. Those Lamanites who become converted—the majority of them—are firm and steadfast in their faith. Samuel testifies that the Lord will be merciful to the Lamanites in the latter days.

INTERESTING FACTS ABOUT CHASTENING The Lord chastens those He loves (see Hel. 12:6), because the purpose of chastening is to help people reform, repent, and purify their lives. Righteous chastening is always based on love for the individual (see D&C 95:1–2). The Lord wants

PROMINENT PEOPLE

• Samuel the Lamanite

to do all He can to help us repent and stay on the straight and narrow path; He may even use external means—such as famine, pestilence, and other hardships—to humble us so we can be persuaded to change our ways. Apathy is not part of the character of the Lord; He diligently does all things to provide for the benefit of mankind.

MAIN THEMES

• A knowledge of and belief in the scriptures lead us to faith, repentance, and a change of heart.

• True repentance and a steadfast testimony result in righteous behavior.

• After being scattered, hunted, and smitten, the Lamanites will be brought to a true knowledge of the Lord in the last days.

• Had the Lamanites known the truth from the beginning rather than being influenced by the evil traditions of their fathers, they never would have dwindled in unbelief.

• If we refuse to repent, we will be destroyed.

HELAMAN

600 BC

90 BC

334

Lord, concerning the people of the Nephites: If they will not will, I will utterly destroy them . . . because of their unbelief works which I have done among them. . . ." (Hel. 15:17)

KEY INSIGHTS ABOUT THE SAVIOR

- The Lord chastens those He loves.
- The Lord is merciful and prolongs the days of those who are the victims of evil traditions, giving them an opportunity to hear and accept the truth.
- The Lord fulfills the prophecies He causes to be spoken by His prophets.
- In the last days, the Lord will bring the Lamanites to a true knowledge of their Redeemer, the True Shepherd.
- The Lord will utterly destroy those who do not repent.

Helaman 16

Major Concept

Satan is irrevocably committed to countering and overcoming the Spirit of Jesus Christ and will do everything he can to persuade us from good.

OVERVIEW Though many of the people are angry at Samuel, they are unable to hurt him with their stones and arrows; when they try to capture and kill him, he flees into his own country and is never heard of again among the Nephites. The Nephites who believe his words go to Nephi and are baptized. While some of the Nephites see angels, others harden their hearts and refuse to believe, saying it is not reasonable to believe in Jesus Christ and His coming to Jerusalem.

INTERESTING FACTS ABOUT HARDENED HEARTS People with hardened hearts discount any evidence of the divine in human affairs; they look to their own limited understanding and depend exclusively on their own senses as the source of

Prominent People

• Samuel the Lamanite
• Nephi

their knowledge. In essence, they follow the philosophy of Korihor, the anti-Christ: "Behold, ye cannot know of things which ye do not see" (Alma 30:15) and that "every man prospered according to his genius, and that every man conquered according to his strength" (Alma 30:17). The reaction of hardhearted people to Samuel parallels the reaction of hardhearted people to Joseph Smith. They claimed that the prophets simply guessed right when it came to some of the prophecies; that what the prophets preached simply wasn't reasonable; that the prophecies were simply traditions; and that the prophets were speaking by the power of the devil.

Main Themes

• It's not important for a prophet to say things with which we agree; it is important for us to bring ourselves in full accord with what the prophet says.

• Satan's purposes are always directly opposite those of the Lord.

• Satan's desire is to destroy us.

• If our hearts are hardened, we refuse to believe anything we can't see with our own eyes.

• Satan stirs people up to iniquity through rumors and contention and tries to convince them that signs from the Lord are meaningless.

HELAMAN

600 BC

90 BC

for Satan did stir them up to do iniquity continually; yea, he did contentions upon all the face of the land, that he might harden the which was good and against that which should come." (Hel. 16:22)

3 Nephi 1

"Lift up your head and be of good
the sign be given, and on the morrow
that which I have caused to be spoken

MAJOR CONCEPT

Signs flow from faith and are a product of faith; their chief purpose is not to produce faith, but to reward it.

OVERVIEW Nephi, the son of Helaman, departs out of the land and entrusts the sacred records to his son Nephi. Just as those who believe in the coming Messiah are about to be killed for their belief, the signs of His birth are given, and a new star arises. Despite the signs and wonders, iniquity abounds and the Gadianton robbers slay many.

WHO WAS NEPHI? Nephi, the son of Nephi, bridged the transition to a new dispensation in which the Savior fulfilled the law of Moses and the resurrected Messiah brought a new covenant of salvation and exaltation. Nephi came through a line of faithful progenitors that included Alma the Elder, Alma the Younger, Helaman (who led the two thousand stripling

PROMINENT PEOPLE

- Nephi, son of Helaman
- Nephi, son of Nephi

warriors), Helaman (the chief judge), and Helaman's son Nephi. In approximately AD 1, Nephi's father entrusted him with the sacred records—records that prophesied of the Savior's birth and ministry on earth. For years Nephi preached, expounded, exhorted, baptized, and invoked the powers of heaven

MAIN THEMES

- The wicked rejoice when it seems that the faith of the righteous is in vain.

- Prophets sorrow over and plead for their people.

- When signs appear and prophecies are fulfilled, the wicked fear because of their iniquity.

- Even in the face of remarkable signs, Satan works to convince the hearts of men that such signs are not divinely given.

- Baptism causes remission of sins.

- Satan and his followers work through lies and flattery.

- Signs don't convert people.

3 NEPHI

cheer; for behold, the time is at hand, and on this night shall come I into the world, to show unto the world that I will fulfill all by the mouth of my holy prophets." (3 Ne. 1:13)

to bring others to the fold of Christ. With his fellow Saints, Nephi survived the upheavals following the Savior's crucifixion; when the resurrected Lord appeared in Bountiful, the first leader He called forth was Nephi. Nephi was the first to be given the power to baptize in this dispensation and was the first of the Savior's twelve disciples mentioned by Mormon. Nephi was a central participant in the Savior's church on the American continent and lived to enjoy the peace that followed the Savior's ministry. He died during the first generation following that ministry.

KEY INSIGHTS ABOUT THE SAVIOR

- The Savior was born in mortality, and great signs of His birth were seen by the people on the American continent.
- The Lord fulfilled the law of Moses.
- The voice of the Lord was heard by Nephi, assuring Nephi that the sign of His birth would be given as prophesied by Samuel.
- The signs of the Savior's birth happened precisely as Samuel said they would.
- The law of Moses was not fulfilled at the sign of Jesus' birth, but would be fulfilled after His death and resurrection.

3 Nephi 2

> "Satan did go about, leading away the them and causing them that they the land." (3 Ne. 2:3)

MAJOR CONCEPT

Satan is determined to capture the souls of men and is constantly battling against righteousness.

OVERVIEW Wickedness and iniquity increase among the people, and the Nephites and Lamanites unite to defend themselves, their families, and their liberty against the Gadianton robbers. The Lamanites who convert join with the Nephites; the curse (being cut off from the Lord) is lifted, their skin becomes white (meaning the mark has also been removed), and they are called Nephites.

INTERESTING FACTS ABOUT RECKONING OF TIME Throughout their history, the Nephites used three different systems of reckoning time; each was used consecutively. The first system measured time in the number of years since Lehi left Jerusalem. That system was abandoned in favor of the second system, which measured time in the number of years since the beginning of the reign of judges. The third and final system began in AD 9 and measured time in the number of years since the signs were given of Christ's birth.

PROMINENT PEOPLE

• Nephi

MAIN THEMES

- Conversion based on signs dissolves as time passes.
- As time passes, we tend to forget even the miraculous things that happen in our lives.
- Satan can convince us that signs and wonders were imaginary or unimportant.
- All that is evil comes from Satan.
- We need to unite against the forces of evil for our own safety.
- When we are not living righteously, it becomes easier for the forces of evil to overcome us.
- We are destroyed as a result of our iniquity.

600 BC

90 BC

340

hearts of the people, tempting should do great wickedness in

Image: Mayan calendar.

KEY INSIGHTS ABOUT THE SAVIOR

- The Savior removes curses from those who repent and abandon their evil practices.
- The Lord destroys those who practice iniquity.

3 Nephi 3

"[Lachoneus] was a just man, and . . . cry unto the Lord for strength against come down against them." (3 Ne. 12)

MAJOR CONCEPT

A key in the deliverance of the Nephites was the righteousness of their leaders.

OVERVIEW Giddianhi—the leader of the Gadianton robbers—demands that the chief judge, Lachoneus, and the Nephites surrender their lands and themselves to the robbers. Lachoneus appoints Gidgiddoni as chief captain of the armies, and they assemble the Nephites in Zarahemla and Bountiful to defend themselves against the robbers.

WHO WERE GIDDIANHI AND LACHONEUS? Giddianhi was the leader of the Gadianton robbers following the birth of the Savior. The people began to lapse into prideful and wicked ways, and the Gadianton robbers concurrently emerged as a growing threat, requiring the people to unite to protect themselves and their families. Lachoneus, chief

judge and governor, was a just man who was not frightened by Giddianhi's threats. While the Nephites had some success, they were not able to permanently defeat the robbers. In AD 16, Giddianhi sent an epistle to Lachoneus, demanding that his people yield up their lands and themselves—in

MAIN THEMES

- Satan and his evil forces often use flattery to entice.

- The forces of evil want us to join them and often threaten us with destruction if we will not.

- Our true source of protection is the Lord and His righteousness.

- We are not justified in attacking, but we may fight to defend ourselves, our families, our homes, our liberties, and our religion.

- We should appoint the most righteous people possible as our leaders.

- We should pray to the Lord for strength to overcome evil.

- If we are prepared, we need not fear.

did cause that this people should
the time that the robbers should

other words, unite with the robbers—or suffer extinction. Lachoneus responded by pleading with the people to immediately repent, cry unto the Lord, and gather themselves into a place of safety. He built fortifications and placed guards to protect his people. Filled with the spirit of prophecy, he refused to launch an offensive against the enemy. Two years later the robbers invaded the cities but found them left desolate; as a result, the robbers had to rely on scarce provisions in the wilderness. Finally, having no other choice, they attacked the Nephite stronghold; an immense battle ensued, in which the Nephites succeeded in driving out the robbers and Giddianhi was killed.

Image: Nephites assemble in Zarahemla and Bountiful.

Key Insights about the Savior

- The Lord delivers His people.
- The custom of the Nephites was to appoint chief captains who had the spirit of revelation and prophecy; the spirit of prophecy is the testimony of Jesus.

"And their hearts were swollen with repentance and their humility that destruction." (3 Ne. 4:33)

MAJOR CONCEPT

The defeat of evil requires solid strategy and great righteousness.

OVERVIEW Gathered in a central place in unity and strength, the Nephites succeed in defeating the Gadianton robbers. Giddianhi, the leader of the robbers, becomes exhausted from battle and is overcome and slain. His successor, Zemnarihah, is captured and hanged. The Nephites praise the Lord, thanking Him and giving Him the credit for their victories.

INTERESTING FACTS ABOUT EXECUTION The Nephites' public execution of Zemnarihah adheres to ancient ceremony and law. Zemnarihah was hanged from the top of a tree until he was dead, and then the tree was chopped down—felled to the earth. By Jewish law, if a criminal was

PROMINENT PEOPLE

- Gidgiddoni
- Zemnarihah
- Giddianhi

hanged, the tree on which he was hanged had to be buried with him so it would not remind the people of the person executed on it. Paralleling the ancient practice of announcing an important execution, the Nephites "cried with a loud voice" after Zemnarihah's death, urging the righteous to similarly execute all such criminals and thanking the Lord for His protection (see *Echoes*, 366–369). While the common form of execution under the law of Moses was stoning, one of the Dead Sea Scrolls explains that someone who "curses his own people" or "causes evil against his own people" should be hanged (see *Echoes*, 249–251).

WHO WAS ZEMNARIHAH? When Giddianhi (leader of the Gadianton robbers) was slain in battle, Zemnarihah became his successor. He attempted to besiege the capital, but the Nephite stronghold proved to be impenetrable. The

MAIN THEMES

- In times of need we should call upon the Lord for help.
- When we receive help from the Lord, we need to remember Him, thank Him, and praise Him.
- We are delivered from destruction through our repentance, our humility, and the strength of the Lord.

joy . . . and they knew it was because of their
they had been delivered from an everlasting

Nephite military sent out troops at night to decimate Zemnarihah's robbers and prevent their escape; those who were not slain were taken prisoner, and Zemnarihah was captured. He was subsequently hanged from the top of a tree, and when he was dead the tree was cut down. At that time the people offered a mighty prayer that all who came against them because of secret combinations would also be felled to the earth.

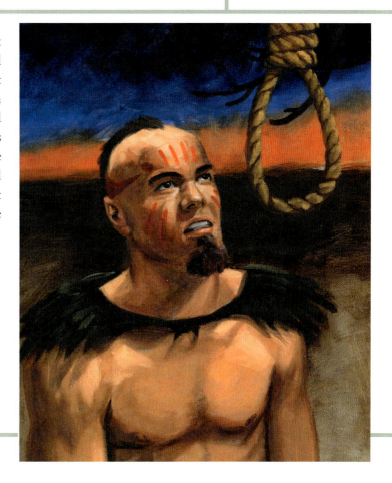

KEY INSIGHTS ABOUT THE SAVIOR

- The Lord will spare, protect, and deliver His people as long as they call on His name for protection.
- The Lord strengthens His people against their enemies.
- The Lord preserves His people in their righteousness.
- The Lord delivers His people when they repent and are humble.

"And now behold, there was not a who did doubt in the least the words knew that it must needs be that they

MAJOR CONCEPT

Powerful repentance and widespread conversion among a people can lead to the eradication of wickedness and evil influences.

OVERVIEW The Nephites repent and forsake their sins; so powerful was their repentance that they believed firmly in the words spoken by all the prophets. The Gadianton robbers who have not escaped are put into prison and taught the gospel; those who accept it and covenant to murder no more are liberated from prison. Mormon inserts in this chapter his own words, in which he declares the truthfulness of the gospel and prophesies that in the last days Israel will eventually be brought to a knowledge of the Savior and will be gathered from her long dispersion.

WHO WAS MORMON? Mormon was born around AD 310; he commanded the Nephite forces from the time he was

PROMINENT PEOPLE

• Mormon

sixteen until the final battle at Cumorah, in which he witnessed the destruction of close to a million of his people (see Morm. 6). Mormon compiled a number of records and abridged many others, including 3 Nephi. Mormon himself kept his eye single to the glory of God and remained faithful to the end, eventually turning over the sacred commission as a record keeper to his son Moroni. Both prophets were administered to by the tarrying disciples of Christ until even those were withdrawn by the Lord because of the universal wickedness of the people (see Morm. 8:10–11). Mormon was killed by the warring Lamanites around AD 385 (see Morm. 8:3, 5), leaving Moroni alone to finish the work of the Lord. More information on Mormon will be given in later chapters.

MAIN THEMES

• Great good results when we listen to and believe in the words of the prophets.

• We need to repent of and forsake any gross sins before we can serve the Lord with all diligence.

• The gospel is key to establishing peace and overcoming secret combinations.

• Most of those who kept the sacred records have given us their testimony that the records are true.

living soul among all the people of the Nephites of all the holy prophets who had spoken; for they must be fulfilled." (3 Ne. 5:1)

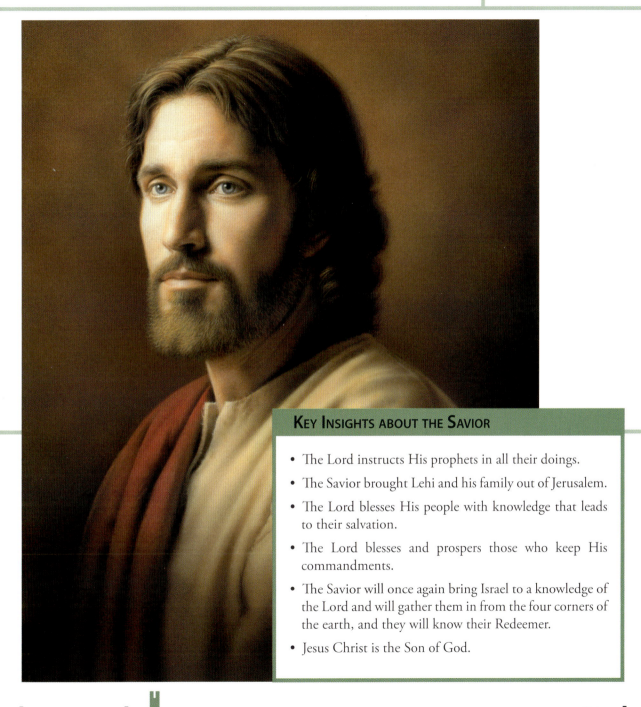

KEY INSIGHTS ABOUT THE SAVIOR

- The Lord instructs His prophets in all their doings.
- The Savior brought Lehi and his family out of Jerusalem.
- The Lord blesses His people with knowledge that leads to their salvation.
- The Lord blesses and prospers those who keep His commandments.
- The Savior will once again bring Israel to a knowledge of the Lord and will gather them in from the four corners of the earth, and they will know their Redeemer.
- Jesus Christ is the Son of God.

"Now they did not sin ignorantly, for had been taught unto them; therefore

MAJOR CONCEPT

Widespread rebellion—casting aside the truths we have been taught—opens the door to evil influences.

OVERVIEW After repenting and living in peace and unity in their stronghold against the Gadianton robbers, the Nephites return to their homes and begin to prosper. As they increase in wealth, pride and class distinctions arise. The church begins to suffer from widespread dissension, and Satan leads the people in open rebellion against their leaders. Many prophets cry repentance and are secretly put to death; those who murder the prophets conspire to take over the government.

WHO WAS LACHONEUS, SON OF LACHONEUS? Lachoneus, son of Lachoneus, succeeded his father as chief judge and governor in AD 30. His father was responsible, along with

PROMINENT PEOPLE

- Gidgiddoni
- Lachoneus, son of Lachoneus

army commander Gidgiddoni, for putting a stop to the rise of secret combinations and restoring peace between AD 26 and 27. But that peace was soon imperiled as the people began to forget the principles of righteousness and elevate themselves in arrogance and pride. During the second

MAIN THEMES

- Pride leads to class distinction and inequality.
- Pride causes us to seek for power, authority, riches, and the vain things of the world.
- Satan is the source of all iniquity; that which is evil comes from him and causes the Church to be broken up.
- Willful rebellion is a casting aside of the things we know to be true.
- The only effective tool against evil and darkness is truth and light.
- Secret combinations have the ability to infiltrate the entire government.

they knew the will of God concerning them, for it they did willfully rebel against God." (3 Ne. 6:18)

Lachoneus's tenure, inspired men were sent forth to preach repentance to the people, but angry judges and lawyers of high rank had them killed and then conspired in a secret combination to protect the assassins against any action by Lachoneus as chief judge and governor; in fact, they plotted to murder Lachoneus and have him replaced by a king. In AD 30, they did murder him; at that point the government disintegrated and the people separated themselves into self-governing tribes.

KEY INSIGHTS ABOUT THE SAVIOR

- The Lord inspires His prophets to teach those things that we need.

- The Lord will redeem His people.

- The covenants that people enter into through secret combinations are counterfeit to the Lord's covenants.

MAJOR CONCEPT

The demarcation between righteousness and wickedness is stark and separates the good from the evil.

OVERVIEW Lachoneus, chief judge and governor, is murdered as a result of secret combinations; the government is overthrown, and the people divide into self-governing tribes. Jacob, an anti-Christ, becomes king over the secret combination and tries to lure various tribes to join him in the north so they can become great enough in numbers to attack the other tribes. Nephi preaches repentance and faith in Christ, and many listen to him, repent, and are baptized. Angels minister to Nephi daily, and he raises his brother Timothy from the dead.

INTERESTING FACTS ABOUT NEPHI AND JACOB The contrasting portraits of Nephi and Jacob provide a stark

PROMINENT PEOPLE

- Lachoneus, son of Lachoneus
- Jacob
- Nephi
- Timothy

MAIN THEMES

- Satan is the source of all iniquity.
- Great missionaries are bold and unflinching in bearing testimony of the truth.
- When prophets speak with power and authority it is not possible to disbelieve their words.
- Great miracles are done in the name of Jesus Christ.
- Although people witness miracles, miracles alone do not produce conversion.

demarcation between the light of the gospel and the eclipsed bleakness of satanic evil. Nephi's daily companions are angels of God; Jacob's daily work involves plotting and scheming to destroy. Nephi proclaims the redeeming word of Christ; Jacob maintains that there is no Christ. Nephi commands the people to repent that they might be redeemed and works mighty miracles among them; Jacob commands those who will listen to murder their countrymen.

WHO WAS JACOB? Wickedness was so rampant in the land of Zarahemla from AD 29 to 30 that the people no longer had a central government. The people had separated into self-governing tribes following the murder of their chief judge and governor. When a group of tribes formed a league, they chose Jacob—an anti-Christ who had vocally opposed the prophets—as their leader and king. Jacob's strategy was to retreat to his northern stronghold and lure members of

600 BC

90 BC

people had nearly all become wicked; yea, there them." (3 Ne. 7:7)

other tribes until his numbers were sufficient to come to battle against those same tribes. Meanwhile, many were converted and baptized through the preaching of Nephi. When significant natural disasters occurred at the time of the crucifixion of the Savior, cities were destroyed and the followers of secret combinations—including Jacob—perished.

Image: Central American ruins.

KEY INSIGHTS ABOUT THE SAVIOR

- The Lord sends angels to minister to those who need them.

- The Savior enables His servants to perform great miracles in His name.

- The events prior to Jesus' appearance to the Nephites parallel the events that will precede His Second Coming (see Ezra Taft Benson, *A Witness and a Warning*, 21, 22).

3 Nephi 8

> "And there could be no light, because neither could there be fire kindled there could not be any light at all."

MAJOR CONCEPT

Unmistakable signs of the Savior's Crucifixion were given on the American continent in direct fulfillment of prophecy.

OVERVIEW The signs of the Savior's Crucifixion are given, as prophesied by Samuel the Lamanite. Tempests, earthquakes, whirlwinds, fires, and destruction testify of the death of Jesus Christ. Highways are broken up and cities are burned or buried in the sea; many people are destroyed. Impenetrable darkness covers the land for three days. Those who survive the destruction sorrow in their fate.

INTERESTING FACTS ABOUT GEOLOGY The destruction described in this chapter provides yet more evidence that Joseph Smith translated ancient records instead of writing the Book of Mormon himself. The Prophet lived in an area

PROMINENT PEOPLE

• Nephi

that was very quiet in a geologic sense; he probably never felt an earthquake of any notable magnitude, and he never saw a volcano. Due to his humble circumstances and his limited access to books, it is extremely improbable that Joseph Smith did any research on earthquakes or

MAIN THEMES

• Just as people began to doubt the truth of prophecies concerning the Savior's death, the signs they had been looking for appeared.

• A great storm accompanied by terrible thunder, sharp lightning, and tempests—violent wind often accompanied by rain, hail, or snow—was the initial sign.

• The city of Zarahemla burned.

• The city of Moroni sank into the depths of the sea, and its inhabitants drowned.

• The city of Moronihah was buried in the earth.

• A great earthquake changed the whole face of the land; many cities were sunk into the ground.

• People were carried away in a whirlwind.

• Impenetrable darkness covered the land for three days, during which time those who had survived groaned, mourned, and howled.

• Those who survived expressed great regret that they had not repented before the sign was given.

of the darkness, neither candles, neither torches;
with their fine and exceedingly dry wood, so that
(3 Ne. 8:21)

volcanoes, either. Yet this chapter includes amazingly detailed descriptions of the cataclysmic earthquake that occurred after the Savior's crucifixion (see *Echoes*, 198).

KEY INSIGHTS ABOUT THE SAVIOR

- The Lord fulfills prophecies.
- The Savior was crucified; nature itself testified of this pivotal event.

3 Nephi 9

"Behold, I am Jesus Christ the Son of
am Alpha and Omega, the beginning
to bring redemption unto the world,

MAJOR CONCEPT

Jesus Christ is the light and life of the world and came into the world to save the world from sin.

OVERVIEW As the people wait in darkness, the voice of the Savior proclaims the destruction of many people and cities because of their wickedness. He also proclaims His divinity and testifies that in Him the law of Moses has been fulfilled. He invites men to come unto Him and be saved.

PROMINENT PEOPLE

• Jesus Christ

INTERESTING FACTS ABOUT THE LORD'S DESTRUCTION

From Adam until this final dispensation, the Lord has warned His children to repent and live righteously or they will be destroyed. In some cases that destruction has involved not only losing the blessings of eternal life but being physically swept off the face of the earth in stark fulfillment of prophecies made by the Lord or through His servants, the prophets. Just a few examples of such destruction include the cities of the plains (see Gen. 19:29), the Canaanites (see Num. 2:3), the cities of Sodom and Gomorrah (see Gen. 13:10), the cities on the American continent (see 3 Ne. 8–9), and the civilizations of the Jaredites and the Nephites (see Ether 15, Morm. 6, and Moro. 9). Modern-day revelation indicates that the destruction in our day will be just as terrible (see D&C 29:14–21; 43:19–25; 45:39–42; 88:87–91; 133:41–49).

MAIN THEMES

• Iniquity leads to destruction.

• Those who reject and cast out the prophets will be destroyed.

• Those who are converted and follow righteousness are healed from their iniquities.

• Those who receive the Lord become the sons and daughters of God.

• Those who believe on the Savior's name will be redeemed.

• We are to offer as a sacrifice to the Lord a broken heart and a contrite spirit.

WHAT IS THE DIFFERENCE BETWEEN A BROKEN HEART AND A CONTRITE SPIRIT?

Elder D. Todd Christofferson explains that a broken heart is a repentant heart, while a contrite spirit is an obedient spirit (see Conference Report, Apr. 2008, 10).

God. . . . I am the light and the life of the world. I
and the end. . . . Behold, I have come unto the world
to save the world from sin." (3 Ne. 9:15, 18, 21)

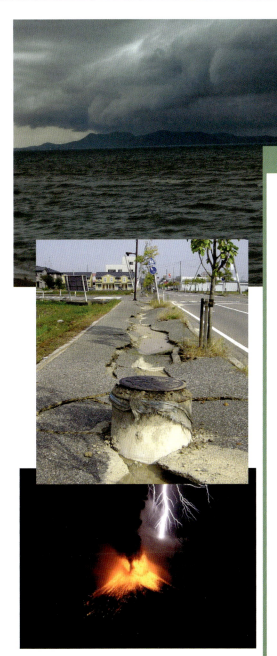

KEY INSIGHTS ABOUT THE SAVIOR

- The Lord destroys the wicked.
- The Lord invites us to repent and come unto Him.
- Jesus Christ created the heavens and earth and all things in them.
- The Lord was with the Father in the beginning.
- The Lord is in the Father and the Father is in Him.
- Through the Lord the Father glorified His name.
- The Savior came to His own, and they did not receive Him.
- The Savior is the source of redemption.
- The Lord fulfilled the law of Moses.
- The Savior is the light and life of the world, the beginning and the end.
- The Lord will baptize with fire and with the Holy Ghost those who come to Him with a broken heart and a contrite spirit.
- The Lord came into the world to save the world from sin.
- The Lord will receive all who repent and come unto Him as little children.
- The Lord laid down His life and took it up again in the Resurrection.

MAJOR CONCEPT

The Lord will gather all those who repent and come unto Him with full purpose of heart.

OVERVIEW After a period of silence lasting many hours, the voice of the Savior is heard again. He promises to gather His people as a hen gathers her chicks if they will repent and come unto Him. The darkness is dispelled, the light returns, and the earth is healed. The Savior explains that the more righteous part of the people have been preserved and saved from destruction.

INTERESTING FACTS ABOUT PROPHETS Much of the Book of Mormon describes people who were privileged to have prophets but who rejected the words of those prophets. In the time period described in this part of the Book of Mormon, many who heard the prophets thought they were wrong—but when the destruction came, and it was too late, it became immediately obvious exactly how right the prophets had been. Karl G. Maeser, while leading a group of missionaries in the Swiss Alps, told them that prophets are like the poles stuck into the glacier to mark the safe path. If we step aside from the mark, he taught— if we fail to heed the words of the prophets—we are lost (see Burton, 22).

PROMINENT PEOPLE

• Jesus Christ

MAIN THEMES

• It is we who move away from the Lord, not the Lord who moves away from us.

• As we are healed by the Lord, we turn to Him in thanksgiving and praise.

• We who have the scriptures can search them and see in them the fulfillment of prophecy.

• Many of the prophets who testified of the coming of the Savior were slain for doing so.

gathereth her chickens under her wings, if with full purpose of heart." (3 Ne. 10:6)

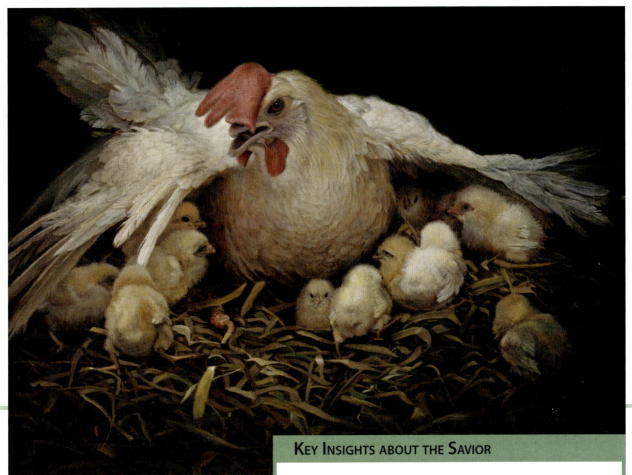

KEY INSIGHTS ABOUT THE SAVIOR

- The Lord gathers His people and nurtures them in the same way a hen gathers and nurtures her chicks.
- The Lord will gather and nurture those who repent and return to Him with full purpose of heart.
- The Lord saves the righteous and those who heed the prophets.
- The Lord fulfills His prophecies.
- The Lord pours out great blessings upon the righteous.

MAJOR CONCEPT

Jesus Christ is the source of life, light, and truth, and we must look to Him for those things.

OVERVIEW The voice of God the Father testifies of His Beloved Son. Christ appears to a crowd of 2,500 people at Bountiful and proclaims His Atonement. The people feel the wounds in His hands, feet, and side and cry "Hosanna" (from a Hebrew word meaning "Oh, grant salvation"; see *LDS Bible Dictionary*, 704). The Savior gives Nephi and others the power to baptize in this dispensation as the fulness of the gospel begins and teaches the proper way to baptize. He testifies that the spirit of contention is of the devil and teaches His doctrine, which is that men should believe in Him, be baptized, and receive the Holy Ghost.

PROMINENT PEOPLE

- God the Father
- Jesus Christ
- Nephi

INTERESTING FACTS ABOUT FALSE DOCTRINE
In this chapter, we learn that the Savior cautioned the people against disputations concerning the points of doctrine. President Joseph F. Smith taught that among the Latter-day Saints, preaching of false doctrine disguised as truth comes from only two types

MAIN THEMES

- The central message of every prophet through the ages has been the divinity of Jesus Christ.

- We must focus on and have the spirit of revelation if we are to understand the voice of the Lord.

- Jesus gave very specific details on how to baptize properly that are not found in the Bible, accounting for the confusion over the doctrine of baptism in the world today.

- Those who repent and desire to be baptized should be baptized by immersion by those

who have proper authority.

- The spirit of contention is of the devil, who is the father of contention; he stirs up the hearts of men to contend in anger with each other.

- We must repent, become as little children, and be baptized in order to inherit the kingdom of God.

- Those who build upon anything other than the doctrine of Christ build on a sandy foundation, and the gates of hell stand open to receive them when the floods and winds come.

I am well pleased, in whom I him." (3 Ne. 11:7)

of people: those who don't know the doctrine (and are too lazy to learn it) and the proud and self-vaunting who interpret it by their own conceit—which is much more dangerous than those who simply don't know. He taught, "Beware of the lazy and of the proud; their infection in each case is contagious; better for them and for all when they are compelled to display the yellow flag of warning, that the clean and uninfected may be protected" (*Gospel Doctrine*, 373).

KEY INSIGHTS ABOUT THE SAVIOR

- The Savior drank the bitter cup and glorified the Father in taking upon Himself the sins of the world.

- The Lord suffered the will of the Father in all things from the beginning; the first principle He taught was obedience.

- The Savior has allowed 2,500 people to feel the wounds of His Crucifixion so they would know He is the Lord and was slain for the sins of the world.

- The Father, the Son, and the Holy Ghost are one; the Son is in the Father, and the Father is in the Son, and they are one in unity and purpose.

- The Father and the Holy Ghost bear record of the Savior; those who believe in the Lord also believe in the Father and in the Holy Ghost.

- The Lord saves those who are baptized and believe in Him.

MAJOR CONCEPT

If we hope to be perfected, we must follow the higher law and covenant to live a Christ-like life.

OVERVIEW Jesus calls and commissions the Twelve to minister to the people on His behalf. He then delivers in the Beatitudes in a sermon very similar to the Sermon on the Mount that He delivered in the Holy Land during His mortal ministry (compare to Matthew 5). He testifies that His teachings transcend and take precedence over the law of Moses.

INTERESTING FACTS ABOUT THE SERMON ON THE MOUNT

The Savior came to the world not only to atone for our sins, but to exemplify how we should live and to teach the standard of perfection of God's law. A significant part of that teaching is contained in the Sermon on the

PROMINENT PEOPLE

• Jesus Christ
• Nephi

Mount, which President Harold B. Lee called the Lord's blueprint for perfection (see *Decisions for Successful Living*, 55–62). The account given in 3 Nephi 12–14 is much more complete and leads to greater understanding than that given in Matthew 5–7 for several reasons. The New

MAIN THEMES

• We will be blessed if we give heed to the words of the Apostles and prophets.

• Those who are baptized receive a remission of their sins.

• We will be blessed if we sincerely adopt the traits described by the Savior in the Beatitudes.

• A true Saint accepts persecution patiently, prayerfully, and humbly.

• We should let our testimony and gifts shine before others so they will be inspired to learn of and glorify the Father.

• In order to enter the kingdom of heaven we must keep the commandments.

• We cannot come to the Savior if there is anger in our hearts.

• Those whose marriage ends should be legally divorced before they enter into a relationship with someone else.

• Our communication should be inspiring and free of profanity.

• We should love our enemies and do good to those that hate us, use us, and persecute us.

before this people, that they may see
Father who is in heaven." (3 Ne. 12:16)

Key Insights about the Savior

- The Lord calls servants to minister to His people and gives them authority to act in His name.
- The Lord blesses those who believe on His name and are baptized; the beatitudes apply to those who come unto Him.
- The Lord blesses those who are poor in spirit, who mourn, who are meek, who are merciful, who are pure in heart, who are peacemakers, and who hunger and thirst after righteousness.
- The Lord blesses those who are persecuted for His name's sake.
- The Lord fulfilled the law of Moses.
- The Lord gives us commandments so we will repent and come to Him with a broken heart and a contrite spirit.
- The Lord condemns adultery and the lust that leads to it.
- The Lord sets the example of the type of perfection for which we should strive.

Testament teachings were given before the Savior performed His Atonement; the Book of Mormon teachings followed the Atonement and occurred after the law of Moses had been fulfilled. In addition, the sermon in the New Testament was delivered to twelve people, while the Book of Mormon account was taught to 2,500.

MAJOR CONCEPT

The Savior provided the patterns for living that will bring us the greatest joy.

OVERVIEW The Savior continues His sermon to the Nephites, similar to His Sermon on the Mount; compare this chapter to Matthew 6. The Savior teaches the Lord's Prayer and counsels the people to lay up treasures in heaven instead of on the earth. He prepares the Twelve for their ministry and advises them to take no thought for temporal matters.

INTERESTING FACTS ABOUT THE LORD'S PRAYER In the version of the Lord's Prayer taught to the Saints at Bountiful there are two interesting omissions. First is the phrase *Thy kingdom come*, which was left out of the Bountiful version because the Savior was in the process of establishing and delivering His kingdom to His "other sheep" in America. The

Matthew version also contains the phrase *Give us this day our daily bread*, because in that sermon the Savior was addressing the Twelve who were about to leave on full-time missions without purse or scrip—and who needed to petition the Father for the food and drink they needed to sustain their daily

PROMINENT PEOPLE

• Jesus Christ

MAIN THEMES

• As we give of our goods to help those less fortunate, we should do so quietly and without grandiose display.

• Hypocrites who make a show of their offerings are rewarded by men but not by the Lord.

• We should pray in an attitude of reverence in places where we are not seen by others and should not make ourselves look deprived when we fast.

• In our prayers, we should not use "vain repetitions" (words or phrases used without real thought, feeling, or intent).

• We must forgive others if we expect to be forgiven.

• We should lay up treasures in heaven by spending time and energy on things of eternal value.

• We should live so that we are filled with light, not darkness.

• No man can serve two masters; if we want to serve the Lord, we cannot serve man or the devil at the same time.

• Before anything else, we must seek the kingdom of God and His righteousness.

will your heart be also . . . But seek ye first righteousness. . . ." (3 Ne. 13:21, 33)

lives. In Bountiful, however, the Savior was addressing a multitude of more than two thousand people who were sustained by their daily work (see *Doctrinal Commentary on the Book of Mormon,* 4:83). In addition, the impersonal pronoun *which* is changed to the personal pronoun *who;* the translator, Joseph Smith, knew that God is a living person. The Book of Mormon version also clarifies that it is Satan, not the Lord, who leads people into temptation.

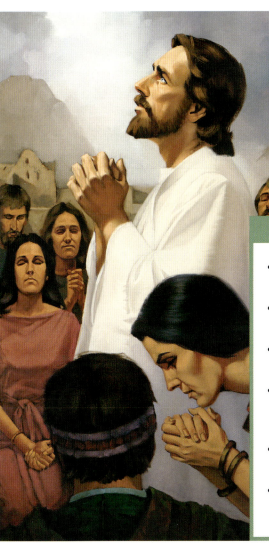

KEY INSIGHTS ABOUT THE SAVIOR

- The Lord will reward us openly for the good things we do in secret.

- The Lord and our Father in Heaven know what we need before we ask.

- The Savior taught us how to pray by teaching us the Lord's Prayer.

- The Lord didn't teach the Nephites to pray in His name because He was with them; only later did He teach them to pray in His name.

- The Lord will forgive those who have forgiven others of their trespasses.

- The Savior will help provide the daily needs of those who serve Him.

3 Nephi 14

"Ask, and it shall be given unto you; opened unto you." (3 Ne. 14:7)

Major Concept

The Savior has given us the principles and teachings we need to return to live with our Father.

OVERVIEW To conclude His sermon (compare to Matthew 7), the Savior commands the people of Bountiful not to judge others, to ask of God in faith, to treat others as they would wish to be treated, to follow the strait and narrow pathway to eternal life, to beware of false prophets, and to do the will of the Father.

Prominent People

- Jesus Christ

INTERESTING FACTS ABOUT THE WORD *STRAIT* In this and many other places in the scriptures, we are told that the way to eternal life is *strait*—clearly a different spelling from the word *straight*. While the path to eternal life is undoubtedly also straight, the Savior teaches that the path that leads into the presence of God is strait—it is restricted and narrow, and does not allow for us to take with us the things that don't apply or fit into the kingdom of heaven. We need to leave behind all such things "when we enter into this narrow way which leads into the presence of God, where we can receive life eternal" (Joseph Fielding Smith, *Doctrines of Salvation*, 2:13).

Main Themes

- We are to avoid judging people, but should only judge situations.
- We should judge a righteous judgment—guided by the Spirit, within our stewardship, according to righteous standards, and only after we have all the facts (see Dallin H. Oaks, CES Fireside, Mar. 1, 1998).
- We should focus on improving ourselves rather than trying to improve others.
- We should protect those things that are holy and sacred and not put them out for public display or consideration.

- We should ask Heavenly Father in faith for We should treat others as we want to be treated ourselves.
- We should follow the strait and narrow pathway to eternal life by leaving behind those things that are unimportant in an eternal perspective and by obeying the commandments.
- We should beware of false prophets and those who teach false doctrines.
- Saying we believe is not enough; we must be doers of the word.

600 BC

90 BC

364

seek, and ye shall find; knock, and it shall be

Image: The strait way.

KEY INSIGHTS ABOUT THE SAVIOR

- Those things that are good come from the Lord, and those things that are evil come from Satan.

- The Lord will not recognize those who have taught of Him but have failed to serve Him and obey His commandments.

- The rock upon which we should build our house—in other words, our life—is Jesus Christ.

"Behold, I am the law, and the endure to the end, and ye shall endureth to the end will I give

MAJOR CONCEPT

The law of Moses was given by the Savior to prepare the people for His coming; through His teachings and His atoning sacrifice, He fulfilled the law of Moses and ushered in the fulness of the gospel.

OVERVIEW Jesus finishes His sermon to the Saints at Bountiful and is inspired to know that they wonder about the law of Moses. He announces that He has fulfilled the law of Moses. He testifies to them that they are the "other sheep" to which He referred when teaching the people in the Holy Land—and that because of the iniquity of the Jews, they are not aware of the existence of the people on the American continent.

INTERESTING FACTS ABOUT THE LAW AND THE PROPHETS

In this chapter (see verse 10), the Savior explains that His commandments are "the law and the prophets." This phrase actually refers to two of the three sections of the Jewish scripture, which is our Old Testament. "The law" (the Torah) consists of the five books of Moses: Genesis, Exodus, Leviticus, Numbers, and Deuteronomy. "The prophets" includes the writings of various prophets, including but not limited to Isaiah, Jeremiah, Ezekiel, and Daniel. Elder Neal A. Maxwell taught that the spirit of the law demands more of us than the actual letter of the law, which the Jews tended to emphasize. The spirit of the law, Elder Maxwell taught, consists of giving our attention and focus to what matters most while still doing the rest (see *For the Power Is in Them*, 46–47). Although the law has been fulfilled, many of the prophets' words are not yet fulfilled, nor has the covenant given to Abraham been completely fulfilled.

PROMINENT PEOPLE

• Jesus Christ

MAIN THEMES

• The law of Moses was fulfilled by the Savior; the new law is the gospel of Jesus Christ.

• The prophecies of all the prophets since the beginning are still valid.

• We must endure to the end in righteousness if we want to gain eternal life.

• We must keep the commandments of the Savior.

light. Look unto me, and live; for unto him that eternal life." (3 Ne. 15:9)

KEY INSIGHTS ABOUT THE SAVIOR

- The Savior fulfilled the law of Moses and gave the new law through His gospel.

- The Lord is the law and the light.

- The Savior will give eternal life to those who endure to the end.

- The Lord calls Apostles to testify of Him.

- The Lord was never commanded to tell the people in Jerusalem of the people on the American continent or of the ten tribes—and it was because of their iniquity.

- The people on the American continent are numbered among those the Father gave the Lord.

- Jesus came only to the house of Israel, not the Gentiles; they will learn of Him through the Holy Ghost.

"And verily, verily, I say unto you this land, neither of the land of round about whither I have been

MAJOR CONCEPT

At the last day, the Savior will gather all His people, including those of the ten lost tribes, and they will be united when He establishes Zion.

OVERVIEW Addressing the 2,500 gathered at the temple in Bountiful, the Savior tells them he has other sheep that are not in their land nor in Jerusalem or its vicinity and that He will visit them. These are the lost tribes of Israel, who will be numbered among His people, and there will be one fold and one shepherd. He testifies that in the latter days the gospel will go to the Gentiles and that His people will be united when He reestablishes Zion.

INTERESTING FACTS ABOUT THE LOST TRIBES OF ISRAEL

In his 1825 book, *A View of the Hebrews*, Ethan Smith theorized that the American Indians are the "lost ten tribes" of Israel, using various arguments and citing many

PROMINENT PEOPLE

- Jesus Christ
- The Gentiles

commonalities between the Indians and the ancient Israelites. In contrast, the Book of Mormon relates a lengthy, detailed story of Lehi's descendants and declares that they descended from the Israelites. The Book of Mormon specifically states that the Nephites and Lamanites are a remnant of the house of Joseph and that "the other tribes of Israel . . . are not of this land, neither of the land of Jerusalem" (3 Ne. 16:1). While they descended from two of the lost tribes (Ephraim and Manasseh), the Book of Mormon peoples cannot be considered to represent all the descendants of all ten lost tribes (see *Echoes*, 312–313).

MAIN THEMES

- There were people other than at Jerusalem and on the American continent at the time of the Savior's Resurrection.

- The Gentiles—those not of the house of Israel who do not have the gospel—will receive and accept the gospel during our day.

- Those Gentiles who repent and return to the Lord will be numbered among His people.

that I have other sheep, which are not of Jerusalem, neither in any parts of that land to minister." (3 Ne. 16:1)

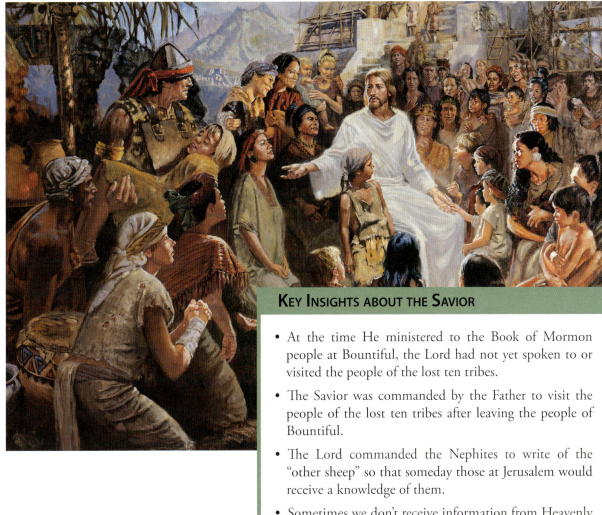

KEY INSIGHTS ABOUT THE SAVIOR

- At the time He ministered to the Book of Mormon people at Bountiful, the Lord had not yet spoken to or visited the people of the lost ten tribes.

- The Savior was commanded by the Father to visit the people of the lost ten tribes after leaving the people of Bountiful.

- The Lord commanded the Nephites to write of the "other sheep" so that someday those at Jerusalem would receive a knowledge of them.

- Sometimes we don't receive information from Heavenly Father through the Lord because we fail to ask.

- The Lord will gather the Gentiles at the last day.

- The Savior will take the gospel from those Gentiles who reject it.

- All the ends of the earth will eventually see the salvation of the Savior.

"The eye hath never seen, neither saw and heard Jesus speak unto our souls at the time we heard

MAJOR CONCEPT

The Savior has great love for His children and desires to bless them.

OVERVIEW The Savior tells the people to go to their homes and ponder and pray concerning the things they have heard and promises to return the next day. He tells them He will then leave to minister to the lost tribes of Israel. He is moved by compassion to bless the infirm among the people. He gathers their children around Him and prays marvelous and unspeakable things to the Father. Jesus then blesses the children, and angels descend and minister unto them.

INTERESTING FACTS ABOUT THE LOST TEN TRIBES Elder Bruce R. McConkie wrote, "The Lost Tribes are not lost unto the Lord. In their northward journeyings they were led by prophets and inspired leaders. They had their

PROMINENT PEOPLE

• Jesus Christ

Moses and their Lehi, were guided by the spirit of revelation, kept the law of Moses, and carried with them the statutes and judgments which the Lord had given them in ages past. They were still a distinct people many hundreds of years later, for the resurrected Lord visited and ministered unto them following his ministry on this continent among the Nephites. . . . In due course the Lost Tribes of Israel will return and come to the children of Ephraim to receive their blessings. This great gathering will take place under the direction of the President of The Church of Jesus Christ of Latter-day Saints. . ." (Bruce R. McConkie, *Mormon Doctrine,* 457–458).

MAIN THEMES

• Pondering is an important way to prepare our minds to absorb things of the Spirit.

• The Savior has compassion for all of us.

• With sufficient faith, we can be healed.

• The Savior delights in our faith and desires to bless us.

• The faith and purity of little children qualifies them for the ministration of angels.

hath the ear heard, before, so great and marvelous things as we the Father; . . . and no one can conceive of the joy which filled him pray for us unto the Father." (3 Ne. 17:16–17)

KEY INSIGHTS ABOUT THE SAVIOR

- The Savior had not yet appeared to the lost ten tribes but He knew where they were; they were not lost to the Father.
- The Savior has the power to heal us of our afflictions.
- The Savior is troubled over the wickedness of the house of Israel.
- The Savior's prayer for the people of Bountiful was so magnificent that it could not be written.
- The Savior's joy was full over the faith of the Nephites at Bountiful.
- The Savior has a particular love for little children.
- Just as the Savior blessed the children one by one, He cares for us individually.

3 Nephi 18

"And this shall ye do in
it shall be a testimony unto the
remember me ye shall have my

MAJOR CONCEPT

The sacrament was instituted by the Savior Himself among the Nephites.

OVERVIEW The Savior institutes the sacrament among the Nephites and cautions them that whoever partakes of it unworthily will be damned. He commands the Nephites to pray always in His name. All are invited to come to the meetings of the Saints to be nourished and nurtured. He gives the Twelve the power to confer the Holy Ghost upon those who have been baptized. A cloud overshadows the Savior and He departs from them.

INTERESTING FACTS ABOUT THE SACRAMENT The order of breaking and blessing the bread in the Book of Mormon and the Joseph Smith Translation is opposite that of the New Testament: the bread is broken first, then blessed, symbolic of

PROMINENT PEOPLE

• Jesus Christ

Christ's body being broken to bring about the blessing of the Atonement. According to Elder Dallin H. Oaks, worthily partaking of the sacrament not only qualifies a person for the Holy Ghost, but also for the ministering of angels (see Conference Report, Oct. 1998, 50, 51).

MAIN THEMES

- The sacrament is to be given to all who believe, repent, and are baptized in the Savior's name.

- The sacrament is a witness to the Father that we will always remember the Savior.

- Those who partake of the sacrament unworthily eat and drink damnation to their souls; only those with keys and stewardship (in our case, priesthood leaders) should restrict people from taking the sacrament.

- We covenant through the sacrament that we are willing to keep the Lord's commandments.

- If we worthily partake of the sacrament, we are built upon the rock of the Savior.

- We must watch and pray always that we may resist the devil.

- Satan desires to lead us into temptation so he can have us.

- Whatever we ask the Father in the Savior's name will be given to us if we believe and if we ask for that which is right.

- We should always pray to the Father in the name of Jesus Christ.

- We should meet together often as Saints.

600 BC

90 BC

remembrance of my body, which I have shown unto you. And Father that ye do always remember me. And if ye do always Spirit to be with you." (3 Ne. 18:7)

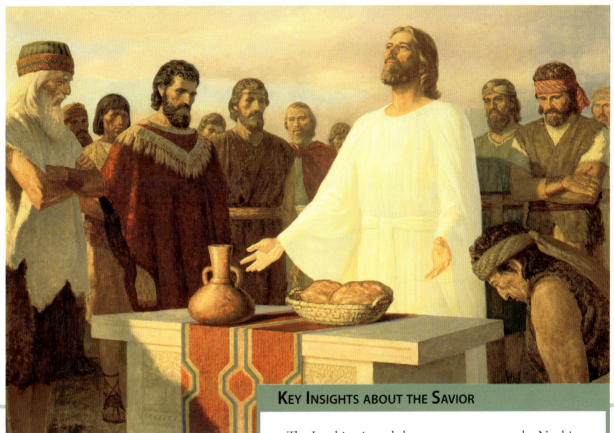

KEY INSIGHTS ABOUT THE SAVIOR

- The Lord instituted the sacrament among the Nephites.
- The Lord pours out His Spirit on those who always remember Him, as covenanted through the sacrament.
- The Lord commands that we partake of the sacrament.
- The Lord blesses those who obey His commandments.
- The Savior has set the example for all.
- The Lord is the light that we should hold up to the world.
- The Lord has commanded that we come unto Him.
- The Lord casts out those who refuse to repent.

3 Nephi 19

MAJOR CONCEPT

We experience baptism by fire when we receive the Holy Ghost.

OVERVIEW Many more people gather at the temple the second day, and the multitude is divided into twelve groups. The Twelve minister to the people and pray for the Holy Ghost. Nephi is baptized; then he baptizes the Twelve. They receive the Holy Ghost and the ministering of angels. Jesus prays to the Father for the people, using words too sacred to be written. He confirms the great faith of the Nephites.

INTERESTING FACTS ABOUT REBAPTISM In this chapter, we learn that Nephi was baptized again. That second baptism was necessary because Nephi's original baptism was under the law of Moses, and Jesus now brought a new

PROMINENT PEOPLE

- Jesus Christ
- The Holy Ghost
- Nephi
- Timothy
- Jonas
- Mathoni
- Mathonihah
- Kumen
- Kumenonhi
- Jeremiah
- Shemnon
- Jonas
- Zedekiah
- Isaiah

dispensation that contained the fulness of the gospel. Old covenants were done away at the ushering in of a new church and a new dispensation (see *Answers to Gospel Questions,* 3:205, 206). Because the Lord had now organized His Church among the Nephites, Nephi needed to be baptized a member of the newly organized Church. The same thing happened at the beginning of this dispensation—Joseph Smith, Oliver Cowdery, and others who had already been baptized were baptized again when the Church was organized on April 6, 1830.

MAIN THEMES

- Those who are called by the Lord as His servants teach and minister under His direction.

- The Holy Ghost is given to those who believe in the Savior.

- In prayers that are inspired, the Spirit reveals what is to be said.

- The three members of the Godhead are one in purpose; when we become like Them, we become one with Them.

- Faith allows our hearts to open so we can understand things of the Spirit.

3 NEPHI

them, and they were filled with the Holy Ghost and with fire. And if it were by fire; and it came down from heaven, and the multitude . . ." (3 Ne. 19:13–14)

KEY INSIGHTS ABOUT THE SAVIOR

- The Lord is grateful for the Holy Ghost.
- The Savior chose the Nephite disciples because of their great faith in Him.
- The Lord's countenance and clothing are exceedingly white—more so than anything found on the earth.
- The Lord purifies those whom He chooses because of their faith.
- The Savior, God the Father, and the Holy Ghost are one in purpose.
- The Lord was able to perform mighty miracles among the Nephites because their faith was so great.
- So great and marvelous were the words of Christ as He prayed that they cannot be written.

MAJOR CONCEPT

The house of Israel, which was scattered because of iniquity and unbelief, will be gathered at the last day as they learn of and accept the Savior as their Redeemer.

OVERVIEW The Savior miraculously provides bread and wine and again administers the sacrament to the people at Bountiful. He testifies that the covenant of the Father with His people will be fulfilled. All prophets have spoken of the coming Messiah; we are the children of the prophets and the covenant. The remnant of Jacob will come to a knowledge of the Lord and will receive the land of their inheritance.

INTERESTING FACTS ABOUT SCATTERING AND GATHERING Numerous references to Israel's scattering appear in scripture; it was written about by Isaiah, Jeremiah, Ezekiel, and Nephi, among others. The

PROMINENT PEOPLE

• Jesus Christ

scattering—imposed by the Lord to punish His covenant people—occurred in three primary phases: the Assyrian captivity of the northern kingdom of ten of the tribes of Israel (around 722 BC); the Babylonian captivity of the kingdom of Judah (around 587 BC); and the Roman

MAIN THEMES

• We should pray continually in our hearts.

• When we partake of the sacrament worthily, our souls are filled with the Spirit.

• The Nephites were given the American continent as the land of their inheritance.

• The sword of justice will hang over us if we fail to repent.

• All the prophets testified of the Savior.

• The Nephites are descendants of Israel and are entitled to the blessings of the Abrahamic covenant, which means we can become gods.

• Those who are baptized are the children of the prophets and of the covenant.

• Through us, as through Abraham, all the people of the earth will be blessed.

• In order to preach the gospel or administer its ordinances, we must be clean.

600 BC

90 BC

the time cometh, when the fulness of my gospel shall be believe in me, that I am Jesus Christ, the Son of God, and name." (3 Ne. 20:30–31)

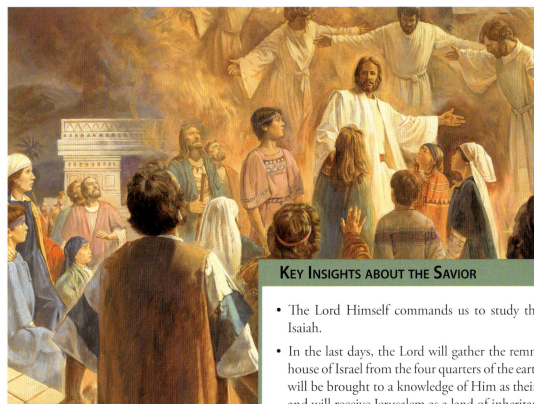

Key Insights about the Savior

- The Lord Himself commands us to study the words of Isaiah.

- In the last days, the Lord will gather the remnants of the house of Israel from the four quarters of the earth, and they will be brought to a knowledge of Him as their Redeemer and will receive Jerusalem as a land of inheritance.

- The Lord will establish His covenant people in the New Jerusalem on the American continent, and the powers of heaven will be in the midst of them.

- Jesus announced that He is the prophet of whom Moses spoke (see Deut. 18:15–19, footnote 23a).

- The Lord will pour out the Holy Ghost upon the Gentiles as they accept the gospel.

- The Lord is God.

- The Lord will go before us and will be at our rear as we proclaim the gospel.

- All of the Lord's covenants with His people will be fulfilled.

destruction of the Judean state and second temple (AD 66–70). In His mercy, the Lord has made arrangements for gathering His people again in the latter days as they come to the knowledge of their Redeemer.

3 Nephi 21

"And they shall assist my people Jerusalem. And then shall they the power of heaven come down

MAJOR CONCEPT

New Jerusalem will be built in the last days as a gathering place for all those who have been scattered.

OVERVIEW The Restoration of the gospel—including the coming forth of the Book of Mormon—is to be a sign that the latter-day work of the Father has begun. The Gentiles will be established as a free people in America and will be saved only if they believe and obey the Lord; if they refuse to repent, they will be cut off and destroyed. Israel will build New Jerusalem, and the lost tribes will return.

INTERESTING FACTS ABOUT GATHERING The Prophet Joseph Smith taught that the gathering of Israel began with the restoration of the gospel and the re-establishment of the Church and kingdom of God. He said that the

PROMINENT PEOPLE

• Jesus Christ

Lord has gathered His people in every age of the world and is gathering them today for the same purpose: "to build unto the Lord a house to prepare them for the ordinances and endowments, washings and anointings, etc. . . . If a man gets a fullness of the priesthood of God, he has to get it in the same way that Jesus Christ obtained it, and that was by keeping all the commandments and obeying all the ordinances of the house of the Lord" (*History of the Church,* 5:424).

MAIN THEMES

- The publication of the Book of Mormon and the conversion of the Gentiles are signs that the Father's work of the gathering in this dispensation has begun.

- A city will be built on the American continent called the New Jerusalem; the Second Coming will occur after that city is built.

- The house of Israel and the remnant of Jacob will be gathered at New Jersualem along with the Gentiles who have converted; the majority of Israel will be gathered after the Millennium begins (see *The Millennial Messiah,* 217, 323–327).

. . . that they may build a city, which shall be called the New assist my people that they may be gathered in . . . And then shall among them; and I also will be in the midst." (3 Ne. 21:23–25)

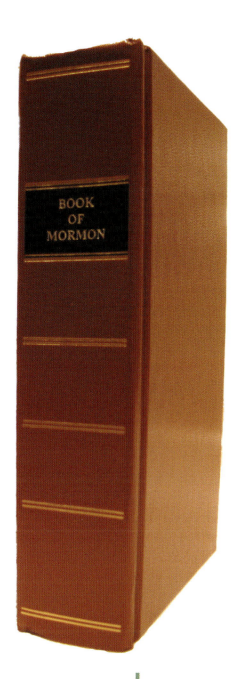

KEY INSIGHTS ABOUT THE SAVIOR

- The Lord will gather the house of Israel in the last days and will establish them in Zion.
- Jesus taught that the free land of America was established so the Restoration could come forth.
- The Lord will number among His people those Gentiles who repent, come unto the Savior, get baptized, and know His doctrine.
- The Lord held Joseph Smith's life in His hands.
- The Lord will cut off and cast out those who refuse to repent and believe on His name; they will forfeit the opportunity to become gods.
- The Lord will be in the midst of those at New Jerusalem.
- In our day the Lord will begin to gather the lost ten tribes.

"No weapon that is formed against judgment thou shalt condemn. This is of me, saith the Lord." (3 Ne.

MAJOR CONCEPT

In these the last days, the scattered of Israel will be gathered through the tenderness and mercy of the Lord.

OVERVIEW The Savior quotes Isaiah 24 to the people gathered at Bountiful. In the last days Zion and her stakes will be established and strengthened, and Israel will be gathered through the mercy and tenderness of the Lord. Israel will have safety through righteousness, and her children will be taught of the Lord, have peace, and receive a glorious inheritance.

INTERESTING FACTS ABOUT THE CHURCH AND GATHERING

Emanating from the Lord's dealings with His people over the millennia is the constant promise of the ultimate gathering of the house of Israel in the last days. Those who do not have the gospel will be taught and endowed with

PROMINENT PEOPLE

• The Lord

truth. Elder Matthias Cowley taught, "The Church of Jesus Christ of Latter-day Saints is the organization through which the Lord is accomplishing the declaration of the Gospel in the last days, gathering Israel, administering the ordinances of salvation, and, in short, is accomplishing the work of redemption—that accomplishment which has been predicted by the mouths of all His holy prophets since the world began" (*Cowley's Talks on Doctrine*, 45).

INTERESTING FACTS ABOUT THE TENT MOTIF

Using the symbolism of a tent is instructive. The tent represents the gospel. We strengthen the stakes by baptizing people into our stakes, and we lengthen the cords by filling the world with stakes. Once the world is filled with stakes, the center pole will be put up from the central place—Independence, Jackson County, Missouri (see Bateman, 65).

MAIN THEMES

• Personal righteousness and family solidarity are key to our protection.

• We must strengthen our families.

• Our faith in the Lord will help keep us safe.

600 BC

90 BC

thee shall prosper; and every tongue that shall revile against thee in is the heritage of the servants of the Lord, and their righteousness 22:17)

Key Insights about the Savior

- The Lord's relationship to the Church is like that of a bridegroom to his chosen. The desolate wife is represented by unconverted, scattered Israel; the married wife represents gathered Israel.

- The Lord will pour out great mercies upon those to be gathered.

- The Lord has already gone through our trials with us.

- The Lord intimately knows the adversary.

- The Lord will protect His servants and His people against the destruction of Satan.

- During the Millennium, all will be taught of Christ and peace will prevail.

MAJOR CONCEPT

The scriptures are of tremendous value, and we should speak, teach, write, and testify of them.

OVERVIEW The Lord approves the words of Isaiah and counsels the people to search them diligently. He also commands that they search the words of all the prophets, and commands that the words of Samuel the Lamanite be added to their sacred records.

PROMINENT PEOPLE

- Jesus Christ
- Samuel the Lamanite
- Isaiah

INTERESTING FACTS ABOUT OUR READING OF ISAIAH Gospel scholar Victor L. Ludlow pointed out that fifty-three of the sixty-six chapters of Isaiah deal exclusively with the latter days and point to our time. Nephi also testified that they would be of great worth to us in the last days (see 2 Ne. 25:8). Ludlow said, "Jews reading Isaiah miss the messianic references, which apply to Jesus Christ, while the traditional Christian readers usually overlook the glorious message of the Restoration. Latter-day Saints stand apart in their perspective of Isaiah because, with their fuller understanding of the gospel, they should be able to see how Isaiah's prophecies can find a full range of fulfillment and application" (*Isaiah: Prophet, Seer, and Poet*, 56).

MAIN THEMES

- We should study the words of Isaiah; the Lord has testified that all of Isaiah's prophecies will be fulfilled.

- The words of the scriptures will go forth to the Gentiles.

- All the prophets testified of the Messiah.

- The major focus of the scriptures is the mission of Jesus Christ.

unto you that ye search these things of Isaiah." (3 Ne. 23:1)

KEY INSIGHTS ABOUT THE SAVIOR

- The Lord Himself commands us to search the words of Isaiah.

- The Lord commanded the Nephites at Bountiful to write additional scripture and to include the prophecies of Samuel the Lamanite, all of which had been fulfilled.

- The Lord spoke, taught, and testified of all the scriptures and commanded that they be taught to others.

- The Nephite record contained Samuel's prophecy that people on the American continent would be resurrected (see Hel. 14:25). What was left out was that Samuel's prophecy had been fulfilled. Jesus commanded that because the prophecy had been fulfilled, it should be added to the record.

3 Nephi 24

MAJOR CONCEPT

When we pay a full tithing and generous fast offerings, blessings are poured out upon us in abundance.

OVERVIEW The Savior quotes Malachi 3 to the Saints at Bountiful and commands that Malachi's words be recorded. Malachi prophesies that the Lord will come to His temple in the latter days and testifies that the sons of Levi will be purified and offer an offering in righteousness. The people are commanded to pay tithes and offerings. Those who fear the Lord will be delivered and included in the book of remembrance.

WHO WAS MALACHI? Malachi delivered his prophetic message to the Jews around 430 BC—long after Lehi left Jerusalem for the promised land. The words of Malachi—including truths about the law of tithing and the sealing

PROMINENT PEOPLE

- Jesus Christ
- Malachi

commission of Elijah—are so important that the resurrected Savior quoted them to the ancient Americans during His visit to them and commanded that they be written down. Malachi was the last of the Old Testament prophets; the central purpose of the book of Malachi was to call the people and their priests to repentance for gross shortcomings and remind them to prepare for the Second Coming and the judgments of the Lord. Malachi was included among the elect seen by President Joseph F. Smith during his vision of the work of salvation going on in the spirit world (see D&C 138:46). He is remembered especially for his teachings about the law of tithing. President Harold B. Lee said that revelation to tithe payers is the blessing that will be poured out when the windows of heaven are opened as a result of paying tithing (see "The Way to Eternal Life," 16).

MAIN THEMES

- If we fail to be charitable to the widow and fatherless, and if we turn away the stranger, we will be judged by the Lord.

- We are commanded to pay tithes and offerings; if we fail to do so, we have robbed God.

- It may seem at times that the wicked are happy and spared from destruction, but in the end those who are righteous will be chosen and blessed.

- Our names will be kept in a book of remembrance if we worship the Lord and walk in righteousness.

storehouse, that there may be meat in my house; and prove of Hosts, if I will not open you the windows of heaven, and shall not be room enough to receive it." (3 Ne. 24:10)

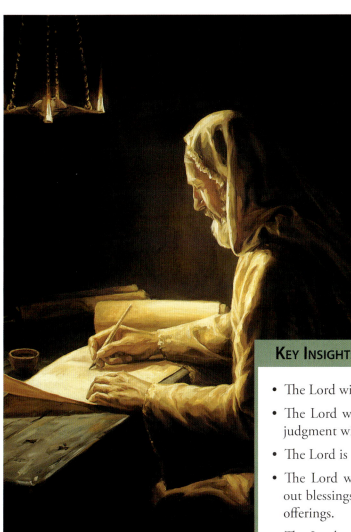

Key Insights about the Savior

- The Lord will appear in the temple at the last day.
- The Lord will sit in judgment at the last day, and His judgment will be swift against those who do iniquity.
- The Lord is unchanging.
- The Lord will open the windows of heaven and pour out blessings in abundance for those who pay tithes and offerings.
- The Lord will protect us against destruction if we pay tithes and offerings.
- The Lord considers those who keep the commandments to be His jewels.
- The Lord will discern between those who are righteous and those who are not.

"Behold, I will send you Elijah the Lord; And he shall turn the heart to their fathers, lest I come and

Major Concept

The sealing power of Elijah—which unites families for eternity—fulfills the purpose of the earth.

OVERVIEW The Lord quotes Malachi 4 to the people in Bountiful. At the Second Coming, those who are proud and wicked will be burned as stubble. In the last day, the Lord will send the prophet Elijah to restore the sealing power and to instill the spirit of family.

WHO WAS ELIJAH? Elijah the Tishbite is a singularly imposing figure in a long line of extraordinary prophets. He began his ministry around 926 BC among the northern tribes of Israel. His history is recounted in 1 Kings 17 through 2 Kings 2; his ministry included many themes and doctrines of the gospel of salvation; he defeated the priests of Baal (see 1 Kgs. 18:37–40)

Prominent People

- Jesus Christ
- Elijah

and supplicated the Lord during a forty-day fast. The prophet Elijah occupied a central position in the design of God as the one holding the keys of the power of turning the hearts of the fathers to the children, and the hearts of the children to the fathers, leading to the incredible latter-day work of family history. His influence was felt with compelling force among the people of his day and continued to be felt long afterward. He was called forth again on the Mount of Transfiguration (see Matt. 17:1–11) and restored the keys of the sealing power in our dispensation to Joseph Smith on April 3, 1836, in the Kirtland Temple, along with the authority to administer all the ordinances of the priesthood (see D&C 110:13–16).

Main Themes

- If we are to be saved at the last day, we must obey the commandments and walk in righteousness.

- Because of Jesus Christ's Atonement and the restoration of the sealing keys by the prophet Elijah, we are able to be sealed as families in units that will last throughout eternity.

- The promises made to the fathers—Abraham, Isaac, and Jacob—enabled them to become gods; that same promise is ours (see D&C 132:30–31).

600 BC

90 BC

prophet before the coming of the great and dreadful day of the of the fathers to the children, and the heart of the children smite the earth with a curse." (3 Ne. 25:5–6)

KEY INSIGHTS ABOUT THE SAVIOR

- At the last day the Lord will burn the wicked as stubble, and they will have neither ancestors nor posterity (roots and branches).

- The Lord will tread down the wicked.

- The Lord will nurture and protect the righteous with healing in His wings.

- The Lord sent the prophet Elijah to restore the keys of the sealing power, that the purpose of the earth would be fulfilled.

3 Nephi 26

MAJOR CONCEPT

We are given truths as we are prepared to receive them.

OVERVIEW The Savior expounds all things from the beginning to the end and testifies that on the day of judgment all will be judged of their works according to the Lord's justice and holiness. The Lord explains that we are given truth in a measure that accords with our faith. He loosens the tongues of children and babies, and they utter marvelous and unspeakable things. The disciples teach and baptize people into the church, and those in the church are united.

INTERESTING FACTS ABOUT THE SEALED PORTION In 1961, President Joseph Fielding Smith counseled that we as a people are currently on probation; we need to show

PROMINENT PEOPLE

- Jesus Christ
- Mormon

that we will obey the commandments we have been given and exercise faith in what is taught in the "lesser part" (verse 8)— in other words, the Book of Mormon as we have it—before the Lord will give us the rest (the sealed portion and other truths). He testified that we will receive the rest when we have read and followed the counsels of the Book of Mormon. President Spencer W. Kimball and Elder Bruce R. McConkie both became a second witness of that truth when they said that in order to qualify for the two-thirds of the Book of Mormon record that was sealed, we need to read and obey what we already have.

MAIN THEMES

- If we are righteous, we will be resurrected to everlasting life; if not, we will be resurrected to everlasting damnation.

- Our current Book of Mormon contains the "lesser part" (only 1 percent) of what the Savior taught the Nephites at Bountiful; if we are to qualify for the rest, we must believe and obey what we have.

- We need to listen to and obey the teachings of the prophets, because they are taught by the Lord.

[the Book of Mormon], which is expedient that they should
it shall so be that they shall believe these things then shall the
unto them." (3 Ne. 26:9)

Key Insights about the Savior

- The Lord expounded all things to the Nephites at Bountiful.
- The Lord revealed to the Nephites at Bountiful all things from the beginning to the end, when He will come in glory.
- The Father commanded Jesus to give the Nephites Malachi 3 and 4 so future generations would have them.
- The Lord will judge us by our works at the last day.
- If we don't believe and obey the part of the Book of Mormon we have, the Lord will withhold the rest from us, and it will be to our condemnation.
- The Lord forbade Mormon from including all the writings on the plates of Nephi in the abridgement of the Book of Mormon to try the faith of the people.
- The Lord loosed the tongues of babies and children at Bountiful, and they spoke things too marvelous to be written.
- The Savior worked mighty miracles among the people at Bountiful.

"Now this is the commandment: baptized in my name, that ye may stand spotless before me at the

MAJOR CONCEPT

Through the atoning sacrifice of Jesus Christ, the faithful and obedient will be sanctified and cleansed of sin through faith, repentance, baptism by water and fire, and enduring to the end.

OVERVIEW The Savior appears to His Twelve, specifies that the church is to be called by His name, and teaches that the gospel is the divine plan for lifting and saving God's children through His atoning sacrifice. Jesus testifies that He gave His life that all might be resurrected and that the faithful and obedient might be able to dwell in the kingdom of God forever. He commands that the Saints are to be even as He is.

INTERESTING FACTS ABOUT SANCTIFICATION Sanctification, the purification that cleanses us from all sin, is the result of two things. First, the Atonement of the Savior provided a way for the Savior to take upon Himself all our sins, giving us the opportunity to have those sins forgiven if we repent.

PROMINENT PEOPLE

- Jesus Christ
- The Twelve Disciples

The second great element of sanctification is the cleansing influence of the Holy Ghost. Christ's Atonement made sanctification possible; the Holy Ghost actually cleanses us from the effects of sin (see 2 Ne. 31:17, Moro. 6:4). Together these elements bring about an actual sanctification in our behalf.

MAIN THEMES

- Whatever we do is to be done in the Lord's name.

- Ours is the Church of Jesus Christ; the addition of "Latter-day Saints" distinguishes us from the original church.

- If the Church is built upon the gospel, then the Father will show forth His good works through the Church.

- We will all stand before the Lord to be judged by our works; if we are to be held guiltless, we must repent, be baptized, and endure to the end.

- No unclean thing can enter into the kingdom of God.

- We must do what we have seen the Savior do in the scriptures and live as He taught.

- Few will find the gate of baptism in this life.

- We will be judged by what is written in the scriptures.

- We are to ask for those things we need.

600 BC

90 BC

Repent, all ye ends of the earth, and come unto me and be be sanctified by the reception of the Holy Ghost, that ye may last day." (3 Ne. 27:20)

KEY INSIGHTS ABOUT THE SAVIOR

- The Lord Himself specified that the Church should be called by His name, both then and in the latter days.

- The Lord will destroy those who establish a church that is not built upon His gospel but is built on the works of men or of the devil.

- The Lord defined His gospel as faith, repentance, baptism, receiving the Holy Ghost, and faithfulness to the end; therefore, the Book of Mormon contains the fulness of the gospel.

- The Lord was sent to earth to perform the Atonement.

- The Lord will judge all of us according to our works.

- The Lord will hold those guiltless at the last day who have repented, been baptized in His name, and endured to the end.

- God the Father and Jesus Christ do not lie.

- The Lord has commanded us to be as He is.

- The Lord grants those things for which we ask in faith.

"Behold, I was about to write the Nephites], but the Lord forbade; But behold, I [Mormon] have seen

MAJOR CONCEPT

Three of the Savior's disciples asked to remain on the earth until He comes again; they minister among us as translated beings who are working to bring souls to Christ.

OVERVIEW The Savior asks the Twelve what they desire of Him after He returns to the Father; nine ask to come to Him speedily, while the other three ask to remain on the earth and bring souls to Him. He grants their desire. The Three Nephites are transformed and rendered immune to death and temptation, are caught up into heaven and experience sacred things, and serve the people with devotion and love. Following the day of judgment, they will change from translated beings to resurrected beings and will dwell with God eternally.

INTERESTING FACTS ABOUT TRANSFIGURATION AND TRANS-LATION We sometimes mistakenly refer to *transfiguration* and *translation* interchangeably, as if they are the same thing. In

PROMINENT PEOPLE

• Jesus Christ
• The Three Nephites
• Mormon

actuality, there are important differences. Transfiguration is a special change in appearance and nature that is brought about by the power of God. The transfigured person is able to see things of eternity that we cannot see in the flesh. It is a temporary condition. Translation, on the other hand, is a condition that

MAIN THEMES

• The Three Nephites wanted to remain on earth to bring souls to Christ.

• The Three Nephites will not pass through death until the Second Coming and will live to see all things fulfilled.

• The Holy Ghost bears witness of the Savior and of God the Father.

• The Three Nephites were transfigured and caught up into heaven, where they experienced things so sacred they cannot be written.

• The Three Nephites have been cast into prison, down into the earth, and into a

furnace, but they cannot be destroyed.

• The Three Nephites ministered to Mormon, and he knew them.

• The Three Nephites will minister to the Nephites, Gentiles, Jews, and all the scattered tribes of Israel; Satan has no power over them.

• The Three Nephites are as the angels of God and can show themselves to man as it is necessary and deemed good.

• The Three Nephites were sanctified in the flesh, or made holy, and the powers of earth could not hold them.

600 BC

90 BC

names of those who were never to taste of death [the Three therefore I write them not, for they are hid from the world. them, and they have ministered unto me." (3 Ne. 28:25–26)

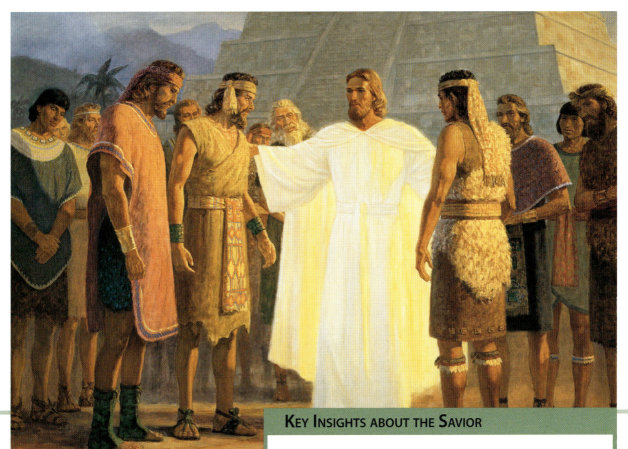

lasts until the judgment day. Those who are translated never endure pain or temptation, have power over the evil things of the earth, and are filled with a fullness of joy; the only sorrow they feel is for the sins of the world. At the Second Coming, they are changed in the twinkling of an eye from mortality to immortality; death will be sweet.

KEY INSIGHTS ABOUT THE SAVIOR

- The Lord granted the desire of nine of His disciples to come speedily to Him and of three of His disciples to remain on the earth until His Second Coming—the same desire that John the Beloved had.

- The Lord is as the Father, and they are one in purpose and unity.

- The Lord will not receive at the last day those who do not hearken unto His words and those of His servants; it would be better for those unbelievers had they not been born.

"And now behold, I say unto you that come unto the Gentiles according to hath made with the children of

MAJOR CONCEPT

The coming forth of the Book of Mormon is a sign that the work of the Lord in the latter days has begun.

OVERVIEW The coming forth of the Book of Mormon is a sure sign that the Lord has commenced His work in the latter days to gather Israel and fulfill His covenant promises. Those who reject the work of the Lord and His revelations will be cursed.

INTERESTING FACTS ABOUT "WO" The word *wo* refers to grief, sorrow, misery, or great calamity. When the Lord issues a categorical "wo," it constitutes a grave warning as to what will happen if we do not heed His words. There are more than thirty-eight incidences of "wo" in the Book of Mormon—eight alone in Jacob's address concerning the Atonement (see 2 Ne. 9) and three in

3 Nephi 29. We need to remember that the Lord issues warnings because He loves us and wants us to understand the severity of the consequences of sin and the importance of keeping the commandments so He can protect us.

PROMINENT PEOPLE

• Jesus Christ

MAIN THEMES

- The coming forth of the Book of Mormon signaled the beginning of the Lord's work of the gathering in the latter days.

- It is our responsibility to heed the words of the Lord and recognize His works.

600 BC

90 BC

when the Lord shall see fit, in his wisdom, that these sayings shall his word, then ye may know that the covenant which the Father Israel . . . is beginning to be fulfilled." (3 Ne. 29:1)

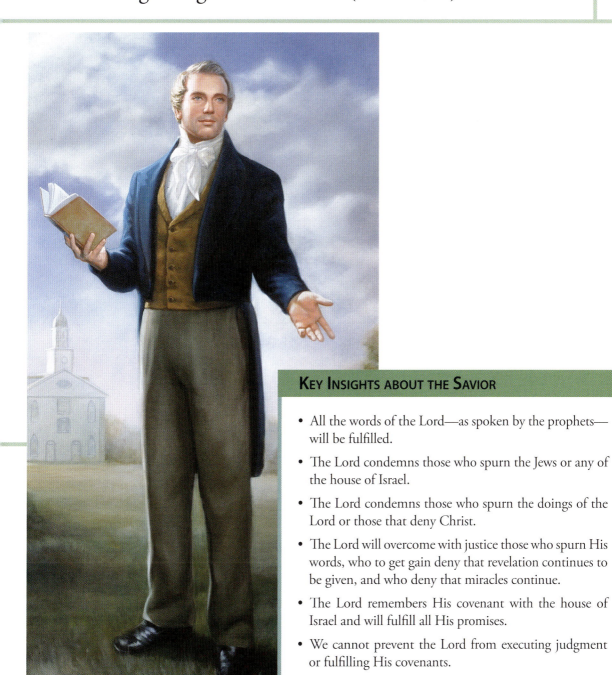

KEY INSIGHTS ABOUT THE SAVIOR

- All the words of the Lord—as spoken by the prophets—will be fulfilled.

- The Lord condemns those who spurn the Jews or any of the house of Israel.

- The Lord condemns those who spurn the doings of the Lord or those that deny Christ.

- The Lord will overcome with justice those who spurn His words, who to get gain deny that revelation continues to be given, and who deny that miracles continue.

- The Lord remembers His covenant with the house of Israel and will fulfill all His promises.

- We cannot prevent the Lord from executing judgment or fulfilling His covenants.

MAJOR CONCEPT

The Gentiles of the latter days are invited to repent, come unto Christ, and be accepted into the house of Israel.

OVERVIEW The Gentiles of the latter days are commanded to repent, come unto Christ, and be numbered among the house of Israel.

INTERESTING FACTS ABOUT THE SAVIOR'S VISIT TO THE NEPHITES The Savior's visit to the Nephites on the American continent forever set an agenda we can follow in charitable and purposeful home teaching and visiting teaching. In His visit—a pattern for our visits—He bore testimony, taught the fundamentals of the gospel, brought enduring gifts and a life-changing influence, taught us who we are and how to gain a fulness of truth, provided priesthood blessings to those in need, and taught us how to endure to the end. As we do these things in our own visits, we will emulate His example and have a positive and uplifting influence on the lives of those we are called to serve.

PROMINENT PEOPLE

• The Gentiles

MAIN THEMES

• We need to repent and turn from our evil ways.

• Baptism brings a remission of our sins.

• Those who repent, are baptized, and receive the Holy Ghost are numbered among the house of Israel.

• We are to cease evil, lying, deceiving, immorality, secret abominations, idolatry, murder, priestcraft, envyings, and strife.

wicked ways . . . and come unto me, and be baptized in my remission of your sins. . . ." (3 Ne. 30:2)

KEY INSIGHTS ABOUT THE SAVIOR

- The Lord gives direction to His servants for the blessing of His people.
- The Lord commands us to repent and turn from our wicked ways.
- The Father commanded Jesus to call us (the Gentiles) to repentance.

"There began to be among them those who
goods and their substance no more common
to build up churches unto themselves to get

MAJOR CONCEPT

An entire civilization moved from complete righteousness to total wickedness in just two
hundred years.

OVERVIEW In this book, which is an account of the people of Nephi, Mormon abridges approximately 285 years of writings—by Nephi, Amos, and his sons Amos and Ammaron—into just 49 verses. It averages 72 years of history per page; almost one-third of the total years covered by the Book of Mormon are in 4 Nephi. The Nephites and Lamanites are all converted, work miracles, and prosper in the land. After two hundred years, divisions, evils, and false churches arise. After three hundred years, both the Nephites and the Lamanites are wicked.

WHO WAS AMMARON? Ammaron and his brother Amos were the sons of Amos and the grandsons of Nephi, the first

PROMINENT PEOPLE

- Nephi
- Amos
- Ammaron
- Amos, son of Amos

of the original disciples of Jesus Christ on the American continent (see 4 Ne. 1:19, 21, 47). Ammaron—the record-keeper of the Nephite records just before Mormon—received the commission to preserve the records around AD 306, at a time when the Gadianton robbers had taken over the entire

MAIN THEMES

- Hallmarks of a righteous society are lack of contention, the law of consecration (resulting in no poor among them), prosperity, the working of miracles, the partaking of heavenly gifts, and obedience to the commandments.

- The key to widespread peace is the love of God and each other, which results in great happiness.

- The wickedness of just a few can impact an entire people.

- Pride has the ability to prevent us from righteousness.

- Wickedness is usually accompanied by persecution of the righteous.

- Those who willfully rebel and who teach their children to not believe are the source of false traditions that can impact many generations.

600 BC

90 BC

were lifted up in pride. . . . And from that time forth they did have their ⟨goods and their substance no more common⟩ among them. And they began to be divided into classes; and they began ⟨to build up churches unto themselves to get⟩ gain, and began to deny the true church of Christ." (4 Nephi 1:24–26)

land and the only righteous people in the nation were the Savior's disciples. Around AD 321, Ammaron was constrained by the Holy Ghost to hide up the sacred records to protect them until the Lord would bring them forth again (see 4 Ne. 1:48–49). Shortly after Ammaron hid the plates in the hill Shim (see Morm. 1:3), he directed ten-year-old Mormon to retrieve the plates when he reached the age of twenty-four. Mormon accepted the commission and carried on the work of writing and abridging the records with diligence.

A PATTERN FOR THE MILLENNIUM 4 Nephi is a pattern for the Millennium and provides parallels for that 1,000 years of peace. It took more than two years after Jesus' appearance before all were converted; the same will be true at the start of the Millennium. In addition, the people of 4 Nephi lived the law of consecration; were attended by miracles; rebuilt the cities that had been damaged; had lots of marriages and the birth of many children; and established a "Zion society." Christ did not personally dwell among the Nephites, just as He will not dwell on earth during the Millennium (see *Teachings of the Prophet Joseph Smith*, 288–289). The steps to the downfall of the Nephites (see 4 Ne. 20–46) parallel the downfall of Satan's casualties at the end of the Millennium when he will be loosed for a short season.

KEY INSIGHTS ABOUT THE SAVIOR

- The Lord prospers righteous civilizations.
- The Lord delights in righteousness and blesses the righteous in all ways.
- When people profess to know Christ but deny parts of the gospel, they open the door to the re-emergence of evil practices and secret combinations.

Mormon 1

MAJOR CONCEPT

The greatest weapon against the righteous is their own tendency to decline into unrighteousness.

OVERVIEW Ammaron has hidden the sacred records in the hill Shim; they include the large plates, the small plates, the plates of Ether, and the plates of brass. He instructs Mormon to retrieve them and keep them when he reaches the age of twenty-four. The Nephites and Lamanites go to war at the borders of Zarahemla, and wickedness, unbelief, sorceries, and witchcrafts prevail throughout the land. The Three Nephites are removed from among the people because of their iniquity.

WHO WAS MORMON AS A RECORD-KEEPER? Born around AD 310, Mormon was called of God to serve as chief administrator in finalizing the ultimate structure and

PROMINENT PEOPLE

- Ammaron
- Mormon
- The Three Nephites

content of the Book of Mormon. With the help of his son Moroni, he compiled for the latter days the plan of salvation as contained in the Book of Mormon. His compilation included the contents of the smaller plates of Nephi in unabridged format (1 Nephi, 2 Nephi, Jacob, Enos, Jarom, and Omni), which served as a replacement for his abridgement of the large plates of Nephi (the 116 lost manuscript pages). His abridgement of records in the current Book of Mormon includes Mosiah, Alma, Helaman, 3 Nephi, and 4 Nephi. That material is contained between Mormon's "bookends," which consist of the Words of Mormon and the book of Mormon; the book of Mormon is a record of the things Mormon personally observed. He eventually turned the records over to his son Moroni; Mormon was killed by the warring Lamanites around AD 385, leaving Moroni to finish the work alone.

MAIN THEMES

- Mormon was told about his commission to keep the records when he was only ten years old.
- When the Lord's servants are taken away, miracles and healings cease.
- Those who are wicked do not have the companionship of the Holy Ghost.
- Unrighteousness and hardened hearts open the way for secret combinations to flourish.
- The wickedness among the Nephites fulfilled the prophecies of both Samuel and Lamanite and the prophet Abinadi.

MORMON

the face of the whole land, insomuch that disciples, and the work of miracles and of iniquity of the people." (Morm. 1:13)

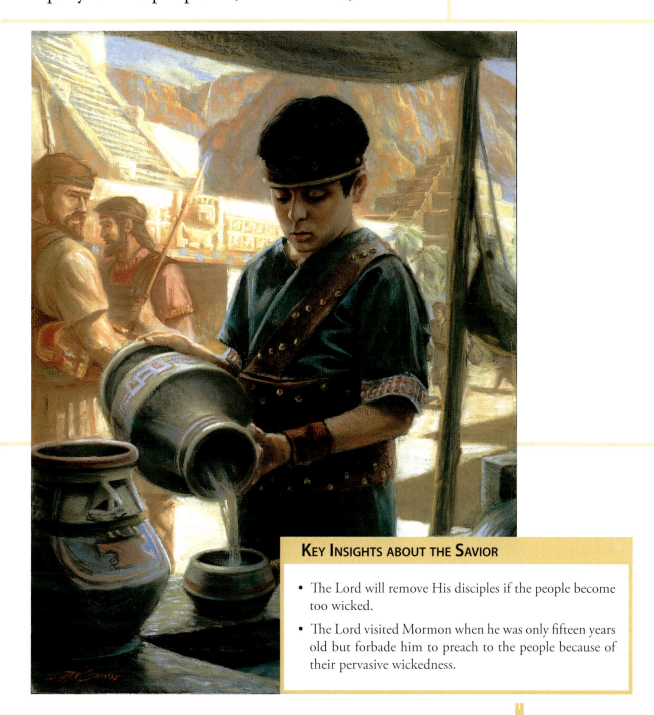

KEY INSIGHTS ABOUT THE SAVIOR

- The Lord will remove His disciples if the people become too wicked.
- The Lord visited Mormon when he was only fifteen years old but forbade him to preach to the people because of their pervasive wickedness.

Mormon 2

MAJOR CONCEPT

Those whose hearts are not broken experience sorrow that causes them to curse God, not sorrow that leads to repentance; Godly sorrow is the only way to arrive at a broken heart and a contrite spirit.

OVERVIEW Mormon is appointed to lead the Nephite armies at the age of sixteen; while they have some success against the Lamanite armies, their lives are filled with emptiness because they lack gospel perspective and have to fight without the strength of the Lord. Mormon sorrows over the wickedness of all the people. A treaty between the Nephites and the Lamanites is made.

WHO WAS MORMON AS A COMMANDER? When he was sixteen, Mormon—being "large in stature" (Morm. 2:1)—was appointed commander of the armies of the Nephites. Despite their wickedness, he loved the people, which enabled him to fight in their defense. He commanded the Nephite

PROMINENT PEOPLE

- Mormon
- Aaron

forces from the time he was sixteen until the final battle at Cumorah, where he witnessed the destruction of nearly half a million of his people. Thereafter he continued to keep his eye single to the glory of God and remained faithful to the end; during that time, he was ministered to by the Three Nephites. He was eventually killed in battle by the warring Lamanites around AD 385.

INTERESTING FACTS ABOUT THE PLATES

Ammaron hid the plates in the hill Shim; Mormon removed the large plates from the hill Shim and put a full account on them. Verse 18 indicates that by this time Mormon had made the gold plates, but "forbears" to make a full account on the gold plates (not wanting to record all the wickedness and abominations). Mormon later removed all the plates—including now the small plates, the plates of Ether, and the plates of brass—from the hill Shim because the Lamanites were about to overtake the land. Mormon

MAIN THEMES

- Widespread iniquity leads to destruction.
- It is possible to be beyond the ability to repent as a result of intense and long-term iniquity.
- Repentance involves proper sorrow for sin; any other kind of sorrow is of the world and does not lead to repentance.
- If we remain righteous we have the assurance of being lifted up at the last day.

MORMON

repentance, because of the goodness of
of the damned, because the Lord would
happiness in sin." (Morm. 2:13)

put all but the gold plates in the hill Cumorah so they would not fall into the hands of the Lamanites and be destroyed (see Morm. 6:6). He then gave the gold plates with the small plates attached (see W of M 1:6) to Moroni, who made additional engravings on them before burying them in the hill Cumorah with the other plates.

Image: Tikal, thought to be a city of the Lamanites around 350 A.D.

KEY INSIGHTS ABOUT THE SAVIOR

- The Lord is merciful and long-suffering.
- The Lord destroys those who are in open rebellion against Him.
- The Lord withdraws His strength from the wicked.

Mormon 3

MAJOR CONCEPT

Those who persist in wickedness pave the way for their own destruction.

OVERVIEW Mormon cries repentance unto the Nephites, and they enjoy a significant victory over the Lamanites. However, they glory in their own strength instead of acknowledging the Lord's help. Mormon prays for them in love and compassion, but they refuse to obey; he wearies of their iniquities and resigns as their commander. He prophesies of their destruction. Mormon compiles a message of repentance and salvation (the Book of Mormon), inviting all to believe the gospel.

WHO WAS MORMON AS A PROPHET? Even before he was called to be a prophet, Mormon's character was confirmed in the scriptures. Ammaron, archivist of the sacred records,

PROMINENT PEOPLE

• Mormon

came to ten-year-old Mormon and said, "I perceive that thou art a sober child and art quick to observe" (Morm. 1:2). At that time Mormon was commissioned to take over the sacred records when he turned twenty-four. He became commander of the Nephite armies at the age of sixteen, and he spent the rest of his life balancing the demands of military service with his commission to guard, preserve, keep, and abridge the sacred records. He loved his people despite their wickedness, and his love of the Lord kept him firm in his assignment. He kept his eye single to the glory of God until the end of his days and was ministered to by the Three Nephites because of his great righteousness.

MAIN THEMES

• We should constantly recognize and acknowledge the Lord's hand in our lives.

• Prophets generally pray without ceasing for their people.

• By associating constantly with wicked people, we risk being drawn into wickedness ourselves.

• When people are left to fight without the strength of the Lord, they are doomed to destruction.

• Righteous people are occasionally called on to witness against the wicked.

all ye ends of the earth to repent and prepare of Christ." (Morm. 3:22)

Key Insights about the Savior

- The Lord commands His prophets to cry repentance to the people.
- The Lord spares people so they will have an opportunity to repent.
- The Lord justifies us in fighting to defend ourselves, our families, our lands, and our religion but does not justify offensive war for the sake of vengeance.
- The Lord cuts off those who refuse to repent.
- Every soul of the human family of Adam will stand before the judgment seat of Christ.
- The Jews will receive other witnesses besides Jesus Himself that Jesus is the Christ.

Mormon 4

MAJOR CONCEPT

The wicked are punished when the Lord withdraws from them; left to themselves, the people then punish and destroy each other.

OVERVIEW Wickedness and carnage continue between the Nephites and the Lamanites, with the wicked punishing and destroying their own. Greater wickedness exists among this people than among any other in all of Israel's history; they are so wicked that women and children are sacrificed to idols. The Nephites begin to be heavily defeated by the Lamanites. Fearing because of the intensity of battle, Mormon retrieves the sacred records. He calls the land Desolation because this is where the desolation of the Nephite nation begins.

INTERESTING FACTS ABOUT HUMAN SACRIFICE Ceremonial human sacrifice by the Lamanites—such as in this

PROMINENT PEOPLE

- Mormon

chapter—along with cannibalism among both the Lamanites and the Nephites is recorded toward the end of the Book of Mormon. Recent archaeological digs provide evidence that human sacrifice and cannibalism were indeed practiced in Mesoamerica during the time period covered by the Book of Mormon. That evidence was not available at the time the Book of Mormon was translated, however, giving further credence to Joseph Smith's translation of ancient records as opposed to his creation of the Book of Mormon (see *Echoes*, 298–299). Although the Lamanites engaged in human sacrifice, the depravity of the Nephites was worse (see Moro. 9:8–9, which is part of Mormon's letter to Moroni).

MAIN THEMES

- The wicked punish themselves and each other.
- The wicked boast in their own strength.
- Left to our own devices, we are weak and vulnerable.

wickedness among all the children of Lehi, Israel, according to the words of the (Morm. 4:12)

KEY INSIGHTS ABOUT THE SAVIOR

- The judgments of the Lord will overtake the wicked.
- The Lord testified that never had there been so much wickedness among Lehi's descendants or among the house of Israel as there was during this time.

Image: Hill Shim, thought to be the location where Mormon retrieved the records.

Mormon 5

MAJOR CONCEPT

The Book of Mormon came forth in the latter days as another witness of Jesus Christ.

OVERVIEW Mormon repents of his oath to abandon his troops and again leads the Nephite armies. In contrast to the wickedness surrounding him, Mormon's righteousness is bright. The Lamanites become a dark, filthy, and loathsome people as a result of their iniquity; it is prophesied that they will receive the gospel from the Gentiles in the latter days. The Book of Mormon will come forth to convince all that Jesus is the Christ.

INTERESTING FACTS ABOUT CONTRASTS IN THE BOOK OF MORMON The Book of Mormon abounds in contrasts. For the two centuries following the Savior's appearance to the Nephites in Bountiful, the people were delightsome, being led by the Father and the Son; now they are as chaff before the wind or as a ship without sail or steerage. The Lamanites, who several hundred years earlier had been a righteous and peaceful people, are now dark, filthy, and loathsome, filled with pride and iniquity; they are rudderless and without noble aims.

PROMINENT PEOPLE

- Mormon
- The Lamanites
- The Gentiles

MAIN THEMES

- No matter how bad things get, we should never give up on those we love or stop trying to improve conditions.

- Those who are wicked struggle through adversity without calling on the Lord for help.

- The Book of Mormon testifies that Jesus is the Christ, the Son of the living God.

- The Gentiles will use the Book of Mormon to bring the gospel to the Lamanites.

- The Lamanites were once led by the Lord, but their iniquity later caused them to be driven and scattered by the Gentiles.

MORMON

shall go unto the unbelieving of the Jews; and for this intent shall that Jesus is the Christ, the Son of the living God; that the Father Beloved, his great and eternal purpose. . . ." (Morm. 5:14)

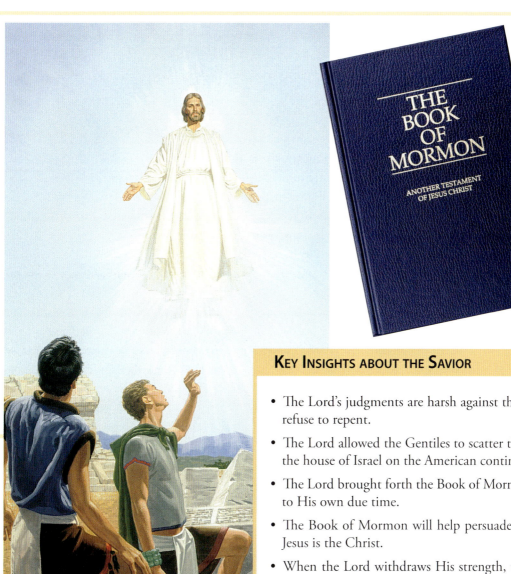

KEY INSIGHTS ABOUT THE SAVIOR

- The Lord's judgments are harsh against the wicked who refuse to repent.
- The Lord allowed the Gentiles to scatter the remnant of the house of Israel on the American continent.
- The Lord brought forth the Book of Mormon according to His own due time.
- The Book of Mormon will help persuade the Jews that Jesus is the Christ.
- When the Lord withdraws His strength, the people are driven about as chaff before the wind.
- If a people no longer qualifies for blessings, the Lord will give those blessings to others.
- The Lord remembers the prayers of the righteous.

Mormon 6

MAJOR CONCEPT

Complete iniquity leads to great destruction.

OVERVIEW All of the Nephites and their families gather to the land of Cumorah for the final battles, with Mormon as their commander. Mormon is seriously wounded, but finishes his record and is commanded by the Lord to bury most of the records in the Hill Cumorah so they will not fall into the hands of the Lamanites. In a monumental battle around AD 385, the Nephite nation is destroyed (the hill where the Nephites are destroyed, Cumorah, is the same hill—Ramah—where the Jaredites were destroyed). An estimated number of nearly a million—230,000 Nephite men, along with all their women and children—were destroyed. Mormon laments the loss of his people in one of the most beautiful and moving passages in the Book of Mormon.

MAIN THEMES

- Mormon's soul was rent with anguish when he saw the destruction of his people.
- We will all stand before the judgment seat of Christ and will be judged by our works.

PROMINENT PEOPLE

- Mormon
- Moroni

INTERESTING FACTS ABOUT THE WRATH OF THE LORD "When the Lord pours out his wrath without measure, the wicked suffer the vengeance of a just God in exactly the same proportion. It is their day of reckoning: they are given measure for measure as their deeds warrant; it is a day of retribution and avengement. It is 'the day when the Lord shall come to recompense unto every man according to his work, and measure to every man according to the measure which he has measured to his fellow man' (D&C 1:10)" (Bruce R. McConkie, *The Millennial Messiah*, 500).

MORMON

600 BC

90 BC

departed from the ways of the Lord! O ye fair ones, who stood with open arms to receive you! Behold if have fallen." (Morm. 6:17–18)

Key Insights about the Savior

- The Lord protects the sacred records of His people.
- The Lord is merciful and just and will judge us fairly.
- The Nephite nation fell because they rejected Jesus, who stood with open arms to receive them.

Mormon 7

Major Concept

The Book of Mormon reinforces the Bible and was brought forth that we might believe that Jesus is the Christ.

OVERVIEW In his farewell testimony, Mormon invites the Lamanites of the latter days to believe in Christ, accept the gospel, and be saved through the atoning sacrifice of the Lord. The Book of Mormon will confirm the truth of the Bible, and the Bible will confirm the truth of the Book of Mormon.

INTERESTING FACTS ABOUT THE BIBLE AND THE BOOK OF MORMON Both the Bible and the Book of Mormon—the sticks of Judah and Joseph (see Ezek. 37:15–23)—establish the divinity of Jesus Christ and act as two witnesses to the truth of the Atonement and the plan of salvation. The effect is to unify the word, or gather all things pertaining

Prominent People

• Mormon

to the covenant of God, as Paul declared: "That in the dispensation of the fulness of times he might gather together in one all things in Christ, both which are in heaven, and which are on earth; even in him" (Eph. 1:10). Quoting Elder Bruce R. McConkie, President Ezra Taft Benson said that 10,000 times more people would be saved in the kingdom of God as a result of the Book of Mormon than as a result of the Bible (see Conference Report, Oct. 1984, 7). President Brigham Young said, "No one can say that this [the Bible] is true . . . and at the same time say that the Book of Mormon is untrue. . . . If one be true, both are true. If one be false, both are false" (*Journal of Discourses,* 1:38). Both the Book of Mormon (see Moro. 10:4–5) and the Bible (see James 1:5) contain the promise that one can ask God and the truthfulness of the writings will be made manifest.

Main Themes

• As descendants of Abraham, the Lamanites inherit both the blessings and the responsibilities that come with that heritage.

• Unless we repent, we cannot be saved.

• We should not go to war unless commanded to do so by God.

• We will all be raised from the dead to stand before the Savior at the judgment seat.

• We must repent and be baptized in the name of Jesus Christ and lay hold on His gospel.

• The Book of Mormon was written to testify of Jesus Christ.

knowledge of your fathers, and repent
believe in Jesus Christ, that he is the

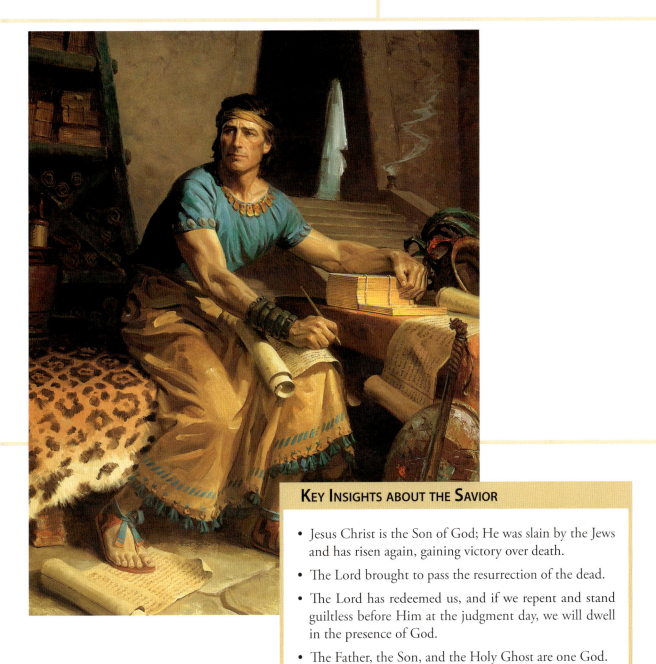

KEY INSIGHTS ABOUT THE SAVIOR

- Jesus Christ is the Son of God; He was slain by the Jews and has risen again, gaining victory over death.

- The Lord brought to pass the resurrection of the dead.

- The Lord has redeemed us, and if we repent and stand guiltless before Him at the judgment day, we will dwell in the presence of God.

- The Father, the Son, and the Holy Ghost are one God.

Mormon 8

"Behold, I speak unto you as if ye behold, Jesus Christ hath shown you (Morm. 8:35)

MAJOR CONCEPT

The Book of Mormon was intended to come forth in our day to coincide with the restoration of the gospel.

OVERVIEW The Lamanites seek out the rest of the Nephites and destroy them; Moroni clarifies that his father, Mormon, was killed by them. Moroni verifies that he is the last of his people; he completes the record of his father and buries it in the Hill Cumorah, prophesying that it will come forth in the last days during a time of great wickedness, upheaval, and apostasy. The only ones on the earth other than Moroni who know the Lord are the Three Nephites, who have ministered unto Mormon and Moroni.

INTERESTING FACTS ABOUT OTHER HIDDEN RECORDS
In verse 4, Moroni says that he is going to "hide up the records in the earth." Joseph Smith reported that he found

PROMINENT PEOPLE

• Moroni

the gold plates in a stone box buried in the ground, a claim that most of his critics did not believe (and that many still fail to believe). However, in the mid-1900s, such discoveries became quite common. In 1945, several volumes of Christian writing from the fifth century AD were discovered

MAIN THEMES

- Whoever receives the Book of Mormon and does not condemn it because of any errors that are in it will have great knowledge.

- The Book of Mormon plates themselves were not of great worth—it was the record contained on the plates that is of priceless worth.

- No one had power to bring the Book of Mormon records to light save by God's will.

- The Book of Mormon will be brought out of the earth and will shine forth out of darkness by the power of God.

- The Book of Mormon was prophesied to come forth in a day when people had ceased to believe in miracles, the power of God had been denied, the churches had become defiled by those who wanted to get gain, and there were great pollutions on the face of the land.

- Moroni saw our day in vision and spoke to us as if we were present.

- The Book of Mormon was written for us in our day; the ancient Americans did not have it.

600 BC

90 BC

were present, and yet ye are not. But unto me, and I know your doing."

in Egypt, followed two years later by the discovery of more than eight hundred scrolls in caves near the Dead Sea. Many of the Dead Sea Scrolls, which contain ancient religious writings including the Old Testament, were concealed inside fired clay pots. Recently discovered writings speak of hundreds of ancient records hidden away for future discovery—many of them written on metal plates and buried in stone boxes (see *Echoes*, 232–233).

Top Image: The Great Isaiah Scroll.
Bottom Image: Qumran Caves, where the Dead Sea Scrolls were found.

KEY INSIGHTS ABOUT THE SAVIOR

- It was the hand of the Lord that destroyed the Nephites.
- It was by the Lord's will that the Book of Mormon records were brought forth by Joseph Smith.
- The Lord will destroy those who condemn the Book of Mormon.
- Judgment and vengeance are the Lord's, not ours.
- The purposes of the Lord will roll on until all His promises have been fulfilled.
- The Lord will never forget the covenants He makes with His people.
- The Lord allows people to work miracles through their great faith in Him.
- The praise of the Lord is of much greater value to us than is the praise of the world.

Mormon 9

"Doubt not, but be believing, and unto the Lord with all your heart, fear and trembling before him."

MAJOR CONCEPT

The Lord continues to pour out revelation and miracles as He did in ancient times.

OVERVIEW Moroni prophesies that those who see the Lord at the last day will no longer be able to deny Him. He calls upon all who believe in Christ to repent and follow Him. He testifies that the Lord is a God of miracles who pours out gifts to the faithful and gives revelations to those who believe; he clarifies that miracles cease only because of unbelief. He exhorts us to be wise and to keep the commandments. Moroni speaks to us as if he were here because he knew we would have his words.

INTERESTING FACTS ABOUT REFORMED EGYPTIAN In verse 32, Moroni verifies Nephi's explanation that the records of the Book of Mormon were written in reformed

PROMINENT PEOPLE

• Moroni

Egyptian in order to get more on the plates, even though the Nephites used the Hebrew language in their everyday lives. In Joseph Smith's day, many critics of the Book of Mormon stated that there was no such thing as "reformed Egyptian." But twentieth-century scholars were introduced

MAIN THEMES

- We will be more miserable in the Lord's presence than being in hell if we have not repented and believed on Him.

- We need to turn to the Lord and repent so we can be found spotless at the last day.

- If we fail to believe in revelation, we do not know the Lord and have not studied the scriptures.

- At the judgment, those who are filthy will still be filthy, but those who have repented and are righteous will always be righteous.

- If we believe in Christ, doubting nothing,

we will be given whatever we ask of the Father in the Savior's name; therefore, we must ask for those things of which we stand in need.

- We must preach the gospel to all people.

- We must repent and resist temptation.

- We should not be baptized or partake of the sacrament unworthily.

- We should doubt not, but believe.

- We should work out our own salvation.

begin as in times of old, and come and work out your own salvation with (Morm. 9:27)

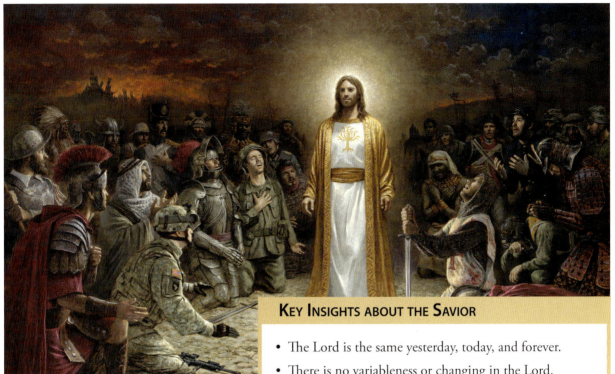

KEY INSIGHTS ABOUT THE SAVIOR

- The Lord is the same yesterday, today, and forever.
- There is no variableness or changing in the Lord.
- The Lord is a God of miracles, and He has not ceased doing miracles.
- The Lord created the heavens and the earth and all things in them.
- The Atonement of the Lord redeems us and brings everyone back to God's presence to be judged.
- The death of the Savior brought about the resurrection of all men.
- The Lord will confirm all His words to those who believe in Him, doubting nothing.
- The Lord knew the plates were written in reformed Egyptian, which was not widely known, and He provided for the interpretation of the plates.

to numerous ancient Hebrew texts written in Egyptian. Many of these, written on papyri, used a type of cursive or reformed version of the hieroglyphic characters most people think of as Egyptian writing—in other words, a "reformed" Egyptian (see *Echoes*, 233–235).

Ether 1

MAJOR CONCEPT

The Lord will bless and direct those who come to Him in faith, trusting in Him completely.

OVERVIEW The book of Ether contains the records of the Jaredites, who had left Jerusalem and gone to the promised land around 2200 BC; they continued to live there for about 1,500 years (including during the time Lehi and his family arrived in 600 BC). The record of Ether was taken from the twenty-four gold plates found by the people of Limhi in the days of King Mosiah. In this chapter, Ether's genealogy is spelled out. The Jaredites are at the Tower of Babel, but the brother of Jared pleads with the Lord not to confound their language. The Lord preserves their language for them and promises to lead them to a choice land, where He will make them a great nation.

MAIN THEMES

- Those things that we ask of the Lord in faith and righteousness will be granted.
- We must trust in the Lord fully and completely.

PROMINENT PEOPLE

- Jared
- The brother of Jared

WHO WAS JARED? Jared was the first leader associated with the civilization known as the Jaredites. He and his family were at the Tower of Babel when the Lord scattered the people and confounded their language. Jared asked his brother to plead with the Lord to spare their family and friends from the confounding of languages. The Lord responded by directing Jared and his family and friends to go with their provisions to a valley northward, where they should wait for instructions. Jared and his followers were eventually led across the water to the promised land, where they gave thanks to the Lord and built up a great civilization. In their final years, Jared and his brother asked the people what blessing they might leave; the people asked for a king, which greatly concerned both righteous men. While the brother of Jared resisted, Jared acquiesced and told the people to choose a king. In the end, wicked kings and secret combinations led to the utter extinction of the Jaredite civilization.

male and female, of every kind; and also of the seed of the earth of
will I meet thee, and I will go before thee into a land which is
there I will bless thee and thy seed. . . ." (Ether 1:41–43)

KEY INSIGHTS ABOUT THE SAVIOR

- The Lord will direct His righteous people.
- The Lord desires to bless those who trust in Him.
- The Lord went before the Jaredites and led them to the promised land.
- The Lord blessed the brother of Jared because of the length of time he spent in prayer.

Ether 2

"Behold, this is a choice land, and whatsoever and from captivity, and from all other nations land, who is Jesus Christ. . . ." (Ether 2:12)

MAJOR CONCEPT

America is a land of promise, choice above all other lands, whose people need to serve God if they are to maintain their freedom.

OVERVIEW The Jaredites prepare for their journey to a land of promise; the Lord testifies that it is a choice land where the inhabitants must serve the Lord or be swept off the face of the land. The Savior chastens the brother of Jared for three hours. By direction from the Lord, the brother of Jared builds barges to carry the Jaredites over the sea; the Lord asks the brother of Jared to propose how the barges will be lighted during the journey.

INTERESTING FACTS ABOUT DESERET In verse 3, we learn that among the provisions carried by the people was "deseret, which, by interpretation, is a honey bee." Since Ether (or perhaps Moroni) had to interpret it, it obviously

PROMINENT PEOPLE

- Jared
- The brother of Jared

comes from the Jaredite language. Hugh Nibley explained that *deseret,* or a word similar to it, was used in ancient Egypt and was associated with the symbol of the bee (see *Echoes,* 462–463).

WHO WAS NIMROD? Nimrod was the son of Cush, who was the son of Ham. Nimrod is described in the Old Testament as "a mighty hunter before the Lord" (Gen. 10:9). As the Jaredites left the Tower of Babel, they were directed by the Lord to go to a valley northward, where they would receive further instructions. We learn in Ether 2:1 that the Jaredites camped in a valley known as Nimrod, after the mighty hunter of the Old Testament.

IS THE NAME OF THE BROTHER OF JARED IN THE BOOK OF MORMON? In Ether 2:13 we are told that the name of the place where the Jaredites pitched their tents was *Moriancumr.* In Alma 8:7 (listed in the

MAIN THEMES

- We should carefully prepare for all contingencies.
- In order to qualify for the Lord's blessings, we must serve Him in righteousness.
- We must call on the Lord always.
- We are to reason things out and think for ourselves before seeking direction from the Lord.

nation shall possess it shall be free from bondage, under heaven, if they will but serve the God of the

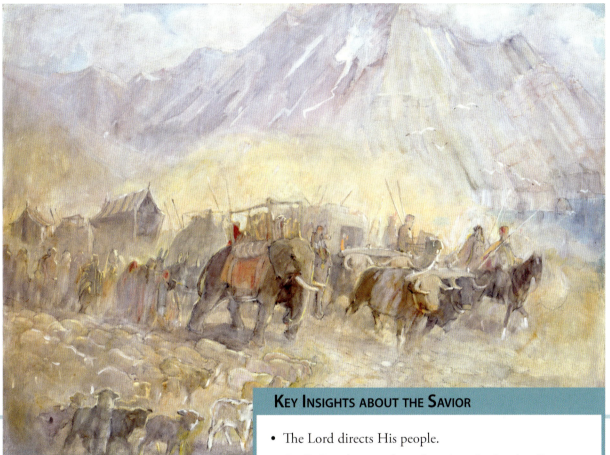

footnote to Ether 2:13), we learn that it was tradition to name a place after the first person to inhabit it. As the Jaredites were led by the brother of Jared, the place they pitched their tents—Moriancumr—was named after him. Therefore, the name of the brother of Jared *is* found in the Book of Mormon.

KEY INSIGHTS ABOUT THE SAVIOR

- The Lord directs His people.
- God's "everlasting decree" is that the Lord will protect His people as long as they are righteous; if they fail to serve Him, they will be swept off the land.
- The Lord will not always strive with man, and the fullness of the Lord's wrath is exercised upon those who are ripened in iniquity.
- The Lord chastened the brother of Jared because he had forgotten to call on the Lord.
- The Lord expects us to come up with potential solutions before seeking His direction.

Ether 3

"And the Lord said unto him: Because of thy
and blood; and never has man come before me

MAJOR CONCEPT

The brother of Jared had a sound understanding of the power and attributes of the Lord, and his great faith enabled him to ask that the Lord illuminate the stones.

OVERVIEW The brother of Jared presents sixteen stones to the Lord that he hopes to use to light the barges; the Lord touches each stone with His finger, providing light. The Savior shows His spirit body to the brother of Jared and testifies that those who have a perfect knowledge cannot be kept from within the veil. The Lord commands the brother of Jared to write the records, and He prepares the Urim and Thummim for their interpretation. The Lord shows the brother of Jared all the inhabitants of the earth from the beginning to the end.

USING STONES TO LIGHT THE BARGES Where did the brother of Jared get the idea to use stones to light the

PROMINENT PEOPLE

- The brother of Jared
- Jesus Christ

barges, which we are told had no windows? In Ether 6:7 we learn that Noah's ark was tight like the Jaredite barges and that it had no windows. But in the LDS Bible, the footnote for Gen. 6:16 says that the translation of "window" is *tsohar,* which means "a stone that shone in the dark." Because the brother of Jared had access to the Biblical record, he possibly got the idea of glowing stones from Noah's account. The Lord had revealed to the brother of Jared how to get air (see Ether 2:20) but not light, possibly because the brother of Jared already had access to such information. The Prophet Joseph Smith said, "We never inquire at the hand of God for a special revelation—only in the case of there being no previous revelation to suit the case" (*Teachings of the Prophet Joseph Smith,* 22).

MAIN THEMES

- We are commanded to call upon the Lord continually.
- Faith no longer exists in the presence of perfect knowledge.
- The brother of Jared saw in vision the whole history of the world from its beginning to its end.
- The experience of the brother of Jared was the actual experience that is taught through symbolism in LDS temples.

faith thou hast seen that I shall take upon me flesh with such exceeding faith as thou hast. . . ." (Ether 3:9)

KEY INSIGHTS ABOUT THE SAVIOR

- The Lord has all power and can do whatever He wills for the benefit of man.
- When the Lord came into mortality, He took upon Himself a body of flesh and blood; before that, His spirit body was in the form of a man.
- The Lord is a God of truth and cannot lie.
- The Savior was prepared before the foundation of the world to redeem all mankind.
- Those who believe on the Lord's name will have eternal life and will become His sons and daughters.
- We are created in the Lord's image.
- The Lord prepared the Urim and Thummim for the interpretation of ancient records.
- The Lord will show all things to those who believe on His name.

Ether 4

"And whatsoever thing persuadeth men to be of me. . . . For behold, I am the Father, world." (Ether 4:12)

MAJOR CONCEPT

Great and marvelous things are opened up to those who believe and have mighty faith.

OVERVIEW Moroni is commanded to seal up the writings of the brother of Jared until the Gentiles have repented and accepted the gospel. The Savior commands that men believe His words and those of His disciples, and that they repent, believe the gospel, and be saved.

PROMINENT PEOPLE

- Moroni
- The brother of Jared
- Jesus Christ

WHO WAS THE BROTHER OF JARED? The brother of Jared lived at the time of the Tower of Babel—approximately two thousand years before the Savior was born—and was a contemporary of Abraham and an aged Noah. He was a man of such extraordinary faith that he beheld first the finger, and then the entire body, of the Lord. By nature, the brother of Jared was a large and mighty man who was highly favored of the Lord (see Ether 1:34); as a result, Jared asked him to petition the Lord for guidance and protection. Directed by the Lord, he built barges and led his people across the waters to the promised land, where they established the nation of the Jaredites. At the end of his days,

MAIN THEMES

- Those who believe the Lord will be given the manifestations of His Spirit.
- Those who do not believe the *words* of the Lord will not believe the Lord Himself.
- When we do not receive the things of the Lord it is because of our unbelief.
- The sealed portion of the Book of Mormon contains the vision seen by the brother of Jared.
- The sealed portion of the gold plates will help us better understand the book of Revelation.

- We will not receive the sealed portion of the Book of Mormon until we repent and become sanctified like the brother of Jared.
- The coming forth of the Book of Mormon is a sign that the Lord has commenced His work in the last days.
- We must repent, come unto the Lord, believe in His gospel, and be baptized.

do good is of me; for good cometh of none save it
I am the light, and the life, and the truth of the

the brother of Jared was distressed when his people wanted a king; he accurately prophesied that such would lead to captivity (see Ether 6:23). Though the full name of the brother of Jared was not given in the Book of Mormon, Joseph Smith indicated that his name was Mahonri Moriancumer (see *Times and Seasons*, 362).

KEY INSIGHTS ABOUT THE SAVIOR

- The Lord will manifest to us all things that were manifest to the brother of Jared when we have that same level of faith.
- Jesus Christ is the Son of God.
- The Lord will not show great things to those who contend against the word of the Lord or who deny the things of God.
- By the Lord's command are all things done.
- Whatever persuades us to do good is of the Lord.
- The Lord will lift up to the kingdom of God those who are faithful and believe.

Ether 5

"And unto three shall [the plates] be shown of a surety that these things are true. And in established. . . ." (Ether 5:3–4)

MAJOR CONCEPT

Three witnesses testified of the existence of the plates from which the Book of Mormon was translated.

OVERVIEW In a chapter addressed to Joseph Smith, Moroni testifies that three witnesses and the work itself will stand as a testimony of the truthfulness of the Book of Mormon. (The Three Witnesses were Oliver Cowdery, David Whitmer, and Martin Harris.)

INTERESTING FACTS ABOUT WITNESSES In this chapter, Moroni reveals to Joseph Smith that there will be three witnesses to the Book of Mormon and that they will play a providential role in establishing the book. The law of witnesses provides that everything is established on the earth in the mouth of two or three witnesses (see Matt. 18:16; 2 Cor. 13:1; 2 Ne. 11:3). In the Godhead, the Father, Son, and Holy Ghost witness of each other (see 3 Ne. 11:32–36; 1 John 5:7–9) and also of the truthfulness of the Book of Mormon (see Ether 5:4). The Lord uses witnesses to establish truth; there are always two witnesses for all priesthood ordinances of exaltation and salvation. Those who repent witness of their accepting the word of God and being willing to come unto the Father in the name of the Son and they will be received into the kingdom of God. Several other witnesses are listed in Ether 5: verse 2 refers to the Eight Witnesses who helped bring the Book of Mormon forth; verse 3 refers to the Three Witnesses; verse 4 shows that the work itself is a witness; verse 4 also teaches that the Holy Ghost is a witness; and verse 6 reminds us that Moroni himself is a witness.

PROMINENT PEOPLE

• Moroni

MAIN THEMES

• The sealed portion of the Book of Mormon will not be translated until the Lord commands it; Moroni commanded the future translator (Joseph Smith) to not touch or translate the sealed portion.

• Three witnesses were shown the plates by the power of God.

• The Book of Mormon will stand as a testimony against the world at the last day.

• Those who repent will be received into the kingdom of God.

by the power of God; wherefore they shall know the mouth of three witnesses shall these things be

KEY INSIGHTS ABOUT THE SAVIOR

- The Lord is over all, and we have no authority on our own in directing the things of the kingdom.

"And it came to pass that the Lord God face of the waters, towards the promised to blow towards the promised land . . . and

MAJOR CONCEPT

When the people desired a king, Jared and his brother resisted, knowing that a king would lead the people into captivity. Following this experience, we need to follow the counsel of prophets rather than our own desires.

OVERVIEW The Lord causes the stones to give light for the barges. The Jaredite barges are driven across the waters to the promised land, and the people praise the Lord for His goodness in delivering them. The people multiply and prosper. As Jared and his brother near the end of their lives, the people ask for a king; Jared and his brother resist. The brother of Jared prophesies that a king will lead the people into captivity. The sons of the brother of Jared refuse to be king, and Jared's son Orihah is finally appointed king. Jared and his brother die.

INTERESTING FACTS ABOUT THE PROBLEMS WITH KINGS
In 1 Samuel 8:9, the people plead with Samuel to give them a king like those of other nations. But the prophet Samuel knew better. He told the people that a king taxes the people excessively (see 1 Sam. 8:15, 17), drafts a labor force (see 1 Sam. 8:11–13, 16), and seizes private land (see 1 Sam. 8:14–15). King Mosiah also gave a discourse about the problems with kings and suggested that the people be ruled by judges instead (see Mosiah 29). In our day, President Spencer W. Kimball compared us to Israel in our desire for a king "like the other nations" instead of being willing to follow the prophet of God; he maintained that such a desire works to our detriment (see *Church News,* 14).

PROMINENT PEOPLE

- Jared
- The brother of Jared
- The Jaredites
- Orihah

MAIN THEMES

- We must have enough trust in the Lord that we commend ourselves into His hands.
- Even when conditions are hard, we should never stop praising the Lord.
- We should always remember to thank the Lord for His tender mercies.
- We should follow the counsel of the prophet and our other leaders rather than our own desires.

Bottom Images: Olmec (Jaredite) Stela showing a "monster of the sea."

caused that there should be a furious wind blow upon the land; . . . And it came to pass that the wind did never cease thus they were driven forth before the wind." (Ether 6:5, 8)

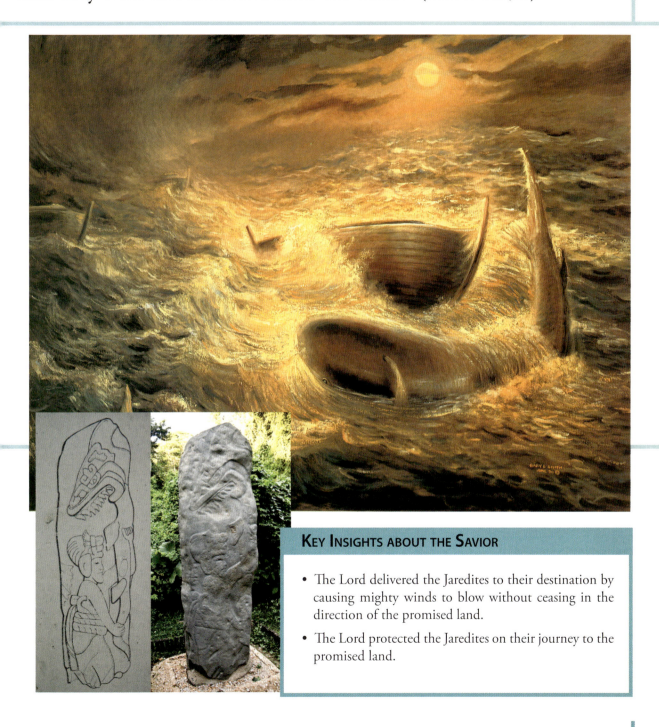

KEY INSIGHTS ABOUT THE SAVIOR

- The Lord delivered the Jaredites to their destination by causing mighty winds to blow without ceasing in the direction of the promised land.

- The Lord protected the Jaredites on their journey to the promised land.

"And . . . there came prophets among the prophesying that the wickedness and idolatry upon the land, and they should be destroyed

MAJOR CONCEPT

The brother of Jared's prophecy that a king would lead to captivity was fulfilled numerous times during the succeeding generations.

OVERVIEW Many years of Jaredite history are condensed into this chapter; Moroni gives only the highlights. King Orihah rules in righteousness over the Jaredites. Following his reign a period of power-mongering and intrigue erupts, and rival factions battle for control, just as the brother of Jared prophesied. The country is divided into two major factions—one under Shule and another under Cohor. Shule prevails and restores unity and peace; prophets come among the people and persuade them to repent. The history of the Jaredites is like that of the Nephites: both were driven by wind, desired a king, led into bondage by a king, warned by prophets, brought to repentance, subjected to secret oaths, and destroyed by secret combinations.

MAIN THEMES

• Unrighteous leadership leads to divisions and captivity.

PROMINENT PEOPLE

- Orihah
- Kib
- Corihor
- Shule
- Cohor

WHO WAS SHULE? Shule was the great-grandson of Jared, founder of the Jaredite nation. Kib, the grandson of Jared, had a son named Corihor who rebelled against and imprisoned his father; Corihor's brother Shule was born during Kib's captivity. Shule made weapons and came against his brother, regaining the kingdom for his father; out of gratitude, Kib then bestowed the kingdom on Shule, who received the repentant Corihor back into the circle of leadership. Corihor's son Noah rebelled and gained power over part of the kingdom; he took Shule captive and planned to execute him. Instead, Shule's sons murdered Noah, and the people returned Shule to the throne. Despite continued efforts by others to dethrone him, Shule maintained control over the kingdom, supported the ministry of prophets, and reigned in peace and righteousness all his days.

people, who were sent from the Lord, of the people was bringing a curse if they did not repent." (Ether 7:23)

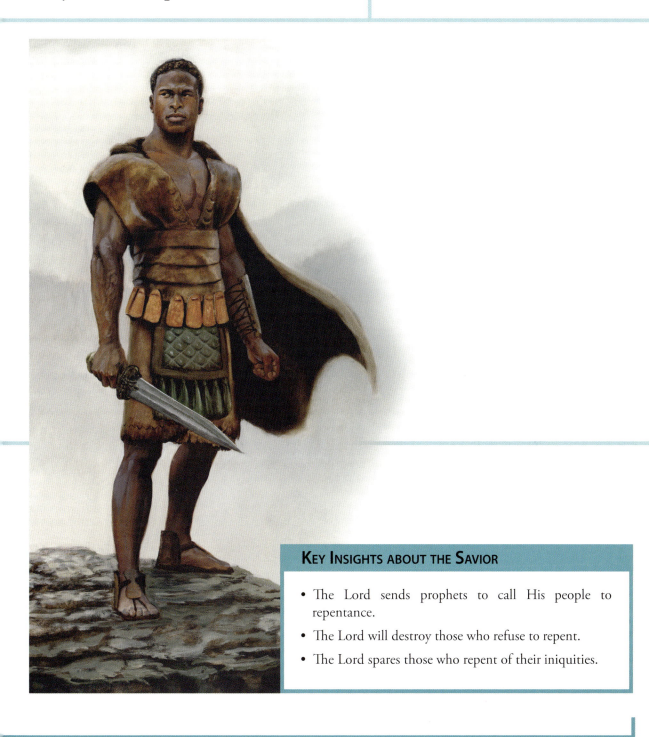

KEY INSIGHTS ABOUT THE SAVIOR

- The Lord sends prophets to call His people to repentance.
- The Lord will destroy those who refuse to repent.
- The Lord spares those who repent of their iniquities.

Ether 8

"And whatsoever nation shall uphold such and gain, until they shall spread over the destroyed. . . ." (Ether 8:22)

MAJOR CONCEPT

Secret combinations are of the devil, and any nation that upholds secret combinations will be destroyed; we are shown the effects of them so we will not fall victim to them.

OVERVIEW Moroni pauses in his rapid summary of Jaredite history to give great detail about how secret combinations were instituted among the Jaredites, because these secret combinations caused the complete downfall of the entire Jaredite (and Nephite) civilization. He testifies that secret combinations are of the devil. Akish forms an oath-bound secret combination to slay the king. We are warned against secret combinations that will seek to overthrow the freedom of all nations.

WHO WAS AKISH? Akish is infamous among the Jaredites for launching a murderous secret combination to get power and gain. He was a friend of Omer, the king who had been

PROMINENT PEOPLE

• Omer
• Jared
• Akish

deposed and imprisoned by his rebellious son Jared. When Jared's brothers rose up in support of their father and defeated Jared's forces, Jared became extremely sorrowful—at which point his daughter reminded him of the secret combinations of antiquity, which she had read about in

MAIN THEMES

• Secret combinations are inspired and fueled by Satan.

• Evil people prosper by taking advantage of human weakness.

• The oath sworn by secret combinations is the same oath that originated with Satan and Cain.

• Secret combinations are the most abominable and wicked above all in the sight of God.

• Secret combinations are had among all people.

• When we see secret combinations among us, we must wake up and do whatever possible to expose and defeat them.

• We stand in danger of losing our liberties if we allow secret conspiracies to overthrow our freedom.

• We must be certain that the only covenants we make are with the Lord.

• Satan never upholds his own.

secret combinations, to get power nation, behold, they shall be

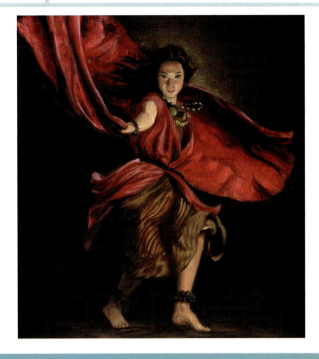

the records the Jaredites brought with them to the promised land (see verse 9). She seduced Akish with her dancing, and he desired her as his wife; she then convinced Akish to use secret combinations to defeat the righteous and regain the kingdom for Jared, which he did in order to win her hand. Omer fled for his safety, and Akish then murdered Jared as he sat on his throne. Akish then became embroiled in a civil war that eventually destroyed all but thirty people, who returned with Omer when he recovered the throne. We can combat secret combinations in our day by preaching the word of God, electing honest and wise people to office, raising our families in light and truth, and heeding the words of Apostles and prophets.

KEY INSIGHTS ABOUT THE SAVIOR

- The Lord does not work in secret combinations and forbids that one man kill another.
- The Lord will destroy any nation that upholds secret combinations.

Ether 9

"For so great had been the spreading of this had corrupted the hearts of all the people. . ."

MAJOR CONCEPT

Secret combinations have the power to destroy an entire civilization, but cannot thrive unless they are supported by the people.

OVERVIEW Jared gains the throne but is murdered by his son-in-law, Akish. Omer is warned by the Lord and flees with his family to safety. The sons of Akish rise up against their father, and civil war erupts, destroying most of the nation. Omer is restored to the throne; he dies, and his son Emer reigns in righteousness and sees the Lord. The Jaredites live in wealth, prosperity, and peace for more than 225 years because of their righteousness. After several kings in succession, Heth comes to power and rules in wickedness. The people decline in spirituality and reject the prophets; the Lord sends a famine and a plague of poisonous serpents, and the people repent. Prosperity returns.

MAIN THEMES

- The evil of secret combinations can tear apart families.

- The evil of secret combinations can be pervasive enough to destroy entire nations.

- Righteousness among people and their leaders results in peace and prosperity.

- An established pattern of apostasy often seen after prosperity is that the people become wicked, the prophets preach repentance, the people reject the prophets, the Lord sends judgments, the people are humbled and repent, and the Lord again blesses the people with prosperity.

PROMINENT PEOPLE

- Jared
- Akish
- Omer
- Emer
- Heth

INTERESTING FACTS ABOUT HORSES AND ELEPHANTS Horses and elephants are both mentioned in Ether 9 (see verse 19). Scientific evidence of horses and elephants having inhabited the American continent during the time of the Jaredites was not available in Joseph Smith's day, and early critics of the Book of Mormon tried to use that fact to discredit Joseph Smith and the book. However, the skeletal remains of both animals—dating to the approximate time of the Jaredite civilization—have since been found in the La Brea Tar Pits in California.

WHO WAS EMER? Emer came five generations after Jared, the first of the Jaredite rulers. Like his father, Omer, Emer was a righteous monarch (see verse 16); the people heeded his warning that whoever possessed the promised land must do so in righteousness, and they enjoyed a great abundance of blessings

wicked and secret society that it
. . ." (Ether 9:6)

under Emer. He was so righteous and
faithful that he saw the Lord (see verse 22).
He continued to rule in righteousness,
rejoiced in the condition of the people,
and died in peace. He was succeeded by
his son Coriantum, who also reigned in
righteousness.

Images: Olmec (Jaredite) artifacts.

KEY INSIGHTS ABOUT THE SAVIOR

- The Lord warns and protects His people from the forces that would destroy them.
- The Lord sends judgments upon those who have forgotten Him and who reject the prophets.
- The Lord blesses those who repent.

Ether 10

MAJOR CONCEPT

Nations who live in righteousness and remember the Lord are prospered by Him; those who reject the prophets and live in wickedness are cursed by Him.

OVERVIEW In this chapter, Moroni traces the linear succession of rulers during the middle and later period of Jaredite history. While some of the kings rule in righteousness, others are wicked; many spend most of their days in captivity, in fulfillment of the prophecy of the brother of Jared. During periods of righteousness, the people flourish through the blessings of the Lord and enjoy a high state of civilization.

WHO WAS RIPLAKISH? Riplakish was one in a sequence of Jaredite leaders toward the beginning of the middle period. He was the son of Shez, who ruled in righteousness and walked in the ways of the Lord. But unlike his father,

PROMINENT PEOPLE

- Shez
- Shez, son of Shez
- Riplakish
- Morianton
- Lib
- Com

Riplakish became a man of whoredoms and wickedness who placed heavy tax burdens on the people to support his extravagant tastes (see verses 6–7). After forty-two years of such treatment, the people revolted and killed Riplakish, driving his descendants

MAIN THEMES

- Riplakish resembled wicked King Noah (see Mosiah 11); both were very immoral, levied heavy taxes on their people, and were killed by their own people.

- Indications of the refinement of the Jaredite civilization include their aggressive trade practices; their work with all kinds of ores and metals; their silks, linens, and other fine cloths; the abundance of tools with which they tilled the earth; and the various weapons they manufactured.

- Material things aren't bad, but the love of material things can corrupt.

blessed than were they, and more prospered by a land that was choice above all lands, for the

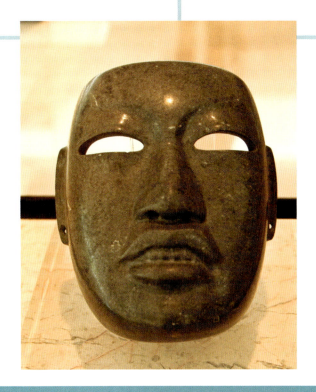

from the land. Eventually one of his descendants, Morianton, rose up in power and took over leadership of the country; while he was not morally decent, he eased the burdens of the people and reigned in justice for many years.

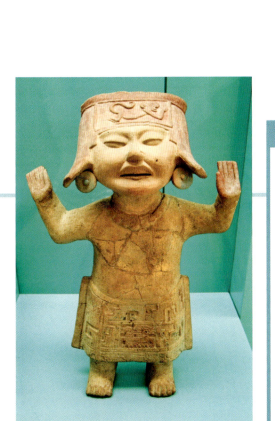

Images: Olmec (Jaredite) artifacts.

KEY INSIGHTS ABOUT THE SAVIOR

- Those who are wicked are cut off from the presence of the Lord.
- The Lord blesses and prospers the righteous.
- The Lord declared the promised land to be choice above all other lands.

Ether 11

MAJOR CONCEPT

Wickedness and dissension lead to apostasy and destruction.

OVERVIEW In this chapter, the Jaredite civilization takes its final decline into apostasy. The Jaredite nation is dominated by wars, dissensions, and wickedness among both its leaders and its people. The prophets who labor among the people predict the utter destruction of the Jaredites unless they repent; the people reject the prophets. A law is enacted to execute the prophets; calamity reigns.

WHO WAS COM? Com, the son of Coriantum, drew away half of the nation of the Jaredites and ruled over it for forty-two years. Eventually he defeated the king, Amgid, and gained control over the entire land. During the reign of Com, secret combinations began to rise up again, administering evil oaths

PROMINENT PEOPLE

- Com
- Shiblom
- Seth
- Ahah
- Ethem
- Moron
- Coriantor
- Ether

and seeking to destroy the kingdom; Com fought against the secret combinations but was unable to prevail against them. Many prophets arose during Com's reign, calling the people to repentance, but they were rejected by the people and sought protection from Com, which he provided. Com was blessed all the remainder of his days.

MAIN THEMES

- The Lord never destroys a people without first warning them through His prophets.
- Secret combinations bring about war, contentions, and destruction.
- Wickedness can cause the downfall and destruction of even the greatest nations.
- Prophets mourn over the wickedness of the people.
- Secret combinations are built up for power and gain.
- Killing of prophets is one of the final steps that leads to complete apostasy and destruction.

of the Lord, because of their wicked combinations; wherefore, there land, and also many famines and pestilences, insomuch that there was had been known upon the face of the earth. . . ." (Ether 11:7)

Images: Olmec (Jaredite) artifacts.

KEY INSIGHTS ABOUT THE SAVIOR

- The Lord sends His prophets to warn the people of the consequences of wickedness.
- The Lord causes famines, pestilences, and destruction among people who reject the prophets and refuse to repent.
- The Lord has mercy on those who repent.
- The Lord first speaks by the mouth of His servants; when they are rejected, He uses the voice of thunderings, tempests, earthquakes, famine, and pestilence (see also D&C 43:25).

MAJOR CONCEPT

Faith, hope, and charity are attributes essential to salvation.

OVERVIEW The prophet Ether exhorts the people to believe in God. Moroni inserts into the record his great teachings on Christlike attributes. He testifies that wonders and marvels are done by the power of faith and asserts that faith, hope, and charity are essential to salvation. Moroni sees Jesus face to face.

PROMINENT PEOPLE

- Ether
- Coriantumr
- Moroni

WHO WAS ETHER? The brother of Jared was the first of the Jaredite prophets; Ether was the last—living some 1,500 years after the brother of Jared, probably around 500 BC. As specified in verse 2 of this chapter, Ether's faith was so strong that he could not be restrained because the Spirit of the Lord was with him. His diligence caused him to cry all day, preaching repentance to the people, but they rejected him because their hearts were turned to the things of the world. He prophesied of the New Jerusalem, but the people could not see beyond their own wretched, war-torn conditions. Ether's situation was so perilous that he had to hide

MAIN THEMES

- All things are fulfilled by faith.
- Those who believe in God can with surety hope for a better world.
- Hope and faith anchor our souls, making them sure.
- Faith is things that are hoped for but not seen, and we receive a witness after the trial of our faith.
- All miracles are accomplished by faith.
- Faith leads to hope.
- Our weaknesses help us be humble, but they can be made into strengths through the Lord.
- Faith, hope, and charity create all righteousness.
- Unless we have faith, hope, and charity, we cannot receive the inheritance the Lord has in store for us.
- We are to seek Jesus.
- We must have faith before we can receive the Second Comforter, who is Jesus Christ.

not seen; wherefore, dispute not because ye see not, for ye receive faith." (Ether 12:6)

in the cavity of a rock and venture out only under the cover of darkness. From his hiding place in the rock, he recorded the downfall of his civilization, then hid the record in a place where it would later be discovered by Limhi (see Mosiah 8:9). The entire Jaredite nation was destroyed except for Coriantumr, who discovered the descendants of the Mulekites in Zarahemla.

Top Image: Olmec (Jaredite) artifact.

Key Insights about the Savior

- The Lord showed Himself to mortals because of their great faith.
- The Lord and His Atonement was given as a gift by the Father, and those gifts were accomplished by faith.
- The Lord gives us weaknesses that we may be humble; if we come unto Him, He will show us our weaknesses and will make weak things become strong.
- The Lord has prepared a house for us in the mansions of His Father.

MAJOR CONCEPT

The city of New Jerusalem will be built in America and will be a dwelling place for the pure and righteous.

OVERVIEW Ether prophesies of a New Jerusalem that will be built in America by the seed of Joseph. Because of the wickedness of the people and the hardness of their hearts, they cast Ether out and threaten his life. He hides in the cavity of rock during the day and goes out during the night to observe the conditions of the people. He prophesies the destruction of the Jaredite civilization. War rages throughout the land.

INTERESTING FACTS ABOUT THE NEW JERUSALEM There will be two holy cities during the Millennium: Jerusalem of old and the New Jerusalem on the American continent (which will include the city of Enoch that was translated).

MAIN THEMES

- America is a land choice above all other lands and has been so since the waters of the flood receded.

- The city of New Jerusalem will be built in America and will be a holy sanctuary for the pure and righteous.

- Real peace does not exist among those who reject righteousness.

PROMINENT PEOPLE

- Ether
- Coriantumr
- Shared

The characteristics of the New Jerusalem, according to the prophecies of Ether, are that it will be a holy sanctuary of the Lord; it will be built on the American continent by the remnant of the seed of Joseph; it will be a holy city like Jerusalem; it will stand until the earth is celestialized; and it will be a city for the pure and righteous. When the earth dies, New Jerusalem will be taken up during the cleansing period of the earth according to John the Beloved's prophecy (see Rev. 21:10–27). Elder Bruce R. McConkie said that to envision what is meant by the New Jerusalem, we must know five facts: (1) Ancient Jerusalem will be rebuilt and become one of two great world capitols during the Millennium. (2) A New Jerusalem (Zion) will be built in America. (3) Enoch's city was taken to heaven. (4) Enoch's city with its resurrected inhabitants will return as New Jerusalem and will join the city of the same name. (5) New Jerusalem will be lifted off the

and blessed are they who dwell therein, for it is they whose the Lamb. . . ." (Ether 13:10)

earth at the final cleansing of the earth, but will descend again from heaven when the earth becomes celestial (see *Doctrinal New Testament Commentary,* 3:580, 581).

Bottom Image: Olmec (Jaredite) stela.

KEY INSIGHTS ABOUT THE SAVIOR

- The Lord will preserve the New Jerusalem as His holy sanctuary.

- The Lord destroys the wicked.

- The Lord told Coriantumr through the prophet Ether exactly what would happen to him if he failed to repent: if he repented, his people and his household would be saved; if he didn't repent, he alone would survive and he would see another people inherit the land.

MAJOR CONCEPT

The wickedness and the iniquities of the Jaredite people paved the way for their destruction.

OVERVIEW The wickedness of the Jaredites brings a great curse upon the land. Secret combinations rage. Blood and carnage cover the land as Coriantumr and his armies engage against Gilead, then Lib, then Shiz.

INTERESTING FACTS ABOUT ASIATIC WARFARE Hugh Nibley taught that there were several circumstances peculiar to Asiatic warfare. First, since every war was a strictly personal contest between kings, battles had to continue until one of the kings was killed. Second, the king must be the very last person to fall; the entire army existed for the sole purpose of defending the king. In the book of Ether, there were many instances in which the kings were kept in prison for many years but were never executed; as long as the king was alive, the war could continue—but as soon as the king died, the war was over and that king's side lost, no matter how strong the surviving forces were (see "The World of the Jaredites").

MAIN THEMES

- We cannot expect to be blessed by the Lord if we refuse to repent and follow the prophets.

- We are given the same "everlasting decree" as was given the Jaredites: we must serve the God of this land—Jesus Christ—or be swept off the land.

- Secret combinations play a major role when wicked kings rule.

visit them in the fulness of his wrath, and their wickedness and their everlasting destruction." (Ether 14:25)

Key Insights about the Savior

- The Lord curses those people who refuse to repent and who persist in iniquity.

Ether 15

MAJOR CONCEPT

Great wickedness and secret combinations led to the utter destruction of the Jaredite civilization.

OVERVIEW In the final battle of the Jaredite nation, Shiz and Coriantumr assemble all the people—including women and children—into mortal combat. Because of their iniquities, the Lord ceases striving with them. The entire Jaredite nation is utterly destroyed. The only survivors are Coriantumr and Ether.

WHO WAS CORIANTUMR? Coriantumr was the last of the Jaredite kings—kings that spanned a period of time from approximately 2000 BC to possibly as late as 250 BC. During the days of Coriantumr, a period of great wickedness, the Lord sent the prophet Ether to preach repentance and prophesy of destruction if the people did

PROMINENT PEOPLE

• Coriantumr
• Shiz

not repent. Coriantumr, who was expert in the science of war, was too occupied with military maneuvers to maintain his power and position in the face of constant attacks from rival factions. Ether declared that if Coriantumr would repent, the Lord would preserve him in his position, but the king rejected the message. The Lord visited the people in all His wrath, and millions of Jaredites were slain in a final battle. (According to Hugh Nibley, wars of extinction were a standard institution in the history of Asia; see "The World of the Jaredites.") Coriantumr and Ether were the sole survivors. As Ether had prophesied, Coriantumr was discovered by the Mulekites in the land of Zarahemla.

MAIN THEMES

• Our only protection is righteousness and obedience to the words of the prophets.

• Satan has full power over the wicked.

• The most important thing over all else is that we are saved in the kingdom of God.

• Moroni identified the hill Ramah where the Jaredites were destroyed as the same hill, called Cumorah, where the Nephites were destroyed. In other words, both nations ended in destruction on the same battlefield.

ceased striving with them, and Satan had full power over the hearts

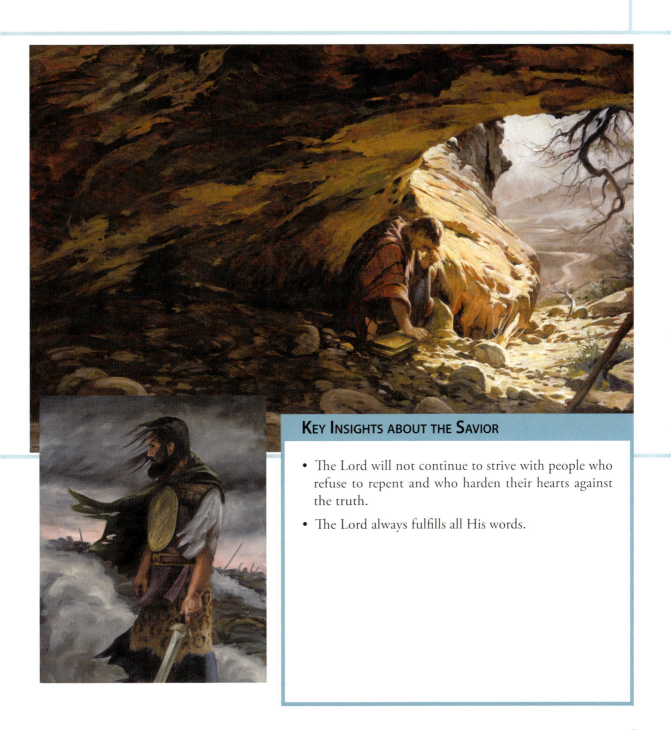

KEY INSIGHTS ABOUT THE SAVIOR

- The Lord will not continue to strive with people who refuse to repent and who harden their hearts against the truth.
- The Lord always fulfills all His words.

Moroni 1

MAJOR CONCEPT

While written for the Lamanites, the sacred truths in the book of Moroni are of great worth to all our Father's children.

OVERVIEW In this brief first chapter of the book of Moroni—a book that was written while Moroni was hiding from the Lamanites, waiting to be destroyed—he specifies that he has finished abridging the records of the Jaredites. He explains that the Lamanites have put to death every Nephite that will not deny Christ and testifies that he will not deny the Savior and so is wandering to avoid being detected. He expresses the hope that what he has written will be of worth to the Lamanites in some future day. The book of Moroni seems to have at least two purposes: to testify of the need for a formal church organization with its ordinances, and to witness of the unchanging nature of Christ and His Church. This may be because Moroni saw our day and witnessed the confusion among different churches about their organizations and ordinances.

PROMINENT PEOPLE

• Moroni

MAIN THEMES

• Some who have stood firm in their testimony of the Savior have been martyred for their belief.

• Moroni refused to deny the Christ.

• The Book of Mormon records were written for us in our day.

• Covenants and ordinances are essential (see also Boyd K. Packer, Conference Report, Oct. 1985, 105–106).

INTERESTING FACTS ABOUT THE PATTERN OF ANCIENT TEXTS Moroni wrote his text on metallic plates in reformed Egyptian (see Morm. 9:32–34), according to the pattern set by previous archivists of the Book of Mormon. Of the three earliest existing manuscripts that contain biblical text, one was transcribed on small metal scrolls, one was written in reformed Egyptian, and the third was hidden to be recovered at a later date. These facts demonstrate that the Book of Mormon fits an ancient pattern: it was written on thin gold plates, was written in reformed Egyptian, and was buried in a hillside by Moroni, who expressed the hope that it would be of worth to his brethren in some future day (see Moro. 1:4) (see *Echoes*, 235–236).

perhaps they may be of worth unto future day, according to the will of

- It is by the Lord's will that all things are accomplished.

Major Concept

The gift of the Holy Ghost must be given by one who has been authorized to confer that gift.

OVERVIEW Moroni gives the words of Christ that He spoke when conferring upon the Nephite disciples the power to bestow the gift of the Holy Ghost.

INTERESTING FACTS ABOUT THE HOLY GHOST A house may be wired with all the components essential for electricity, but until the power company connects the house to a source of power, no electrical power exists. In a similar way, the Holy Ghost is our power source—the thing which we must have in order to illuminate His gifts in our life. The Prophet Joseph Smith testified that the Holy Ghost is necessary to make and to organize the priesthood and that the gifts of prophecy, tongues, visions, revelations, gifts, and healings cannot be enjoyed without the Holy Ghost.

Main Themes

- The gift of the Holy Ghost is conferred only by one having authority.
- The gift of the Holy Ghost is given in the name of Jesus Christ.
- The Holy Ghost is conferred by the laying on of hands (see also Acts 8:18).

Prominent People

- Jesus Christ

WERE THE TWELVE NEPHITE DISCIPLES "APOSTLES" LIKE THOSE IN JERUSALEM?
Statements by three Church leaders indicate that the twelve chosen by Jesus in Bountiful were Apostles. In the Wentworth Letter, Joseph Smith said of the Nephites "they had Apostles" (see *History of the Church,* 4:538). John Taylor testified that "Apostles lived on this [the American] continent" (see *The Gospel Kingdom,* 353). And Joseph Fielding Smith said that the twelve chosen by the Savior in Bountiful "were virtually Apostles" (see *Answers to Gospel Questions,* 1:122). Also note that in 4 Nephi 1:14, we are told that new disciples were ordained to replace those who died—a practice that indicates they were Apostles (compare to Acts 1:26–29).

hands, ye shall give the Holy Ghost; and do mine apostles." (Moro. 2:2)

KEY INSIGHTS ABOUT THE SAVIOR

- The Savior laid His hands upon the heads of His Twelve and gave them the power to confer the gift of the Holy Ghost.
- The Savior spoke things to His disciples that He did not tell the multitudes.
- The Savior gave specific instructions and wording for the ordinance in which the Holy Ghost is to be conferred.

Moroni 3

MAJOR CONCEPT

Ordinations are to be done by the laying on of hands and by the power of the Holy Ghost.

OVERVIEW Moroni explains the procedure used by the disciples to ordain priests and teachers.

WHO WAS MORONI? Moroni, the son of Mormon, lived from around AD 350 until around AD 421. He and his father had experienced the cataclysmic battle of nations at Cumorah around AD 385, where nearly half a million Nephite warriors were slain (along with countless women and children), including the ten thousand commanded by Moroni (see Morm. 6:12). Mormon himself was slain shortly thereafter by the Lamanites. Moroni was then left alone for the better part of thirty-five years, wandering in the wilderness to protect his own life during a period

PROMINENT PEOPLE

• Moroni

of universal warfare among the existing Lamanite factions. He devoted his final years to preserving and adding to the sacred records. Notwithstanding the bleakness of his lonely existence, Moroni was sustained by the Spirit of God, and his strength in the Lord derived from a confirmation of the mission given him to speak eternal truth to future generations who would face the challenge of overcoming pride and embracing the plan of happiness. During Moroni's solitary years he added to the sacred records invaluable information about Church administration as taught to the people by the resurrected Christ. He also included three treatises from his father: a speech explaining the miracle of the Spirit of Christ and the power of faith, hope, and charity (see Moro. 7); an epistle on the falsehood of infant baptism (see Moro. 8); and a report of the atrocities rampant among the wicked Nephites before their extinction (see Moro. 9). Moroni was

MAIN THEMES

• Ordinations in the Church are done by the laying on of hands by those who are in proper authority and in the name of Jesus Christ.

priests and teachers, according to the
and they ordained them by the power
them." (Moro. 3:4)

Key Insights about the Savior

- All ordinations are done in the name of Jesus Christ.
- Jesus gave the Nephites the full gospel, so the priests and teachers referred to in this chapter (see verse 1) would have been offices in the Aaronic Priesthood. (This is in contrast to the "priests and teachers" referred to in Jacob 1:18; they would not have been offices in the Aaronic Priesthood because the Nephites at that time had only the Melchizedek Priesthood. Those priests, then, would have been high priests, and the teachers would have been similar to school teachers, not holders of a priesthood office.)

entrusted with the keys of restoring the divine message of hope and exaltation in the latter days, and was viewed in vision by John the Revelator (see Rev. 14:6–7). Moroni's last words—the final words of the Book of Mormon—declared that he would be on hand at the judgment bar of God following the resurrection to greet each of his readers in person.

"O God, the Eternal Father, we ask Son, Jesus Christ, to bless and sanctify of all those who partake of it. . . ."

MAJOR CONCEPT

The sacramental bread is blessed using a prayer administered by the Savior.

OVERVIEW Moroni gives the prayer that is to be used to bless the sacramental bread.

INTERESTING FACTS ABOUT THE SACRAMENT "The weekly opportunity of partaking of the sacrament of the Lord's Supper is one of the most sacred ordinances of The Church of Jesus Christ of Latter-day Saints and is further indication of His love for all of us. Associated with the partaking of the sacrament are principles that are fundamental to man's advancement and exaltation in the kingdom of God and the shaping of one's spiritual character" (David B. Haight, "The Sacrament," 12–14).

PROMINENT PEOPLE

• Elders and priests blessing the sacrament

MAIN THEMES

• We partake of the sacrament to remember the flesh and blood of Christ.

• We partake of the bread to remember the body of the Savior.

• In partaking of the sacramental bread, we witness that we are willing to take upon ourselves the name of Jesus Christ and always remember Him.

• In partaking of the sacramental bread, we covenant that we will always keep the commandments the Lord has given us.

thee in the name of thy
this bread to the souls
(Moro. 4:3)

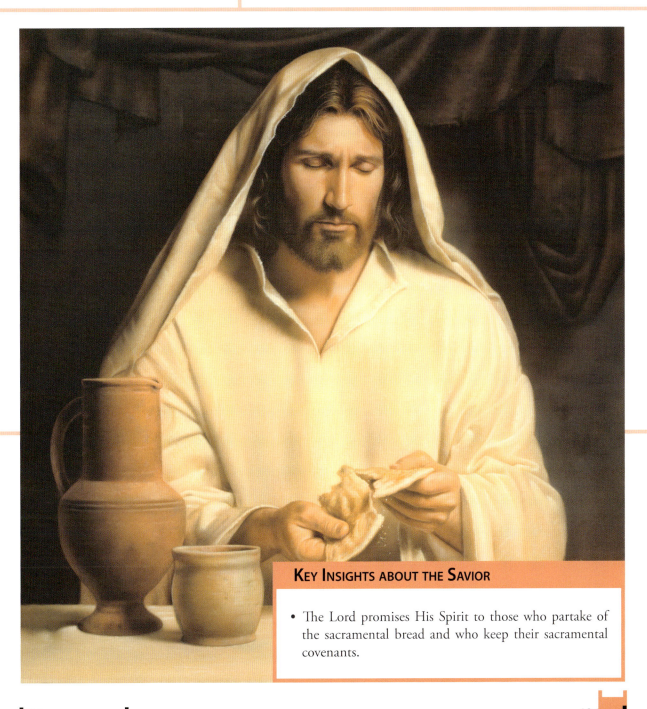

KEY INSIGHTS ABOUT THE SAVIOR

- The Lord promises His Spirit to those who partake of the sacramental bread and who keep their sacramental covenants.

MAJOR CONCEPT

The sacramental water is blessed using a prayer administered by the Savior.

OVERVIEW Moroni gives the prayer that is to be used to bless the sacramental water.

INTERESTING FACTS ABOUT THE SACRAMENT President Gordon B. Hinckley, in speaking about our partaking of the sacrament, said that we "should rethink the contract which exists between [us] and the Lord under which we take upon ourselves His name and agree to keep His commandments and He, in turn, promises that His Spirit will be with us. If we could bring about the consummation of that covenant in the lives of our people with a renewal each week, what a marvelous thing it would be" (*Teachings of Gordon B. Hinckley*, 565). President Spencer W. Kimball said in refer- ence to the sacrament, "The most important word in the dictionary could be 'remember.' Because of the covenants we've made, our greatest need is to remember" (see *Circles of Exaltation*). And Elder Dallin H. Oaks said that by partaking of the sacrament, we witness our willingness to participate in the sacred ordinances of the temple (see Confer- ence Report, Apr. 1985, 102, 103, 105).

PROMINENT PEOPLE

- Those who administer the sacrament

MAIN THEMES

- We partake of the sacramental water in remembrance of the blood of the Savior, which was shed for us.

- In partaking of the sacramental water, we witness that we will always remember the Savior.

thee, in the name of thy Son, Jesus Christ, to
of all those who drink of it. . . ." (Moro. 5:2)

KEY INSIGHTS ABOUT THE SAVIOR

- The Lord promises His Spirit to those who partake of
  the sacramental water and who keep their sacramental
  covenants.

Moroni 6

MAJOR CONCEPT

Those who repent with a broken heart and a contrite spirit are to be baptized, and we are to fellowship them and nourish them with the good word of God.

OVERVIEW Moroni sets forth the requirements for baptism: repentance, a broken heart and a contrite spirit, and the willingness to take upon ourselves the name of Christ and serve Him all our days. He declares that Church members who repent are to be forgiven and teaches that Church meetings are to be conducted by the power of the Holy Ghost.

INTERESTING FACTS ABOUT BEING "WROUGHT UPON" In verse 4, Moroni refers to those who are "wrought upon" by the power of the Holy Ghost. To be "wrought upon" means to be changed in a basic or essential way—usually by hand tools—through twisting, beating, or embellishing. This refers to the change that occurs when the Spirit changes us to new people. Later in that verse, Christ is called the author and finisher of our faith. As the author, He enables us to have faith only as we rely on His merits; as the finisher, He makes it possible for us to repent and endure to the end.

PROMINENT PEOPLE

• Members of the Church

MAIN THEMES

• We need to demonstrate our worthiness for baptism before we can be baptized.

• Those who are to be baptized must have a broken heart and a contrite spirit.

• Those who are to be baptized must have repented of all their sins.

• In baptism, we take upon ourselves the name of Jesus Christ and promise to serve Him throughout our lives.

• The names of those who are baptized are recorded as members of the Church.

• Following baptism, we are cleansed by the power of the Holy Ghost.

• We should meet together often in our Church meetings.

• We have a responsibility to fellowship and nourish those who are baptized.

• Those who commit gross iniquity and refuse to repent are excommunicated, but those who repent with real intent are forgiven.

• Our Church meetings should be conducted after the manner of the workings of the Spirit.

save they took upon themselves the name
serve him to the end." (Moro. 6:3)

KEY INSIGHTS ABOUT THE SAVIOR

- The Lord makes it possible for us to have faith through His merits.
- The Savior's Atonement made it possible for us to repent and gain forgiveness.

Moroni 7

"But charity is the pure love of Christ, possessed of it at the last day, it shall

MAJOR CONCEPT

Faith, hope, and charity are essential to salvation.

OVERVIEW In this chapter, Moroni includes an epistle written by his father, Mormon, on the subjects of faith, hope, and charity. Mormon testifies that the peaceable followers of Christ have sufficient hope that they can enter into His rest. He demonstrates the way to judge good from evil and testifies that faith comes from God and enables the operation of miracles. He teaches that faith, hope, and charity work together unto salvation and he defines charity as the pure love of Christ.

INTERESTING FACTS ABOUT FAITH, HOPE, AND CHARITY
The Prophet Joseph Smith taught that faith is the first great governing principle, and that it has power, dominion, and

PROMINENT PEOPLE

- Mormon
- Moroni

authority over all things (see *Lectures on Faith*). Hope and faith are intertwined. Elder Bruce R. McConkie taught that hope is not a flimsy, ethereal desire that is without an actual assurance; instead, it is desire coupled with full expectation of receiving the coveted reward (see *Mormon*

MAIN THEMES

- Peaceable followers of Christ will enter His rest.
- If a man offers a gift or prays without real intent it profits him nothing.
- We can determine those who are good by their works—a man who is evil cannot do good, and a man who is good cannot do evil.
- We should be very careful in our judgments and can be given a perfect knowledge of what is right through the Spirit of Christ.

- By faith, we can lay hold on every good thing.
- Miracles have not ceased; they are wrought by faith.
- Satan persuades no man to do good.
- We are commanded to have faith, hope, and charity.
- Charity is the pure love of Christ; we should pray with all the energy of our hearts that we can be filled with this love.
- We can be saved only through faith in Christ.

and it endureth forever; and whoso is found
be well with him." (Moro. 7:47)

Doctrine, 365). Elder McConkie also
testified that charity is a love so centered in
righteousness that we have no aim or desire
except for the eternal welfare of our own
soul and for the souls of those around us
(see *Mormon Doctrine,* 121).

KEY INSIGHTS ABOUT THE SAVIOR

- All things that are good come from the Lord, and that
  which is evil comes from the devil. The way to judge is
  that if something invites you to do good, it is sent forth
  by the power of Christ.

- The Spirit of Christ is given to all men.

- The Lord knows all things.

- The Lord is from everlasting to everlasting.

- The Savior sends angels to minister to men and to testify of
  Him; God sends angels to manifest the coming of Christ.

- Through Christ will come every good thing.

- Because He atoned for our sins, the Lord has the right
  to prescribe how we will receive the benefits of His
  Atonement.

Moroni 8

"Little children are whole, for they are
Adam is taken from them in me, that it
in Christ, and also all they that are

MAJOR CONCEPT

The Savior's Atonement covers infants and children before the age of accountability, and they do not require baptism for a remission of sins.

OVERVIEW In this chapter, Moroni includes an epistle his father wrote to him right after he was called to the ministry. Mormon testifies that little children are alive in Christ and that His Atonement covers them, declaring that infant baptism is evil. He also testifies that salvation is earned through faith, repentance, meekness of heart, receiving the Holy Ghost, and enduring to the end.

INTERESTING FACTS ABOUT THOSE "WITHOUT LAW" In verse 22, Mormon explains that those "without the law" are under no condemnation, cannot repent, and thus are not required to be baptized. President Joseph Fielding Smith explained that "without the law" refers to those who are mentally handicapped or unaccountable under age eight and are therefore incapable of understanding the law of the gospel. He taught that they need no baptism and will enter the celestial kingdom, where all deficiencies will be restored (see *Answers to Gospel Questions*, 3:20–21).

PROMINENT PEOPLE

- Mormon
- Moroni

MAIN THEMES

- Infant baptism is a gross error and a mockery of God.

- Little children and those who are incapable of understanding the law are saved by the Savior's Atonement.

- Little children are not capable of committing sin and cannot repent.

- Parents must repent and be baptized in order to be saved with their children.

- The Holy Ghost—the Comforter, who brings hope and perfect love—comes to those who are meek and lowly of heart.

- Salvation is earned through faith, repentance, baptism, meekness, and enduring to the end.

- Those who reject the Lord and His word will perish.

- The pride of the Nephites proved to be the destruction of the entire nation.

not capable of committing sin; wherefore, the curse of hath no power over them . . . all little children are alive without the law." (Moro. 8:8, 22)

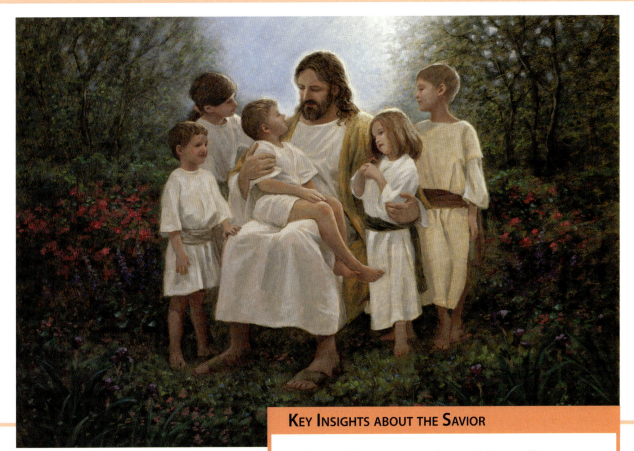

THE DOCTRINE ABOUT LITTLE CHILDREN

Little children are not capable of sin because they are unaccountable; if a child younger than eight does something wrong, it is a transgression, not a sin, and does not require repentance. It is a mockery to baptize children younger than eight because the Atonement pays for their transgressions. The curse of Adam is taken from them, and as heirs to the celestial kingdom, they will be restored to God's presence (see Hel. 14:17).

KEY INSIGHTS ABOUT THE SAVIOR

- The Lord came into the world to call sinners to repentance.
- The Savior's Atonement removes the curse of Adam from little children, and His mercies and redemption provide them exaltation.
- The Savior's Atonement covers those whose mental handicaps make them incapable of understanding the law of the gospel.
- The Lord does not change and is not a respecter of persons.

Moroni 9

"Be faithful in Christ; and may not the but may Christ lift thee up, and may his mercy and long-suffering, and the hope

MAJOR CONCEPT

When the Spirit of the Lord is completely withdrawn, people become savage and unfeeling, unreceptive to spiritual insights and the needs of others.

OVERVIEW Mormon's epistle to his son Moroni outlines the universal degeneration and depravity of both the Nephites and the Lamanites. Even though the Spirit has ceased to strive with the people, Mormon and Moroni continue to serve them. Mormon prays that grace and goodness may rest upon Moroni forever.

INTERESTING FACTS ABOUT WITHDRAWING OF THE SPIRIT The words written in this chapter comprise Mormon's final admonition to his son as well as to all of us in the latter days. It outlines the conditions of the people at a time when the Spirit had completely withdrawn from them and shows what happens when people totally lose the Spirit of the Lord. In describing such a condition, Elder Neal A. Maxwell testified that those who are "past feeling" have suffered an inevitable dulling of the capacity to feel, rendering them impervious to conscience, to the needs of others, and to both intellectual and spiritual insights (see "The Stern but Sweet Seventh Commandment").

PROMINENT PEOPLE

• Mormon
• Moroni

MAIN THEMES

• Thirst for blood and loss of love is an abomination in the sight of the Lord.

• Satan stirs up anger and contention.

• We should not give up on people, regardless of their hardened condition.

• Gross iniquity and depravity can lead to the destruction of an entire civilization.

• Those who completely lack the Spirit of the Lord are past feeling and delight in abomination.

• Those who refuse to repent will perish.

things which I have written grieve thee, to weigh thee down unto death; sufferings and death, and the showing his body unto our fathers, and his of his glory and of eternal life, rest in your mind forever." (Moro. 9:25)

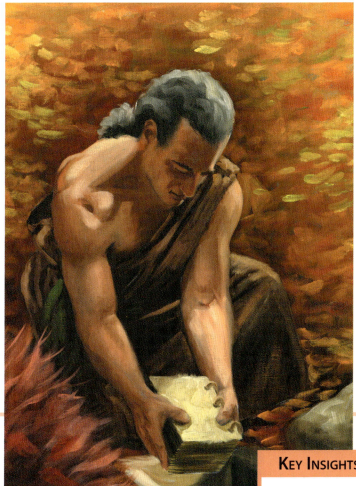

KEY INSIGHTS ABOUT THE SAVIOR

- The Lord stops striving with those who refuse to repent and are hardened to the things of the Spirit.

- The Lord destroys those who refuse to repent.

- The Lord's Atonement is a source of great hope.

- Jesus Christ sits on the right hand of God.

- Although the horrible things of the world grieve us, Christ can lift us up.

Moroni 10

MAJOR CONCEPT

The gifts of God are given for our benefit and will help us gain eternal life.

OVERVIEW Moroni gives us the formula by which we can know the truthfulness of the Book of Mormon and of all things. He lists the gifts of the Spirit and testifies that they are given to the faithful. He also testifies that his voice will speak as one from the dust. Moroni's final admonition is for us to come unto Christ, be perfected in Him, and sanctify our souls.

INTERESTING FACTS ABOUT GIFTS OF THE SPIRIT In verses 8–16 of this chapter, Moroni lists the gifts of the Spirit—signs and miracles that are reserved for the faithful. Gifts of the Spirit are bestowed upon us by the grace of God following devotion, faith, and obedience on our part. The

PROMINENT PEOPLE

• Moroni

receipt of these gifts is always predicated on obedience to the laws and ordinances of the gospel. The purpose of these gifts is to enlighten, encourage, and edify the faithful and to guide them toward eternal life; they are proof of the Lord's divinity. These gifts will exist among the faithful and believing

MAIN THEMES

- In order to know the truthfulness of the Book of Mormon, we must first read it with a sincere heart and real intent. We must also ponder, ask God in Christ's name with a sincere heart, exercise faith, and deny ourselves all ungodliness, then let the Lord determine how the answer will come.

- The Holy Ghost will testify to us of the truthfulness of the Book of Mormon.

- The formula for learning the truthfulness of the Book of Mormon applies to learning the truthfulness of all things.

- We should seek—and not deny—the gifts of God.

- We must strive for faith, hope, and charity, all of which are necessary if we are to be saved in the kingdom of God.

- We must come unto Christ and be perfected in Him.

- We must love God with all our might, mind, and strength.

- Moroni will meet us at the judgment bar of God.

things, I would exhort you that ye would ask God, the [...]
if these things are not true . . . And by the power of the [...]
of all things." (Moro. 10:4–5)

as long as the earth continues in its present state; once we and the earth are exalted, there will be no more need for the gifts of the Spirit (see 1 Cor. 13).

Key Insights about the Savior

- The Lord is the same yesterday, today, and forever.
- The Lord works by power according to our faith.
- Every good gift comes from Christ.
- The Lord will deny the gifts of God to those who are unbelieving.
- The grace of the Lord is sufficient for those who love Him and deny themselves of all ungodliness.
- The Savior will sanctify us if we strive to obey the commandments and do not deny His power.

SOURCES

Bateman, Merrill J. "Stretching the Cords of the Tent," Ensign, May 1994.

Benson, Ezra Taft. "A Witness and a Warning," Ensign, Nov. 1979, 31.

_____. "Rely on the Book of Mormon." Ft. Collins Colorado Regional Conference, June 19, 1988.

_____. The Teachings of Ezra Taft Benson. Salt Lake City: Bookcraft, 1988.

Black, Susan Easton. "Finding Christ in the Book of Mormon." Ensign, July 1978, 60–61.

Book of Mormon Student Manual: Religion 121, 122. Salt Lake City: The Church of Jesus Christ of Latter-day Saints, 1979.

Brown, S. Kent. Voices from the Dust. American Fork: Covenant Communications, 2004.

Burton, Alma P. Karl G. Maeser: Mormon Educator. Salt Lake City: Deseret Book, 1953.

Cannon, George Q. Juvenile Instructor, Jan. 1890.

Clark, J. Reuben, Jr. "The Charted Course of the Church in Education." Address to Seminary and Institute of Religion Leaders, Aug. 8, 1938, Brigham Young University Summer School, Aspen Grove, Utah.

Cowley, Matthias. Cowley's Talks on Doctrine. Chattanooga, TN: Ben. E. Rich, 1902.

Haight, David B. "The Sacrament." Ensign, May 1983.

Hinckley, Gordon B. "A Testimony of the Son of God." Ensign, Dec. 2002.

_____. Teachings of Gordon B. Hinckley. Salt Lake City: Deseret Book, 1997.

History of the Church.

Journal of Discourses.

Kimball, Edward L., ed. The Teachings of Spencer W. Kimball. Salt Lake City: Bookcraft, 1982.

Kimball, Spencer W. Church News, Oct. 15, 1960, 14.

_____. Circles of Exaltation (pamphlet). Salt Lake City: The Church of Jesus Christ of Latter-day Saints.

_____. "God Will Not Be Mocked." Ensign, Nov. 1974.

_____. "Prayer." BYU Speeches of the Year, 1961.

_____. The Miracle of Forgiveness. Salt Lake City: Bookcraft, 1969.

Largey, Dennis L. Book of Mormon Reference Companion. Salt Lake City: Deseret Book, 2003.

Lane, Jennifer Clark. "The Lord Will Redeem His People: Adoptive Covenant and Redemption in the Old Testament and Book of Mormon." FARMS Journal of Book of Mormon Studies, Vol. 2, No. 2, Fall 1993.

Lee, Harold B. Decisions for Successful Living. Salt Lake City: Deseret Book, 1973.

_____. "The Way to Eternal Life," Ensign, Nov. 1971.

Ludlow, Daniel H. A Companion to Your Study of the Book of Mormon. Salt Lake City: Deseret Book, 1976.

Ludlow, Daniel H., ed. Encyclopedia of Mormonism. New York: Macmillan, 1992.

Ludlow, Victor L. Isaiah: Prophet, Seer, and Poet. Salt Lake City: Deseret Book, 1982.

Maxwell, Neal A. For the Power Is in Them. Salt Lake City: Deseret Book, 1973.

_____. Not My Will, But Thine. Salt Lake City: Bookcraft, 1988.

_____. "The Stern but Sweet Seventh Commandment." New Era, June 1979.

McConkie, Bruce R. Mormon Doctrine, Salt Lake City: Bookcraft, 2nd edition, 1966.

_____. Sermons and Writings of Bruce R. McConkie. Salt Lake City: Bookcraft, 1998.

_____. The Millennial Messiah: The Second Coming of the Son of Man. Salt Lake City: Deseret Book, 1982.

McConkie, Joseph Fielding and Robert L. Millet. Doctrinal Commentary on the Book of Mormon. Salt Lake City: Bookcraft, 1987–1992.

McKay, David O. Gospel Ideals: Selections from the Discourses of David O. McKay. Salt Lake City: Improvement Era, 1953.

Nibley, Hugh. An Approach to the Book of Mormon. Salt Lake City: The Church of Jesus Christ of Latter-day Saints, 1957.

_____. "The World of the Jaredites," Improvement Era, 1951–1952.

Nyman, Monte S. and Charles D. Tate, Jr. Mosiah: Salvation Only through Christ. Provo: Religious Studies Center, 1991.

Parry, Donald W., Daniel C. Peterson, and John W. Welch, eds. Echoes and Evidences of the Book of Mormon. Provo: FARMS, 2002.

Petersen, Mark E. The Great Prologue. Salt Lake City: Deseret Book, 1975.

Pinegar, Ed J. and Richard J. Allen. Book of Mormon Who's Who. American Fork: Covenant Communications. 2007.

_____. Commentaries and Insights on the Book of Mormon: Alma 30–Moroni. American Fork: Covenant Communications, 2008.

_____. Commentaries and Insights on the Book of Mormon: 1 Nephi–Alma 29. American Fork: Covenant Communications, 2007.

_____. Old Testament Who's Who. American Fork: Covenant Communications. 2009.

Pratt, Parley P. Key to the Science of Theology. Salt Lake City: Deseret Book, 1855.

Reynolds, Noel B., ed. Book of Mormon Authorship Revisited: The Evidence for Ancient Origins. Provo: FARMS, 1997.

Romney, Marion G. Look to God and Live. Salt Lake City: Deseret Book, 1971.

Smith, Joseph Fielding, comp. Teachings of the Prophet Joseph Smith. Salt Lake City: Deseret Book, 2006.

Smith, Joseph. Lectures on Faith. Salt Lake City: Deseret Book, 1993.

_____. Times and Seasons, Vol. 2, No. 11, April 1, 1841.

Smith, Joseph Sr. "Patriarchal Blessing Given by Joseph Smith, Sr., Patriarch of The Church of the Latter Day Saints, to His Son, Joseph Smith, Jr., on 9 December 1834." Patriarchal Blessing Book, No. 1. Salt Lake City: Historical Department, The Church of Jesus Christ of Latter-day Saints.

Smith, Joseph Fielding. Answers to Gospel Questions. Salt Lake City: Deseret Book, 1960.

_____. Doctrines of Salvation. Bruce R. McConkie, ed. Salt Lake City: Bookcraft, 1954–1956.

_____. Gospel Doctrine: Selections from the Sermons and Writings of Joseph F. Smith. Salt Lake City: Deseret Book, 5th edition, 1939.

Sorenson, John L. and Melvin J. Thorne. Rediscovering the Book of Mormon. Salt Lake City and Provo: Deseret Book and FARMS, 1991.

Sperry, Sidney B. "Types of Literature in the Book of Mormon: Epistles, Psalms, Lamentations." Journal of Book of Mormon Studies, Vol. 4, Issue 1.

_____. The Voice of Israel's Prophets. Salt Lake City: Deseret Book, 1953.

Talmage, James E. The Articles of Faith. Salt Lake City: Deseret News, 1899.

Taylor, John. The Gospel Kingdom: Selections and Sermons from the Writings and Discourses of John Taylor. G. Homer Durham, comp. Salt Lake City: Bookcraft, 1984.

Welch, John W., ed. Reexploring the Book of Mormon. Salt Lake City and Provo: Deseret Book and FARMS, 1992.

Wirthlin, Joseph B. Finding Peace in Our Lives. Salt Lake City: Deseret Book, 1995.

Woodruff, Wilford. Deseret Weekly, Nov. 7, 1896.

Young, Brigham. Discourses of Brigham Young.

ART CREDITS

Page 3—*Lehi Prophesying to the People in Jerusalem* by Del Parson © Intellectual Reserve, Inc.

Page 5—*Wadi_Shaab* © Imbâbah22. Courtesy of wikimedia commons; for more information, visit www.commons.wikimedia.org.

Page 7—*I Did Obey the Voice of the Spirit* © Walter Rane. For more information, visit www.WalterRane.com.

Page 9—*Zoram* © James Fullmer. For more information, visit www.JamesFullmer.com.

Page 11—*Their Joy was Full* by Walter Rane. © By the Hand of Mormon Foundation.

Page 11—Map © Covenant Communications, Inc.

Page 13—*In His Glory* © Del Parson. For more information visit www.delparson.com.

Page 13—*Nephi* © James Fullmer. For more information, visit www.JamesFullmer.com.

Page 15—*Ishmael* © James Fullmer. For more information, visit www.JamesFullmer.com.

Page 17—*Tree of Life* © Jon McNaughton. For more information, visit www.mcnaughtonart.com.

Page 19—*Martin Harris* by Charles Roscoe Savage.

Page 21—*Olive Tree Fruit August* © Rodrigo Nuno Bragança da Cunha. Courtesy of wikimedia commons; for more information, visit www.commons.wikimedia.org.

Page 21—*Destruction of Jerusalem* by Gary Kapp © Intellectual Reserve, Inc.

Page 23—*Izapa Stela 5 drawing* © Clifford F. Dunston.

Page 23—*Izapa Stela 5 photograph* © Sheryl Lee Wilson.

Page 24–25—*Christ Appears to the Nephites* by John Scott © Intellectual Reserve, Inc.

Page 27—*First landing of Columbus on the Shores of the New World, at San Salvador, W.I., Oct. 12th 1492* by Dióscoro Teófilo Puebla Tolín. Courtesy of wikimedia commons; for more information, visit www.commons.wikimedia.org.

Page 29—*Saint John on Golgotha Hajdudorog,* artist unknown. Photograph © Jojojoe. Courtesy of wikimedia commons; for more information, visit www.commons.wikimedia.org.

Page 31—*By Small Means* © Joseph Brickey. For more information, visit www.josephbrickey.com.

Page 31—*Empet d'olivera 2009* © Chixoy. Courtesy of wikimedia commons; for more information, visit www.commons.wikimedia.org.

Page 33—Map © Covenant Communications, Inc.

Page 33—*Nephi's Broken Bow* © Jeremy Winborg. For more information, visit www.jeremywinborg.blogspot.com.

Page 35—*Salalah Oman* © Mary Paulose. Courtesy of wikimedia commons; for more information, visit www.commons.wikimedia.org.

Page 35—*Moses Seeing Jehovah* © Joseph Brickey. For more information, visit www.

visit www.mcnaughtonart.com.

Page 75—Breitling Jet Team 2 by Karelj. Courtesy of wikimedia commons; for more information, visit www.commons.wikimedia. org.

Page 75—Sarganska Osmica © Herbert Ortner. Courtesy of wikimedia commons; for more information, visit www.commons.wikimedia.

Page 77—*Isaiah* by Ted Henninger © Intellectual Reserve, Inc.

Page 79—Assyrian battering ram, photograph © Iglonghurst. Courtesy of wikimedia commons; for more information, visit www. commons.wikimedia.org.

Page 81—Isaiah Bible Card. Courtesy of wikimedia commons; for more information, visit www.commons.wikimedia.org.

Page 81—Degel Maoz © עצמי. Courtesy of wikimedia commons; for more information, visit www.commons.wikimedia.org.

Page 83—*Behold the Lamb of God* © Walter Rane. For more information, visit www. WalterRane.com.

Page 85—Jehu-Obelisk-cropped. Photograph © Steven G. Johnson. Courtesy of wikimedia commons; for more information, visit www. commons.wikimedia.org.

Page 85—*Sennacherib's Army Is Destroyed* by Gustave Doré. Courtesy of wikimedia commons; for more information, visit www. commons.wikimedia.org.

Page 87—Stem of Jesse. Photograph © SteveK. Courtesy of wikimedia commons; for more information, visit www.commons.wikimedia. org.

Page 89—*Song of the Heart* © J. Kirk Richards. For more information, visit www.jkirkrichards. com.

Page 91—Babylon 1932. Courtesy of wikimedia commons; for more information, visit www. commons.wikimedia.org.

Page 93—*Get Thee Behind Me* © Walter Rane. For more information, visit www.WalterRane. com.

Page 95—*The Bible and Book of Mormon Testify of Christ* by Greg Olsen © Intellectual Reserve, Inc.

Page 97—*Prophet and Seer* © Simon Dewey. Courtesy of Altus Fine Arts. For print information, visit www.altusfinearts.com or call 801-763-9788.

Page 99—Charles Anthon. Courtesy of wikimedia commons; for more information, visit www.commons.wikimedia.org.

Page 101—Scriptures. Photograph © Covenant Communications, Inc.

Page 103—*The Prophet Ezekiel* by Lyle Beddes © Intellectual Reserve, Inc.

Page 105—*Go Ye Into the Wilderness* by Robert T. Barrett © Intellectual Reserve, Inc.

Page 107—*Baptism of Christ* © Robert T. Barrett. For more information, visit www. roberttbarrett.com.

Page 109—*She Taught Me to Pray* © Ben Sowards. For more information, visit www. bensowards.com.

Page 111—*Ye Shall Have My Words* © Judith Mehr. For more information, visit www. judithmehr.com.

Page 113—*Jacob* © Robert T. Barrett. For more

information, visit www.roberttbarrett.com.

Page 115—Coins Lot by AB. Courtesy of wikimedia commons; for more information, visit www.commons.wikimedia.org.

Page 117—*Lehi's Landing* © Clark Kelley Price. For more information, visit www.clarkkelleyprice.com.

Page 119—Dead Sea Scrolls Amman Museum, photograph by Pufacz. Courtesy of wikimedia commons; for more information, visit www.commons.wikimedia.org.

Page 121—Olive Groves in Syria © High Contrast. Courtesy of wikimedia commons; for more information, visit www.commons.wikimedia.org.

Page 123—*I Am* © Simon Dewey. Courtesy of Altus Fine Arts. For print information, visit www.altusfinearts.com or call 801-763-9788.

Page 125—*Sherem* © James Fullmer. For more information visit www.JamesFullmer.com.

Page 127—*I Did Raise My Voice that It Reached the Heavens* by Walter Rane © By the Hand of Mormon Foundation.

Page 129—*Moses Comes Down from Mount Sinai* by Gustave Doré. Courtesy of wikimedia commons; for more information, visit www.commons.wikimedia.org.

Page 131—Map © Covenant Communications, Inc.

Page 131— *Mosiah Interprets the Jaredite Stone* by Minerva Teichert *(*1888–1976), ca. 1935, oil on masonite, 36 x 48 inches. Gift of the artist, 1969. For more information, visit http://moa.byu.edu/

Page 133—*Character Study* © Adam Abram. For more information, visit www.adamabram.com.

Page 135—*King Benjamin Confers the Kingdom on Mosiah* by Robert T. Barrett © Intellectual Reserve, Inc.

Page 137—*King Benjamin's Address* © Jeremy Winborg. For more information, visit www.jeremywinborg.blogspot.com.

Page 139—*Nativity* © Simon Dewey. Courtesy of Altus Fine Arts. For print information, visit www.altusfinearts.com or call 801-763-9788.

Page 141—*King Benjamin Adresses His People* by Gary Kapp © Intellectual Reserve, Inc.

Page 143—*Men of Galilee* © Simon Dewey. Courtesy of Altus Fine Arts. For print information, visit www.altusfinearts.com or call 801-763-9788.

Page 145—*King Benjamin* © James Fullmer. For more information, visit www.JamesFullmer.com.

Page 146—Map © Covenant Communications, Inc.

Page 147—*Zeniff* © James Fullmer. For more information, visit www.JamesFullmer.com.

Page 149—Etching by Fredrick Catherwood.

Page 151—Map © Covenant Communications, Inc.

Page 153—*King Laman* © James Fullmer. For more information, visit www.JamesFullmer.com.

Page 155—*King Noah* © James Fullmer. For more information, visit www.JamesFullmer.com.

Page 157—*Abinadi* © James Fullmer. For more information, visit www.JamesFullmer.com.

Page 159—*Moses San Pietro in Vincoli* by Michelangelo Buonarroti. Photograph © Prasenberg. Courtesy of wikimedia commons; for more information, visit www.commons.wikimedia.org.

Page 161—*Not My Will But Thine* © Walter Rane. For more information, visit www.WalterRane.com.

Page 163—*The First Vision* by Minerva K. Teichert (1888–1976), 1934, oil on canvas, 102 x 78 inches. Brigham Young University Museum of Art. For more information, visit http://moa.byu.edu/

Page 165—*Abinadi* © Jeremy Winborg. For more information, visit www.jeremywinborg.blogspot.com.

Page 167—*Abinadi Seals His Testimony* © Ronald K. Crosby.

Page 169—Lake Atitlan © Sheryl Lee Wilson.

Page 171—*Courageous Daughters* © James Fullmer. For more information, visit www.JamesFullmer.com.

Page 173—*Escape to Zarahemla* © Dr. Steven Lloyd Neal. For more information, visit www.nealmd.com.

Page 175—Wood carving, photograph by Leon Woodward.

Page 177— *Escape of King Limhi and His People* by Minerva Teichert (1888–1976), ca. 1950–1951, oil on masonite, 35 7/8 x 48 inches. Gift of the artist, 1969. For more information, visit http://moa.byu.edu/

Page 179—*Amulon* © James Fullmer. For more information, visit www.JamesFullmer.com.

Page 179—Photograph © Cortney Boice.

Page 181—Men with Burdens on their Backs © Sheryl Lee Wilson.

Page 181— *Escape of Alma's People* by Minerva Teichert (1888–1976), ca. 1935, oil on masonite, 35 15/16 x 48 inches. Gift of the artist, 1969. For more information, visit http://moa.byu.edu/

Page 183—The Grijalva River © Sheryl Lee Wilson.

Page 185—*A Book of Mormon Prophet* © Michael Malm. For more information, visit www.michaelmalm.com.

Page 187—*Alma Arise* © Walter Rane. For more information, visit www.WalterRane.com.

Page 189—*Four Sons of Mosiah Kneeling in Prayer* by Harold (Dale) T. Kilbourn. © Intellectual Reserve, Inc.

Page 191—*Alma* © James Fullmer. For more information, visit www.JamesFullmer.com.

Page 193—*Nehor* © James Fullmer. For more information, visit www.JamesFullmer.com.

Page 195— *Alma Overcomes Amlici* by Minerva Teichert (1888–1976), ca. 1935, oil on board, 36 x 48 inches. Gift of the artist, 1969. For more information, visit http://moa.byu.edu/

Page 197—Maori Chief. Courtesy of wikimedia commons; for more information, visit www.commons.wikimedia.org.

Page 201—*He Will Make It More* © Simon Dewey. Courtesy of Altus Fine Arts. For print information, visit www.altusfinearts.com or call 801-763-9788.

Page 251—*Korihor Before Alma* © Robert T. Barrett. For more information, visit www.roberttbarrett.com.

Page 253—*Zoram* © James Fullmer. For more information, visit www.JamesFullmer.com.

Page 255—Drawing taken from Pacal's sarcophagus at Palenque, photograph © Sheryl Lee Wilson.

Page 255—Pacal's sarcophagus at Palenque, photograph © Sheryl Lee Wilson.

Page 257—*Christ's Prayer* © Derek Hegsted. For more information, visit www.hegsted.com.

Page 259—Duraeuropa, courtesy of wikimedia commons; for more information, visit www.commons.wikimedia.org.

Page 259—*Gethsemane* © Liz Lemon Swindle. For more information, visit www.foundationarts.com.

Page 261—Etching by Fredrick Catherwood.

Page 263— *An Angel Appears to Alma and the Sons of Mosiah* by Minerva Teichert (1888–1976), ca. 1935, oil on board, 36 x 48 inches. Gift of the artist, 1969. For more information, visit http://moa.byu.edu/

Page 265—Etching by Fredrick Catherwood.

Page 267—*He Lives* © Simon Dewey. Courtesy of Altus Fine Arts. For print information, visit www.altusfinearts.com or call 801-763-9788.

Page 269—Etching by Fredrick Catherwood.

Page 271—*Here Is Not Here* © Walter Rane. For more information, visit www.WalterRane.com.

Page 273—*Prodigal Son* © Liz Lemon Swindle. For more information, visit www.foundationarts.com.

Page 275—Ambox Scales, courtesy of wikimedia commons; for more information, visit www.commons.wikimedia.org.

Page 277— *A Battle at the River Sidon* by Minerva Teichert (1888–1976), ca. 1935, oil on masonite, 36 x 48 inches. Gift of the artist, 1969. For more information, visit http://moa.byu.edu/

Page 279—*Moroni Prays* © Paul Mann. For more information, visit www.paulmannwesternart.com.

Page 281—*Alma the Younger Counseling His Son* by Darrell Thomas © Intellectual Reserve, Inc.

Page 283—*The Title of Liberty* © Jeremy Winborg. For more information, visit www.jeremywinborg.blogspot.com.

Page 285— *The Treachery of Amalickiah* by Minerva Teichert (1888–1976), ca. 1950–1951, oil on masonite, 35 15/16 x 48 inches. Gift of the artist, 1969. For more information, visit http://moa.byu.edu/

Page 287—*Captain Moroni* © Ken Corbett. For more information, visit www.kencorbettart.com.

Page 289—*Becán* © Sheryl Lee Wilson.

Page 289—Becán Map, photograph © Sheryl Lee Wilson.

Page 291—*Teancum Slaying Amalickiah* © Joseph Brickey. For more information, visit www.josephbrickey.com.

Page 293—*Jacob* © James Fullmer. For more information, visit www.JamesFullmer.com.

Page 295—*Farewell My Stripling Warrior* © Del Parson. For more information, visit www.delparson.com.

Page 297—*Standard of Liberty* © Joseph Brickey. For more information, visit www. josephbrickey.com.

Page 299—*Mother and Sons* © Joseph Brickey. For more information, visit www. josephbrickey.com.

Page 301—*It's True, Sir—All Present and Accounted For* © Clark Kelley Price. For more information, visit www.clarkkelleyprice.com.

Page 303—*Pahoran* © James Fullmer. For more information, visit www.JamesFullmer.com.

Page 305—*The Ancient Mariner* © Dr. Steven Lloyd Neal. For more information, visit www. nealmd.com.

Page 307—Etching by Fredrick Catherwood.

Page 309—*Kishkumen* © James Fullmer. For more information visit www.JamesFullmer.com.

Page 311—Teotihuacán © Sheryl Lee Wilson.

Page 313—Stela in Chiapa de Corzo © Sheryl Lee Wilson.

Page 315—*Nephi and Lehi Encircled by Fire* © Gary Kapp. For more information, visit www. garykapp.com.

Page 317—*Gadianton* © James Fullmer. For more information, visit www.JamesFullmer.com.

Page 319—Etching by Fredrick Catherwood.

Page 321—*Moses and the Brass Serpent* by Judith Mehr © Intellectual Reserve, Inc.

Page 323—*Seantum* © James Fullmer. For more information, visit www.JamesFullmer.

Page 325—Etching by Fredrick Catherwood.

Page 327—*Nephi & Lehi* © James Fullmer. For more information, visit www.JamesFullmer.com.

Page 329—*The Last Judgment* by Albrecht Dürer. Courtesy of wikimedia commons; for more information, visit www.commons. wikimedia.org.

Page 331—*He Did Bring Glad Tidings to My Soul* by Walter Rane. © By the Hand of Mormon Foundation.

Page 333—*Silent Night* © Liz Lemon Swindle. For more information, visit www. foundationarts.com.

Page 335—*Samuel the Lamanite* by Jerry Thompson © Intellectual Reserve, Inc.

Page 337—*Samuel the Lamanite* © James Fullmer. For more information, visit www. JamesFullmer.com.

Page 339—*Shepherds* © Simon Dewey. Courtesy of Altus Fine Arts. For print information, visit www.altusfinearts.com or call 801-763-9788.

Page 341—Mayan Calendar © Hannah Gleghorn. Courtesy of istockphoto.com.

Page 343— *The Answer of Lachoneus* by Minerva Teichert (1888–1976), ca. 1935, oil on linen affixed to masonite, 36 x 48 inches. Gift of the artist, 1969. For more information, visit http:// moa.byu.edu/

Page 345—*Zemnarihah* © James Fullmer. For more information, visit www.JamesFullmer.com.

Page 347—*Divine Redeemer* © Simon Dewey. Courtesy of Altus Fine Arts. For print information, visit www.altusfinearts.com or call 801-763-9788.

Page 349—*Lachoneus* © James Fullmer. For more information, visit www.JamesFullmer. com.

Page 393—*The Mission of the Three Nephites* © Gary Kapp. For more information, visit www.garykapp.com.

Page 395—*Brother Joseph* © David Lindsley.

Page 397—*Lamb of God* © Liz Lemon Swindle. For more information, visit www.foundationarts.com.

Page 399—*Ammaron* © James Fullmer. For more information, visit www.JamesFullmer.com.

Page 401—*Mormon at Age Ten* © Scott Snow.

Page 403—Tikal © Sheryl Lee Wilson.

Page 405—*Mormon the Nephite Prophet Warrior* © Joseph Brickey. For more information, visit www.josephbrickey.com.

Page 407—Hill Shim © Sheryl Lee Wilson.

Page 409—*Christ Visits the New World* by Jerry Thompson © Intellectual Reserve, Inc.

Page 411—*The Nephites' Final Battle* © Gary E. Smith.Page 413—*Mormon Abridging the Plates* by Tom Lovell © Intellectual Reserve, Inc.

Page 415—Great Isaiah Scroll, photographs by Ardon Bar Hama. Courtesy of wikimedia commons; for more information, visit www.commons.wikimedia.org.

Page 415—Qumran Caves, photograph © Grauesel. Courtesy of wikimedia commons; for more information, visit www.commons.wikimedia.org.

Page 417—*Peace Is Coming* © Jon McNaughton. For more information, visit www.mcnaughtonart.com.

Page 419—*The Tower of Babel* by Gustave Doré. Courtesy of wikimedia commons; for more information, visit www.commons.wikimedia.org.

Page 421— *Journey of the Jaredites Across Asia* by Minerva Teichert (1888–1976), ca. 1957, oil on linen on masonite, 35 15/16 x 48 inches. Gift of the artist, 1969. For more information, visit http://moa.byu.edu/

Page 423—*Selecting Stones, the Brother of Jared* © Nathan Florence. For more information, visit www.nflorencefineart.com.

Page 425—*The Brother of Jared Conversing with the Lord* by Jerry Thompson © Intellectual Reserve, Inc.

Page 427—*An Angel Shows the Gold Plates to Joseph Smith, Oliver Cowdery and David Whitmer* © William L. Maughan.

Page 429—*Jaredite Barges* © Gary E. Smith.

Page 429—Olmec Stela at La Venta, photograph © Sheryl Lee Wilson.

Page 429—Sketch of Olmec Stela at La Venta, photograph © Sheryl Lee Wilson.

Page 431—*Shule* © James Fullmer. For more information, visit www.JamesFullmer.com.

Page 433—UA_Flight_175_hits_WTC_south_tower_9-11 © TheMachineStops. Courtesy of wikimedia commons; for more information, visit www.commons.wikimedia.org.

Page 433—*Jared's Daughter* © James Fullmer. For more information, visit www.JamesFullmer.com.

Page 435—Olmec Artifacts, photograph © Sheryl Lee Wilson.

Page 435—Olmec Artifacts, photograph © Sheryl Lee Wilson.

Page 437—Olmec Artifacts, photograph © Sheryl Lee Wilson.

About the Author

The managing editor at Covenant Communications, Kathryn B. Jenkins loves the scriptures and is a gospel doctrine teacher in her ward in Orem, Utah. With thirty-eight years of professional experience in corporate and internal communications, public relations, media relations, marketing communications, and publications management, she has been press secretary for a U.S. Congressman; vice-president of a Salt Lake City publishing company; manager of strategic communications for Novell, Inc.; director of public relations at a private college in Salt Lake City; and has held communications management positions at a variety of national and international corporations.

Former president-elect of the Association of Utah Publishers, she was also on the board of directors of the Mental Health Association of Utah County and the Constitutional Principles Policy Council. She has held membership in the Consortium of Utah Women in Higher Education, the Council for the Advancement and Support of Education, the International Association of Business Communicators, the National Association of Earth Science Editors, and the National Association of State Poetry Societies. She is the author or co-author of more than seven dozen published books and wrote an award-winning book-length poetry manuscript recognized by the governor of Utah. A former member of Sigma Delta Chi, she was named an Outstanding Young Woman of America.

Her interests include reading, writing, cooking, traveling, and doing family history. She has met five presidents of the United States, sailed up the Nile River, prayed in the Garden of Gethsemane, eaten tempura in Tokyo, and received a dozen long-stemmed red roses from a stranger on the street in Athens.